Archaeology:
A Cultural-Evolutionary Approach

Frank W. Eddy

University of Colorado

Prentice-Hall, Inc., Englewood Cliffs, New Jersey 07632

Library of Congress Cataloging in Publication Data

EDDY, FRANK W.
   Archaeology, a cultural-evolutionary approach.

   Includes bibliographies and index.
   1. Archaeology. 2. Social evolution. 3. Anthropology, Prehistoric. 4. Man, Prehistoric. I. Title.
CC165.E32 1984   930.1   83–11006
ISBN 0–13–044057–4

Printed in the United States of America

10   9   8   7   6   5   4   3   2   1

Editorial/production supervision and
interior design: Joan L. Stone
Manufacturing buyer: Ron Chapman

ISBN 0-13-044057-4

PRENTICE-HALL INTERNATIONAL, INC., *London*
PRENTICE-HALL OF AUSTRALIA PTY. LIMITED, *Sydney*
EDITORA PRENTICE-HALL DO BRASIL, LTDA., *Rio de Janeiro*
PRENTICE-HALL CANADA INC., *Toronto*
PRENTICE-HALL OF INDIA PRIVATE LIMITED, *New Delhi*
PRENTICE-HALL OF JAPAN, INC., *Tokyo*
PRENTICE-HALL OF SOUTHEAST ASIA PTE. LTD., *Singapore*
WHITEHALL BOOKS LIMITED, *Wellington, New Zealand*

Contents

(Age) (AD/BC)	Cultural Stages	Geological Calendar	Glacial Calendar	Age (mya)
AD 1 —	Iron Age	Holocene (Recent) Epoch	Post-glacial Modern Climates — Neoglaciation	
1200 BC —	Bronze Age			
3000 BC —	Neolithic		Thermal Maximum	
7000 BC —			Deglaciation	
8000 BC	Mesolithic			

(scale change)

Paleolithic	Upper	Pleistocene Epoch — Upper	Würm III	0.001
			Würm II	0.03
			Paudorf Interstadial	0.04
	Middle		Würm I	0.07
			Eemian Interglacial	0.10
	Lower	Middle	Riss Glaciation	
			Holsteinian Interglacial	
			Mindel Glaciation	
			Cromerian Interglacial	
		Lower	Gunz Glaciation	0.70
			Donau Glaciation	
			Biber Glaciation	
				1.90
		Pliocene Epoch	Pre-glacial	
				2.5

Legend: ⌇ = Scale change

mya = millions of years ago

The time span of cultural stages, the epochs of the geological calendar, and the named episodes of the glacial calendar. Note that the time scale for the Holocene epoch is in terms of thousands of years of Christian calendar time, whereas the Pleistocene epoch is measured in millions of years ago (mya).

Preface

The aim of this study is to integrate the field of archaeology with the scholarly discipline of anthropology. This goal is accomplished from an evolutionary perspective that traces the growth and development of society from the simplest primitive bands through tribes, chiefdoms, states, and early conquest empires, a progression that covers more than two million years. The special brand of theory employed by most (but not all) anthropological archaeologists to explain these social developments is materialism. Basically materialism proposes that new forms of economic production generate larger and larger human populations on the face of the earth. Ever more complex systems of human organization are developed to control and regulate these enlarged human communities. And finally, new systems of economic production are rationalized by appropriate belief systems. In this thesis, change spreads upward from the economic base of society through the sociological level until finally the ideological beliefs of human beings are affected.

Although not all materialists see the natural environment as playing a significant role in cultural evolution, cultural ecologists such as Julian Steward (1955) point to the role of adaptation as paramount in driving the cultural system toward ever more complex states of functional integration. Thus, changes in the natural environment and colonization of new environments, for example, during the several million-year-long ice ages, were conditions that stimulated new and more advanced systems of production—the prime means by which a society interacts with both its natural habitat and with neighboring peoples.

Although the various parts of this materialist theory of society have been proposed by many individual theorists, both archaeologists and cultural anthropologists, it was not until the writings of Marvin Harris (1969) that all of the pieces were put together into a macro-theory of cultural evolution in which each contribution was shown to be a functional and functioning part of the larger society (Price 1982).

This text, then, introduces the reader to the field of modern scientific archaeology as the means by which much of the evidence to test the materialist theory of cultural evolution has been collected. Individual sections of the text treat the research procedures of the archaeologist, the resulting unit concepts, dating and environmental reconstruction, and all means by which fossil data is gathered, analyzed, put in a time frame, and interpreted as to its evolutionary significance. In addition, other sections of the book examine the biological evolution of humans from the perspective of our enlarging capacity for culture, the prime means by which our species has adapted to its natural and social habitat. Next, summary reviews are presented covering the archaeological evidence of prehistory taken from both the Old and New Worlds, essentially parallel but independent case studies of cultural evolution that demonstrate the cultural system's remarkably strong drive to increase in complexity as the result of adaptation. Further evidence for the course of evolution is next treated from the standpoint of social complexity. And finally, materialism is tested against the evidence of archaeology and found to form a valid and insightful theory explaining the growth and development of society. Besides clarifying the past, the theory helps to predict the future of our society, which strives for ever larger and more complex states of organization that are of necessity burdensome to the well-being of the individual citizen.

An expression of appreciation is due many people and institutions who have provided support in bringing this endeavor to completion. Chief among them are the editors: Stan Wakefield first provided assistance, followed by Susan J. Taylor and Joan Stone. These staff members of Prentice-Hall, Inc., patiently guided me through the various steps by which the concept of a manuscript becomes the reality of a textbook. Not least among these steps is the role of many anonymous reviewers who read and provided comments on the original prospectus and were followed by other readers who examined two successive drafts of the actual product. Of outstanding assistance was Carol King, who painstakingly performed the comprehensive editing of the text.

Special thanks are offered to John L. Montgomery, graduate student in the Department of Anthropology, University of Colorado, who provided assistance by making arrangements for illustration permissions, indexing, and preparation of the glossary.

And finally, thanks are extended to Debbie Tyler, staff member for the Department of Anthropology, University of Colorado, who provided draft typing, mailing of manuscripts, and xeroxing among other clerical services. Further thanks are due the Department of Anthropology, University of Colorado, for their support through Ms. Tyler's services, not to mention office equipment and space.

1

Archaeology as Anthropology

Anthropology is the study of the cultural and biological evolution of humankind over the entire globe during the last two million years of the earth's history. It is a wide-ranging discipline that overlaps many of the social and natural sciences. Furthermore, it draws on the humanities, which contribute to the study of our artistic and intellectual humanness, over the last 5000 years, the period of history that began with the invention of writing.

Central to the study of anthropology are the twin concepts of culture and society, for anthropologists are primarily concerned with the study of human group behavior. The culture concept, a unique creation of anthropology, embraces beliefs, values, and ideas held in common by a local community of people and leading to predictable behavior on the part of the members of that group.

Defined in this fashion, culture is explicitly separated from behavior. Unlike culture, which is mentalistic and must be inferred, behavior can be observed directly by the social scientist. All members of the human species carry cultural ideas about the preferred and approved forms of behavior. On the other hand, many of life's situations prevent us from attaining these ideal customs, so that real behavior may deviate considerably from the sanctioned norms. Therefore, actual behavior is carried out within the constraints of a practical world to produce less than perfect results. Defined as organized group behavior, society exhibits a range of individual behaviors that are both acceptable and unacceptable to the group.

In North American colleges, universities, and high schools, anthropology is traditionally organized into four subdivisions: archaeology, ethnology (cultural anthropology), human biology (physical anthropology), and linguistics. Elsewhere in the world, particularly in England and on the European continent, archaeology is often separated as an independent department within a college or school.

In a broad sense that includes the full range of archaeological practitioners, archaeology "consists of a method and a set of specialized techniques for the gathering or production of cultural information" (Taylor 1948, p. 44). In this sense, the archaeologist is first and foremost a technician trained to recover and classify artifacts. The archaeologist becomes something more than a technician, however, by applying the artifactual data, or "cultural information," to research in a specific discipline. A fragment of pottery, for example, might convey one message to the art historian and another message to the anthropologist.

To a member of the History Department, the artifactual evidence becomes the basis for enlarging and verifying information contained in written documents, that is, for writing history. As a member of a Classics Department, the archaeologist uses the artifactual information in humanistic research that focuses primarily on the civilizations of ancient Greece and Rome. In the Language Department, the archaeologist deciphers ancient texts to understand the development of writing in such pre-classic civilizations as the Egyptian, Sumerian, Babylonian, and Assyrian. In a Fine Arts Department, the archaeologist studies art history of early civilizations on a world-wide basis. And finally, the anthropologist uses archaeological data for social science research. Consequently, this textbook defines archaeology as the anthropology of the past (Willey and Phillips 1958).

In contrast to the ethnologist, the linguist, and at times the physical anthropologist, the archaeologist is most concerned with the study of society and culture within a historical context, that is, the investigation of group behavior from the viewpoint of change or persistence over time. In this sense the archaeologist is a cultural historian. But unlike the traditional historian who relies on written documents and archival research for a data base, the archaeological anthropologist reconstructs cultural history from worn and discarded objects imperfectly perserved from the past.

The Anthropological Archaeologist

To the archaeologist, society is group behavior expressed within a framework of time (historical context) and space (geographical context). Furthermore, society is made up of three kinds of behavior: verbal, social, and material (Fig. 1-1). Verbal behavior is the spoken and written language coupled with more subtle forms of nonverbal communication, all of which are ephemeral and, as a rule, lost to the archaeologist except under rather special circum-

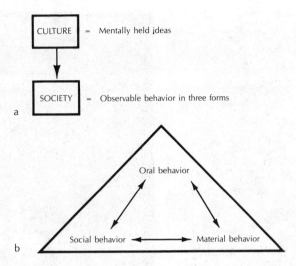

FIGURE 1-1   The relationship between culture and society. (a) The manner in which culture generates societal behavior. (b) The behavioral components of society.

stances. For instance, linguistic evidence may be preserved from past civilized societies in the form of inscriptions carved on stone monoliths, such as the Central American Mayan stelae, or impressed into baked clay tablets, such as the Near Eastern Sumerian cuneiform texts (Fig. 1–2). Texts such as these are important to the classical and historical archaeologist. Anthropological archaeologists, however, generally deal with prehistoric (before the advent of writing) or illiterate societies so that language is not usually important in their research.

Social behavior consists of group customs dealing with political, religious, familial, and economic activities. Evidence for social behavior is preserved indirectly in certain kinds of material objects, such as paintings on tombs or carvings on rock cliff faces. Still other examples are toys, ornaments, items of dress or hair styling, and objects of office, which indicate the sex, age, and social rank of the individual user (Fig. 1–3). Such material trappings are called status symbols, that is, indicators of social position. Architectural forms that reflect the nature of past social behavior include buildings with specialized function, such as temples, palaces, courts, and markets. Occupational tools provide inferences concerning the range of skilled craftsmen and such other specialists as priests or bureaucratic administrators.

Material behavior, the third and last aspect of society, is expressed as physical objects manufactured and used by humans. These objects of human manufacture and use are called *artifacts* by the archaeologist to distinguish them from natural objects, sometimes called *ecofacts*, which display no evidence of human use. Evidence of material behavior consists mostly of artifacts

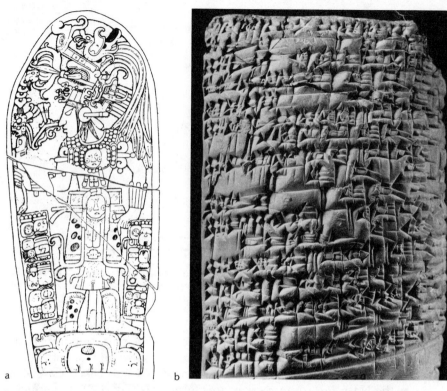

FIGURE 1-2   Evidence of ancient languages preserved as written texts. (a) Stela 4, Machaquila, Guatemala, dating to the Late Classic period of the Mayan civilization. (b) Cuneiform tablet giving information on the farmer's almanac, Sumerian civilization.

Source: (a) From *The Maya* by Michael Coe. Copyright © 1966 by Praeger Publishers. Reprinted by permission of Holt, Rinehart and Winston. CBS College Publishing. (b) Reprinted from *The Sumerians* by Samuel N. Kramer by permission of The University of Chicago Press. Copyright © 1973 by The University of Chicago Press.

employed as tools to satisfy human needs for food, clothing, and shelter. Additional evidence of material behavior consists of symbolic objects that relate to social and verbal behavior. A symbol, an object that stands for an idea, is just as much an artifact as a tool or implement, but the meaning attached to the physical form is not always obvious from the shape of the specimen. Whereas the function of a prehistoric tool may be inferred from its size, shape, and wear characteristics, discovering the purpose of a symbolic artifact is far more difficult. The meaning of symbolic artifacts is interpreted by inference from their setting within a site of human occupation or by analogy with objects of similar shape used in a contemporary society.

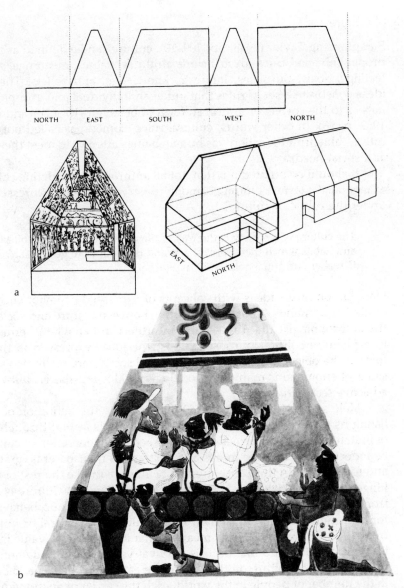

NORTH   EAST   SOUTH   WEST   NORTH

EAST   NORTH

a

b

FIGURE 1-3   Mural from a temple at Bonampak, Classic Maya civilization. (a) The mural scheme from Bonampak's Room 1 is outlined at right and shown with one end removed at left. (b) The chief and his ladies sit on a large stone table for a blood-letting rite. The chief is pricking his tongue with a sharp thorn or bone. Their social status is indicated by clothing and hair styles.

Source: (a) From Great Ages of Man/*Ancient America.* Drawings by Otto Van Eersel. Time-Life Books Inc., Publisher. © 1967 Time Inc. (b) Mayan paintings copied by Antonio Tejeda for the Carnegie Institution of Washington, D.C. Print property of Time Inc. Reproduction forbidden without express consent. Photo credit: Kafka.

The Study of Culture

Paraphrasing Taylor (1948, pp. 109–10), culture can be defined as ideas about proper behavior. Such ideas include attitudes, values, meanings, sentiments, feelings, goals, purposes, interests, knowledge, and beliefs. These cultural ideas constitute a set of rules that guide an individual and groups of individuals as to the correct or approved form of behavior (Kroeber and Kluckhohn 1952, p. 98). In other words, cultural rules, sometimes called norms, constitute a "blueprint for action" as human beings attempt to meet their biological and social needs.

It should be pointed out that not all anthropologists define culture solely in mentalistic terms. Linton is among those who include expressed behavior under the rubric of culture:

> The culture of a society is the way of life of its members, the collection of ideas and habits which they learn, share, and transmit from generation to generation (Kroeber and Kluckhohn 1952, p. 96).

Here Linton mixes ideas with concepts of expressed behavior such as "way-of-life" and "habits." But the distinction between culture and society enables the anthropologist first to describe an artifact in behavioral terms and then to explain its cultural purpose, that is, the ideas expressed in the physical form of the object. Since in fact culture and society are really two sides of the same phenomenon, many anthropologists side-step the issue by using the adjective *sociocultural*.

Hole and Heizer (1969, pp. 40–42) elaborate the definition of culture by listing its five central characteristics: (1) Culture is *learned* through processes of imitation and oral instruction so that each new generation of children must be indoctrinated into the mores and customs of their parents, grandparents, and forefathers. In this sense, human beings are unlike the rest of the animal kingdom, whose behavior is innate and instinctive. (2) Culture is *transmitted* from generation to generation, so that traditions of group behavior endure for centuries and even millenia if uninterrupted by natural or human catastrophe. (3) Culture is *adaptive*, meaning that it has survival value in the physical and social environment. This survival value is amply demonstrated by the longevity of culture on the face of the earth and the remarkable increase in the number of people in the world, each the carrier of an individual version of a culture. (4) Culture is *patterned*, which means that each individual tends to reproduce, in large part, the ideas of other members of society. A personalized or idiosyncratic culture would lead to social chaos as each individual failed to coordinate activities with the activities of others of the same community. (5) Finally, culture is an organized *system*. By this characteristic, Hole and Heizer indicate that a culture's ideas are integrated, rather than in conflict with one another. If the individual's system of cultural beliefs becomes too inconsistent, to relieve psychological strain the person may have to give up an entire belief system, such as a religious philosophy that has become out of touch with a changing life-style.

The Goals of Anthropological Archaeology

Immediate goals of the anthropological archaeologist are to solve particular research problems that bear on current anthropological interests. For instance, the archaeologist may examine the behavior of an extinct society concerning the following subjects:

1. The ability to work with stone and other raw materials
2. Changing fashions in artifact styles
3. Diet and nutrition
4. Hunting ability and other subsistence skills
5. Butchery techniques and other food-preparation routines
6. Physical appearance and cosmetic customs
7. Burial practices
8. Settlement arrangements
9. Size and composition of the work force
10. Aesthetic concepts
11. Supernatural beliefs
12. The age of the past human community
13. Nature of the prehistoric environment inhabited by ancient man

The ultimate goals of the anthropologist-historian can be organized under five questions beginning with what, how, why, where, and when. The archaeologist asks: (1) What is the nature of cultural ideas? (2) How does culture function on a day-to-day basis? (3) Why does culture exist? This question applies both to its origin and to its growth and development through time. (4) Where did culture originate and in what order did humankind spread culture to the far corners of the earth? (5) When did culture originate as a special means of adapting to the environment?

The Use of Inferential Logic

The anthropological archaeologist answers questions about culture by employing inferential logic. An inference is a logical conclusion derived from given data or premises. In archaeology, conclusions are drawn from basic data consisting of the artifact and its provenience, the three-dimensional position of the object within geographical space. As shown in Figure 1–4, the archaeologist-observer analyzes the fossil record of past human behavior and from this data infers the nature of past societal behavior. A second inferential leap is made from the ancient behavior to an interpretation of the beliefs comprising the cultural system (Thompson 1958). Each level of inference, in turn, helps to explain the artifact and provenience data by answering the questions

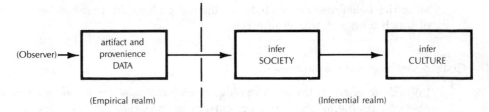

FIGURE 1-4   The nature of inferential logic as applied to intepretations of archaeological data.

of why and how the object came to be—not only in its physical form but also in its spatial location.

The validity of the individual sociocultural inference is checked by comparing it with all other inferences for "goodness of fit." Since cultural ideas are related within a system, a high degree of congruence produces an integrated reconstruction of a past society and its culture (Taylor 1948; Eddy 1974). For instance, archaeological evidence indicates that during the Pleistocene epoch of geological time—the ice ages—society was organized as bands of families that subsisted by hunting herd animals and collecting wild plant foods. Furthermore, these primitive humans held a cultural belief system based on magic control of animal fertility and the movements of wild game. Thus, each aspect of society was functionally related to all others to form a cultural system. If inferences about the fossilized remains of such an early society do not yield evidence of this systemic organization, the validity of the inference is called into question, and the archaeologist re-examines artifactual evidence for correctness of interpretation.

The research methods of archaeology include three procedures: (1) site survey, (2) excavation, and (3) laboratory analysis. Survey is an extensive research method in which the archaeologist observes and records ancient remains exposed on the ground surface. Usually teams of researchers systematically sweep the countryside to find each place of historic and prehistoric occupation; each find spot is called a *site*. Artifacts found between archaeological sites indicate how the land surrounding places of habitation was used. The research goal of site survey is to discover and record systematically each evidence of human landscape modification within a locality, region, or culture area.

Site excavation is a scientific procedure in which observations on artifacts and their three-dimensional location are made by systematic digging below the ground surface. Excavation may entail a single hole in the ground, called a *test pit*, whose purpose is to explore the depth, thickness, and structure of an archaeological deposit, or it may entail an extensive operation in which subsurface layers, each of a different age, are traced horizontally to reveal distribution of ancient remains. But unlike the survey, which is regional, excavation focuses on the single archaeological site.

After the primary artifactual data have been removed from the field, by either site survey or excavation, the recovered artifacts are inspected and classified in the laboratory. Traditionally, classification was performed by sorting artifacts on large table tops. Today, however, the modern archaeologist relies on multivariate statistical programs operated by high-speed computers to classify artifact data into types.

The Nature of Society

All societies of the world, whether national states, industrial powers, feudal monarchies, or primitive groups, hold certain properties in common. In every society people are organized into groups to meet material, biological, and emotional needs for survival. The material needs of the members of society are for food, clothing, and shelter. The biological needs are for reproduction and socialization of the young. Procreation of offspring insures perpetuation of society from one generation to another, whereas socialization pertains to care and raising of children to become effective members of the local community. Emotional needs include: (1) the need of people for one another, (2) the need to reduce fear of the unknown universe, and (3) the need to reduce fear of one's neighbors.

Social Institutions

A society meets its primary and secondary needs by organizing its members into subgroups called *institutions,* whose purpose is to satisfy specific needs. For instance, needs for food, clothing, and shelter are met by economic institutions made up of the organized work force. Labor functions to extract materials and energy from the natural environment and to manufacture tools, facilities, equipment, processed food, and fuels. The economic institution also distributes these goods and services to consumers.

Biological needs of society are met by the family, whose primary role is to produce children and raise them. The basis of the family is socially recognized marriage, which leads to the nuclear or biological family composed of husband, wife, and children. In many cultures, the definition of the family is considerably expanded to include kin far removed from the nuclear family. This expanded family is organized by descent relationships made up of ties extending both across generations (parent-offspring) and within generations (siblings, cousins) to produce a very large support group.

Emotional needs of society are met by political and religious institutions that organize people for secular leadership and sacred purposes. The political institution has the following characteristics: (1) The members form a local group or community. (2) The members share a common culture. (3) The members hold a self-image identifying themselves as a distinctive people. (4) The political community owns property and is a corporate entity. (5) The political group conducts its own affairs, meaning that it is self-determinative. As a corporate group, the political institution holds a continuous territory with defended borders and public facilities including a seat of government.

The religious institution organizes people into a church with the following characteristics: (1) The members share beliefs concerning the nature of supernatural forces. (2) They also share beliefs about how to manipulate these forces through magic or prayer. (3) The church is usually led by a formally organized set of religious specialists, such as shamans (witch doctors, magicians) or priests (ministers, rabbis) who are trained in ritual, dogma, and knowledge.

Institutional Organization

In each of these basic social institutions, people are formally organized into a series of statuses or social positions. Among these are one or more leaders, permanent members forming a cadre of fully trained personnel, and apprentice trainees or young neophytes. In addition, each basic institution of society holds material equipment (artifacts) specially designed for the group's purposes and a body of knowledge concerning how to carry out the institutional functions and thereby fulfill the needs of society.

The conduct of institutional activities involves scheduling in space and time (Flannery 1968). Scheduling in space prevents congestion of all members of the community in one place. The strategy is to disperse the different institutional activity groups by placing them conveniently near sources of raw materials or control points along lines of communication and transport. In this arrangement the members of society minimize their energy outlay and maximize the work accomplished. Furthermore, the social institutions are organized in space so as to avoid conflict with one another and with other communities.

The conduct of institutional activities is also regulated by diurnal, seasonal, and annual scheduling. Diurnal, or once daily, scheduling refers to activities performed at a specified time of the day or night so as to avoid conflict with those performed at other times. Seasonal activities are those scheduled by environmental changes, for example, spring planting, fall harvest, winter hunting, or summer ceremonies. And finally, annual scheduling involves once yearly activities such as "rites of intensification" or "rites of passage." The former are annual ritual events in which community members meet to renew old acquaintances and maintain community solidarity. The latter are annual social events in which young candidates pass from one social status in an institution to another. An example of a rite of passage would be the initiation of a novice into full membership within a secret society such as a war sodality or the priesthood.

In actual fact, all institutionalized activities of society are scheduled simultaneously in both time and space to maximize efficiency of subgroup effort and to avoid between-group competition for usable space. An example of such composite scheduling is the programming of university classes by room and hour. Understanding the composite scheduling of institutional events helps archaeologists to explain the differential density distributions of artifacts within an archaeological site.

Artifacts and Living Societies

Human-made objects are the only durable evidence of past preliterate communities. Therefore, what we know about many ancient societies is based entirely on our ability to interpret accurately the meaning of their artifactual remains.

An artifact is any object made or used by humans, either a portable item or a fixed feature. Artifacts may be tools or symbols. As a tool, an artifact is used to manipulate and extract raw materials, energy, or both from the physical world. Raw materials include organic products and minerals. Energy sources are fuels such as coal, oil, uranium, water, sun or wind power.

Symbols are divisible into two classes, those signifying social status and those reflecting philosophical ideas. Examples of status symbols are a king's crown, the mortar board of a university professor, or a military uniform. Philosophical symbols are exemplified by the Christian cross or Nazi swastika.

Economic Artifacts

Artifacts reflecting the nature of the economic institution have to do with production, distribution, and consumption of goods and services. The nature of the productive economy is signified by raw materials, partially processed products, finished items, discarded manufacturing waste, and the tool technology necessary to convert resources into finished products.

The distributional aspects of the economy are interpreted from the presence of transportation lines such as roads, waterways, railways, and bridges. The actual movement of goods is proved by the appearance of exotic (foreign made) artifacts as demonstrated by manufacture in nonlocal styles and materials. The existence of import trade is verified when complementary nonlocal goods are found in the export center.

Use of economic produce is reflected by both subsistence and conspicuous consumption. Subsistence consumption is most easily interpreted from food refuse such as animal bones and human coprolites (fossil feces), while conspicuous consumption is reflected in ostentatious housing or burial offerings, such as food and wearing apparel placed within the tomb of a king.

Family Artifacts

> Certain artifacts function as status symbols that indicate family structure. Among primitive people, for instance, the head-of-household usually is indicated by clothing. Sex-specific jewelry often signifies married women, while children's toys commonly reflect the age of the subadults and their intended future occupations. The association of such status symbols with specific individuals is most apparent in cemetery burials where the artifact interpretation of sex, age, and occupational status can be verified by the physical anthropologist from the skeletal remains found in the grave. Pertinent observations include tooth eruption, fusion of long-bone caps, and pelvic configuration.
>
> A second line of evidence concerning the organization of the family can be taken from the layout of residential architecture. In this case, the organization of the family group is derived from the shape, size, and interior arrangement of dwellings, that is, settlement characteristics.

Political Artifacts

> The nature and organization of the polity can be inferred from a variety of portable and fixed artifacts. For instance, a political office is often indicated by a status symbol such as the scepter of a prime minister. Burial of the political elite is signified by ostentatious graves as exemplified by the tombs of the ancient Egyptian pharaohs (Fig. 1–5). Public monuments, such as monolithic statues depicting a king or chief, are symbolic of political status. And

FIGURE 1-5   A reconstruction of the pyramids of Abu Sir, Egypt.

Source: Figure 18 redrawn by Penguin Books from W. M. Flinders Petrie, medum, Plate IV from I. E. S. Edwards: *The Pyramids of Egypt* (Pelican Books, Revised edition 1980), p. 135. Copyright 1947, 1961 by I. E. S. Edwards. All rights reserved. Reprinted by permission of Pelican Books Ltd.

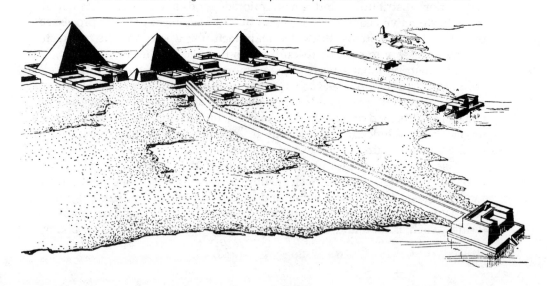

finally, public buildings such as a county courthouse or city hall reflect the nature of the political institution.

Religious Artifacts

Evidence of religious life is preserved in the form of ritual artifacts, such as the stylized fish, the ancient symbol of Christianity. Easier to identify are buildings constructed for prayer such as a Christian cathedral, the pyramid-temple of prehistoric Mexico, or the ziggurat of ancient Mesopotamia (Fig. 1–6). Other sacred places include shrines where prayer offerings are made,

FIGURE 1-6   Ancient religious buildings. (a) The ziggurat of Ur-of-the-Chaldees, Sumerian civilization. (b) The ceremonial center at Copan, Honduras, Mayan civilization. Dominated by massive temple-pyramids, the center also contains administrative buildings, elite residences, and plazas where the populace must have gathered on ceremonial occasions.

Source: (a) From Jacquetta Hawkes (editor) *Atlas of Ancient Archaeology,* Figure on p. 173 by Dr. Vincenzo di Grazia; New York: McGraw-Hill Book Company, 1974. ©Rainbird/Robert Harding Picture Library. (b) Figure 16 from page 61 of *The Lost Civilization: The Story of the Classic Maya* by T. Patrick Culbert. Copyright © 1974 by T. Patrick Culbert. Reprinted by permission of Harper & Row, Publishers, Inc.

a

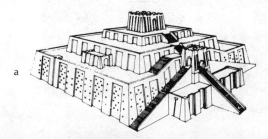

b

FIGURE 1-7   A view of the central pit of a royal tomb excavated at Wu Kuan Ts'un, near the Shang capital of Anyang, northern China. The skeletons of human, sacrificed, funeral victims were buried on the ledge surrounding the central pit.

Source: Plate 12 from *The Prehistory of China* by Judith M. Treistman. Copyright © 1972 by Judith M. Treistman. Rerinted by permission of Doubleday & Company, Inc.

which may be human-constructed buildings or natural features such as hot springs or natural wells recognized for their supernatural qualities. An example of the latter is the sacred cenote, a natural sinkhole in the limestone bedrock of the peninsula of Yucatan, Mexico, where human sacrifices, incense, and gold offerings were cast to bring rain from the Chacs, the rain gods of the prehistoric Maya indians.

Excavation sometimes reveals specialized burials of religious practitioners. In these cases, grave offerings identify the deceased as a shaman (magician) or a priest who lived in a high civilization of ancient times. In fact, cemeteries in general provide an excellent record of both the religious and political institutions of a society because burials of ranked and class-organized societies were usually segregated by their respective social statuses and occupations. Usually commoners were interred in one portion of the cemetery while the elite members of society and their retainers were grouped in another sector of the graveyard or even in a separate, high-status cemetery. As a rule, the king or queen was surrounded by fellow aristocrats in descending order of importance moving away from the royal tomb. Thus spatial patterning of the graves is a direct mirror of social distance during life. Furthermore, the occupation of the individual is often marked by the tools of trade, such as a carpentry kit, brewery equipment, or kitchen utensils.

The king, the preeminent individual of all ancient civilizations, was lavishly supported in death by his royal furnishings, treasury, and retainers, the men and women who served him in life. In order to insure their willingness to travel with him in death, these servants were given a poisonous potion or otherwise executed so that they would continue to serve during life-after-death (Fig. 1–7). To provide for the well-being of the royal household, lavish displays of food, both prepared meals and stored foodstuffs, were included as part of the tomb furnishings.

Preservation of Artifacts

By a process called *death transformation*, a society is converted into a fossil record, and the ethnographic community is converted into an archaeological site. But in order to reverse the death direction and reconstruct the once living community from its dead remains, the archaeologist must consider the nature of the dead (fossil) site, and the death process in Figure 1–8. In this manner, the inert objects of the fossil record can be used to breathe life into the dry bones of archaeology; the quick can be recreated from the dead. An understanding of the death process is essential for institutional reconstruction. The death process includes three subprocesses: discard, emplacement, and fossilization.

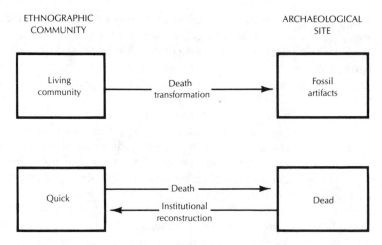

FIGURE 1-8   Death transformation and institutional reconstruction.

Discard

Discard removes an artifact from its living, institutional setting, either by accident or by intention. Accidental loss of an artifact may happen while people are at work or play. The stray stone arrow point found by an archaeologist miles from the nearest habitation site was lost by a hunter far away from camp in prehistoric times. Often these isolated projectile points have a broken tip with a characteristic fracture resulting from impact with the ground after the missile missed the quarry, a deer or elk. Another example of accidental loss is a burned house filled with household utensils partially consumed by the fire. These objects have particular significance to the archaeologist since they reflect family activities stopped in an instant by the conflagration.

Another kind of discard results from intentional disposal. Examples are worn-out artifacts found in a garbage dump, a favorite digging spot for archaeologists. Other examples of intentional discard are objects placed with a burial as offerings for the after-life, such as food or job-specific tools. Then there is ritual disposal such as a sealed offering that served to appease gods of the household, ensuring protection for all those who dwelt there. These fetishes were placed under a major roof support timber, in a cache under the floor or behind the wall, or under the eaves. Sometimes the cache was hidden against loss or theft and never recovered. Prehistoric traders and tinkers were in the habit of secreting some of their wares in the ground or in a rock crevice while making the rounds of the clientele. Some other artifacts were intentionally destroyed because of social custom. A modern example is the ceremonial burning of an American flag that has become too tattered for further use.

Emplacement

Emplacement describes the manner in which objects, once freed from society, were buried in the ground. This covering may have occurred by cultural means such as accumulation of garbage leading to deep, layered trash deposits. The collapse of a building buries artifacts that were resting on the floor, hung from rafters, resting on shelves, or located on the roof of the structure. In the renovation of a house, when a new floor was laid over an old one, whole or broken artifacts were covered.

Many natural agencies lead to the covering of artifacts by sediment. Archaeological remains may be buried by water-laid deposits (alluvium), deposits washed from a slope (colluvium), debris at the base of a cliff (talus build-up), and wind deposits (dune formation). Usually the stratigraphy, or sequence of layered deposits, in archaeological sites results from mixed sediment sources. This combination of cultural and natural matrix may be expressed in alternate layering or in simultaneous sedimentation. Or in another stratigraphic situation, sediment sources may vary in their input with one speeding up only to slow down again during a later interval of time. Where the sedimentation rates are exceedingly variable in time and space, the density distributions of artifacts varies enough to make interpretation difficult. The only way to control for these erratic aspects of archaeological site formation is to perform a very detailed study of the minute stratigraphy (called *microstratigraphy*).

Fossilization

The third subprocess of death transformation is fossilization, the actual preservation of an artifact once it is in the ground. Of all the worn-out and thrown-away objects discarded by society, only a small fraction are actually preserved as a record for future generations to study. And even these are fossilized in very unequal proportions to the original manufacture because of the vagaries of preservation in the ground—particularly when the artifacts were made of organic materials such as wood, fiber, hides, or animal tissue, which are highly subject to destruction by decay. On the other hand, artifacts preserved in disproportionately greater ratios are those made of inert mineral materials like stone, metal, glass, and fired clay.

Fossilization is a subprocess that consists of opposing forces acting on the preservability of the artifact record. One set of factors favors preservation once the object has been covered by sediment. Charring of organic artifacts, for example, converts them to chemically inert charcoal. Roof timbers or furnishings of a house might be burned, but not consumed. Other favorable circumstances are permeation of a specimen by soil minerals such as carbonates or even replacement of organic cell structure by such mineral matter. However, the latter form of fossilization is rare except for a few examples from very old Pleistocene-age sites with a high groundwater table.

Soil environments favorable for artifact preservation are those with moderate hydrogen ion activity. For instance, slightly acidic soils favor preservation of fossil plant pollen while slightly basic soils favor preservation of bone, both food refuse and bones used as tools. Soils of arid lands preserve perishable artifacts such as wood, paper, fiber, and human remains through desiccation. At the other extreme are arctic soils that preserved the Pleistocene mammoths of Siberian Russia and Alaska through freezing (Clark 1964, pp. 94–95). Again water-logged soils, such as those of north European bogs, have preserved iron-age sacrificial victims through the exclusion of oxygen that otherwise would have led to decay (Glob 1971). All conditions that stop, or inhibit, chemical and biological activity leading to decomposition serve archaeology by preserving otherwise perishable objects.

In contrast, certain adverse factors lead to artifact decay and thus provide an imperfect material record of the past. In general, all or partial destruction of perishable artifacts by decay is common. Decay agents include both chemical and biological factors. Particularly unfavorable conditions are provided by alternate wetting and drying of the site soil leading to oxidation of objects, commonly recognized in breakdown by rust and leaching. Again, extreme hydrogen ion activity of the soil is detrimental to preservation. Very acidic soils usually lead to low bone recovery, while quite alkaline (basic) soils are low in plant pollen preservation. Again, biological agents, the decomposing microorganisms such as fungi and bacteria, are highly destructive of organic artifacts.

Other adverse factors that destroy the archaeological record are various forms of mechanical randomization that disturb the distributional patterns of artifacts. Natural agents of randomization include burrowing mammals and insects, plant root disturbance, frost heave, and river bank erosion. Human-induced randomization is created by foot traffic, plowing, rebuilding so that earlier constructions are disturbed, and archaeological field work itself. The result of these mechanical factors is that randomization of the artifact distribution biases the structure of the artifact associations, thereby destroying information.

Analysis of Artifacts

From an imperfect record of the past, the archaeologist must determine the significance of tools and symbols. To decode a message from these inanimate objects, the archaeologist uses four kinds of inference: formal analysis, distributional analysis, experimental analysis, and ethnographic analogy.

Formal Analysis

The archaeologist uses formal analysis to learn how an artifact took on its present form and why it was shaped as it is. First, the investigating archaeologist reduces an artifact to its elemental parts, called *attributes,* through close inspection and specimen-to-specimen comparison (Fig. 1–9). Each minimal observation, the attribute, is the result of a single act of the artisan or user. Next one determines the order in which these manufacturing steps were executed through study of the attribute overlap. And finally, the investigating archaeologist infers the production recipe beginning with the raw material

FIGURE 1-9   Attributes of ceramic vessels. *Upper,* attribute variations in field of design. *Lower,* attributes of a necked jar.

Source, upper: Anna O. Shepard, *Ceramics for the Archaeologist.* Washington, D.C.: Carnegie Institution publication 609, 1957.

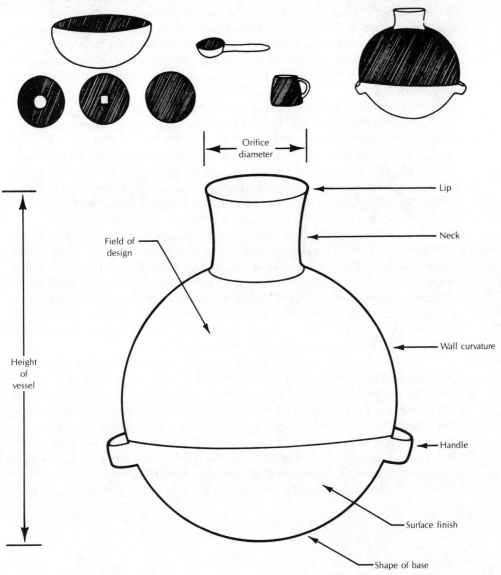

and proceeding through the tool assembly (manufacturing stages) to the finished product.

In short, one goal of formal analysis is to determine the method of artifact manufacture from the shape, size, and manufacturing marks left on the object. The second goal is to determine the use of ancient objects based on marks of wear. Use of an artifact will generate telltale wear on the working edge such as rounding, polish, striations, pitting, and cracks, all attributes which can be identified under high-powered magnification.

Distributional Analysis

Distributional analysis is a second source of artifact inference. The purpose of distributional studies is to learn why certain classes of artifacts occupy the same location in a site while other classes of artifacts occupy different locations in the site. When two or more classes of artifacts are found together, they are said to be *associated*. In artifact association, the archaeologist's concern is with the object-to-object relationship and the reasons for such spatial togetherness.

Another kind of distributional statement deals with artifact context, the relationship between the artifact and its physical setting. In the study of context, the archaeologist asks the question, why do certain classes of artifacts appear only in specific physical settings and fail to appear in others? Examples of physical settings where artifacts are found are trash deposits, storage pits, workshop locations, or dance plazas. Patterning as to where different kinds of artifacts are found leads the archaeologist to inferences about prehistoric behavior in the use and discard of tools and symbolic objects.

Distributional analysis is performed by mapping the spatial location of each individual artifact and class of artifacts, as illustrated for the burins (stone engravers) found at the Mesolithic site of Star Carr (Fig. 1–10). Such maps, with time held constant, may be constructed using several different techniques including scattergram (point location) or contour representation (areas or lines of equal frequency) (Fig. 1–11). Distributional maps of this nature are called *isochronic plots*. (*Iso-* means "same" and *chronic* means "time"—artifacts dating back to the same time in history.)

The next procedural step in distributional analysis is to superimpose two or more isochronic maps looking for spatial concordance (or lack of it) among the various mapped artifact classes (Fig. 1–11, lower). When comparison shows both artifact classes to display the same spatial spread within the site, then the artifacts are in "direct association." This kind of spatial relationship can be expressed in the logical form, *when A, then B*. A common explanation for direct association is that both tools and symbols are involved in the same institutional activity. Figure 1–12 illustrates a hut of the Mousterian culture, showing the direct association of hearths, animal bones, and mammoth teeth artifacts.

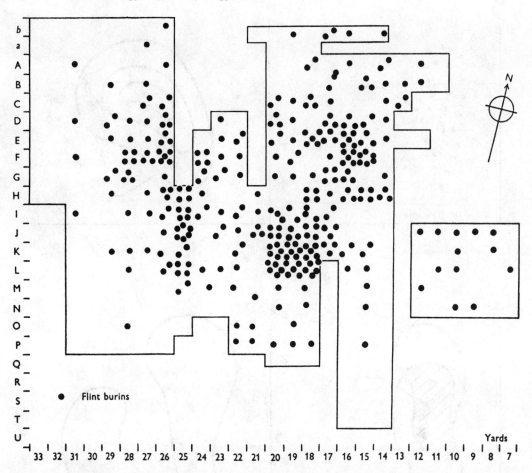

FIGURE 1-10   Scattergram mapping of flint burins found in the Mesolithic site of Star Carr, England.

Source: J. G. D. Clark, 1954, *Excavations at Star Carr*. Cambridge: University of Cambridge Press, p. 23.

On the other hand, when two or more artifact classes show mutual avoidance, then they are said to be in "indirect association." This avoidance relationship is expressed in the logical form, *when A, then not C*. The avoiding tools or symbols are then explained as members of differently scheduled institutional activities (Figure 1–11, lower).

So far artifact association has been presented in terms of mappable spatial patterning, a traditional approach to distributional analysis. But the modern archaeologist, who is seeking to quantify this data, is increasingly turning to statistical procedures to express the strength of associational patterns. Thus, the current technical literature of archaeology shows an increasing use of cor-

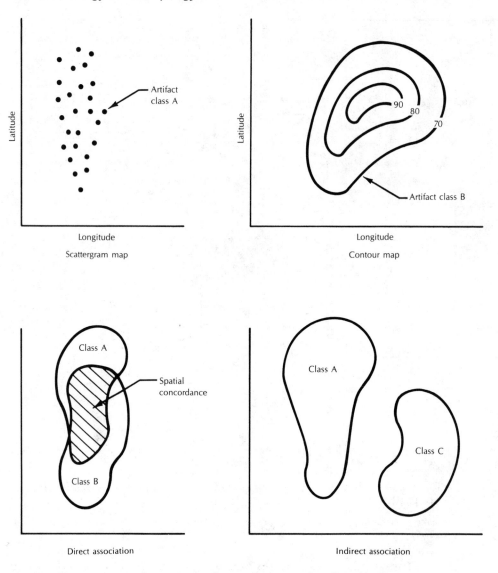

FIGURE 1-11 Isochronic maps showing patterns of artifact distributions.

relation statistics to express relatedness between one artifact class and another. Examples range from simple bivariate correlations like the Pearson R statistic to very complex, multivariate statistical procedures exemplified by factor analysis. Furthermore, because of the great number of calculations required to handle these statistics, the use of high-speed computers is important.

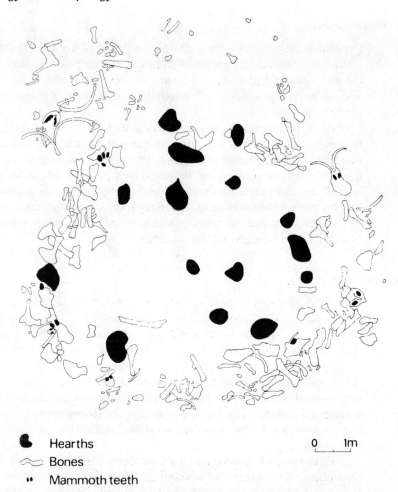

● Hearths

〜 Bones

•• Mammoth teeth

0   1m

FIGURE 1-12   Distributional map of a Middle Paleolithic hut of the Mousterian culture at Moldova, western Russia.

Source: From Francois Bordes, *The Old Stone Age;* London: Weidenfeld & Nicolson Ltd, p. 143.

In summary, the goals of distributional analysis are to define sets of associated artifact classes that were used in the same institutional activity at one location and at one scheduled time. By contrasting the artifacts of one subgroup activity against those of other scheduled institutional tasks, the investigator draws conclusions about the organization of the basic institutions of society.

Experimental Analysis

Experimentation is the manufacture and use of an artifact under controlled conditions to simulate technical behavior of the past. It is carried out to help the archaeologist identify the causes of attributes such as manufacture marks and to build up a body of knowledge about how preindustrial tools were made and used.

Certain controls must be exercised during the experiment. The simulating archaeologist must use the same materials and the same kinds of manufacturing tools as those available to the prehistoric artisan. As a final control, the wear marks and waste debris developed as the experiment proceeds should be compared to those present in the actual archaeological site. Examples of experimental analysis are reproductions of ancient stone tools made of flint and studies on the deterioration of the cutting edges of simulated Neolithic axes used to fell living trees.

Ethnographic Analogy

Inferences derived from the study of the behavior of living primitive peoples are called ethnographic analogy. If the same artifact form is present in both the living and the archaeological context, then the function and meaning of that object also should be the same. But in fact such analogies are not always valid since the form-to-function relationship of an artifact may change through time. For this reason, controls must be exercised by comparing societies, living-to-dead, of the same level of technical evolution and in the same environmental setting. The inference is further strengthened when the modern analog society is of the same historical tradition as the prehistoric society being excavated.

Ethnographic analogy is a particularly useful source of inference in interpreting the meaning of symbolism of ancient artifacts, but the nature of the analogy becomes increasingly dubious with increase in time. For instance, analogies drawn over the last ten thousand years, the Holocene epoch of geological time, are much more likely to be valid than those stretching back to societies dated into the Pleistocene epoch several hundred thousand years ago. And in fact there may well be fossil societies dated to the early Pleistocene, of ages in excess of one million years, for which there are no modern analogies at all.

Traditionally the archaeologist has relied on the expertise of the cultural anthropologist to contribute information on the form, function, and meaning of artifacts used by living primitive peoples. This information forms the modern analog for interpreting the past. In recent decades, however, the research orientation of the field of cultural anthropology has shifted away from the material trappings of society toward more purely social topics, such as studies of preindustrial kinship systems, language, and personality. For this reason, contemporary archaeologists increasingly undertake studies of the material record of living ethnographic peoples. This new development in archaeology is variously called "living archaeology" (Gould 1980), "behavioral archaeology" (Binford 1978, 1980), or "ethnoarchaeology" (Yellen 1977). The purpose of this new field of research is to identify consistent links between the material form of the artifact and its use, meaning, and significance. The archaeologist states a proposition (hypothesis) about the function of an object, then tests it against the fossil record.

Hypothesis Testing

A hypothesis may be derived from any of the four sources of archaeological inference: formal analysis, distributional data, experimental replication, or analogy with a living society. To verify the validity of an inference developed from one source, the archaeologist tests the provisional interpretation against evidence obtained independently from another source.

The hypothesis is a provisional statement explaining the manufacture, use (or purpose), and meaning (symbolism) of an artifact. If the hypothesis is correct, it enables the archaeologist to make reliable predictions. But the prediction should be subject to objective verification before the hypothesis is accepted as fact. Suppose that the shape and wear characteristics of an antler object suggest that it was used as a percussion punch in making stone tools (Fig. 1–13). The archaeologist's hypothesis is that the object was used as a

FIGURE 1-13   Manufacture of flake blades by indirect percussion using two different kinds of punches, hand-held punch (a) and chest-pressure technique (b).

Source: From Francois Bordes, *The Old Stone Age;* London: Weidenfeld & Nicolson Ltd, p. 3.

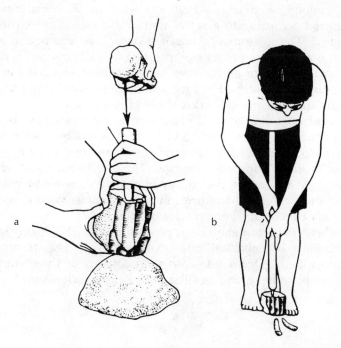

punch. The investigator predicts that other tools employed in the same blade-core technology should be present in the site and located near the antler punch to form a tool kit. Furthermore, this tool kit should be found only in workshop areas identified by waste debris from the knapping activity. The provisional hypothesis is accepted if the artifacts making up the tool kit, raw materials, and debris are found together: a cylinder hammer, special kinds of raw material blocks called *cores*, broken flakes and reject scrap from the manufacturing process, flake blades, and an anvil on which the core was rested as shown in Figure 1–13.

Summary

Anthropological archaeology is the investigation of society and culture within a time-space (or historical) framework. The goal of such study is to develop law-like generalizations about culture change and persistence, based on data obtained by observation and interpretation. Archaeology, itself, is a technical method for gathering cultural information. Its subject matter, which is varied, can be used by any of five departments in a university: Fine Arts, History, Classics, Oriental Languages, and Anthropology. In this textbook, however, the archaeologist is treated as a technician who gathers cultural information about the past for its anthropological uses.

Society is defined as cooperative groups of people organized to meet critical needs for survival, including material, biological, and emotional needs. Society is partitioned into subgroups called *institutions,* each of which is assigned one or more specific tasks to perform. The basic institutional subgroups are: economic, familial, political, and religious. Each institution is internally organized according to a set of ranked statuses to which its members are assigned. The institution also holds specialized equipment and knowledge about how to carry out its assigned tasks. Furthermore, its members follow customary behavior or activities in task performance. The activities of each subgroup are prescribed in time and place to avoid conflict with other such groups and to maximize efficient use of resources.

Understanding the role of artifacts in living societies is essential to the reconstruction of prehistoric social life. Artifacts bear several different relations to society: as elements of technology and the economy, and as symbols of social status and belief systems. These different meanings allow the archaeologist to recreate the culture of ancient societies by making inferences about their behavior. Culture consists of beliefs, values, and ideas held in common by a local community of people.

Death transformation is the process by which the highly structured living community is converted into an incomplete fossil record called an *archaeological site.* Death transformation consists of three subprocesses—discard, emplacement, and fossilization—all of which distort the archaeological data. When articles are discarded, they are removed from the setting where they were used by the living community. Emplacement is the means of artifact burial, whether cultural or natural. Fossilization is the means by which the artifact survives. From an understanding of the death process, the archaeologist can construct a picture of the living community.

The interpretation of fossilized societies is based on four sources of inference: formal analysis, distributional analysis, experimentation, and analogy. Formal analysis is the study of artifact shape and other physical qualities, called *attributes*. Distributional analysis seeks patterns to explain how the artifacts were scattered in space. Through replication, experimentation investigates the way objects were made and used. To derive inferences from analogy, the archaeologist studies living primitive people and links their activities to remains from the past. Each source of evidence concerning the past may provide a testable hypothesis, that is, a provisional explanation of past human behavior. But such hypotheses must be verified in independent bodies of data to be accepted as useful interpretations.

References

BINFORD, LEWIS R.
   1978   Dimensional Analysis of Behavior and Site Structure: Learning from an Eskimo Hunting Stand. *American Antiquity* 43:330–61.
   1980   Willow Smoke and Dog's Tails: Hunter-Gatherer Settlement Systems and Archaeological Site Formation. *American Antiquity* 45:4–20.
CLARK, GRAHAME
   1964   *Archaeology and Society.* London: Methuen.
EDDY, FRANK W.
   1974   Population Dislocation in the Navajo Reservoir District, New Mexico and Colorado. *American Antiquity* 39 (1):75–84.
FLANNERY, KENT V.
   1968   Archeological Systems Theory and Early Mesoamerica. In *Anthropological Archeology in the Americas.* Anthropological Society of Washington, D.C.
GLOB, P. V.
   1971   *The Bog People: Iron-Age Man Preserved.* New York: Ballantine Books.
GOULD, R. A.
   1980   *Living Archaeology.* Cambridge: Cambridge University Press.
HOLE, FRANK, AND ROBERT F. HEIZER
   1969   *An Introduction to Prehistoric Archeology.* New York: Holt, Rinehart and Winston.
KROEBER, A. L., AND CLYDE KLUCKHOHN
   1952   *Culture: A Critical Review of Concepts and Definitions.* New York: Vintage Books.
TAYLOR, WALTER W.
   1948   A Study of Archeology. *American Anthropologist* 50 (3).
THOMPSON, RAYMOND H.
   1958   Modern Yucatecan Maya Pottery Making. *American Antiquity* 23.

WILLEY, GORDON, R., AND PHILIP PHILLIPS
  1958   *Method and Theory in American Archaeology.* Chicago: University of Chicago Press.
YELLEN, JOHN E.
  1977   *Archaeological Approaches to the Present.* New York: Academic Press.

2 Cultural Evolution

Some of the earliest thinking on cultural evolution is attributed to a Chinese writer of AD 52 who proposed a sequence of stone, bronze, and iron ages (Daniel 1967, p. 34). In Europe, ancient Greeks and Romans also speculated about the antiquity of humankind. But modern archaeology, defined as the science of antiquity, began with the Three-Age classification of C. J. Thomsen early in the nineteenth century.

Thomsen, curator of the National Museum in Copenhagen, organized display collections according to their hypothesized ages in the stone-bronze-iron sequence. The artifacts in these collections had been contributed by peasant farmers, who accidentally uncovered the specimens while plowing their fields. The Three-Age hypothesis was still untested, but Thomsen published it in a guidebook to the exhibits when the museum opened in 1819. Thomsen's guidebook marks the beginning of scientific archaeology in the Western world. In fact, all later stage classifications in archaeology are elaborations on Thomsen's basic scheme.

In 1838 J. C. Boucher de Perthes, a customs official and amateur scientist, proved the existence of pre-modern humans. While hiking along the Somme River valley in northern France, de Perthes found fossil bones of ancient animals, such as elephants, and stone tools called *fist-axes*. These artifacts had eroded out of geologically old river deposits called *terraces*. De Perthes concluded correctly that the associated tools, animal bones, and fossil river deposits were all of the same age. And since the bones came from animals that were now extinct in Europe, de Perthes claimed evidence that human life began much earlier than the date accepted by Europeans of his day. Based on the Old Testament account of creation, such clerics as Archbishop James Ussher of England had calculated that the earth was 6000 years old. De Perthes reasoned that the fist-axe users must have been far older than 6000 years. These conclusions precipitated a direct confrontation between the evolutionists and the Biblical scholars of the day. Acceptance of his heretical ideas followed a vigorous campaign in which de Perthes talked before learned societies and conducted field trips for leading geologists.

Thomsen had proposed a developmental world, rather than a static world; de Perthes had proved that although the stone age had great antiquity, pre-modern humans were a part of it. But the succession of human developmental ages was still an untested theory until 1843, when J. J. A. Worsaae published the findings from his studies of Danish antiquities. From English geologists such as Charles Lyle and William Smith, Worsaae borrowed the two important principles of stratigraphy and association (Daniel 1967, p. 96). The principle of stratigraphic succession states that layers of earth are laid down in order with the oldest at the bottom of the series and the youngest at the top (Fig. 2-1). Worsaae applied this principle (sometimes considered a

FIGURE 2-1   Schematic stratigraphic section at Pech de L Aze II, southwestern France, illustrating the nature of layered archaeological cave deposits.

Source: Figure 7 from page 21 of *A Tale of Two Caves* by Francois Bordes. Copyright © 1972 by Francois Bordes. Reprinted by permission of Harper & Row Publishers, Inc.

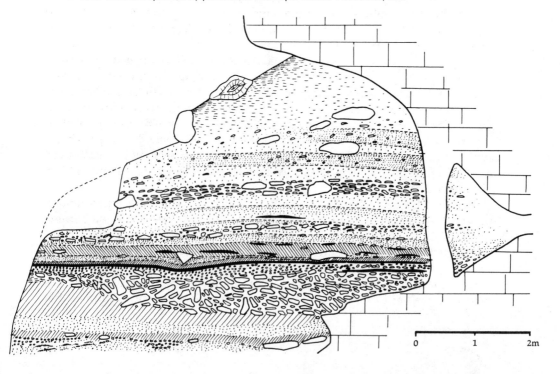

0   1   2m

TABLE 2-1.   Growth and development of successive systems of stage classification.

Artifact Materials (Thomsen 1836)	Manufacturing Technology (Lubbock 1865)	Economic Types (Willey and Phillips 1958)	Social Organization (Service 1962)
Iron Age	Iron age	Post-classic stage	Empires*
Bronze Age	Bronze age	Classic stage	States
	Neolithic stage	Formative stage	Chiefdoms
	Mesolithic stage*	Archaic stage	Tribes
Stone Age	Paleolithic stage	Lithic (Paleo-Indian*) Stage	Bands

*Subsequent addition or substitution to stage classification

scientific rule) to his excavation of artifact-rich peat bogs to prove that Thomsen's Three-Age scheme was correct. The principle of association states that fossils found together in one layer are the same age. Worsaae applied this principle to his study of the mound burials of bronze-age chieftains.

In 1865 Sir John Lubbock of England subdivided the stone age into the Paleolithic or old stone age, and the Neolithic or new stone age. Sometime later the Mesolithic was added to create a stage classification of five ages:

> Iron age (most recent)
> Bronze age
> Neolithic stage
> Mesolithic stage
> Paleolithic stage (earliest)

Further refinements in the stage classifications of antiquities provided new definitions for the strata. Whereas artifact materials had been the basis of Thomsen's Three-Age system, and manufacturing technology formed the criterion for Lubbock's Five-Age scheme, later classifications shifted to stage definitions based on economic developments and social organization. For example, the New World formulation of Gordon Willey and Philip Phillips (1958) is based on a subsistence economy for the early eras and organizational principles for the later strata. And ultimately, the evolutionary stages of Elman Service (1962) are based entirely on the successive appearance of new forms of human organization. A comparative chart showing the growing sophistication of archaeological stage classifications is given in Table 2-1.

Evolutionary Thought in Anthropology

Anthropology, as a distinct discipline, was born in the context of nineteenth-century evolutionary thought in Western Europe. European intellectuals challenged the Biblical view, as detailed in the Book of Genesis, that the earth and all of its life forms had been created in seven days. In the Biblical account, there was no room for trial-and-error or for a progression of social and natural systems from simple to complex. Instead, in the Judeo-Christian view of the nineteenth century, the world was the static, unchanging creation of a Supreme Being. And humankind was perfect until Adam and Eve "fell from grace"—which was not *evolution*, but *devolution* from the purity of the divine creation.

But gradually, a wealth of evidence from many fields showed that forms of life that were once present on earth no longer exist, and that the earth itself has experienced tremendous changes and upheavals not mentioned in the Bible. Evidence of evolutionary growth and development came from many fields—biology, paleontology, astronomy, and geology. At the same time, explorers, colonialists, and missionaries who returned to Europe from foreign lands brought stories of primitive peoples and exotic, pre-industrial civilizations. Scholars asked, how did this cultural diversity arise?

In many scientific fields scholars began to question the adequacy of the Biblical account of the origin of life. Social philosophers such as Herbert Spencer sought to explain European industrial society as the ultimate development of a long line of prior growth stages represented by primitive cultures of different degrees of complexity. At the same time, biologists such as Charles Darwin (1859) and Alfred Russel Wallace explained the diversity of life forms as a product of environmental selection and adaptation to new habitats. And in the field of geology, Charles Lyle explained the present form of the earth as the historical product of prior ages. Although each of these intellectuals worked with a different line of evidence, all put together parallel theories to account for the diversity of the world in terms of an evolution from simple to complex. A single, overriding theory of evolution accounted for many kinds of human and natural diversity.

Classical Cultural Evolutionism

Within this intellectual framework, two nineteenth-century scholars, E. B. Tylor of England and Lewis H. Morgan of the United States, founded the study of anthropology. In keeping with their times, they argued that all societies of the world are steps in human evolution from a primitive (savage) to a modern (civilized) condition. The primitive tribes were then explained as survivals left behind in the race for progress toward civilization, the ultimate goal in evolution. To Tylor and Morgan, advancement was by slow, imperceptible steps along many parallel lines of development leading to the same end. The stages marking the degree of human advancement were savagery, barbarism, and civilization. Morgan's (1877) criteria for sorting living, ethnographic peoples into these stages included: (1) inventions and discoveries, (2) forms of government, (3) family and social institutions, and (4) property ownership. To this list, Tylor (1871) included moral principles and beliefs dealing with magic and religion. Morgan's stage criteria were as follows:

Savagery
1. Emergence of humans
2. Discovery of fire
3. Invention of the bow and arrow

Barbarism
1. Invention of pottery
2. Domestication of animals
3. Smelting of iron ore

Civilization
1. Invention of writing
2. Invention of the alphabet (Daniel 1968, p. 29).

Although the classification was based largely if not entirely upon ethnographic data, the historical order of technical events is reasonably well supported by the findings of modern archaeology. Today, only the trait of iron metallurgy would be reordered, from barbarism to civilization. Furthermore, the invention of writing is still used to mark the beginning of civilization.

American Historical School

Classical evolutionism was the principal explanatory theory in anthropology until the 1920s and '30s, when it came under attack by Franz Boas and his students. Boas, founder of the American Historical school of thought, shifted attention away from the general evolutionism of Tylor and Morgan to emphasize the unique historical development of each individual society, a focus of study called *specific evolution*. Boas vigorously attacked classical evolutionary theory, saying that it was based on comparative study of contemporary ethnographies and thus could not be proved with historical data (Wolf 1964). This was a particularly telling argument since archaeology was not then in a position to provide much supporting evidence. Absolute chronologies were lacking for most of the world's prehistoric sequences. Boas reinforced his critique by stating that the theory of evolution did not take into account the spread of traits between societies. As a result, the Boasians, as they became known, successfully discredited the evolutionists, at least for the moment, and explained each particular culture as a unique historical outcome of its prior contacts with other cultures (Garbarino 1977).

British Social Anthropology

In turn, the American Historical school was criticized during the 1930s and '40s by two British social (cultural) anthropologists, A. R. Radcliff-Brown and B. Malinowski, who pointed out that oral, ethnographic data is not amenable to historical study. Furthermore, many philosophers of science do not accept a historical explanation as valid; that is, the fact that one event precedes another does not prove that the earlier event caused the later one. Instead, said

Brown and Malinowski, the proper approach to the study of anthropology is to investigate the contemporary structure (organization) and function (behavior) of society. Both men viewed society as an integrated system in which each trait and item was interrelated to all others. The investigator can enter such a system at any point, and by tracing out the interrelationships, eventually examine the entire system. Brown emphasized the contribution that each part of society makes to the maintenance of the whole, while Malinowski modeled society as a series of interrelated parts, essentially the basic institutions described in Chapter 1.

The systems model used by the Functionalists, as they are called, is homeostasis. This kind of system is often compared to a heating system in which the thermostat is set for an ideal equilibrium. Any disruption of this equilibrium is followed by an attempt on the part of this system to regain the ideal state. Thus, historical accidents that upset the cultural system are mere inconveniences, followed by a rapid return to the ideal equilibrium among the component parts. Such a model of society allows very little room for historical studies and none at all for the process of evolution. It ignores the vast body of data that relate to the growth history of individual societies and world culture in general.

Neo-Evolutionism

Despite these two major attacks, there has been a recent resurgence of interest in evolutionary theory because of two developments that have occurred since the 1950s. First, archaeology has put its chronological house in order through radiometric dating, particularly using carbon-14. Carbon-14 dating, explained more fully in Chapter 5, measures time elapsed since the death of an organism, such as wood, bone, or shell, by the decay rate of radioactive carbon isotope 14. By this means, prehistoric archaeology for the first time has been able to contribute massive independent proof of the course of evolution. And second, once again anthropologists are concerning themselves with similarities rather than differences among world cultures. According to Wolf (1964), they are seeking to construct a science of culture rather than an inventory of particulars. Wolf has described the basis of the new evolutionism, termed *neo-evolution*, as an integration of the previous approaches of scientific anthropology. This synthesis includes the most useful concepts of classical evolutionism, the American Historical school, and the British social anthropologists.

Neo-evolutionism is founded on the theories of three men: V. Gordon Childe, Julian H. Steward, and Leslie White. Childe contributed the concept of revolutions in human economy. Steward is concerned with evolution along many parallel lines (called *multilinear evolution*) through environmental adaptation. White believes that universal evolution is the consequence of the technical capture of energy (Wolf 1964; Garbarino 1977).

The Nature of Cultural Change

Anthropological research has identified three aspects of society that change through time: style, institutional arrangements, and culture. Style is a year-to-year fashion change, that is, short-term change in artistic decoration. Change in institutional function, which occurs in approximately a decade, is the result of variation in the individual's adaptive relations with the social and physical environment. Cultural evolution is long-term change on a scale of centuries or even millenia. Evolution is the cumulative effect of many successful adaptations leading to irreversible growth and development in the structure and function of society as a whole.

Style Change

Style change affects both craft decoration and fine art. Traditionally craft decoration has been investigated by both anthropologists and specialists in particular crafts, such as textiles and ceramics (Bunzel 1972). On the other hand, fine art has been the special provenience of art historians. To the anthropologist, stylistic or fashion change is the product of what Kroeber (1948) has called the "play instinct." Art historians conceive of the great art traditions as expressions of the individual genius of particular civilizations. But all scholars agree that artistic change follows its own canons or laws. The principal generalization is that such change is cyclical, and major fashions repeat themselves in a wave-like manner. Art styles have a tendency to evolve bi-directionally from simple to complex and back to simple again through elaboration and simplification of the decorative detail.

The aesthetic products of a community of artists always show a range of expression in which some are archaic, others modal, and still others are prototypical. Most of the contemporary artistic output is modal, or fashionable. In contrast, a smaller proportion of art works, generally the products of the older generation of artists, are recognized as somewhat archaic, or outmoded. At the other end of the scale an equally small proportion of aesthetic products are created "before their time." These prototypical examples inspire the modal art forms of the next generation. Often they are the creations of younger artists and are not appreciated by "traditionalists." Clarke (1968) has expressed these concepts in systems theory terms in which the archaic, modal, and prototypical examples are states of an ongoing and continuously oscillating art system (Fig. 2–2).

Changes in the quality of art forms are coupled with changes in quantity. A few examples of a new art style appear early in time as the output of a single innovative craftsman. As the artistic idea catches on and becomes popular, more and more examples are produced until the new style becomes the standard followed by virtually every member of the art community. Still later in time, this style is practiced by only a few aged artisans until all have died, leaving only a few extant examples of their work to linger as "heirloom" pieces of what was once fashionable in a bygone day. This kind of history is called a *popularity curve* with five recognized points: origination, frequency increase, climax, decreasing frequency, and extinction.

Both the qualitative and quantitative aspects of stylistic change are employed in archaeology and art history as aids in dating. Stylistic dating was first introduced into archaeology by Sir Flinders Petrie in 1899 as a means of chronologically ordering a large series of pre-Dynastic Egyptian graves he was then excavating in the delta region of the Nile river. Petrie's dating was based on the presence or absence of certain style attributes at a specific time in history. For example, in a decorative series made up of ceramic types lettered A through E, an early grave would contain Types A and B in association with a pre-Dynastic skeleton. A slightly younger grave would contain funeral offerings consisting of ceramic Types B and C, while the latest grave in the

FIGURE 2-2   A distribution of artifacts or attributes within an assemblage—two alternative portrayals of the same data. The subdivision of the distribution into archaic, modal, prototypical sections is valid only in cases where a moving mode may be traced.

Source: From David L. Clarke, 1968, *Analytical Archaeology.* London: Methuen, p. 149.

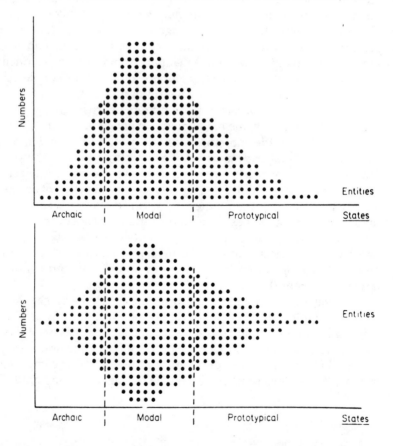

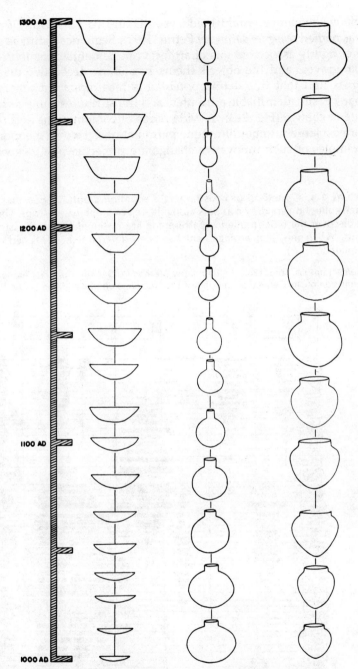

FIGURE 2-3   The gradual change of vessel shapes through time.

Source: James A. Ford, 1962, *A Quantitative Method for Deriving Cultural Chronology.* Reprinted by permission of the General Secretariat of the Organization of American States.

relative sequence would hold Types D and E. This form of stylistic dating was named *sequence dating* by Petrie (1899). Sequence dating is possible whenever tightly associated lots of artifacts can be defined, as in the sealed Egyptian graves, and the objects themselves show decorative details. Archaeologists find that this dating potential is most apparent where objects yield many easily identifiable attributes, and the attributes show a steady, constant rate of change (Fig. 2–3). A wide range of combinations and recombinations forms a large number of unique permutations. Two of the more outstanding examples of such innovative change are projectile points, such as the stone

FIGURE 2-4   Method of constructing a seriation graph. Frequencies of the types in each collection are drawn as bars along the top of graph-paper strips. These are arranged to discover the type-frequency pattern and are fastened to a paper backing with paper clips. When the final arrangement has been determined, a finished drawing may be prepared.

Source: James A. Ford, 1962, *A Quantitative Method for Deriving Cultural Chronology.* Reprinted by permission of the General Secretariat of the Organization of American States.

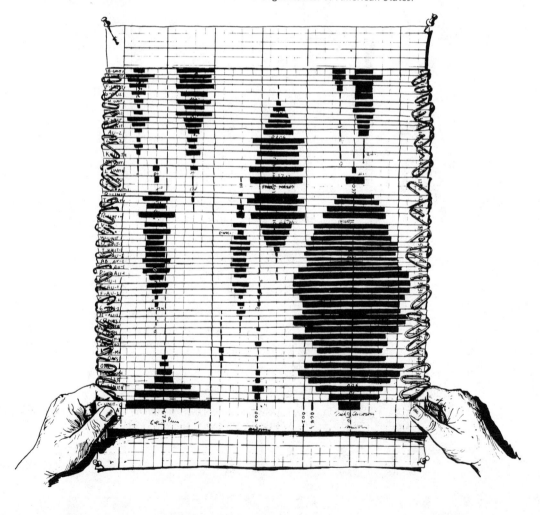

tips of darts and arrows, and the shape and decorative attributes of ceramic vessels.

The history of stylistic attributes is used to date archaeological sites and deposits in a graph technique called *chronological seriation*. Figure 2–4 shows a bar graph in which each collection of datable artifacts is plotted in percentage frequencies. These bars are then arranged in series so that the members of each artifact type trace out a double-convex pattern, which statisticians call a *battleship curve*. The most perfect arrangement orders each artifact collection in chronological series (Ford 1962). Recent improvements on the graphic display have been in the form of matrix manipulation of similarity coefficients sorted either by hand or by means of computerized programs (Brainerd 1951; Hole and Shaw 1967).

Functional Change

Functional change is brought about by alterations in the component parts of the cultural system. These components are the basic institutions of society, such as economics, family, government, and religion. Change takes place in a number of different ways. The structure of the institution changes when the statuses of members are redefined in terms of their respective duties and obligations. Changes in the function of the institution consist of modifications in the roles of personnel, the tasks assigned to the institution, the available technology to do work, and the knowledge needed for task performance. Alterations in the intensity of effort also create change; examples include increase in the number of work hours, the scheduling of additional tasks, and growth of the labor force. And finally, the relationships between institutions may change.

Functional change results from the process called *adaptation* in which society seeks a more perfect fit with both its physical environment and the neighboring cultures. Adaptation, then, links the institutional components of society to the external world. As a process, adaptation is performed by a combination of technical and social adjustments. Technical adjustments include the invention and use of new means of extracting materials and energy from the natural environment in order to run the cultural system. Social adjustments consist of the reorganization of social institutions, and in particular the economy, for the manufacture, distribution, and consumption of goods and services. Change results when new adaptive relationships have been established. Relationships change when colonization of a new environment takes place, when the environment itself changes, and when the society adopts improved social and technical means of exploiting natural resources. According to Clarke (1968, pp. 57–59), adaptation creates a dynamic equilibrium between culture and environment. Change in one system produces concomitant change in the other until a new equilibrium is obtained. The interchange is sometimes compared to a two-party game in which a move by one player is met by a countermove of the other.

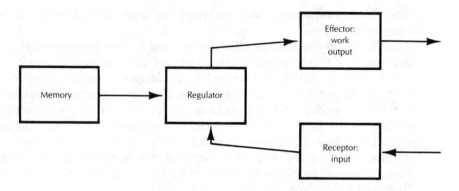

FIGURE 2-5   Adaptive qualities of a cultural system.

Society can be described as a system consisting of (1) an input receptor, (2) a regulator, (3) work output or an effector, and (4) a memory unit (Fig. 2-5). The input receptor takes in food and fuel to run the system; basically input is the function of the economic institution. The receptor also monitors the environment to sense change requiring rescheduling of institutional activities.

The system regulator is a control unit that makes decisions such as the volume of resources to acquire from the environment, utilization of new technologies, organization and work assignments of personnel, schedule of work and celebrations, and the distribution and consumption of products and services. The political and religious institutions are responsible for most of these decision-making actions.

The memory component of society serves as an archive of information on past system performance, and a repository for plans to handle future environmental contingencies. Memory in illiterate, primitive societies consists of myth, legend, oral history, and personal anecdotes. For example, the bard in a preliterate society acts as a memorizer of past cultural experience, which can be drawn on for future reference. On the other hand, memory in civilized societies consists of written records like census lists, tax rolls, and business accounts.

And finally, the effector or work output unit produces goods and services for the cultural system. Examples of products are artifacts, repair and maintenance services, fuel, human population, and movement of the community itself.

Central to a successful adaptation is the decision-making process performed by the system regulator. Constant adjustment is necessary to keep the system performance fine-tuned to environmental changes: (1) seasonal changes in an annual cycle, (2) year-to-year variations in the environment, (3) short-term catastrophes, and (4) long-term effects such as a decade of drought. To make a successful decision, the system regulator must receive information from the receptor on the behavior of the opponent, either the natural environment or competitive neighboring peoples. Next the regulator searches its memory for like situations and successful solutions from the past, like a ruler consulting the expertise of advisors and councilors. Next a decision is made that solves the problem at hand. In a bronze-age civilization, an autocrat sent a directive down to his underlings. In a loosely organized band society, the decision might be reached individually as a consensus among many citizens.

Decisions, themselves, consist of day-to-day tactics or long-term strategies for adaptation. An example of a tactical decision might be where to move a hunting-gathering band for the most profitable foraging. Strategies, on the other hand, are policies held by rulers as to how best to play the game of adaptation. Strategies represent trade-offs of risk versus winnings. Optimizer strategies attempt to acquire the maximum possible gain from an array of alternative courses of action regardless of the risk involved. Such strategies are practiced by "gamblers" who play a game of winner-take-all, but few successful societies can afford such high risk and long endure. Instead, most cultures practice satisficer (from *satis*fy and sacri*fice*) strategies, which pick a prudent but less than optimum course of action to minimize the risk involved (Clarke 1968, p. 94). Satisficer strategies are satisfactory and safe but are not optimal in earnings.

Satisficer strategies have been classified into three types: (1) mixed or blend strategies, (2) randomized strategies, and (3) minimax strategies. The blend strategies are those in which several courses of action are followed simultaneously. A Pueblo Indian farmer of the American desert West, for example, plants fields in a number of different locations to insure against total crop failure in the face of unpredictable year-to-year rainfall (Forde 1963). A randomized strategy is one in which the responses are made to search the outcomes for advantages. Such strategies are exercised when little is known about the opponent, for instance, in the case of colonizers entering an unexplored continent. The minimax, maximin, or most prudent kind of strategy aims at maximizing returns for the minimum risk taken. Minimax strategies are employed by highly vulnerable primitive band societies, whose simple technologies offer little protection against the extremes of the environment.

Several different expressions of functional change leave an imprint in the fossil record. One example is variation in the numbers and kinds of tools comprising an artifact assemblage. This kind of change record has been observed from the Lower Paleolithic site of Olorgesailie, Kenya (Fig. 2–6). Here a percentage analysis of tool types from 13 stratified land surfaces indicates a cyclical shift from use of small tools on Surface 1 to large cutting tools on Surfaces 7 to 9, and return again to the initial pattern by Surfaces 12 and 13. Kleindienst (1961, p. 44) has attributed these differences to functional variability, that is, changing activities at the same spot.

OLORGESAILIE

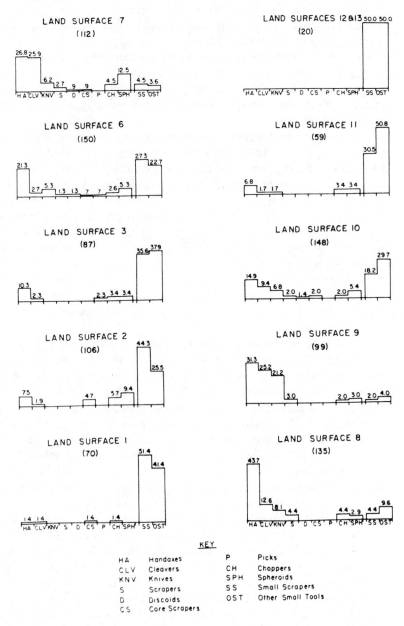

KEY

HA	Handaxes	P	Picks
CLV	Cleavers	CH	Choppers
KNV	Knives	SPH	Spheroids
S	Scrapers	SS	Small Scrapers
D	Discoids	OST	Other Small Tools
CS	Core Scrapers		

FIGURE 2-6   Percentages of major types of shaped tools at Olorgesailie, Kenya.

Source: From Maxine R. Kleindienst, "Variability Within the Late Acheulian Assemblage in Eastern Africa," Figure 3; *The South African Archaeological Bulletin* 16:35–52; Cape Town: The South African Archaeological Society, 1961.

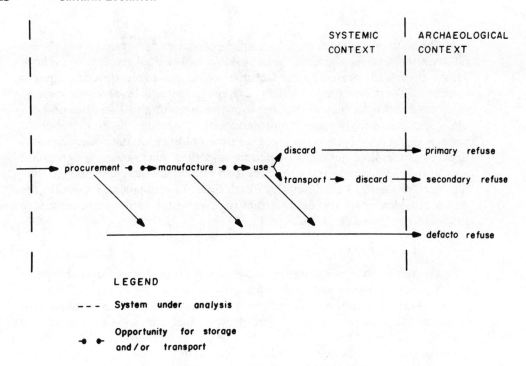

FIGURE 2-7   A simplified flow model shows the differences among primary, second-ary, and de facto refuse.

Source: Michael B. Schiffer, "Archaeological Context and Systematic Context," reproduced by per-mission of Society for American Archaeology from *American Antiquity* 37(2):156–65, 1972.

The spatial configuration of artifacts also indicates functional change. Schiffer (1972, 1976) has diagrammed the flow pattern of artifacts as they pass through society, termed the *systemic context,* and become refuse, the *archaeological context* (Fig. 2–7). Three different kinds of refuse are identifiable, each the product of a different institutional function. Primary refuse is discarded worn-out artifacts thrown away at the place of use. Secondary refuse is waste deposited at a dump following transport from the place of use. And "de facto refuse" consists of tools, facilities, and other cultural materials that, although still usable, are abandoned within an activity area (1976, p. 33). Functional change is recognizable by the relocation of dump refuse through time.

Evolutionary Change

Cultural evolutionary theory seeks to explain the growth and development of culture through time. It traces the long-term trends or patterns of growth and development and attempts to explain them.

The following generalizations are long-term trends in prehistory: (1) Evolutionary change is *directional* (goal seeking) rather than random or cyclical. This pattern is illustrated by the fact that society has evolved from simple to complex. (2) Evolutionary change is *adaptive* because it involves an increasingly closer fit with the environment for the extraction of materials and energy, and increasingly more structured relations among human members of society. (3) Change progresses toward *survival* of the human species as measured by increasing numbers of people and their ever wider geographical spread over the face of the earth. (4) And finally, the *rate* and pace of evolutionary change has accelerated through time. Two opposing models in the anthropological literature express this regularity: the ramp versus the step model of change (Adams 1971, p. 17).

MODELS OF CHANGE

The ramp model of change expresses the concept that evolution has been steadily increasing in a curvilinear fashion. The graph line of Figure 2–8a portrays the idea that culture, as a system of information storage, is cumulative—it builds on what went before. Furthermore, this growth is exponential; it increases by a power rather than a simple linear relationship. Although individual societies may decline and die, most societies survive and incorporate knowledge, which is passed on to future, evolving societies.

The step model of change (Fig. 2–8b) expresses the same accumulating growth of society, but differs from the ramp model by indicating an uneven

FIGURE 2-8   Two opposing models expressing the accelerating pace of culture evolution: (a) the ramp model of change; (b) the step model of change.

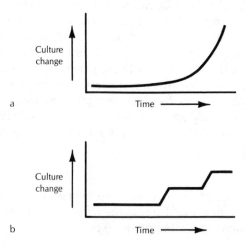

pace of growth. The step model shows periods of abrupt change, upward surges to new plateaus of organizational complexity. During these plateaus, little change occurs, and information acquired during the growth spurt is integrated into the cultural system. Because these spurts seemed to appear suddenly in the archaeological record, V. Gordon Childe (1961) saw them as revolutions. Childe identified three major evolutionary advances: the Neolithic, urban, and industrial revolutions.

The model of economic revolutions has a step form in which the treads represent minimal cultural and population growth (i.e., system stability). In contrast, the step risers represent spurts of cultural and population growth. Each step riser has three phases of change. In the first phase new inventions in food production generate a shift to the growth phase. Growth, itself, is sustained by positive feedback in which population expansion creates a further need for elaboration of the productive economy and more social contol. The growth spurt shuts down in the third phase as the ruling elite of society stifles further technical inventions as their appetite for luxuries is satiated by tribute, taxation, and plunder (Childe 1961).

The Development of Culture

In the past, anthropologists explained cultural evolution mentalistically in terms of the creation of new ideas (or norms) isolated in time and space. The invention of the airplane, for example, was a new idea that has had profound effects on culture. Recently, however, anthropologists have turned to materialistic systems—especially changes generated from the technological and economic system of society—to account for cultural evolution.

Mentalistic Explanations

Mentalistic explanations attribute the growth and development of society to new ideas that result from or produce (1) invention, (2) innovation, (3) discovery, and (4) diffusion or acculturation.

Invention is the process by which an individual genius creates new traits or items. After studying Patent Office records, Kroeber (1948) concluded that inventions are a response to the needs of society, rather than the cause of such needs. The steam engine, for example, was invented while people were exploring and settling a vast continent.

Innovation is a creative process in which existing traits or items are recombined to form new artifacts (Barnett 1953). Kroeber's patent study showed that a burst of innovative patents follows the appearance of a brand new invention, as the new idea is combined and recombined in many ways. Ultimately, patents of this class taper off as the pattern's potential is exhausted.

Discovery is a change process involving the finding of an existing element in nature. The element may be as vast as a continent (the discovery of America) or as minute as an atom (the discovery of radioactive radium and uranium).

Diffusion is a change process that results when ideas or traits are transferred from one society to another. This kind of change is called *borrowing*. Usually borrowing spreads outward from the point of origin in concentric

FIGURE 2-9   The diffusion of an attribute or type in time and space.

Source: Illustration from *Invitation to Archaeology* by James Deetz. Copyright © 1967 by James Deetz. Reproduced by permission of Doubleday & Company, Inc.

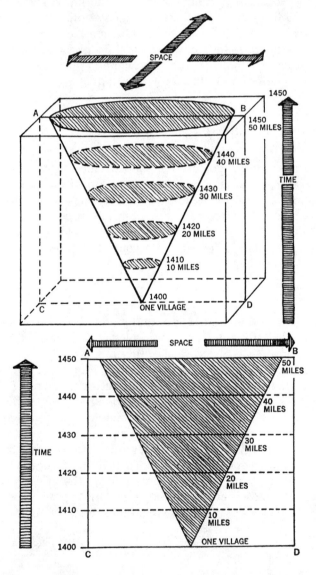

circles, like waves created by the splash of a pebble in a placid pond (Fig. 2–9). As a special case of diffusion, acculturation usually occurs when a dominant culture forces a subordinate culture to change, as illustrated in many colonial societies.

Materialist Explanations

Materialistic explanations for the growth and development of society are all based on the premise that cultural evolution is generated by the application of new technical and economic systems (Harris 1969, 1980; Price 1982). These explanations emphasize the changing of systems, rather than isolated changes such as inventions and discoveries. From the material base, evolutionary change spreads upward to the sociological and ideological realms as each higher level of society undergoes functional adjustment (Fig. 2–10).

Materialism, itself, is founded in the economic determinism of Karl Marx and Frederick Engels (Etzioni and Etzioni 1964), which fostered the revival of the study of cultural evolution, the school of anthropology called *neo-evolutionism*. Although anthropologists such as White, Steward, and Childe deserve credit for this evolutionary revival, it was not until Marvin Harris (1969) had developed his "strategy of cultural materialism" that the component parts of society and the material source of cultural change were outlined by an integrated model. The principles of techno-economic determinism state that: "similar technologies applied to similar environments tend to produce similar arrangements of labor in production and distribution, and that these in turn

FIGURE 2-10   A materialist model of society, showing the source and direction of culture change. Arrows indicate direction of change.

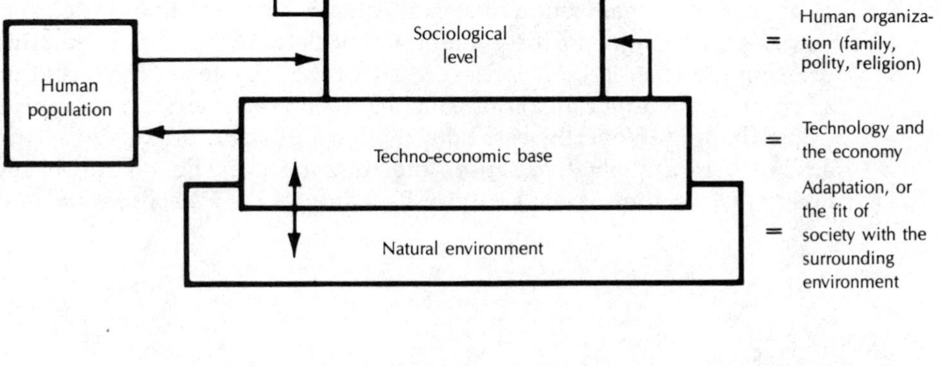

Organization of Society by Levels

call forth similar kinds of social groupings which justify and coordinate their activities by means of similar systems of values and beliefs" (Harris 1969, p. 4). To Harris, change in society is generated by systems modification in the relationship between technology and environment, rather than trait or item invention. The changing systems are technologies for the exploitation of and adjustment to environmental habitats. Thus, they are systems of adaptation.

Some examples of adaptive systems are: (1) hunting and gathering subsistence; (2) food production by dry farming, slash-and-burn agriculture, canal irrigation agriculture, and wet rice agriculture using terraced pools; (3) fishing by hook and line, netting, or use of fish weir and harpoons; (4) nomadic pastoralism, either husbanding semiwild herd animals such as reindeer or herding fully domesticated species on a seasonal cycle of available pasture.

From the adaptive relationship between technology and environment, change spreads upward to the economy where it affects the arrangement of labor. Labor organization includes the size of the work group and its composition by sex and age; it further entails leadership and administration, the number and kinds of specialized workers, and the inclusion of trainees. The means of compensation may be an equal division of produce, or differential payment with a larger share for the foreman, investor, and/or payment to the state in the form of a tax.

The arrangement of labor, in turn, determines the kinds of social groupings, including family, polity, and religious institutions. Organization of these institutions, then, determines the nature of ideologies. Ideologies are rationalizations justifying social reality and regulating the rate and nature of technoeconomic change coming from below. Ideologies include ethics, values, and beliefs—the realm of mental consciousness anthropologists call *world view*.

Childe's (1961) theory of revolutions explains the stages of prehistory as qualitatively new lifestyles brought about by inventions of new food-producing technologies, coupled with new social arrangements of labor. The interaction between these two variables increases the food supply and thereby the number of people. To Childe, three revolutions were significant in the economic history of the world: (1) the Neolithic or food-producing revolution, (2) the urban revolution marked by the appearance of civilization, and (3) the industrial revolution of eighteenth-century England. The basic question Childe asked was, what were the causes that repeatedly transformed small, egalitarian village communities into autocratically controlled urban societies?

Childe used the term *revolution* in two ways: as a qualitative change in the nature and organization of society, and in a quantitative sense, to imply a rapid growth spurt in the evolution of society. Childe has been criticized for using the term in both senses. Many of the changes in the Neolithic age occurred over a long time (approximately 4000 years) rather than abruptly as Childe thought. Nevertheless, both the Neolithic and urban stages are revolutionary in a qualitative sense, and they are even quantitatively revolutionary against the two-million-year backdrop of the Paleolithic stage.

Childe developed the thesis that technology, population, and social organization are causally related by observing the English industrial revolution. During this revolution, England's economic potential was transformed through the energy released from fossil fuels such as coal, gas, and petroleum. The technical device invented to unlock fossil energy was the steam engine, applied to railroads, steamships, and textile mill equipment. Ancillary equipment included gas lighting and ultimately the internal-combustion engine.

The new social arrangement of labor organized to run the industrial machinery was the factory (Heilbroner 1961). The factory is an economic organization composed of owner, management, and skilled labor, trained in mass production of modular products. English textile mills were industrialized first, capitalizing on the invention of the spinning jenny, power loom, and cotton gin. Next came iron and steel mechanization, followed by chemicals in Germany.

Childe next asked the question, how was the food supply affected by the industrial revolution? He found the answer in new forms of applied science, which increased agricultural production. Initially, food production was increased through the application of science rather than by machinery. These scientific techniques involved the application of chemical fertilizers, crop rotation, and selective breeding of livestock. Changes in land tenure took place simultaneously. Small farm holdings were forced into receivership in order to form larger and more efficient consolidated farms. The dispossessed small farmers who were forced off their land migrated to the industrialized cities to swell the work force required by factory development. After 1830, however, industrial machinery was applied to farming in the form of the steel-bladed plow and reaper invented in the United States.

Childe's next question was, what were the consequences of the industrial revolution? The answer was multiple social effects, of which he chose population increase as an index of progress. As shown in Figure 2–11, the population of England in 1750 was 6.5 million persons. From this baseline,

FIGURE 2-11   Graph of the estimated population of Great Britain, 1500–1800.

Source: V. Gordon Childe, 1961, *Man Makes Himself,* p. 18, by permission of Pitman Books Ltd., London.

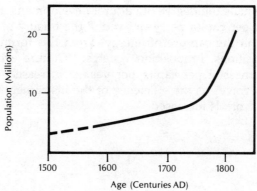

it jumped to 16.3 million by 1801, showing an upward "kink" or surge. When graphed, the line of population growth rotates through about 30 degrees precisely during the decades of industrial growth. From this finding, Childe concluded that new food-producing technologies, coupled with new social arrangements of labor, led to upsurges in population growth.

From this modern model, Childe turned to past economic history, looking for other upward kinks in the world's population curve indicative of successful economic revolutions (Childe 1961, p. 19). The predictive value of his industrial model was confirmed when he observed that past technical stages, such as the Neolithic and bronze ages, led to significant jumps in world populations.

Like Childe, Leslie White (1949) was greatly influenced by the economic determinism of Karl Marx. White called his brand of general evolutionism *universal evolution* because it was based on the assumptions that: (1) all cultures should be averaged together to produce composite accomplishments, and (2) the environment is a constant that does not affect the evolution of culture (White 1949, p. 368 fn). In this respect, he differed from the techno-environmental principle of Marvin Harris and the cultural ecology of Julian H. Steward. Otherwise, White is a party-line materialist.

White views technology as the prime cause of cultural change. He views the sociological and ideological levels of society as dependent variables showing a lag response to the effects of techno-economic determinism. As new technologies are invented to extract new forms and increasing amounts of energy from the constant environment, there is a step-rise in cultural growth. During the Paleolithic stage, humankind had harnessed only manpower, utilized through hunting technology and the band form of social organization. But by the Neolithic and bronze ages, plant and animal energy had been harnessed by domestication. During the industrial revolution, fossil fuels were the principal sources of new energy. The contemporary atomic age is a growth spurt based on splitting the atom, a source of energy harnessed by atomic reactors.

White uses a symbolic model to express the relationship between energy and cultural growth:

$$E \times T \to C$$

where C equals the degree of cultural development, E the amount of energy harnessed per capita per year, and T the quality or efficiency of the tools employed in the capture of energy. From this formulation, White deduces two propositions. Proposition 1 states: "Culture evolves as the amount of energy harnessed per capita per year is increased." Proposition 2 states: "Culture evolves as the efficiency of the instrumental means of putting the energy to work is increased."

Steward (1955) proposed that the evolution of culture along many parallel paths is created by environmental adaptations in the following sequence: (1) a particular exploitive technology operating on a (2) particular environmental habitat (3) generates a particular form of human organization. In contrast to White, who conceives of the environment as a constant, Steward stresses the importance of the interactive role between technology and the useful environment in producing ever more evolved forms of human organization.

Some more recent examples of materialist theories are those of Sanders and Price (1968) and Robert Carneiro (1970). Both theories relate human population size and density to advances in the sociological level of society. The data of the Sanders and Price theory, presented in Figure 2–12, shows that both population size and population density are highly correlated with forms of social organization in the progression from band, to tribe, to chiefdom, and finally civilization. Their thesis is that as the size of human populations increases, the need for political control increases. Thus, larger populations generate more complex forms of human organization.

The cause-and-effect relationship between population size and the level of social complexity has been clarified by Carneiro (1970). In his circumscription theory, he posits that expanding populations encounter constraints of two kinds: natural and social. The natural circumscription consists of geographical barriers (for example, mountains, deserts, and oceans) that stop the spreading of population. Density builds up, leading to warfare as a means of competing for the scarce resources of energy (fuels), land, water, and other raw materials necessary to run a society. As a result, warfare erupts with increasing frequency so that the most elite status in society is that of the war leader. Much the same population packing results from social circumscription as the frontiers of any given society become closed off by the expansion of neighboring peoples.

Among archaeologists, the tendency to follow some variety of materialism is particularly strong. The basic data of archaeology, particularly prehistoric archaeology, is composed of artifacts of which the vast majority relate to technology and economic practices. The symbolic artifacts relating to the sociological and ideological levels of society are far less commonly preserved in the fossil record. For this reason, materialistic explanations of culture evolution are not only easier to apply to archaeological data, but they are more elegant and satisfying in the kinds of cause-and-effect relationships specified.

In review, most archaeological materialists look to some form of adaptation, that is, the fit between the economic base of society and the natural environment, as the causal source of cultural growth and development. Cumulative change of this nature results from the invention of new forms of productive technology. Increased production of food resources in turn expands the number of people and their density on the landscape. Enlarged

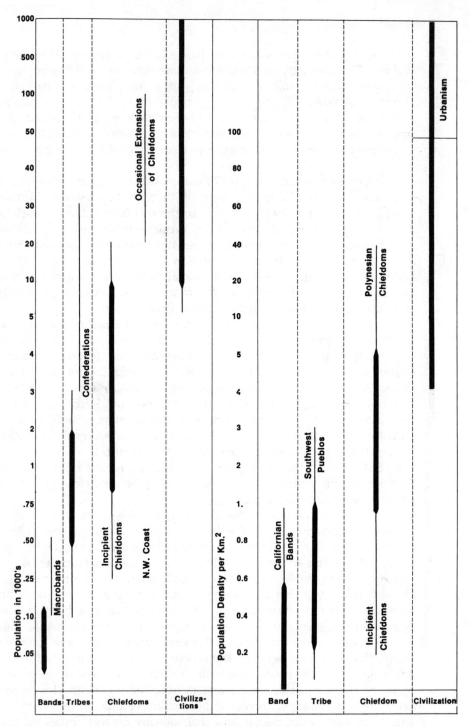

FIGURE 2-12 Chart showing the empirical relationship between societal organization, population size, and population density.

Source: From *Mesoamerica: The Evolution of a Civilization,* by William T. Sanders. Copyright © 1968 by Random House, Inc. Reprinted by permission of publisher.

human populations further create a need for greater social control expressed in more complex arrangements of human organization. This greater complexity in the sociological level of society, in turn, is rationalized and justified by changes in the ideological belief systems. Although this model of society and its levels of organization is basically uni-directional with cause-and-effect change spreading from the concrete base to the abstract top, still return or feedback amplifications take place at every tiered level (Fig. 2–10). Thus an increase in the number of people creates further need for increasing food production. Again, as the organization of society is increased in complexity, the resulting administrative control leads to greater economic productivity and thus more food production, a feedback loop which amplifies the expansion of population. Finally, shifts in the ideological level of society call for and justify ever more structured relationships among people in the direction of the rise of elitism or privileged status that is validated by the new values and attitudes.

Summary

During the nineteenth century, European scholars began to challenge the Biblical story of creation. The finding of stone-age tools provided evidence for the theory of evolution, which proposes that the earth and its inhabitants are developing over time. The first stage theory divided human history into three ages, the stone age, bronze age, and iron age. Evolutionary thought explained the diversity of the world's peoples through the concepts of adaptation and survival. Anthropology was an outgrowth of evolutionary thought in many sciences, including social philosophy, biology, and geology. Anthropologists attempt to explain how culture evolves from simple to complex.

Anthropological research has identified three aspects of society that change over time: style, institutions, and culture. Cultural evolution is described as goal-oriented, adaptive, accelerating over time, and ever increasing the numbers of people to provide for the survival of humankind. Some writers describe this progress as an upward curve, while others see it as a series of steps—spurts of progress followed by periods of adjustment.

In the past, anthropologists explained cultural evolution mentalistically—as the result of new ideas that produced inventions, innovations, and discoveries and led to diffusion of these ideas from one society to another. Today many anthropologists are offering materialistic explanations for cultural evolution. Influenced by the economic determinism of Marx and Engels, materialism contends that changing systems of economic production drive society in the direction of ever more complex forms of human organization. As a society adjusts to new forms of organization, ideology changes to bring the cultural system to a new state of equilibrium.

References

ADAMS, ROBERT McC.
   1966   *The Evolution of Urban Society.* Chicago: Aldine.

BARNETT, HOMER G.
   1953   *Innovation: The Basis of Cultural Change.* New York: McGraw-Hill.

BRAINERD, G. W.
   1951   The Place of Chronological Ordering in Archaeological Analysis. *American Antiquity* 16:301–13.

BUNZEL, RUTH L.
   1972   *The Pueblo Potter.* New York: Dover Publications.

CARNEIRO, ROBERT L.
   1970   A Theory of the Origin of the State. *Science* 169:733–38.

CHILDE, V. GORDON
   1961   *Man Makes Himself.* New York: New American Library.

CLARKE, DAVID L.
   1968   *Analytical Archaeology.* London: Methuen.

DANIEL, GLYN
   1967   *The Origins and Growth of Archaeology.* New York: Penguin Books.

   1968   *The First Civilizations.* New York: Thomas Y. Crowell.

DARWIN, CHARLES
   1859   *The Origin of Species.* London: John Murray.

ETZIONI, AMITAI, and EVA ETZIONI
   1964a   Karl Marx and Friedrich Engels. In *Social Change.* New York: Basic Books.

   1964b   Karl Marx: Historical Materialism Summarized. In *Social Change.* New York: Basic Books.

FORD, JAMES A.
   1962   *A Qualitative Method for Deriving Cultural Chronology.* Washington, D.C.: Pan American Union.

FORDE, C. DARYLL
   1963   *Habitat, Economy, and Society.* New York: E. P. Dutton.

GARBARINO, MERWYN S.
   1977   *Sociocultural Theory in Anthropology.* New York: Holt, Rinehart and Winston.

HARRIS, MARVIN
   1969   *The Rise of Anthropological Theory.* New York: Thomas Y. Crowell.

   1980   *Cultural Materialism.* New York: Vintage Books.

HEILBRONER, ROBERT L.
   1961   *The Inexorable World of Karl Marx.* New York: Time.

HOLE, FRANK, and MARY SHAW
   1967   *Computer Analysis of Chronological Seriation.* Houston: Rice University.

KLEINDIENST, MAXINE R.
   1961   Variability within the late Acheulean Assemblage in Eastern Africa. *The South African Archaeological Bulletin* 16(62):35–52.

KROEBER, A. L.
   1948   *Anthropology*. New York: Harcourt, Brace.

LUBBOCK, JOHN
   1865   *Prehistoric Times as Illustrated by Ancient Remains and the Manners and Customs of Modern
             Savages.*

MORGAN, LEWIS H.
   1877   *Ancient Society or Researches in the Lines of Human Progress from Savagery through Bar-
             barism to Civilization.* New York: H. Holt.

PETRIE, FLINDERS
   1899   Sequences in Prehistoric Remains. *Journal of the Royal Anthropological Institute of Great
             Britain and Ireland* 29:295–301.

PRICE, BARBARA J.
   1982   Cultural Materialism: A Theoretical Review. *American Antiquity* 47(4):709–41.

RATHJE, WILLIAM L.
   1974   The Origin and Development of Lowland Classic Maya Civilization. In *The Rise and
             Fall of Civilizations*, edited by C. C. Lamberg-Karlovsky and Jeremy A. Sabloff. Menlo
             Park, Ca.: Cummings Publishing.

SAHLINS, MARSHALL D., and ELMAN R. SERVICE, eds.
   1970   *Evolution and Culture*. Ann Arbor: University of Michigan Press.

SANDERS, WILLIAM T., and BARBARA J. PRICE
   1968   *Mesoamerica: The Evolution of a Civilization*. New York: Random House.

SCHIFFER, MICHAEL B.
   1972   Archaeological Context and Systemic Context. *American Antiquity* 37:156–65.

   1976   *Behavioral Archeology*. New York: Academic Press.

SERVICE, ELMAN R.
   1962   *Primitive Social Organization: An Evolutionary Perspective*. New York: Random House.

STEWARD, JULIAN H.
   1955   *Theory of Culture Change*. Urbana: University of Illinois Press.

THOMSEN, JURGENSEN
   1836,
   1848   *A Guide to Northern Antiquities.*

TYLOR, SIR EDWARD BURNETT
   1871   *Primitive Culture: Researches into the Development of Mythology, Philosophy, Religion, Art,
             and Customs.* London: J. Murray.

WHITE, LESLIE A.
   1949   *The Science of Culture*. New York: Grove Press.

WILLEY, GORDON R., and PHILIP PHILLIPS
   1958   *Method and Theory in American Archaeology*. Chicago: University of Chicago Press.

WOLF, ERIC R.
   1964   The Study of Evolution. In *Horizons of Anthropology*, edited by Sol Tax. Chicago: Al-
             dine.

3

Research Procedures in Archaeology

The popular press creates a false impression when it pictures the archaeologist as someone who digs for buried treasure. It is true that digging (or site excavation) is an important research method—the archaeologist digs with fingers, whisk broom, trowel, spade, pick and shovel, and occasionally with backhoe. But instead of digging for treasure, the archaeologist digs for information. During the first few weeks of an archaeology course, the lecturer endeavors to replace the treasure-hunter image with a concept of the archaeologist as a social historian who investigates the anthropology of the past.

To gather information from artifacts (objects made or used by humans) and their provenience (location), the archaeologist uses three research procedures: (1) site survey, (2) site excavation, and (3) laboratory analysis. A site survey is a systematic surface inventory of archaeological sites and stray artifacts found in the area. Such an inventory provides a regional background for the more detailed excavation study. Step two is the excavation of a selected number of sites discovered through the survey inventory. Excavation can be defined as the systematic subsurface exploration of a site by digging. Research step three, or laboratory analysis, is the systematic study of the artifactual and provenience data, an operation called *classification*.

Each of these steps forms the basis for the next operation so that the work flows from surface study to underground digging to laboratory investigation. Upon occasion, however, a particular investigation may entail only one or two of these procedures. For instance, a regional site survey may be conducted with the research goal of studying past human settlement, population, and land use. The surface artifacts recovered from many sites are returned to a laboratory for detailed cleaning, labeling, restoration, and classification, thereby bypassing the excavation phase of the research plan. Again, a previously recorded site may be selected for excavation with intensive study of the recovered data, but without the preliminary site survey. Recent federally funded contracts have called for "no-pickup" site surveys, in which artifacts are identified and recorded but left in the field for future generations of archaeologists to study. Such a "no-pickup" survey actually combines the steps of survey and laboratory study. In this case, many more hours are spent in the field recording on-site material, identifying artifacts, and making scattergram maps as a means of observing the spatial patterning of specimens.

Site Survey

The site survey is a systematic collection of archaeological data from the surface of sites. The survey focuses on large blocks of landscape. Extensive surveys may examine several thousands of square miles through a spot check by car, truck, train, or plane to explore the nature of the archaeological remains. Intensive surveys often deal with only tens or hundreds of square miles of countryside. In either case, populations of archaeological sites are studied for their inter-site relationships. In contrast, excavation study focuses on single sites for the intra-site investigation of artifacts.

Survey Goals

The goals of site survey are: (1) the study of site types, (2) study of terrain use, (3) study of site density, and (4) study of site distributions. From a study of site types, the experienced archaeologist can determine the organization of a primitive culture. For band-organized societies, for instance, the archaeologist may find that the site types range among base camps, plant collecting camps, hunting camps, quarry camps, and in-transit camps. In contrast, a primitive state may include a capital city, towns, agrarian villages, hamlets, and farmsteads, not to mention maritime ports, forts, check-points along state roads, canals, and various water control features such as dams, irrigation canals, and field systems.

In the study of terrain use, the investigator classifies the terrain in terms of its usefulness for human subsistence. This land-use typology contains categories such as building sites, arable land for farming, and various resource locations.

The study of site density, a third goal in site survey, is a descriptive procedure in which the archaeologist computes the incidence of sites per unit area (Fig. 3–1a). Such computation defines site clusters, the basis for identi-

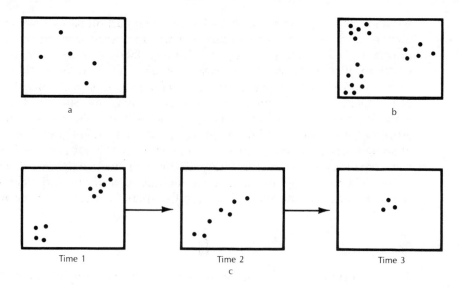

Legend: • = one site

FIGURE 3-1   Density and distributional mapping of sites. (a) Incidence of sites per square area; (b) sites distributed into clusters indicative of past human communities; (c) a time series illustrating changing site distribution.

fying a human community of the prehistoric past. Coupled with a density study is the site distribution study (Fig. 3–1b), in which sites of each age are plotted on maps to reveal their geographical spread by time period. From such period-by-period mapping, it is possible to differentiate the boundaries of ancient communities from the boundaries of contemporary sites. Furthermore, when maps in a time-series are compared, the researcher can identify the patterns of site distribution brought about by immigration, emigration, or population stability (Fig. 3–1c).

An example of community relocation, defined by site density clusters and their distributional shift through time, is illustrated in Figure 3–2. Here prehistoric communities spanning two centuries moved upstream by "leap-frog" movements along the upper San Juan river of Colorado and New Mexico. Each community was forced to relocate because the river eroded the alluvial flood plain, thereby destroying flood-water farming. As the fields of each community were eroded, the community adapted by moving to an upstream site not yet affected by lowering of the water table on which corn agriculture was dependent. By the eleventh century, however, river erosion was so extensive that the entire region was abandoned (Eddy 1974).

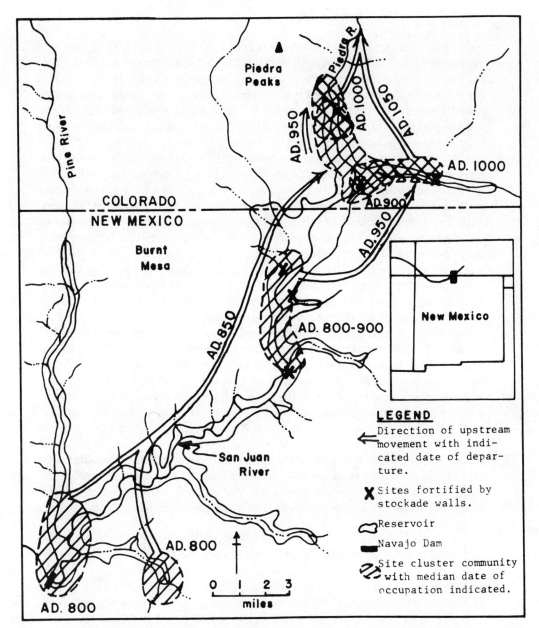

FIGURE 3-2   Map showing prehistoric communities, defined by site clusters, and their upstream relocation in northwestern New Mexico between AD 800 and 1000.

Source: Frank W. Eddy, 1974, Population Dislocation in the Navajo Reservoir District, New Mexico and Colorado. *American Antiquity* 39(1):75–84.

Sampling Procedures

As a rule, archaeologists make observations on only a sample of the data available, rather than running a census, that is, attempting to collect all of the potential sites and artifacts of an area. Sampling is a research procedure for collecting data so that a part is representative of the whole. This part is called a *sample,* whereas the "whole" is called the *population* of sites or artifacts available for study. When the "whole" is defined in terms of area rather than objects, it is labeled the *universe.* Some federal government contracts for site survey identify the universe to be sampled, meaning that a sample is to be drawn from an entire district administered by a government agency (Schiffer and Gumerman 1977). In these contracts, a government request for proposal (RFP) specifies the universe as an administrative district of so many millions of acres of land of which a 10 or 15 percent sample is to be drawn for intensive site survey. The justification for sampling is that limitations in time, money, and effort prohibit collection of all of the data. In fact, the conservation ethic dictates that some data should be preserved for study by future generations, who will undoubtedly have research procedures far more sophisticated than those presently available (Schiffer and Gumerman 1977).

The archaeological profession is now undergoing a revolution. The archaeologists of past generations practiced "hunch sampling" in which they haphazardly followed out leads as to where artifacts and sites might be found. This unsystematic procedure produced large amounts of data for display in museums, but failed to provide samples that were representative of the population or universe from which they were drawn. In contrast, today statisticians devise sampling procedures based on probability theory so that each and every artifact or site in a population has an equal chance of being drawn. Thus, the sample reflects the whole population or universe from which it was obtained. Sampling is employed routinely in many statistical problems involving large numbers of objects. At least two major classes of probability sampling have been applied to cultural and natural phenomena by geographers and plant ecologists: random and systematic sampling (Haggett 1966, p. 195).

Random sampling is an unbiased selection of artifacts or sites according to a table of random numbers (Arkin and Colton 1963). Random numbers are generated by a computer. The human mind is almost incapable of randomization because our cultural training directs us to think in terms of relationships or associations. Simple random sampling is conducted when the population or universe is fairly homogeneous (Fig. 3–3). Should there be a marked heterogeneity in either population or universe, however, some of this imbalance may be reduced by stratifying. The whole is subdivided or partitioned to redistribute the variable creating the heterogeneity. For instance, the sites may be nonrandomly distributed because the area was divided into different vegetation zones. The archaeologist may take this selection into account by randomly drawing from each zone a number of sites proportionate

Sample square randomly drawn from the universe

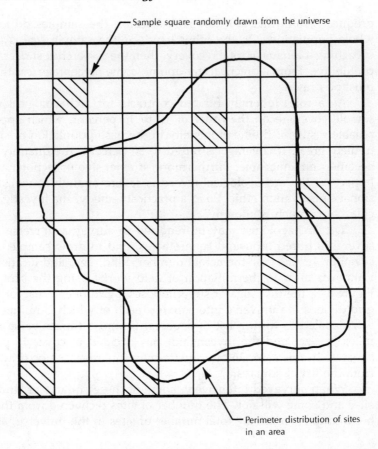

Perimeter distribution of sites
in an area

FIGURE 3-3   The random drawing of sample squares from a universe defined as a large geographical area.

to the percentage of that vegetation type within the total universe. This kind of probability sampling is called a *stratified random sample*.

In a systematic sample, the elements are drawn from the population or universe at uniform intervals. This research procedure can be compared to selecting all of the red squares from a checker board or every fifth item from a list. To employ many statistical tests and achieve "representativeness," however, it is necessary to make a systematic drawing of the area in squares, number the squares, then select the first square to be studied according to numbers drawn from a table of random numbers (Lapin 1975).

The practicing field archaeologist must decide how many squares should be drawn from the universe. Very small samples may consist of 1, 5, or 10 percent of the areal universe, whereas larger, more reliable samples might consist of 15, 25, or 50 percent of the total area. Very small samples may produce results that are unreliable because the samples do not reflect the whole population. On the other hand, as the sample size is increased approaching a census or total recovery, then the research cost rises and becomes prohibitive. From a practical standpoint, some percentage less than the whole must be drawn.

As a rule, federally funded contracts for archaeological work require sample coverage on the order of 10 to 15 percent, which appears to yield reliable results if the heterogeneity in the base population of sites is not extremely great. If coverage is raised to 50 percent, the quantity of data may become unmanageable. Furthermore, if extensive collections are made, the impact on the archaeological record is severe enough to violate the professional conservation ethic. So as a practical remedy, the investigator must decide "how much is enough."

The archaeologist may be required to survey a universe consisting of several hundred thousand square acres, and to draw sample blocks for excavation. In this case the actual number, kind, age, and location of sites are unknown prior to the initiation of field work. Using the sample design in Figure 3–3, the investigator superimposes a grid over a map of the area. The grid divides the universe into squares, each of which is numbered or otherwise labeled to form a list of squares. Suppose the universe is 100 square miles in size, and the investigator has decided to cover 16 percent of the squares. In this case, 16 one-square-mile squares must be drawn at random from the list of squares.

When surveyed intensively, some of these squares of land will contain sites and some will not. The number of sites recovered from the sample can be used to estimate the total number of sites in the universe, as follows:

$$\frac{16\% \ \text{Sample}}{100\% \ \text{Universe}} = \frac{32 \ \text{Sites in sample}}{x \ \text{Sites in population}}$$

$$16x = 3200$$

$$x = 200 \ \text{Sites in the universe}$$

The same estimate can be made using a site-density calculation. Thirty-two sites recovered from 16 square miles yields a site density of two sites per square mile. This density times 100 square miles yields a population estimate of 200 sites. Thus, the actual population of sites can be estimated, with more or less confidence, by extrapolation from the sample recovery.

A different sample problem arises when the survey archaeologist is sampling artifacts from individual sites. In this situation, the site is mapped by some instrument such as an alidade or transit so that each and every artifact is plotted and identified by type and material. In a prehistoric site situated in an open field, the typical artifacts are stone and ceramic fragments called *potsherds.* These sherds, when numbered on the scattergram map, constitute a population of artifacts enumerated by census. From this population, the archaeologist may, as an option, draw a sample for return to the research laboratory for more detailed study. In this "pickup" survey, the recovery of 30 or more specimens allows the use of statistical tests for large samples (Lapin 1975).

Field Techniques

In the past the site survey was not given the importance it deserves as a full-scale archaeological research method. The procedure was merely an ancillary technique for finding excavatable sites, which were considered the primary focus of archaeological research. Now, however, site survey is recognized as a full-scale scientific method, on a par with excavation and laboratory analysis, because of its contributions to regional studies of settlement, human population history, and land use.

To obtain information from surface inspection, special field techniques are tailored to provide intensive inspection of the ground in a systematic manner. For instance, one or more field teams may make systematic sweeps over carefully defined parcels of land. Optimally each crew is composed of two to four crew members and a crew leader. The crew forms a skirmish line and maintains close intervals while it traverses a zigzag path so that each person's field of observation overlaps that of a neighbor. The crew leader guides the sweep by using a compass and making frequent checks on the crew for alignment.

Recent federal contracts have set the interval between crew members at 30 meters. This figure provides reliable coverage in grassland or open shrub country. In woodland and dense forest, however, the team spacing may have to be tightened up considerably to avoid overlooking a small site. In very dense ground cover, such as that found in certain woodland areas of the eastern United States, leaf litter can obscure sites lacking massive mounded features. Here the crew must rely on shovel testing. Although not commonly employed today, the use of air photography, geophysical prospecting equipment, and soil-testing procedures will one day be common for the survey archaeologist.

Ideally, the most reliable manner of covering the ground is the pedestrian or foot survey. In some parts of the world, where archaeological features consist of bulky architectural remains such as ancient cities and fortifications, reliable survey has been conducted on horseback. When extensive rather than intensive survey inspection is the goal, the means of transportation include car, truck, boat, or even low-flying aircraft. In a reconnaissance-type survey in Egypt, a pickup truck was used to cover large areas of the Nile river flood plain in the area now flooded by Lake Nasser. The truck was driven in a zigzag fashion so that crew members were always looking into the sunlight.

The position of epipaleolithic sites could be detected easily by the sun's glint reflected from many chert artifacts, some dating back 20,000 years.

As the survey team sweeps across the landscape, one or more of the members eventually encounters the artifactual debris of an archaeological site. At the moment of discovery, that member calls out the information to the rest of the team who rapidly converge on the find spot. In a well-run party, the crew leader quickly assigns observation and recording tasks to the different members; often these technical jobs are rotated from site to site to vary the crew's routine. There can be no question that much of the routine archaeological field work rests on basic clerical skills. Careful record-keeping is necessary so that site-to-site records are comparable and inter-site analysis is feasible once the field data are returned to the laboratory for processing and technical report writing.

As a rule, crew leaders and project managers maintain a daily journal with entries covering the overall progress of the work, regional observations, weather, and even notations of visitors to the field camp. More germane to the survey are records based on observations at each site. Observations on the site and its surroundings cover a broad range including location, archaeological data, environmental data, and management data.

While one member of the survey team is filling out the site inventory record, another is locating the site position on a good map. In the United States, the U.S. Geological Survey's topographic maps, at a scale of 1:24,000 (7.5 minute series) are deemed adequate for most survey needs. Since not all of the country has been mapped in the 7.5 minute series, however, it is sometimes necessary to utilize other maps or low-altitude aerial photography. When using aerial photographs as maps, it is convenient to mark each site by making a pin hole through the photo, after which the site number can be penciled lightly on the back.

A third team member can be detailed to construct a large-scale map of the site itself. Previous generations of archaeologists often made a quick sketch, sometimes to scale using paced measurements. This rendition showed the site perimeter as well as major features such as housing, ceremonial precinct, civic center, roads, and trash dump. Obviously the architectural contents varied according to the level of organizational complexity exhibited by each ancient society. Today, however, even very simple hunting camps or places of tool manufacture are mapped in considerable detail, often facilitated by transit measurements of each individual artifact if the total number of specimens is not prohibitive. But as the degree of recording precision rises, so does the research cost in terms of hours spent on each site.

Photography is an important part of the record-keeping routine. The site is photographed with both black-and-white and color film. Views should include shots that show the horizon for ease of relocating the site if it should be selected for excavation. In addition, one or more close-up, detailed photographs may be taken if a particular feature warrants recording. Examples might be a fire hearth eroding from a stream bank, mounds containing architecture, or some unique concentration of portable artifacts.

If the research design calls for artifact pickup, the final recording task is specimen collection. In the past, time-sensitive artifacts, such as projectile points (dart or arrow points) or decorated ceramics, were favored for collection because of their utility in dating the site. Today the field archaeologist collects not only stylistically distinctive objects for dating purposes, but also a random selection of all kinds of artifacts to indicate the full range of human activities once conducted at that spot. This kind of procedure may employ a cluster strategy in which the four or five nearest neighbors of a randomly selected specimen are all picked up. The randomly selected cluster yields patterns of nearest-neighbor artifacts. These artifact associations reveal the "tool kits" of the past.

Site Excavation

During excavation, the archaeologist collects data by digging systematically within a single site. The purpose of excavation is to define the artifactual content of the site and explore the intra-site distribution of specimens. In contrast to site survey, which deals with the two-dimensional distribution of artifacts, excavation takes place in three-dimensional space defined by length, width, and depth beneath the ground surface.

Sites for excavation are usually chosen to test a research hypothesis generated from the site survey. Such hypotheses might focus on one or more of the following: (1) further definition of site types, (2) stratigraphic study, (3) definition of tool kits, and (4) study of environmental history. The site type is defined by different kinds of archaeological remains and their spatial organization, provisionally identified by site survey.

Stratigraphic study explores the layered sequence of site deposits in order to write a local history of its occupation. Investigation of tool kits is based on the recovery of artifacts leading to a definition of the industrial activities once conducted on the site. And finally, the recovery of environmental specimens (ecofacts) allow the archaeologist to write a natural history of the site and to define the resource utilization by its occupants. Ecofactual evidence often recovered includes ancient soils, fossil pollen, visible plant parts, and animal bones (fauna).

Kinds of Excavations

As a follow-up to the surface record of the site, underground study is often initiated by means of a "test excavation." A test may consist of a trench or one or two holes put down as "windows" in order to determine the thickness of the subsurface deposits and to recover artifact types that indicate the site's

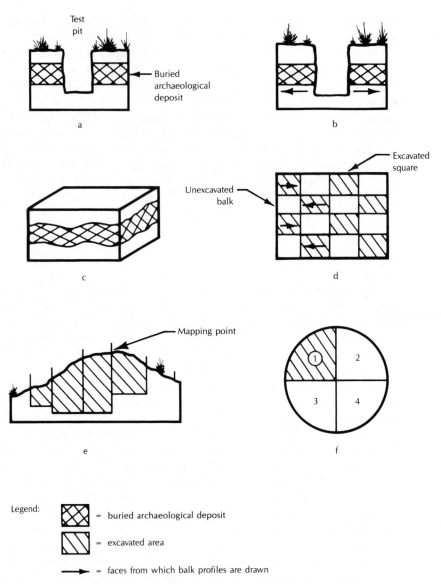

Legend:

⊠ = buried archaeological deposit

⧅ = excavated area

➤ = faces from which balk profiles are drawn

FIGURE 3-4 Excavation strategies. (a) Test excavation bisecting a buried archaeological deposit; (b) extensive excavation opened up horizontally by expansion from a test pit; (c) balk block showing strata exposed on two faces; (d) checkerboard excavation design with arrow showing the method of excavating alternate blocks to create a continuous north-south profile; (e) profiles hung from mapping points; (f) quadrant excavation of pie-shaped slices of a round feature.

age span (Fig. 3–4a). This preliminary testing allows site survey hypotheses to be proved or disproved quickly. If below-ground depth of artifact deposits is found, then a full-scale excavation program can be planned.

Unlike the test pit, which emphasizes vertical relationships, full-scale excavations focus on horizontal tracing of the archaeological deposit (Fig. 3–4b). The archaeologist expects to recover large samples of specimens requiring long-term processing in the laboratory. In the extensive excavation, one defines the horizontal spread of artifacts and discovers the artifact associations that lead to definition of tool kits and activity areas.

Microstratigraphy

At one time many archaeologists dug by arbitrary (10 cm) levels or simply cleared fill from within and around structures. Today the preferred method, proposed by Sir Mortimer Wheeler (1964) and other Europeans, is excavation by natural layers in order to reconstruct long sequences of deposits. This procedure requires close attention to thin (micro) layers. The best technique for examination of microstratigraphy is called *balk excavation*. A balk is an unexcavated block of site fill from which both vertical and horizontal stratigraphy can be "read" (Fig. 3–4c). Balks are not wheelbarrow runways or unexcavated fill left because of laziness.

There are many balk-digging strategies based on the principle of alternate grid squares. Two examples are checkerboard and quadrant digging. Using the checkerboard analogy, either all black or all red squares are dug, leaving the opposite-color squares standing as balks. The stratigraphic profiles made up of layers of deposits are then recorded from the balk face to a standard scale, with symbols to indicate the texture, structure, and color of the soil. These individual profiles are suspended from elevations taken on mapping points (MP of Fig. 3–5) to provide a continuous profile record (Fig. 3–4e). Such profiles, actually composites made up of many individual balk records, allow the field archaeologist to trace horizontal changes in stratigraphy over the entire site as illustrated in Figure 3–5. Here a north-to-south composite profile has been constructed that shows the stratigraphic order of many different kinds of archaeological deposits occurring within and outside of an eleventh-century Anasazi building.

As the profiles are drawn, the standing balks are themselves excavated to provide a 100 percent excavation. On the other hand, if the research plan calls for smaller coverage, the balks can be left in place to provide a sample of 50 percent or less as required by the constraints of time, money, and effort.

Quadrant digging is most applicable to round figures such as pits, earth mounds (called barrows by the English), pit houses, towers, or other circular constructions. The procedure is to excavate alternate pie-shaped slices (Fig. 3–4f).

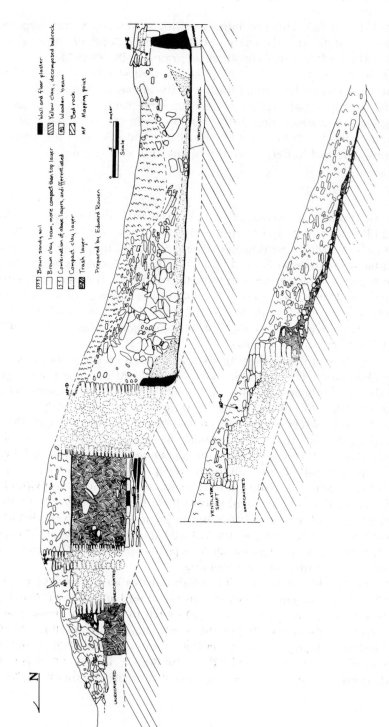

FIGURE 3-5 How individual balk profiles can be matched to create a continuous profile extending entirely across a mound containing eleventh-century Anasazi architecture.

Source: From Frank W. Eddy, *Archaeological Investigations at Chimney Rock Mesa 1970–1972,* Figure 27; Boulder: Colorado Archaeological Society, 1977.

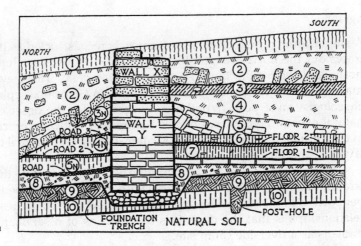

FIGURE 3-6   Balk versus trench-cut excavations. (a) Relationship of stratification to structures is retained by balk excavation; (b) these relationships are obliterated by continuous trenching.

Source: From Mortimer Wheeler, *Archaeology from the Earth.* Middlesex, England: Penguin Books, Oxford University Press, 1954, Figure 16.

The basic principles are relatively simple. The goal is to obtain a continuous record of the strike (trend) and dip (inclination) of the deposits. Excavators should never cut deposits in two without first recording the stratigraphic relation of the residual balks, and should never cut fill from a feature, such as a fixed facility like architecture, without first recording its surface of origin and the stratigraphic relationships (Fig. 3–6).

Site Historiography

A site historiography, or event sequence, is reconstructed as the investigator traces out the microstratigraphic sequence of deposits and orders these deposits and their artifacts into a chain (Taylor 1948). These event chains are made up of depositional, surface contact, and erosional episodes. The archaeologist must posit hypotheses to account for the order of cultural and natural events. Hypotheses of this nature deal with the processes involved in the formation of the stratigraphic context and the artifactual content of each layer or stratum.

As an example, the field description of a layer may state that it is a sandy stratum merging with a clay deposit, with a fire hearth embedded in the upper portion of the sand. The hypothesis offered to explain these stratigraphic relationships is that the deposit is the remains of a sandbar once used by humans as a riverside camp site.

In general an event reconstruction of this nature orders depositional and cultural events into three periods: (1) pre-occupation, (2) occupation, and (3) post-occupation. The pre-occupational period answers the question, what did the landscape look like and how did it develop up to the time of the first human use? The second period details the long sequence of cultural and natural events that took place during human use of the site. And finally, the post-occupational period covers the record of natural events that took place at this site after occupation, for example, the collapse of buildings and the natural succession in which the forest reclaimed the ruined city or village.

Sampling Procedures

Excavation sampling is considerably more complicated than survey recovery because it takes place in three-dimensional space, rather than on the two-dimensional ground surface. Since digging is a discovery process, the site can be divided into representative blocks, and all digging strategies must deal with defining a universe in terms of cubic space. Test excavation plays a role in determining thickness of deposits, and some complementary procedure, such as coring or soil testing, defines the lateral extent of the deposits (Eddy and Dregne 1964). Once the three dimensions of site latitude, longitude, and depth have been determined, estimates of total cubic volume are possible. Next this volumetric universe is partitioned by a grid of cubes that form the sampling frame, or list of excavatable squares. Probability theory requires that each and every one of these squares has an equal chance of being drawn to yield random representativeness. Although elegant in the abstract, true representativeness is difficult to achieve in the field, particularly in cases involving deep deposits in multiple layers of different ages. Inevitably the lower and more ancient layers are slighted in terms of percentage of recovery, while the upper and more recent layers produce a disproportionately high recovery (Mueller 1975).

As a rule of thumb, one might hope to sample through excavation 10 percent of those sites inventoried by site survey, representing 2 to 3 percent of the total archaeology. Excavation constitutes "a sample of a sample," leading to an end result that is merely a tiny fraction of the archaeological resource of a region.

The principle of sample recovery is to obtain both artifacts and ecofacts from every small lens and surface as well as from each horizontal variation within a stratum. Furthermore, specimens of all kinds must be collected from the fill of each feature, such as each pit or room in a coordinated suite, so that each class of evidence can be matched with all others. As a rule, ecofacts should be collected from each layer to record environmental changes between superimposed deposits. The excavator should avoid mindlessly removing samples at equal intervals without regard for the position of strata or features because the multitude of recovered data cannot be coordinated in this fashion.

Field Techniques

Excavation teams can be organized to any size commensurate with the scope of the research job at hand. As a practical matter, however, a ratio of about one crew chief to four or five laborers or field hands is convenient. Since the crew chief is busy deploying workers and recording specimens, a larger crew quickly overwhelms the chief with work. Hierarchies of organization can be constructed in which several higher ranks of supervisors oversee many digging teams.

The actual excavation equipment varies to suit the particulars of the job at hand. On an open-air site, for instance, tools range from trowel and wisk broom for fine clearing around delicate objects to backhoe and other power equipment for massive dirt moving. More standard hand tools include pick and shovel, and a wheelbarrow for dirt removal.

By way of contrast, rock shelter excavation often calls for more specialized equipment to deal with dry deposits, especially in arid lands. Laborers require air-filter or respirator safety equipment because of the dust hazard. Deep in the interior recesses of caves or shelters, excavators need artificial lighting powered by a gasoline-driven generator. This same generator may be used to power exhaust fans to clear the area of dust. Furthermore, special attention must be given the problem of slumpage, resulting from unstable dry deposits. As further safety insurance, workmen are required to wear safety helmets to prevent head injury from falling rocks.

It is always important to remember that archaeological deposits are fragile. Since excavation is a destructive process that analyzes by dissection, any observations not recorded are permanently lost to science. For this reason, careful attention must be given to the various kinds of field recording. Like the site survey, excavation utilizes a daily journal account of the work progress. In addition, supervisory personnel fill out many forms covering the various features and layered deposits, recording each in a standardized manner to insure comparability of observations. In addition, each balk and feature is mapped in plan and profile, and the entire site is mapped topographically. The site map includes surface contours, plan views of features, and the many excavation units.

Laboratory Analysis

Once the data body, made up of artifactual and ecofactual specimens plus their provenience information, has been returned from the field to the laboratory, the routine operations of cleaning, restoring, and labeling begin. Upon completion, the specimens are ready for formal analysis. Formal analysis in archaeology is conducted through artifact classification, the comparative study of the formal attributes of artifacts, searching for similarities and differences among the individual specimens (see Chapter 1).

The output of classification is the artifact type. Types are patterns defined from groupings of artifacts that show a high degree of similarity with one another. Conversely, types are differentiated from one another by a high degree of between-group dissimilarity. The inference to be drawn from the type is that it has resulted from specific human behavior in terms of its manufacture, use, and symbolic meaning in society (Spaulding 1964; Rouse 1960).

Three approaches are employed by the laboratory technician in classifying artifacts: (1) table-top sorting, (2) statistical clustering of attributes, and (3) numerical taxonomy. The traditional table-top sort has been utilized for decades as the primary procedure of the laboratory (Krieger 1944). The process is conducted in the following order: First, the artifacts are spilled out of their collection bags onto some convenient work space such as a large table. Next, the investigator searches for "likes," which are piled together to form physical groups. During this operation it is important to refrain from consulting provenience data because this information can influence the investigator's decisions about the member affiliation of any given group. The laboratory technician must work "blind" of any knowledge of the provenience source of specimens while describing the types of artifacts, based on the shared characteristics of each artifact pile. This provisional description constitutes a type-hypothesis that must be tested for validity, and this testing is accomplished by using the independent body of provenience data. If the type-hypothesis is to be accepted as valid, a frequency plot of specimens from one time and place should display the bell-shaped curve. Randomized distribution in time and space indicate an invalid type-hypothesis. In this case, the table-top classification is repeated with different, more discriminating sorting criteria, which will reveal the normal curve pattern in time or space (Krieger 1944). In summary, then, the artifact type is an abstract unit consisting of a pattern or cluster of attributes that habitually associate, although no single member of the group may exactly duplicate the type description.

In contrast to the traditional table-top sort, the modern, quantitatively trained archaeologist employs statistical procedures to classify artifacts into types. These procedures and tests may be executed by hand calculator if the number of observations and size of the collection is small. The most reliable results are obtained, however, when the list of variables (observations showing variation) and the size of the artifact population are both quite large. Once the collection has been scanned for its research potential, the attributes of each specimen are encoded on punch cards for computer processing. In this operation, the computer searches the punch card deck for highly correlated attribute clusters, which then become artifact types. The computer search of the attribute record uses some form of multivariate statistics, such as factor analysis, if the data are in a metric form comprised of real numbers (that is, continuous measurements in decimal fractions) (Nie and others 1975).

On the other hand, if the observations are counts (integers or whole numbers) made on discrete categories such as color, technical features, use marks, material type, or object shape, then some kind of nonparametric association statistic must be employed to cluster attributes. In archaeology, the chi-square (χ^2) test is commonly employed as a test of significance, to rule out the possibility that the associations in previous tests resulted from coincidence (the null hypothesis) (Spaulding 1953). A large chi-square statistic indicates a nonrandom relationship between the attributes and their quantitative "togetherness" (Noether 1976).

An example of an association test is provided in Table 3–1 where contrived attribute counts for two categories of shape and three categories of stone material are given. The chi-square test measures the difference between an observed value and the value that would be expected if the subjects of the observations were unrelated. To compute chi-square, subtract the expected value from the observed value, square the difference, and divide by each expected value (Noether 1976, p. 113). The chi-square sum is 23.8 which, with two degrees of freedom, yields a significance figure of less than 0.01. This chi-square statistic is large enough to allow rejection of the null hypothesis and acceptance of the alternate hypothesis that the attributes are nonrandom in their distribution. Inspection of the observed-expected differences shows that cylindrical artifacts are most often made of sandstone and quartzite materials, while square objects are usually made of chert. Thus, two artifact types are indicated in this collection. Chi-square is limited to tests made on pairs

TABLE 3-1.   Contrived example of attributes associated by a chi-square test

Stone material	Shape		Row total
	Cylindrical	*Square*	
Sandstone	56.0* 69**	34.0 21	90
Quartzite	46.7 52	28.3 23	75
Chert	62.3 44	37.7 56	100
Column total	165	100	265

* Expected values = col. total × row total/total number of observations
** Observed values (actual counts of specimens)

Degrees of freedom = 2

$$x^2 = \frac{\Sigma (o - e)^2}{e}$$

$$= \frac{(69 - 56.0)^2}{56.0} + \frac{(21 - 34.0)^2}{34.0} + \frac{(52 - 46.7)^2}{46.7} + \frac{(23 - 28.3)^2}{28.3} +$$

$$\frac{(44 - 62.3)^2}{62.3} + \frac{(56 - 37.7)^2}{37.7} = 23.8, P < 0.01$$

of attributes, but by progressively scanning many such pairs the investigator can define types composed of many clustered attributes.

The procedures of numerical taxonomy, whether based on hand sorting or computer processing, constitute a third method of specimen classification lying half-way between hand-sorting and statistical processing of attributes (Sokal 1966; Sokal and Sneath 1963; Johnson 1968). The steps involved in numerical taxonomy are illustrated in Figure 3–7. Some of these procedures are self-evident from the figure drawing, while others require some additional comment. For instance, Step 3, coding of characters, involves compiling an "*n* × *t*" table in which characters (*n* entries) are recorded by specimen (*t* entries or OTU's, standing for *operational taxonomic units*). The calculation of affinity (similarity) between specimens constitutes Step 4, in which each specimen (*t* entry) is compared against other specimens using a measure called a *similarity coefficient*. This measure is calculated by comparing each specimen against all others in the collection and counting the shared attributes over all possible matches to yield a decimal fraction expressing the similarity between each pair of artifacts (OTU's). In Step 5 the similarity matrix or table (*t* × *t* entries) is sorted by placing the highest coefficient values nearest the diagonal of the table, a process involving resorting the specimen (or OTU entries) along the bottom and left margins of the matrix (see Fig. 3–8). This sorted similarity

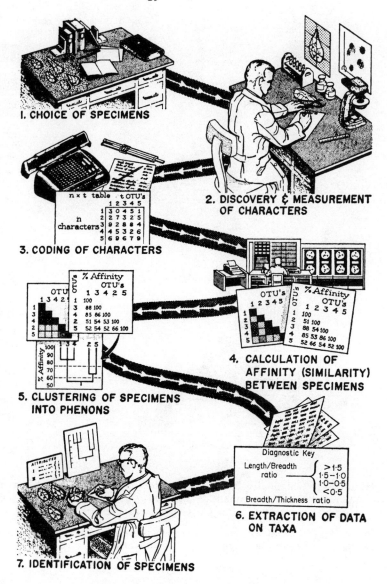

FIGURE 3-7   The operations of numerical taxonomy.

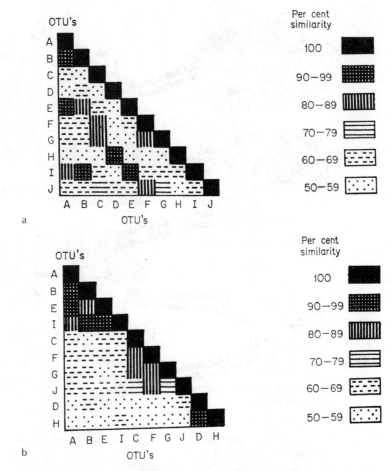

FIGURE 3-8   Similarity matrices with percent similarity shown by shaded squares. (a) Unsorted matrix with haphazard arrangement; (b) sorted matrix with blocks of similar artifacts (OTUs) expressing artifact type groupings or clusters.

Source: From *Principles of Numerical Taxonomy* by Robert Sokol and Peter Sneath. Copyright © 1963 by W. H. Freeman and Company. All rights reserved.

matrix can also be expressed as a tree-diagram or dendrogram, which is another graphic technique to cluster specimens into artifact types (Step 5).

Numerical taxonomy, although pioneered by systematic biologists, has had a comparatively long history in archaeology. Most of the early work dealt not with artifact classification, but with the arrangement of archaeological sites into chronological order, a process called *chronological seriation* that is useful for relative dating of sites and collections (Brainerd 1951; Robinson 1951; Hole and Shaw 1967; Johnson, 1968).

Summary

The archaeologist gathers data on past behavior and analyzes it for classification. Two field procedures for recording cultural information are site survey and site excavation. Site survey is employed to develop an area inventory of site data from which a representative sample will be selected for excavation. Excavation is a research method for making a detailed anatomical investigation of a site by dissecting it (taking it apart) in order to understand the manner in which its artifactual content is organized.

Once the artifacts and provenience data have been collected, they are shipped to the laboratory for cleaning, restoring, and labeling. But the most important laboratory operation is classification, the result of formal analysis. In this operation artifacts are classified into types by techniques such as (1) table-top sorting, (2) statistical analysis of artifact attributes, or (3) a numerical taxonomic approach.

Artifacts can be classified as bone, stone, wood, or pottery. A stone artifact can be classified by substance, such as sandstone, quartzite, or chert. A chert artifact can be classified as cylindrical or square. Categories such as these organize and simplify data so that the archaeologist can use, describe, and compare them easily without endless repetition of details. Such comparisons enable the archaeologist to reconstruct various aspects of ancient societies.

References

ARKIN, HERBERT, and RAYMOND R. COLTON
    1963   *Tables for Statisticians.* New York: Barnes and Noble.

BRAINERD, GEORGE W.
    1951   The Place of Chronological Ordering in Archaeological Analysis. *American Antiquity* 16:301-13.

CRAYTOR, WILLIAM BERT, and LEROY JOHNSON, JR.
    1968   Refinements in Computerized Item Seriation. Eugene: University of Oregon.

EDDY, FRANK W.
    1974   Population Dislocation in the Navajo Reservoir District, New Mexico and Colorado. *American Antiquity* 39(1):75-84.

EDDY, FRANK W., and HAROLD E. DREGNE
    1964   Soil Tests on Alluvial and Archaeological Deposits, Navajo Reservoir District. *El Palacio*, 71(4):5-21.

HAGGETT, PETER
    1966   Locational Analysis in Human Geography. Baltimore: St. Mary's Press.

HOLE, FRANK, and MARY SHAW
    1967   Computer Analysis of Chronological Seriation. *Rice University Studies* 53(3):1-166.

KRIEGER, ALEX D.
    1944   The Typological Concept. *American Antiquity* 9(3):271-87.

JOHNSON, LEROY, JR.
1968   *Item Seriation as an Aid for Elementary Scale and Cluster Analysis.* Eugene: University of Oregon.

LAPIN, LAWRENCE L.
1975   *Statistics.* New York: Harcourt Brace Jovanovich, Inc.

MUELLER, JAMES W., ed.
1975   *Sampling in Archaeology.* Tucson: University of Arizona Press.

NIE, NORMAN H., C. HADLAI HULL, JEAN G. JENKINS, KARIN STEINBRENNER, and DALE H. BENT
1975   *SPSS: Statistical Package for the Social Sciences.* New York: McGraw-Hill.

NOETHER, GOTTFRIED E.
1976   *Introduction to Statistics: A Nonparametric Approach.* Boston: Houghton Mifflin.

ROBINSON, W. S.
1951   A Method for Chronological Ordering Archaeological Deposits. *American Antiquity* 16(4):293–301.

ROUSE, IRVING
1960   The Classification of Artifacts in Archaeology. *American Antiquity* 25(3):313–23.

SCHIFFER, MICHAEL B., and GEORGE J. GUMERMAN, eds.
1977   Conservation Archaeology. New York: Academic Press.

SOKAL, ROBERT R.
1966   *Numerical Taxonomy.* San Francisco: W. H. Freeman and Company Publishers.

SOKAL, ROBERT R., and PETER H. A. SNEATH
1963   *Principles of Numerical Taxonomy.* San Francisco: W. H. Freeman and Company Publishers.

SPAULDING, ALBERT C.
1964   The Dimensions of Archaeology. In *Essays in the Science of Culture in Honor of Leslie A. White,* edited by Gertrude E. Dole and Robert L. Carneiro. New York: Thomas Y. Crowell.

STUART, DAVID R., and ROBERT P. RYAN
n.d.   *Recording Colorado Archaeological Sites: The OSAC Inventory Record,* edited by Bruce Rippeteau. Denver: Office of the State Archaeologist.

TAYLOR, WALTER W.
1948   A Study of Archaeology. *American Anthropologist* 50(3):1–256.

WHEELER, SIR MORTIMER
1964   *Archaeology from the Earth.* Baltimore: Pelican Books.

4

Archaeological
Unit
Concepts

The purpose of classification in archaeology is to study culture change and persistence along three dimensions: form, time, and space (Spaulding 1960). By organizing data into the taxonomic units of form, time, and space, the observer reduces a great diversity of data to a manageable number of categories. Inferences about the form, time, and spatial arrangement of artifacts enable the archaeologist to make generalizations about the behavior of ancient cultures.

These simplest units can be combined as sets, including form-time, form-space, and form-time-space units, or broken down into subsets. Subsets of the form unit concept are the artifact attribute, type, industry, and assemblage. Time units are exemplified by the horizon and period. Units of space include the locality, local sequence, and culture area. And finally, conjunctive sets of unit concepts are the tradition, stage, and phase. The tradition is a unit of form-time; the stage is a form-space unit, while the phase is a form-time-space conjunction (Fig. 4–1).

Table 4–1 shows that these unit concepts form a hierarchy of building blocks so that the lowest unit, the artifact attribute, is combined into more complex, higher units such as the artifact type (Clarke 1968). Ultimately, the high-level taxonomic units are employed in studying the nature of cultural evolution; the tradition is used in the study of specific evolution while the stage is used in investigations of general evolution (Sahlins and Service 1970, pp. 12–44).

79

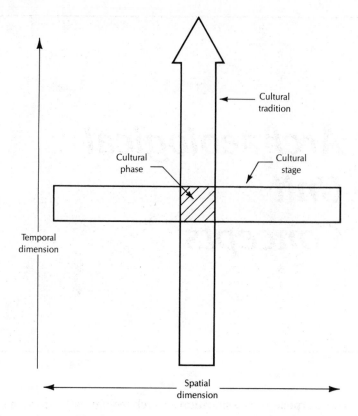

FIGURE 4-1   The conjunctive unit concepts of form-time-space.

TABLE 4-1.   The basic archaeological units of form, time, and space and their common conjunctive sets

Units of Form	Units of Time	Units of Space	Conjunctive Units of Form-Time-Space
			Phase
			Stage
			Tradition
		• Culture Area	
		• Locality	
		• Local sequence	
	• Period		
	• Horizon		
• Assemblage			
• Industry			
• Type			
• Attribute			

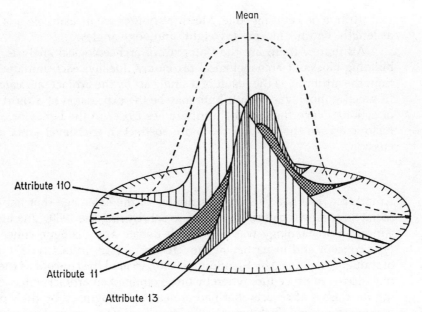

FIGURE 4-2   The tendency of metric attributes to be distributed as a bell-shaped curve. 13 = population of specimen lengths; 11 = specimen weight; 110 = thickness.

Source: From David L. Clarke, 1968, *Analytical Archaeology*. London: Methuen, p. 160.

Units of Form

Observations on artifacts lead to a hierarchy of formal unit concepts that build upward from the attribute successively to higher level units called the type, industry, and artifact assemblage. Units of form are difficult to envision because, although they are based on observations of the physical properties of prehistoric objects, the units measure change and variation occurring simultaneously along many dimensions. This diversity of observations is called *n-dimensional space* where *n* is the ultimate number of observations that can be made on the members of any given class of artifacts (Fig. 4-2). Units of form are constructed while holding time and space constant (invariate).

Attribute

A minimal observation made on an artifact is called an *attribute*. Synonyms for attribute are *characteristics*, *features*, or *physical properties*. Customarily, two kinds of attributes are recognized: nominal (or discrete) and metric. Discrete attributes of shape describe round, oval, or square objects. Technical attributes are characteristics that reveal how an artifact was made or used. Examples of manufacturing attributes are pitting from hammer blows or burnish marks from shaping by grinding. The use of an object is often interpreted from wear attributes such as dulling, polishing, rounding, striating, or general attrition of a cutting edge. Metric attributes are measurable qualities such as length, width, thickness, weight, and edge angles.

Attributes, then, are the "atoms" of archaeological analysis, the basic building blocks of archaeological taxonomy. Ideally, each minimal observation, the attribute, is the result of a single act by the artifact fabricator or user. In practice, however, an attribute may be the expression of a short sequence of actions. Nevertheless, the attribute lies closer to the behavior of the prehistoric artisan than any of the more abstract, higher-level units under discussion.

Type

An artifact type is a cluster of attributes of the same age that habitually associate, forming a pattern or recurrent set. During the 1950s, the literature of American archaeology was filled with debate and dialogue concerning the type concept and in particular the "reality" of an artifact type. One school of thought, espoused by Spaulding (1960), treated the concept as the outcome of a discovery procedure whereby one examined an artifact collection searching for classes of objects that had a meaning recognized by their prehistoric makers and users. Such types, called *functional types,* are recognizable by such tool-use or symbolic names as knife, arrow point, hammer, or "tiponi."[1]

Another class of artifact types, called *descriptive types,* are invented by the archaeologist for purposes of dating and analyzing cultural change below the level of consciousness of the original maker (Ford 1954). Descriptive types are superimposed upon the data, rather than read out of the data as is the case with functional types. Examples of descriptive types abound in the form of pottery or projectile-point types used for dating purposes when the nuances of shape and decorative design are of very little social significance. Such changes represent very minor esthetic alterations through chance recombination and random drift of stylistic attributes largely as a result of what Kroeber called *the play instinct.* Descriptive types can be recognized in the archaeological literature by their geographical place names, such as Cortez black-on-white, a pottery type found principally in southwestern Colorado, dated between AD 900 and 1000 (Breternitz, Rohn, and Morris 1974). Modern archaeology accepts both kinds of types as valid and employs each according to its specific purpose—functional reconstruction of society or chronology building.

Industry

An *artifact industry* is a unit concept coined by Old World archaeologists as a group that includes all of the artifact types of the same age and made of the same material (Braidwood 1967, p. 49). Examples of these materials are stone, bone, ceramics, or bronze. The industry concept is often employed as an or-

---

[1]*Tiponi*—corn mother fetish, a sacred religious symbol to the Pueblo Indians of New Mexico.

ganizational principle in technical monographs reporting excavation or survey data, particularly in discussions of the Lower Paleolithic stage, from which nearly all of the surviving artifacts are made of stone.

Assemblage

The total list of artifact types, of all materials, found at a site or within a single layer of a site, is called an *artifact assemblage*. The artifact types must be the same age and from the same locality. An artifact assemblage is often reported in the literature as a list of types with their numerical counts to form a type frequency list.

The assemblage consists of all of the tools and symbolic objects used by a society at one point in time. In this sense, the assemblage is the basis for reconstructing the basic social institutions and the lifestyle of the entire society.

Frequency Distribution

Spaulding (1960) has summarized his conclusions from the analysis of artifact form in a series of scientific propositions. The first of these generalizations can be paraphrased to the effect that artifact attributes and their clusters (types) tend to vary systematically in form, time, and space. This generalization expresses the idea that human behavior, as expressed physically in artifact form, is consistent and predictable as specified in the theory of culture, rather than chance or random.

The systematic variation in a population of artifacts is made explicit in a proposition stating that "an attribute or type population tends to cluster about a central tendency, taking on the properties of a normal distribution as described by statisticians" (Lapin 1975). The symmetrical shape of such a curve is illustrated in Figure 4–3, in which the metric values of an ideal attribute or type population, such as length, width, or thickness, are plotted against the frequency of artifact specimens. The norm or central tendency of the distribution is indicated by the vertical dashed line. The distribution tails represent the range, or the maximum and minimum values of the population. An actual frequency distribution of late-bronze-age socketed axes is illustrated on Figure 4–3b. Note the mild departure from the normal curve.

Spaulding explains the distribution as the result of the behavior of many artisans, each working to a common concept of what the artifact should look like. This shared concept is sometimes called a *mental template* (Deetz 1967). The norm, or mental template, is reflected in the population distribution as the mean, median, or mode, the ideal toward which all of the artisans of a community are working. On the other hand, aberrant examples of the attribute or type, expressed on Figure 4–3a by artifacts (x's) tucked under the tails of the distribution, are extreme departures from the norm. Such atypical cases are explained as the products of inept artisans or trainees, or even interruptions caused by flaws in the materials. These aberrant examples of craft products are often the inspirational source of new norms during subsequent time

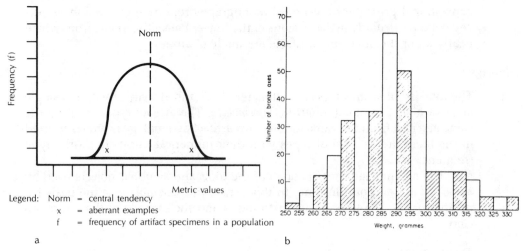

FIGURE 4-3   (a) Formal variation of artifact attributes and types; (b) actual frequency distribution of late-bronze-age socketed axes.

Source: (b) From Jacques Briard, *Les dépôts Bretons et l'Age du Bronze atlantique,* Figure on page 273, Rennes, 1965.

periods. But usually the minimum and maximum values of the frequency distribution are seen as the extremes beyond which the artifact products are unacceptable. Thus, individual artifact products smaller or larger than the range are rejected as unsuitable and often destroyed. For instance, when little girls mimic their mothers in the making of clay pots at San Illdefonso pueblo in New Mexico, their aberrant ceramic vessels are returned to the "melting pot" until their craft skills meet the community standards (Marriott 1948).

Units of Time

The archaeologist constructs units of time on the basis of relative and absolute dating techniques. Relative dating, as discussed in Chapter 5, places events in a serial order. Absolute dating, on the other hand, allows the archaeologist to specify the age-in-years of any one prehistoric event. In this present section, time is considered principally as a yardstick to measure change and persistence in formal units. Two common temporal units are employed by Americanists: horizon and period (Rowe 1962).

Horizon

A horizon is a unit of time defined by the very rapid spread of an art style or technical procedure (Willey and Phillips 1958, pp. 33–34). The distinctive element also changes rapidly so that it endures for only a short time. The concept allows cross-dating of many local sequences to show contemporaneity.

In the Andean cultural history of Peru and Bolivia, six major ceramic
horizons were defined by Bennett and Bird (1949). These horizon styles were
utilized to define time periods and correlate the local valley and subregional
sequences of the coastal and highland zones of the Central Andes as shown
in Figure 4-4. Explanations for the rapid spread of the six master styles are

FIGURE 4-4   Chronological chart for the Central Andes organized into periods by
stylistic and technical horizons shown in the far right column.

Source: Figure 19, page 112, *Andean Culture History* by Wendell C. Bennett and Junius B. Bird (1949)
courtesy of the American Museum of Natural History.

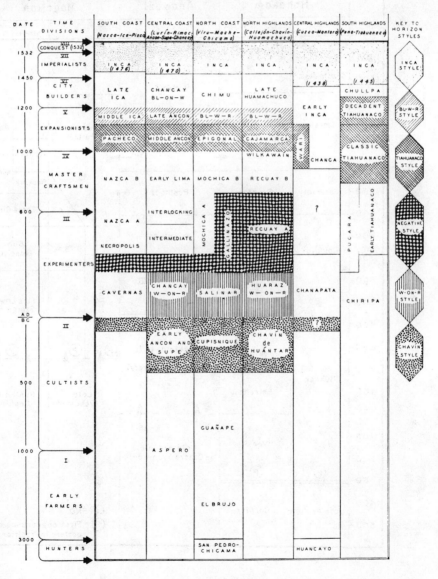

based on: (1) simple diffusion (white-on-red style), (2) a dominating religion (the Chavin cult), or (3) political conquest (formation of the Inca empire).

Despite the potential utility of the horizon concept for chronologically ordering archaeological sequences, little use has been made of it outside of

FIGURE 4-5   Regional sequences of cultural traditions—Anasazi, Mogollon, and Hohokam—found in the southwestern United States. Note the period breakdown of the Mogollon and Hohokam cultures.

Source: William D. Lipe, The Southwest, from *Ancient Native Americans,* edited by Jesse D. Jennings. Copyright © 1978 by W. H. Freeman and Company. All rights reserved.

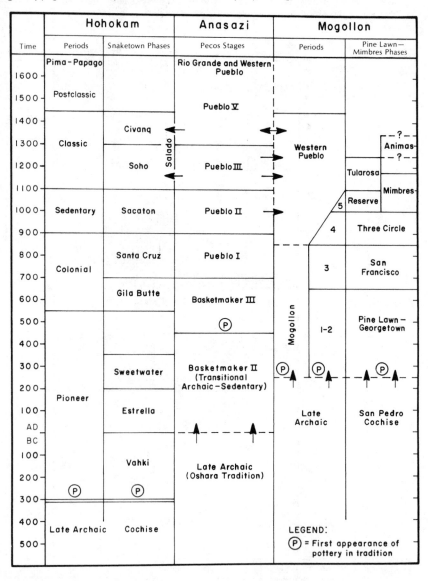

the Andean culture area. But Frison, Wilson, and Wilson (1974) recently applied the concept to the dating of Wyomong archaeology employing projectile point styles. Another example is found in the archaeology of central Mexico, the relative chronology of which is based on wide-spread, named ceramic styles. Furthermore, critiques have pointed out that although the horizons are ideally horizontal when charted, as on Figure 4–4, in reality each shows a minor amount of outward spread from some point of origin toward the perimeter of the distributional circle in conformance with diffusion theory.

Period

When it is possible to date archaeological remains in absolute terms (age in years), a local cultural sequence can be subdivided into time periods. Such a period is measured as a bracket or interval, for example, a particular cultural event that endured for 75 years between AD 1325 and 1400. Time periods may be numbered, as in the American Southwest where the Mogollon cultural tradition is divided into five units labeled *Mogollon I* through *V* (Wheat 1954). Other labels for periods are *early, middle,* and *late.* Some period schemes use names. For the Hohokam cultural tradition of the American Southwest, the breakdown from early to late is: *pioneer, colonial, sedentary,* and *classic.* The Mogollon and Hohokam periods are illustrated on a chart of regional cultural sequences in Figure 4–5.

Lensing

When form, number, and time period are related on a diagram, the result is a frequency distribution that appears in the familiar "battleship" form. This characteristic is sometimes described as lensing because it forms a double-convex curve similar to a lens (Fig. 4–6).

The basic proposition relating artifact form, number, and time states, "An attribute or type population tends to trace out a lensing history through time." This history is sometimes called a *popularity curve* (Ford 1954). The lens or curve expresses five stages of growth and decline: (1) origin, (2) increase, (3) climax or peak, (4) decline, and (5) extinction. The point of origin of an artifact or attribute results from invention, innovation, discovery, or borrowing from a neighboring community. From this single point of origin, the attribute or type increases in frequency because of general acceptance by members of a prehistoric community. Climax or peak comes about as the attribute or type is accepted by all members of the community, who are behaving in one habitual manner. Decline takes place as the attribute or artifact type phases out of popularity and some new alternative gains acceptance. And finally, the attribute type becomes extinct with complete acceptance of some alternative custom. The replacement shift of alternative artifact types is displayed in Figure 4–6, in which Type A is followed by B and ultimately C to produce a time series. The moving mode concept, besides illustrating the

CULTURAL CHANGE PROCESSES

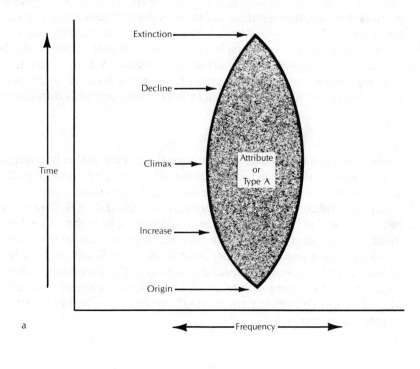

a

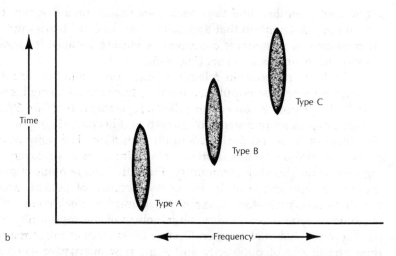

b

FIGURE 4-6 The lensing history of attributes and artifact types. (a) The popularity curve expressing five stages of growth and decline; (b) functionally similar artifact types replacing one another through time.

nature of culture change through time, is useful in chronological seriation, or sequence dating.

Units of Space

Units of geographical space measure cultural change and persistence across the landscape. Spatial units are derived from the study of artifact and site distributions. Two such units are locality and culture area (Willey and Phillips 1958, pp. 18–21).

A locality is the amount of space occupied by a single community, bounded by its territorial limits. The size of the locality varies with the community organization and its subsistence base. For example, a hunting band might occupy hundreds of square miles of territory, while a farming village was confined to a much smaller locality, perhaps tens of square miles in a river flood plain. The size of the village was dictated by the press of neighboring communities in active competition for prime land and resources. Efficiency of the exploitive technology, whether hunting gear or agrarian equipment, limited food production, the size of the local group, and the complexity of human organization necessary to wrest a living from the landscape. Ecologists would say that the interaction between technology, human population, and resource base leads to a particular "carrying capacity" for that community type (Zubrow 1975). In general, simpler communities require larger territories for support, while more complex communities make do with less territory but exploit it more intensely.

A second spatial unit is the culture area, a region occupied by contemporary communities and societies sharing similar cultures (Willey and Phillips 1958, pp. 20–21). Usually culture areas represent common adaptations to particular environments, such as short-grass prairies or deciduous woodlands. Thus the communities' technical base, and by implication their human organization and world view, may be similar. Often culture areas conform to regional provinces such as the great plains or Mississippi drainage system. North American culture areas are shown on Figure 4–7.

The concept of culture areas was largely pioneered by Clark Wissler (1950) as an aid in organizing North American ethnographic collections for display at the American Museum of Natural History in New York City. Wissler's culture-area scheme was based on methods of food production, by which North American tribes adapted to their environment. On the other hand, attempts to apply the culture-area concept outside of North America have met with less success. Historical factors leading to the development of complex, plural societies, such as conquest empires, feudal societies, and industrial states, often override the limitations of environment.

Spaulding (1960) provides the principal proposition relating artifact form and geographical space: "An attribute or type population tends to display

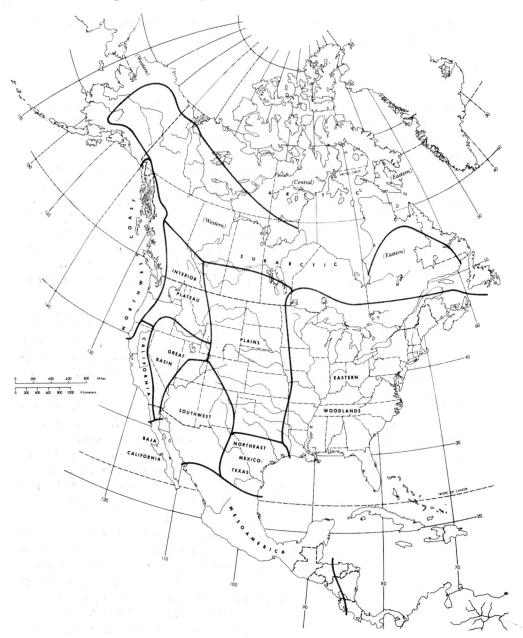

FIGURE 4-7   Archaeological culture areas of North America.

Source: Gordon R. Willey, 1966, *An Introduction to American Archaeology*, Vol. 1. Englewood Cliffs, N.J.: Prentice-Hall.

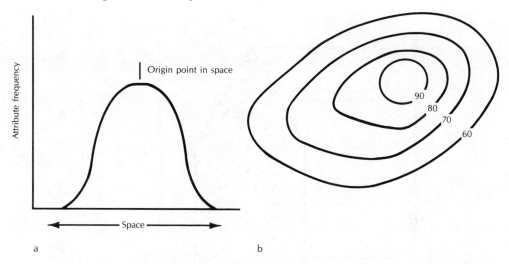

FIGURE 4-8   Diffusion of attributes and artifact types. (a) Frequency distribution of attribute or type in space; (b) contour map showing frequency lapse rate of an attribute or type from point of origin, from 90 specimens per unit area to 60 specimens per unit area.

systematic frequency changes through space." This regularity, which is the basis for diffusion theory, states that both attributes and types originate at a single point in space, where they occur in maximum frequency (Fig. 4–8a). From this point of origin, borrowing spreads outward toward the distributional perimeter of that attribute or type. In terms of attribute frequency, there is a systematic lapse rate from point of origin outward (Fig. 4–8b). These regularities form the age-area law of the Kulturkreis school of Anthropology (Harris 1969, pp. 382–92).

Form-Time-Space
Conjunctive Units

It is possible to discuss the three dimensions of archaeology as separate entities, but in cultural reality, form varies simultaneously in both time and space to produce the effect illustrated by the time-space cone of Figure 2–9. In a controlled experiment, however, any one of the three variables may be held constant in order to see how the other two behave as a set. When space is held invariate, units of form-time result. Tradition is the outstanding example. On the other hand, when time is minimized, the result is conjunctive units of form-space, such as the stage. And finally, the conjunction of all three dimensions—form-time-space—is called a *phase*.

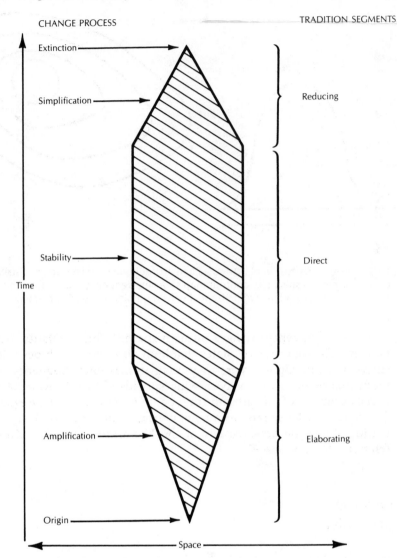

FIGURE 4-9   Tradition segments and their change processes.

Tradition

A tradition is an archaeological unit concept that persists in time but is limited in space (Haury 1956). The term emphasizes continuity and persistence rather than culture change. Furthermore, space is controlled or limited while time is permitted to vary. The concept deals with the evolution of specific attributes, types, industries, or assemblages. The tradition, then, is an evolutionary concept allowing the life-history, or ontogeny, of individual entities to be examined as they grow, peak, and decline. Historians have studied the same kind of regularities in the rise and fall of individual civilizations (Toynbee 1971).

For ease of classification, Haury (1956) has organized traditions into elaborating, direct, and reducing segments (Fig. 4–9).

An elaborating segment is created by increasing complexity as new attributes, tool uses, devices, and tool kits are added to the cultural inventory. These changes lead to new structural organizations. Change is directional in a positive sense as trait gains outnumber losses.

A direct tradition segment results from persistence rather than change. There is minimal trait loss or gain with considerable structural continuity.

The reducing segment is characterized by trait loss and overall simplification. In addition to decline in the number and variety of items composing the cultural assemblage, the organization of these elements is also diminished. Change is directional in a negative sense (Eddy 1972, pp. 55–56).

Examples of long-lived tool-making traditions are found in the Lower Paleolithic stage of the Old World. Braidwood (1967) recognizes five standardized ways of making stone tools, each of which endured for hundreds of thousands of years: (1) pebble tool, (2) core-biface tool, (3) flake tool, and (4) choppers and adze-like tools (1967, pp. 34–38). A fifth tradition, that of blade tools, was added in the Upper Paleolithic stage (1967, p. 60). The core-biface tradition the Abbevillian biface stone tools is shown in Figure 7–3 while the blade tool tradition is shown in Figure 1–13.

Stage

The archaeological stage is a measure of general evolution (Sahlins and Service 1970). Stage is a unit of similar cultural content cross-cutting many local and regional archaeological sequences. The stage emphasizes cultural content, while time and space vary. It organizes the data to emphasize sequential steps in culture change common to many local archaeological cultures. The disadvantage is that when archaeological data is placed in a stage classification, changes may appear as quantum jumps, rather than smooth, continuous advances. Examples of stage schemes in the archaeological literature are: (1) the Three-Age scheme of Thomsen (1836), (2) the classical Old World scheme of Lubbock (1865), (3) the New World scheme of Willey and Phillips (1958), and (4) the sociocultural scheme of Service (1962).

Phase

An archaeological culture appearing within a brief interval of time and restricted in space is called a *phase*. This form-time-space unit is defined by the artifact assemblage of tools and symbolic objects, their numerical frequencies, and subset associations. In describing the length of this unit, archaeologists must depend on the precision of available dating techniques. Consequently, many archaeological phases of the American Southwest average 200 years in length, while phases dated elsewhere in North America may span as much as a millenium. The phase is confined to one locality in many instances so that it takes on the social reality of a community. In some cases, however, a particular phase may appear simultaneously in two contiguous local sequences, leading to the concept of a co-phase (Willey and Phillips 1958, pp. 22–24). Phases are the building blocks of traditions (vertical phase sequences), stages (horizontal phase series), and the master units in writing the historiographies, of culture areas.

Phases, called *foci* in some regions of North America, are named by archaeological convention to enable the investigator to shift them about in time and space until sufficient temporal and spatial data are available to anchor them securely. As a rule, the named labels are taken from geographical places appearing on published maps. When defined in the professional literature, such labels help other archaeologists who may be engaged in comparative studies or simply writing regional cultural histories. Examples of phases from the American Southwest are: (1) the Piedra phase—named for a river in Colorado (Roberts 1930); (2) the Rosa phase—named for a now-abandoned town in New Mexico (Hall 1944); and (3) the Chimney Rock phase—named for a landform in Colorado (Eddy 1977).

Summary

In studying the artifacts of ancient cultures, archaeologists record a vast number of observations. To simplify the description and interpretation of these data, archaeologists have devised unit concepts that group their observations by form, time, and space. These units are frequently discussed in combination or broken down into subsets.

Subsets of form, for example, are attribute, type, industry, and assemblage. The attribute is a characteristic of the artifact, such as shape or color. Type is a cluster of same-age attributes that form a pattern, such as decorative details on pottery. An industry includes all artifacts that are the same age and made of the same material. The assemblage includes all artifact types found at one site or within a single layer of a site.

Units of time include the horizon and the period. A horizon is a comparatively brief time during which a technique or an art style spreads rapidly from its point of origin. The *period* term is used when archaeologists are able to date artifact deposits precisely, for example, AD 1325 to 1400. The terms *early*, *middle*, and *late* are often used to describe periods.

Locality and culture area are units of space. A locality is the space occupied by a single community. A culture area is a region occupied by contemporary communities sharing similar cultures.

The concepts of form, time, and space are combined in the terms *tradition, stage,* and *phase.* In a tradition, space is limited, time varies, and form persists as a particular culture grows, peaks, and declines. Both time and space vary in the stage concept, which applies to the sequential steps of cultural change common to many local communities. The stone, bronze, and iron ages are examples of stages. A phase is defined by the artifact assemblage of a particular culture in a brief period of time and a limited space. Phases, or archaeological cultures, are often named for geographical features of the localities in which they originate.

References

BENNETT, WENDELL C., and JUNIUS B. BIRD
    1949   Andean Culture History. New York: American Museum of Natural History.

BRAIDWOOD, ROBERT J.
    1967   *Prehistoric Men.* Atlanta: Scott, Foresman.

BRETERNITZ, DAVID A., ARTHUR H. ROHN, JR., and ELIZABETH A. MORRIS
    1974   *Prehistoric Ceramics of the Mesa Verde Region.* Flagstaff: Museum of Northern Arizona.

CLARKE, DAVID
    1968   *Analytical Archaeology.* London: Methuen.

DEETZ, JAMES
    1967   *Invitation to Archaeology.* Garden City, N.J.: Natural History Press.

EDDY, FRANK W.
    1972   Culture Ecology and the Prehistory of the Navajo Reservoir District. *Southwestern Lore* (1, 2):1–75.

    1977   Archaeological Investigations at Chimney Rock Mesa. *Memoirs of the Colorado Archaeological Society* (1).

FORD, JAMES A.
    1954   On the Concept of Types. *American Antiquity* 56:42–53.

FRISON, GEORGE C., MICHAEL WILSON, and DIANE J. WILSON
    1974   The Holocene Stratigraphic Archaeology of Wyoming: An Introduction. In *Applied Geology and Archaeology: The Holocene History of Wyoming,* edited by Michael Wilson. The Geological Survey of Wyoming, Report of Investigations No. 10, pp. 108–27.

HALL, EDWARD T., JR.
    1944   *Early Stockaded Settlements in the Gobernador, New Mexico.* Columbia Studies in Archaeology and Ethnology, Vol. 2. New York: Columbia University Press.

HARRIS, MARVIN
    1969   *The Rise of Anthropological Theory.* New York: Thomas Y. Crowell.

HAURY, E. W. (chairman)
    1956   An Archaeological Approach to the Study of Cultural Stability. In *Seminars in Archaeology: 1955,* edited by R. Wauchope. Memoirs of the Society for American Archaeology, No. 11, pp. 31–57.

LAPIN, LAWRENCE L.
    1975   *Statistics*. New York: Harcourt Brace Jovanovich, Inc.
LUBBOCK, JOHN
    1865   Prehistoric Times as Illustrated by Ancient Remains and the Manners and Customs of Modern Savages.
MARRIOTT, A.
    1948   *Maria: The Potter of San Illdefonso*. Norman: University of Oklahoma Press.
ROBERTS, FRANK H. H., JR.
    1930   *Early Pueblo Ruins in the Piedra District, Southwestern Colorado*. Washington, D.C.: Bureau of American Ethnology, Bulletin No. 96.
ROWE, JOHN HOWLAND
    1962   Stages and Periods in Archaeological Interpretation. *Southwestern Journal of Anthropology* 18:40–54.
SAHLINS, MARSHALL D., and ELMAN R. SERVICE
    1970   *Evolution and Culture*. Ann Arbor: University of Michigan Press.
SERVICE, ELMAN R.
    1962   *Primitive Social Organization: An Evolutionary Perspective*. New York: Random House.
SPAULDING, ALBERT C.
    1960   The Dimensions of Archaeology. In *Essays in the Science of Culture in Honor of Leslie A. White*, edited by Gertrude E. Dole and Robert L. White. New York: Thomas Y. Crowell.
THOMSEN, JURGENSEN
    1836,   *A Guide to Northern Antiquities*.
    1848
TOYNBEE, ARNOLD J.
    1971   *A Study of History*, vols. 1 and 2. New York: Dell Pub. Co., Inc.
WHEAT, JOE BEN
    1954   Southwestern Cultural Interrelationships and the Question of Area Co-traditions. In *American Anthropologist, Southwest Issue* 56(4):576–86.
WILLEY, GORDON R., and PHILIP PHILLIPS
    1958   *Method and Theory in American Archaeology*. Chicago: University of Chicago Press.
WISSLER, CLARK
    1950   *The American Indian*. New York: Peter Smith.
ZUBROW, EZRA B. W.
    1975   *Prehistoric Carrying Capacity: A Model*. Menlo Park, Calif.: Cummings.

5

Time
and Environment

One of the popular distortions concerning archaeology is the overemphasis on dating, or "How old is it?" In this misconception, the archaeologist is seen as a kind of historian whose research interest is entirely focused on chronology so that the more ancient the find, the more valuable it is. This public view of archaeology is in part the outcome of sensational news reporting, leading to a kind of competitive search for the oldest artifact, site, or fossil human being. In turn, the archaeologist, ever eager to obtain research funds, may actually encourage this attitude in press releases, which further amplifies the overemphasis on dating techniques and their results. On the other hand, curiosity about antiquities is not a bad thing since a lively appreciation of our human heritage is an enrichment to our every-day lives.

To combat this unfortunate overemphasis requires a shift to a chronological perspective in which dating techniques are simply "tools" in the arsenal of the archaeologist. These dating tools are no more or no less important than the microscope in the laboratory or the whisk broom and trowel in the field. In the study of archaeology, time is no more and no less important than environment. Dating is used to generate temporal units such as period and horizons, which in turn are useful in the study of the growth and development of society. Reconstruction of ancient environments is important for the contribution such study makes to chronology building and for insight into adaptations of past cultures to their natural environments.

Time is employed in evolutionary studies in order to measure the direc-

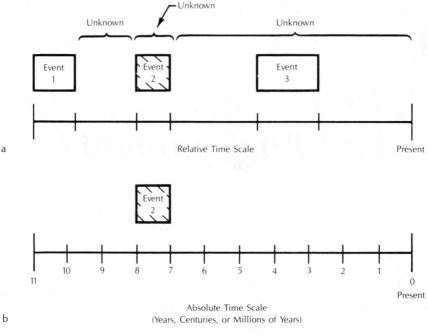

FIGURE 5-1   Comparison of relative and absolute dating.

tion of cultural growth and development as well as rates of change. Ideally, time is a measure based on the year, or one revolution of the earth around the sun, which takes place in approximately 365 days. But in a practical sense, time is defined by the archaeologist-historian as any succession of events whose order can be defined.

If time is the measurement, then "dating" is the assignment of a past event to this dimensional scale. In the archaeological literature, two classes of dating are customarily recognized—relative and absolute (Smiley 1955; Butzer 1976).

When an event is placed before, contemporary, or after another event, it is said to be "dated" in a relative sense. In Figure 5–1a, Event 2 is dated in a relative position as later than Event 1 and prior to Event 3. Examples of such relative ordering of events include (1) stratigraphy, or dating by the order that geological and archaeological deposits were laid down, and (2) sequence dating or seriation, that is, relative dating in terms of style and frequency change among populations of time-sensitive artifacts.

Relative dating is basic to chronology building in that the ordering of events, in the absence of a written record, is the first step in reconstructing prehistory. After such ladders or event chains are defined, however, the relative sequence is ideally upgraded to an absolute chronology by means of various dating techniques that yield an age-in-years.

In relative dating the duration of the event in question is unknown, and the elapsed time between events cannot be determined. Furthermore, the temporal distance between any past event and the present cannot be determined. All of these deficiencies are made up, however, when relative time is transformed into an absolute scale (Smiley 1955).

Dating Techniques

In absolute dating, each event is assigned to a time-in-years scale (Fig. 5–1b). However, the precision of this kind of dating is quite variable. A technique of absolute dating that provides temporal control as fine as a single year or season of a year is tree-ring dating (dendrochronology). On the other hand, the various radiometric dating techniques, like radiocarbon (C–14) or potassium/argon (K/Ar) dating, are statistical estimations in which the degree of confidence attached to a mean age may be quite large, on the order of a century or more for C–14 dates or 0.1 million years (my) or more for K/Ar. Despite this degree of uncertainty, radiometric assays are still classified as absolute dates since they yield an age-in-years measurement.

Absolute dates overcome many of the liabilities mentioned above for relative dating. As shown in Figure 5–1b, Event 2 is dated to one unit in terms of its duration on an age-in-years time scale. It is further anchored to the present by seven units of elapsed time. And furthermore, if other, related events had been dated by placement on the time scale, then the elapsed time between events could be measured for a rate calculation (number of events per unit of time) (Brothwell and Higgs 1963; Smiley 1955).

Since only a few of the more important techniques are described in this book, the reader who is interested in archaeological dating may wish to consult some of the citations in the following list of dating techniques:

> *Relative Dating:*
>   Stratigraphy (Smiley 1955; Rowe 1961)
>   Chronological seriation, or sequence dating (Rowe 1961)
>   Analytical dating of bone: fluorine, uranium, and nitrogen (Aitken 1961)
>   Paleontology (Lance 1955)
>   Pollen dating (Kurtz and Anderson 1955)
>
> *Absolute Dating:*
>   Radiocarbon dating (Willis 1963)
>   Potassium-argon dating (Gentner and Lippolt 1963)
>   Varve dating (Smiley 1955)
>   Geologic-climatic dating (Antevs 1955)
>   Dendrochronology (Bannister 1963; Fritts 1972)
>   Obsidian dating (Bannister and Smiley 1955; Friedman and Smith 1963)
>   Archaeomagnetism (Cook 1963)
>   Thermoluminescence dating (Hall 1963)

Paleomagnetic dating (Cox 1969)
Fission track dating (Michels 1973)

This chapter describes stratigraphy, several of the more common radiometric techniques, and dendrochronology.

Stratigraphy

Stratigraphy is the study of layered deposits. Stratigraphic study is based on the law of superposition, which declares that deposits, whether of natural or cultural origin, form with the oldest on the bottom of the sequence and each overlying stratum younger, or more recent, than the layer below (Rowe 1961). This kind of layering comes about as uplands, or "topographic highs," erode by wind, water, and gravity, to fill troughs or "topographic lows." Cultural factors that lead to stratigraphic layering include collapse of buildings, dumping of trash, and renovation of architecture.

Once the strata have been ordered from early to late, it is possible to date the artifacts and ecofacts of each layer according to Worsaae's law of association (Rowe 1962). This proposition states that objects, both natural and cultural, found together in the same layered deposit are of the same age. Thus, the relative dating of the superimposed deposits also dates their fossil specimens. In this manner, with Stratum 1 on top, long chains of strata and objects can be ordered in time to form the historiography of a site. For instance, a particular fire hearth can be dated to Stratum 6, or the erosional contact lying between Strata 7 and 8. The archaeologist might report that polished black pottery occurs in high frequency relative to all other ceramic types in Strata 1 through 3, after which it is replaced by red-on-buff decorated ceramics in underlying Strata 4 and 5.

The law of association is useful not only in the ordering of site historiographies, but also in the construction of local or regional sequences. Because layers with the same fossil content are of the same relative age, the archaeologist can match many site stratigraphies to form composite sequences that generalize beyond the individual site stratigraphy. Typically, each site contains part of the local prehistory. Only rarely are all archaeological phases present at every site (Fig. 5–2a). The matching procedure is called *cross-dating*.

As an exercise to demonstrate the strength of relative dating, the reader may wish to construct a historiography of the stratified architecture shown in Figure 5–2b. Once the event chain has been fabricated, date the burials or the pots on the floor of the two houses (Haury 1955). Pay particular attention to human-made features such as burial pits and pithouses, which should be relative-dated by their surface of origin. In cross section, such as Figure 5–2b, these features intersect older deposits. Thus, they are to be dated as younger than the intersected layers. If a number of dug features are viewed in plan perspective, it is possible to relative-date them based on their pattern of intersection; the younger features are "bites" taken out of the older features.

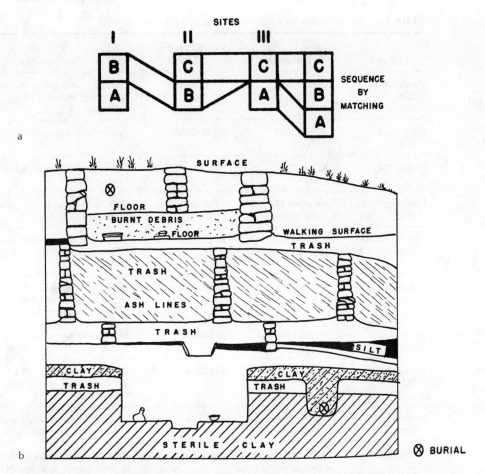

FIGURE 5-2   Examples of stratigraphic archaeology. (a) The manner in which the lettered layers of three numbered sites are cross-dated to yield a composite local sequence; (b) a multi-layered mound containing many stratified layers of architecture.

Source: By permission, from Emil W. Hawry, "Archaeological Stratigraphy," figures on pages 132, 124, in *Geochronology,* Terah L. Smiley, editor; Tucson: University of Arizona Press, copyright 1955.

Radiometric Dating

Absolute dating of fossil residues is based on the proposition that some regularity in nature can be related to an age-in-years scale. One class of such dating procedures is based on the principle of radioactive decay in which an unstable atomic isotope disintegrates at a known, constant rate to produce a stable, daughter product. The term *radiometric* is derived from *radioactive* and *metric,* meaning measurable atomic decay. Unstable isotopes, like carbon–14, differ little from their stable variants, such as carbon–12, except in their atomic weights. Decay of the radioactive isotope is constant through time by the

TABLE 5-1.   Common radiometric dating techniques.*

Parent	Daughter	Parent Half-life (Years)	Applications
Beryllium-10 (Be)	Boron-10 (B)	1.5 million	Oceanic sediments, soils, and cosmic-ray exposure of meteorites
Carbon-14 (C)	Nitrogen-14 (N)	5,730 (5568)	Archeological specimens
Iodine-129 (I)	Xenon-129 (Xe)	17 million	Duration of formation of the solar system
Lutetium-176 (Lu)	Hafnium-176 (Hf)	35 billion	Rare earth minerals and basaltic meteorites
Plutonium-244 (Pu)	Xenon-136, 134, 132 (Xe)	82 million	Very early events (older than 4 billion years) in solar system history
Potassium-40 (K)	Argon-40 (Ar)	1.25 billion	Rocks of all ages, down to those as young as about 0.5 million years, and meteorites
Rhenium-187 (Re)	Osmium-187 (Os)	43 billion	Iron meteorites and very old molybdenite
Rubidium-87 (Rb)	Strontium-87 (Sr)	49 billion	Rocks and meteorites of all ages, including those as young as 10 million years
Samarium-147 (Sm)	Neodymium-143 (Nd)	11 billion	Precambrian rocks and meteorites older than 600 million years
Thorium-232 (Th)	A chain of 9 radio-active daughters ending in stable lead-207 (Pb)	14 billion	Rocks and meteorites of all ages, including those as young as 20 million years
Uranium-235 (U)	A chain of 10 radioactive daughters ending in stable lead-207 (Pb)	704 million	Same as thorium-232
Uranium-238 (U)	A chain of 13 radioactive daughters ending in stable lead-206 (Pb)	4.5 billion	Same as thorium-232

*Wetherill, 1982, Dating Very Old Objects. With permission from Natural History, Vol. 91, #1; Copyright the American Museum of Natural History, 1982.

emission of nuclear particles. A measurement of how much any given sample of isotopes has progressed in its radioactive decay, times the rate of decay, called the *half-life*, provides the laboratory radiochemist with the age estimate of the object under assay. Table 5–1 provides a list of dating processes, along with the materials to be tested, potential age range in years, and the half-life or decay rate of each isotopic substance. Of course, carbon–14 (radiocarbon) and potassium–40/argon–40 are the two most commonly employed radiometric dating techniques in Quaternary studies. The radiometric techniques are often called *atomic clocks.*

Unlike stratigraphy and seriation, which are relative dating techniques conducted by the archaeologist, most physical, chemical, and biological dating techniques require the expertise of other specialists. Thus, the field archaeologist must collect datable materials, record stratigraphic provenience properly, and package and label specimens suitably for shipment to the appropriate laboratory. Radiocarbon dating requires a university or commercial laboratory with appropriate equipment, where technicians can clean the specimen, reduce it to elemental carbon, and count the beta particle emissions for age determination (Wilson 1976). The date, returned to the archaeologist after payment of cost of processing, is a mean age followed by a plus and minus figure called a *confidence interval* (for example, 2000 ± 100 years). It is then up to the archaeologist to interpret the meaning of the date in terms of the stratigraphic context and the artifact assemblage obtained from that layer.

As is true of all absolute dates, a single age estimate is of little value if it cannot be related to the prehistoric event that produced the artifact. Furthermore, suites of dates are more useful than single assays since they can be evaluated for stratigraphic or seriational order. Without this relative age check, individual radiometric assays may contain unnoticed error resulting from false measurement, poor collection practices, or contamination in the ground. In a long stratigraphic column, reversal in the stratigraphic ordering of the radiocarbon assays is comparatively simple to detect and correct for by resampling or submission of alternate carbon samples from the same occupational layer.

Radiocarbon Dating

Since the development of radiocarbon theory in the early 1950s won Willard Libby a Nobel prize, C–14 dating has revolutionized time scales and dating control in archaeology worldwide. C–14 is applicable for age determinations both in the late Pleistocene epoch and throughout the Holocene. All that is required for dating is suitable fossil organic remains, usually wood, charcoal, bone, or shell (see Table 5–1).

The theory of radiocarbon dating is as follows: Isotope 14 of carbon decays to nitrogen by emission of beta particles at a constant and known rate, the half-life figure (Willis 1963). A number of such half-life calculations have been made including the original determination by Libby, one by the National Bureau of Standards in the United States, and several by dating laboratories.

All of these figures range around 5000 years, although the original Libby figure is 5568 years, used as a convention by the dating laboratories of the world. Since all living matter, both plants and animals, contains a fixed ratio of C–14 to C–12, this ratio does not begin to change until the death of the organism. But upon death, this ratio changes in favor of the stable isotopes as the C–14 decays radioactively. Geiger counter determination of the degree of radiocarbon activity in the prehistoric specimen compared to a modern specimen times the decay rate constant (half-life) allows calculation of the age.

Certain limitations are inherent in the radiocarbon technique of dating. The sample may be too young, too old, or contaminated. Very recent organic samples are simply too young to yield accurate calculations. Furthermore, samples older than 70,000 years have too little radiocarbon to measure since it has been converted back to nitrogen–14. In fact, 50,000 years is the maximum age for reliable dating. Various forms of contaminants that may enter the specimen while it lies in the ground include soil carbonates and modern rootlets.

Measurements Before Present (BP) constantly become out-of-date because the present date changes daily. To solve this problem, a convention has been adopted that fixes the present at AD 1950 in honor of the pioneering research by Willard Libby on the radiocarbon clock. Thus, all conversions from radiocarbon BP time to Christian calendar time should be made by subtracting 1950 years from the radiocarbon age determination supplied by the dating laboratory. Thus a BP date of 2050 ± 100 years is to be translated as 100 B.C. ± 100 years. That is, there is a probability of two out of three times that this age determination has bracketed the true age of the event, the growth of the datable organic specimen, within a confidence interval of 200 BC to AD 0.

Since the production of C–14 in the upper atmosphere is a function of cosmic radiation by the sun, any variation in this form of energy causes variations in the production of C–14. Studies of the C–14 age of bristlecone pine tree rings has shown that just this effect has taken place over the last 7000 years (Wilson 1976). A number of correction charts have been compiled to convert radiocarbon years to Christian calendar years (Fagan 1977). These charts show that radiocarbon is too old back to about AD 1000. The two calendars are in reasonable agreement from AD 1000 to 1000 BC, after which the radiocarbon discrepancy becomes increasingly severe. For example, a radiocarbon date of 4500 BC is equivalent to a Christian calendar date (derived from tree-ring dating) of 5350 BC.

Despite these shortcomings, C–14 dating is the most reliable and certainly most nearly universal dating technique on a global scale. It has revolutionized understanding of the rise of Neolithic village farming and the appearance of urban and nonurban civilization throughout the world. With its reach back into the past, it covers all of the postglacial times as well as the Upper and Middle Paleolithic and Late Pleistocene times. And finally, by its theoretical coverage back to 70,000 years, which can be met occasionally with certain enrichment techniques in the laboratory, C–14 virtually links up with K/Ar to provide full coverage in dating the cultural evolution of humanity.

Potassium-Argon Dating

Potassium-argon dating, also identified by its chemical symbols, K/Ar, is a kind of radiometric dating whereby the relative Pleistocene chronology was converted to an absolute age-in-years calendar made up of a dated sequence of glacial and paleomagnetic events. Dating is based on the principle that the radioactive potassium isotope (K–40) decays at a constant and known rate to the gas isotope, argon–40 (Gentner and Lippolt 1963; Michels 1973). Suitable samples are rocks such as lava and tuff (volcanic ash) containing such minerals as muscovite (clear mica), biotite (dark mica), or sanidine (a greenish crystal). The age estimate is a measurement of the ratio of K–40/Ar–40 times the half-life (or decay constant), which equals the amount of elapsed time since the rock crystals first formed as the molten volcanic matter began to cool. When the minerals first form, only K–40 is present. Over time, some of the potassium decays radioactively to its end-product, which is the gas, argon–40. The decay constant, called the *half-life*, is a very large figure equal to 1.25 billion years ± 40 million years.

The form of the K/Ar date is an average age followed by a plus and minus figure that is a statistical confidence interval symbolized by the Greek letter sigma ($\overline{X} \pm \sigma$). This form of date is a statistical interval estimate showing that with 68 percent confidence, the true age of the event being measured (in this case the formation of the volcanic crystal) falls somewhere between the plus and minus figures. To increase confidence in the age estimate to the 95 percent level, double the sigma figure. Virtual certainty in the age estimate can be obtained by tripling the figure to obtain a 99 percent level of assurance. By convention, dating laboratories report K/Ar dates at the one-sigma level.

An important difference between K/Ar and C–14 dating is that with K/Ar the time scale is in millions rather than thousands of years. Thus, the mean date is expressed in decimal fractions times 10^6 (1,000,000 years), which often is abbreviated as millions-of-years-ago (mya). As an example of a K/Ar date, the Zinjanthropus fossil (*Australopithecus boisei*) found in Bed I at Olduvai Gorge, Tanzania, is dated $1.86 \times 10^6 \pm 0.06$ mya (Michels 1973). In actual fact, the assay sample for the date was taken from a volcanic ash layer one foot above the Lower Paleolithic occupational surface, but the association of date and fossil hominid is sufficiently close to warrant extending the age to the proto-human find.

In theory, K/Ar provides an age range from 4.5 billion years ago to 2500 years ago (Michels 1973, p. 168), although some authorities set the more recent age limit at 30,000 years (1973, p. 172). In conclusion, K/Ar dating overlaps radiocarbon dating to cover the entire age of the earth, but especially the late Tertiary and Pleistocene epoch. In this fashion, it provides time control on the early hominid ancestors of modern humankind as well as the Lower Paleolithic stage of cultural evolution.

Dendrochronology

Absolute dating by tree rings, called *dendrochronology*, is based on the principle that many trees and other woody plants of the middle and high latitudes lay down an annual growth ring. Variations in the widths of these annual rings reflect changes in the environment of the tree site, particularly temperature and precipitation fluctuations (Fritts 1972). In general moist, warm years produce wide growth rings and dry, cool years yield narrow rings. Despite the regularity of most tree growth, anomalies in ring widths do occur. For example, some years a tree may produce a double ring by starting, stopping, and then restarting its growth. Other anomalies are incomplete rings or missing rings, which tend to mislead the dendrochronologist.

Ring growth is uneven throughout the life history of any given tree. Young trees express a growth spurt whereas mature trees slow down in their growth rate so that over the lifetime of a tree, growth expresses an exponential curve. This S-shaped curve is standardized by the use of a statistic called *least-squares*. The purpose is to convert the S curve into a linear measure of ring widths so that climate, rather than life history, can be measured.

Synchronized patterns in tree growth allow trees of the same forest to be cross-dated as shown in Figure 5–3. In this way a composite ring sequence is built up by overlapping living tree sequences of wide and narrow rings to wood sequences from historic structures and ultimately specimens from prehistoric times. With this master chronology prepared, the dendrochronologist is then able to date wood specimens excavated from ancient ruins by matching the ring series from the unknown piece against the master chronology and searching for the exact point of perfect match. In this manner, the cutting date can be determined to the precise year. If the last growth ring has been interrupted in its development, then the season of felling also can be determined.

The early research in dendrochronology was conducted by Andrew E. Douglass, an astronomer who was searching for a climatic history that he could relate to sun-spot activity. Douglass, the father of tree-ring studies, ultimately constructed an absolute chronology for the American Southwest based on Douglas fir, ponderosa pine, and pinyon pine, which extends back to 273 BC. Later work in tree-ring studies has shifted to bristlecone pine, which has yielded a chronology spanning nearly 8200 years (Fritts 1972; Wilson 1976).

Besides providing information on the cutting age of the tree, and thus its date, most studies of tree rings provide considerable information on an-

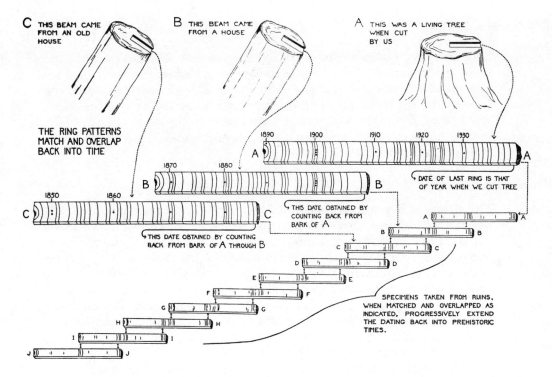

FIGURE 5-3   Cross-dating leading to the construction of a master tree-ring chronology.

Source: By permission, from Bryant Bannister and Terah L. Smiley, "Dendrochronology," Figure 11-3, in *Geochronology*, Terah L. Smiley, editor; Tucson: University of Arizona Press, copyright 1955.

nual climatic patterns in terms of normal rainfall or drought. Not only total annual precipitation is measured by trees, but also seasonal weather variations and ultimately meteorological pressure systems and storm tracks of the past (Fritts 1972). In addition, past runoff from a watershed can be measured as well as variations in geological phenomena such as the age of flood plains, advance and retreat of alpine glaciers, erosion rates, frequency of floods and avalanches, fires, and earthquakes. And finally, recalibration of C-14 production has been accomplished by radiocarbon-dating each individual tree ring of the bristlecone pine series collected from eastern California (Wilson 1976). This correction of the radiocarbon clock has led to far-reaching changes in the dating of European Neolithic and bronze age prehistory (Wilson 1976; Renfrew 1971).

Temporal Calendars

A calendar is a system of fixing the divisions of time. The component parts of a calendar consist of the units of measurement, whether relative or absolute, and the divisions of this scale. Although many such calendars have been invented by the historically minded sciences such as geology, archaeology, and history, only a few will be considered here. In the study of cultural evolution, these calendars are most useful: (1) geological, (2) glacial, (3) paleomagnetic, and (4) Holocene.

Geological Calendar

The history of the earth is subdivided by the geological calendar. Originally this history was organized by the relative age of the various rock formations that comprise the stratigraphic record of the science of historical geology. Later this relative chronology was converted to an absolute chronology by the use of the various radiometric dating techniques. The oldest rocks, of Pre-Cambrian age, have been dated to 4.6 billion years ago by uranium-lead radiometric assays (Butzer 1976; Laporte 1968). Younger subdivisions of the geological calendar are dated in a relative sense by the fossil content of their rock units and in an absolute manner through the broad range of isotopic decay techniques such as those listed in Table 5-1.

The subdivisions of the geological calendar are shown in Figure 5-4 with taxonomic breakdown into eras, periods, and epochs. The Cenozoic, the latest era, is the subdivision during which modern forms of life evolved. The Cenozoic era is subdivided into two periods, the Tertiary and Quaternary, respectively the third and fourth great subdivisions of the geological calendar. The Tertiary period saw the rise of mammals, including primates, during the last 65 million years. The Quaternary is of prime importance to the study of cultural evolution because it is the period of humankind. During the Quaternary, the fossil record shows the biological evolution of humans and their primate relatives over the last 2 million years.

The Quaternary period in turn is subdivided into two epochs, the Pleistocene and the Holocene. The Pleistocene is characterized as the "ice ages" when premodern humans evolved. Fully modern humans, called *Homo sapiens* in biological terminology, appear at the end of the Pleistocene and flourish during the last 10,000 years, the epoch called the *Holocene*. The Holocene epoch is the geological interval following the ice ages and hence is often called *post-glacial*. It has witnessed essentially modern climates and is marked by the appearance first of village agriculture and ultimately of urban civilizations.

Glacial Calendar

The Pleistocene epoch of the geological calendar is subdivided by the glacial calendar as shown for the chronology of Europe and North America in Figure 5-5. In fact, the Pleistocene is characterized as an epoch of widely fluctuating

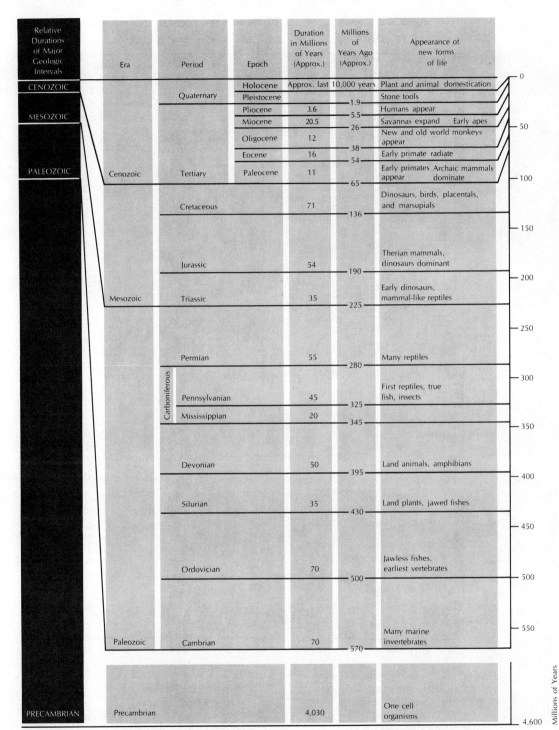

FIGURE 5–4   The geological calendar.

Source: Adapted from Leo F. Laporte, *Ancient Environments,* 2nd ed. © 1979. Reprinted by permission of Prentice-Hall, Inc., Englewood Cliffs, NJ. Data from Jolly and Plog 1982; Zihlman 1982.

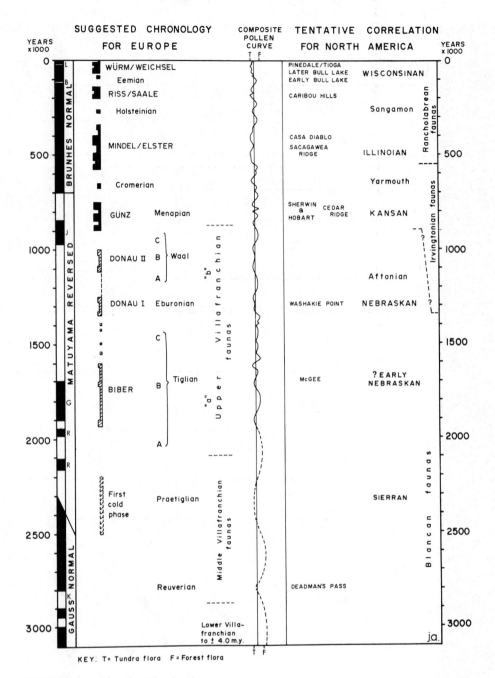

FIGURE 5-5 The glacial calendar.

Paleomagnetic time scale:
  Brunhes Normal epoch
    L = Laschamp event
  Matuyama Reversal epoch
    J = Jaramillo event
    G = Gilsa or Olduvai event
    R̄ = Reunion events

Gauss Normal epoch
  K = Kaena event
■ = normal polarity or magnetic north at present north pole position
□ = reversed polarity with magnetic north at present south pole position

Source: H. B. S. Cooke, "Pleistocene Chronology: Long or Short?" Table 3, *Quaternary Research* 2:206–20; Seattle: University of Washington, 1973.

climates with world temperature averages ranging between 4 and 5°C below today's values. During cold climatic episodes, the polar ice caps thickened and continental glaciers advanced as snow accumulated at high latitudes, while mountain glaciers formed and advanced in middle latitudes (Fig. 5–6). While water was stored in ice sheets, the world's sea levels dropped because of the retention of water at high latitudes. Alternately, during warm, interglacial episodes of the Pleistocene, the ice caps melted, glaciers retreated, and sea levels rose.

The glacial calendar is subdivided according to the oscillation of climates from cold to warm. The cold episodes are called *glacial stages*. In Europe, at least seven glaciations have been recognized and named (Cooke 1973). Three warm-climate phases have been identified and named Cromerian, Holsteinian, and Eemian. The capitalized glacial stage names listed in Figure 5–5 are

FIGURE 5-6   Environmental zonation of Europe during the Würm glaciation (ca. 20,000 years ago).

Source: From Karl W. Butzer, *Environment and Archaeology,* Figure 49; New York: Aldine Publishing Company, 1971.

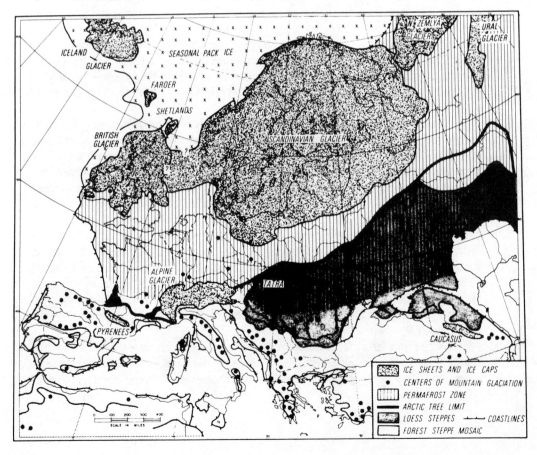

pulses of cold climate with internal variations shown by peaks on the bar graph. These minor oscillations of intense cold are called *stadials* while the intervening, relatively warmer sub-episodes are called *interstadials*. Stadials are given Roman numerals as illustrated by Würm I, II, and III.

Evidence for cold climate glaciation in the past is provided by piles of rock and soil, called *moraines,* which have been pushed ahead of the advancing ice sheet or smeared along the margins of ice-filled mountain valleys. Those moraines piled in front of the glacier, called *end-moraines,* mark the maximum extent of ice advance. The valley margin rock debris is called a *lateral moraine.* Those glaciers forming in high mountain masses pluck rock at the head of a valley to sculpture a sheer wall. Several such valley glaciers converging on one mountain peak form a "matterhorn" relief such as the famous Swiss Alpine landscape. Just in front of the rock headwall of each valley, the ice scours a depression with sill, which later fills with water to form a cirque lake. Furthermore, as the glacier descends to lower elevations, it scours the V-shaped profile of the mountain valley reshaping it to a flat-floored U-shape, and excavates a string of cirque depressions. After retreat and disappearance of the ice, glacial valleys reveal all of these sculptured features including a string of cirque lakes and a lake impounded by the end moraine. These cirque lakes fill with annual layers of mud, called *varves,* and are favorite sampling spots for pollen specialists, or palynologists, who core the muds for a history of the upper forest limit. As the mountain glaciers retreat, the coniferous forest pollen appears in the lake muds. Absolute dating of the succession of forest tree types can often be performed by radiocarbon using the organics of the lake bottom mud. By this means we know that the last major glaciation, the Würm or Weichsel of northern Europe, ended about 10,000 years ago.

Assuming a fixed quantity of water in the earth's hydrosphere, cold climates lock water in the form of ice and snow at high latitudes. World sea levels fall during glacial episodes, as evidenced by now-submerged wave-cut benches and deposits of beach gravels. Thus, glacial advance is inversely related to sea stand. Interestingly, ocean shore archaeological sites of interglacial times are now submarine phenomena requiring the use of dredging or modern scuba diving equipment for their study. Conversely, during warm interglacials, water is unlocked from high latitude and high altitude snow fields. It flows to the seas to produce a high ocean stand marked by raised fossil beaches, sea caves, and wave-cut bench marks. This kind of relative sequence of marine deposits, marked by alternate transgressing and regressing sea deposits, has been used on the North African coast of Morocco and Algeria to date Middle Pleistocene fist axe industries and *Homo erectus* fossils (Howell 1960).

As the sea level fluctuates from high to low, the delta reaches of the major rivers also are affected. The seas serve as base level for streams and rivers so that a high oceanic stand fills the channels with sediment, an effect

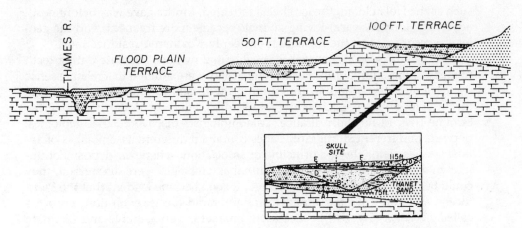

FIGURE 5-7   Cross-section of the Thames river valley showing terraces at the Swanscombe site, England. Inset shows details of the Swanscombe skull with associated artifacts in Layer D.

Source: F. Clark Howell, "Observations on the Earlier Phases of the European Paleolithic," reproduced by permission of the American Anthropological Association from *American Anthropologist* 68(2, Pt. 2):88–201, 1966.

that extends some distance upstream. On the other hand, as the sea level lowers, the rivers cut through their former beds, lowering their channels to reach the new base level and leaving high terraces along the valley flanks. These terraces then become a fossil record of the former valley floor. In general, the older terrace deposits are set back from the modern river channel, and successively younger river terraces are stair-stepped down to the present river. Customarily, fossil river terraces are either labeled by numbering from the modern river (T-0) counting upward toward successively higher and older terraces as T-1, T-2, continuing on to T-*n*, the last in the series, or by measured height above the modern river course as shown in Figure 5-7. In this latter example, the famous Swanscombe hominid find is an early modern human identified taxonomically as *Homo sapiens* but associated with the 100-foot terrace of the Thames river, England, which is dated to Middle Pleistocene times.

During the cold climates of glacial episodes, other aspects of the Pleistocene environment also left a fossil record. For instance, when continental ice sheets advanced southward on the north German plains of Europe, loess deposits formed,* the northern boreal forest limit gave way, and tundra-lov-

---

Loess—a columnar soil formed from wind-blown dust accumulating on the tundra zone in front of a glacial ice sheet.

ing animals predominated. Conversely, during warm interglacial episodes such as the Holsteinian, the ice sheets retreated, tundra gave way before north advancing forests, warm-loving animals became more frequent, and the geological record shows the formation of deeply weathered residual soils.

Before the glacial calendar was calibrated by such absolute dating techniques as potassium/argon, Pleistocene events were ordered in a relative sense by fossil animals, or fauna. In studying the fossilized animal bone of Pleistocene river terraces, such as the faunas discovered by de Perthes along the Somme river in northern France, paleontologists discovered that geological deposits of different stratigraphic ages contained different assemblages of animal species. Thus, by the principle of association, whenever deposits of unknown age containing these same faunal assemblages were discovered, they could be dated to the same relative age. It soon became evident that the Pleistocene was a time of giant animal forms and rapid species evolution, a process called *speciation* (Fig. 5–8). Since tooth enamel is very durable and teeth are highly distinctive to each animal species, the Pleistocene was early subdivided on the basis of its paleontology, particularly the teeth of the various elephant species. One particular faunal assemblage, named the *Villafranchian* after a type-site locale in France, was elected as the horizon marker separating the end of the Tertiary period (Pliocene epoch) from the beginning of the Quaternary period (Pleistocene epoch). This Plio-Pleistocene boundary marker is typified by a list of now-extinct giant animals including an elephant-like animal, rhinoceros, horse, and a huge beaver (Coles and Higgs 1975, p. 44 *ff*). As study of the Plio-Pleistocene fauna continued, it became possible to subdivide the Villafranchian into early, middle, and late periods of evolution. Today we know that the Villafranchian fauna is anything but a discrete horizon boundary. Recent radiometric assays show that the early Villafranchian extends back into the Pliocene epoch more or less to 4 million years ago, whereas the upper Villafranchian fauna endured up to the Gunz glaciation of Europe around 850,000 years ago. Because of this extensive time spread, current dating of the beginning of the Pleistocene epoch is in considerable dispute if not outright turmoil. Cooke (1973) would place the Plio-Pleistocene boundary at 3 million years ago. On the other hand, Brace and others (1979, p. 3) elevated the boundary considerably to 1.8 million years ago on the basis of the first appearance of stone tools, the cobble choppers employed by the various species of *Australopithecus*.

Customarily, the Pleistocene epoch is periodized in a three-fold scheme as Upper (or Late), Middle, and Lower (or Basal). The Lower Pleistocene is marked by (1) the first cold phase, (2) the Biber glaciation, (3) the two Donau glaciations, and (4) the Gunz glaciation. The time interval of the Lower Pleistocene period extends from 700,000 to 2 million years ago (Butzer and Isaac 1974). The Middle Pleistocene contains the Cromerian and Holsteinian interglacials plus the Mindel and Riss glacial stages, according to the terminology of the Swiss Alpine sequence of Europe. The corresponding glacial stages, Elster and Saale, are advances of the Scandinavian sheet that pushed

FIGURE 5–8   Upper Pleistocene mammals of mid-latitude Europe.

Source: From Karl W. Butzer, *Environment and Archaeology,* Figure 51; New York: Aldine Publishing Company, 1971.

down from the Baltic Sea onto the north German plains. And finally, the Late (or Upper) Pleistocene epoch is a comparatively short period of time of approximately 100,000 years including the Eemian interglacial and Würm/ Weichsel glaciation and ending about 10,000 years ago with the final retreat of the world's continental and mountain glaciers.

Paleomagnetic Calendar

The Glacial calendar is the traditional means of subdividing the Pleistocene epoch, but it has shortcomings. Glaciation is directly evident only in high and middle latitudes, whereas the tropics were little affected. Furthermore, marine sediments of the Pleistocene, which contain an important record of oscillating seawater temperatures, are difficult to correlate with terrestrial deposits (Butzer 1976). For these reasons, a more universal calendar without these limitations is now being developed. This new calendar, called the *paleomagnetic* or *geomagnetic calendar*, is applicable everywhere, at all latitudes of the earth and on land or sea floor (Cox 1969; Hay 1973; Cooke 1973). The chronology is made up of dated reversals in the earth's polarity field as these are registered in such volcanic rocks as lava and tuff (volcanic ash). The mineral particles of such rocks behave like little magnets that align with the earth's magnetic field. Upon cooling, these minerals are frozen in place. Study of successive layers of stratified volcanic rock shows repeated reversals in the earth's force field so that a compass would abruptly swing from north to south in its alignment if directional measurements were taken over geological time.

The age of these periods of normal (north alignment) and reversed (south alignment) polarity are derived by dating the volcanic rocks using the potassium–40/argon–40 radiometric technique. Based on hundreds of such polarity measurements, a fine-grained chronology has been erected covering the last 4.5 million years, or the Pleistocene and Late Pliocene epochs of geological time. The calendar consists of two magnitudes of units: epochs and events. Three named epochs subdivided the Pleistocene, as shown on the left side of Figure 5–5. Of these, Gauss and Brunhes are normal polarity epochs with the magnetic north near the present-day north pole position. These two epochs are separated by the Matuyama reversed epoch, dated between 2.43 and 0.69 mya, when the magnetic north was located at the present south pole position in Antarctica. In turn these major polarity episodes are split by named events of very short duration. Polarity events contrast with epochs because of their temporary polarity reversal. For instance, the normal polarity Olduvai event of the Matuyama reversed epoch dates Bed I and the Bed II contact at Olduvai Gorge between 1.7 and 1.9 mya (Hay 1973). These East Africa lake, lake-shore, and flood plain deposits contain some of the oldest tool-using hominids in the world, the *Australopithecus* species (Fig. 5–9). Higher in the stratigraphic column at Olduvai, Bed III is dated by another normal polarity event, the Jaramillo, between 0.89 and 0.95 mya and thus the contained fist-

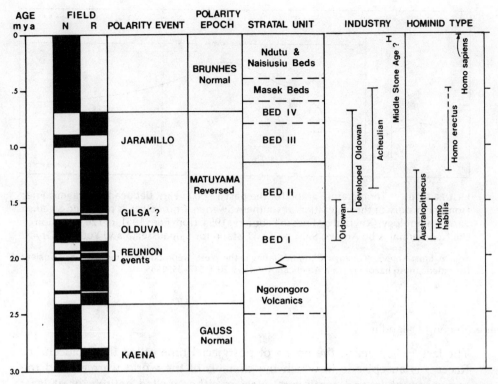

FIGURE 5-9   Stratigraphic and archaeologic units and hominid types of the Olduvai Gorge, Tanzania, matched against the magnetic polarity scale, which is modified after Cox 1969.

Source: From *Geology of Olduvai Gorge,* by Richard L. Hay; courtesy of University of California Press.

axe Acheulean industry and *Homo erectus* hominid fossils are also fixed in absolute time.

A further use of paleomagnetic events is to provide a more precise time marker for the beginning of the Pleistocene epoch than has heretofore been possible. Several Italian marine paleontologists have chosen the upper Reunion event (R of Figure 5–5) as the boundary marker. This dating shortens the Pleistocene to 1.9 mya based on K/Ar dating of volcanic ash from a clay pit sequence in Italy. Here the ash and marine sediments provide good dating and correlation with the paleomagnetic calendar and with marine sea shells used by paleontologists as marker fauna for the Plio-Pleistocene time boundary (Arias, Azzaroli, Bigazzi, and Bonadonna 1980). This convention, which is followed in this textbook, effectively resolves the differences between the long (3 mya) and short (1.8 mya) Pleistocene chronologies in favor of the shorter sequence.

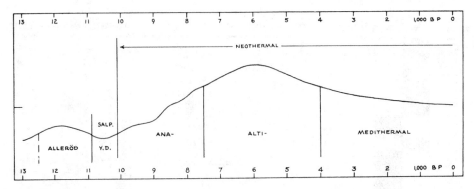

FIGURE 5-10   Temperature graph for the past 13,000 years, deduced by Magnus Fries from the history of the vegetation of southern Sweden. Chronology is the Finno-Swedish varve chronology. (Revised by Fries in February, 1954, from Fries 1951, p. 126.) Division of the Neothermal is by Antevs; Salp. and Y.D. stand for Salpausselkä and Younger Dryas.

Source: Ernst Antevs, "Geologic-Climatic Dating in the West," reproduced by permission of Society for American Archaeology from *American Antiquity* 20(3):317–35, 1955.

Holocene (Recent) Calendar

The last 10,000 years, the epoch of postglacial time called the Holocene or Recent, is an episode in which the climates of the world warmed and the major mountain and continental glaciers either melted entirely or at least shrank to insignificant sizes. The trend is one of global warming progressing from the cool, moist climates of the last major glaciation, either the Würm/Weichsel of Europe or the Wisconsin of North America, with mean annual temperatures climbing to a maximum around 6000 years ago then falling off to values approximating those of today. Antevs (1955), generalizing from geologic-climatic studies he had conducted in Sweden, Northeastern United States, and the semi-arid American West, divided the Holocene climates into three periods: (1) Anathermal, (2) Altithermal, and (3) Medithermal (Fig. 5-10). The Anathermal (10,000–7500 BP) is a period of cool, moist climates representing conditions as the Pleistocene glaciation ended. Antevs called this dying of the glaciers *deglaciation.* The Anathermal period saw the last of the large herd animals such as mammoth, horse, and the forms of bison on which Pleistocene hunters thrived.

The Altithermal, a period of high (alti-) temperature (-thermal) is dated between 4000 and 7500 years ago in the American Southwest. Here it represents the postglacial temperature maximum with changeover from the extinct faunas of the Pleistocene to fully modern animal forms. The desert areas of the world were expanded, though not uniformly. In some parts of the world, such as the Near East and Northern Europe, the mid-Holocene temperature high was a warm, wet period rather than warm, dry period, depend-

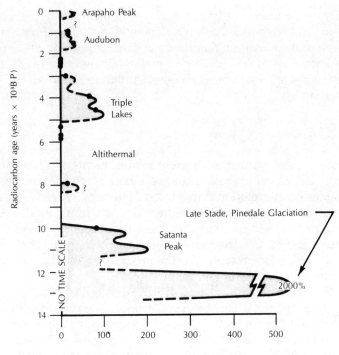

FIGURE 5-11   Diagram showing terminal fluctuations of Holocene glaciers in the Colorado Front range. Distances from cirque headwalls are expressed as a percentage of the maximum length attained during the Triple Lakes advance. The Pinedale glaciation is a local mountain equivalent to the last stadial of the continent-wide Wisconsin glaciation.

Source: James B. Benedict, "Prehistoric Man and Climate: The View from Timberline," In *Quaternary Studies,* edited by R. P. Suggate and M. M. Cresswell. Wellington: The Royal Society of New Zealand, 1975.

ing on the arrangement of meteorological pressure cells and storm tracks. In the American Southwest, the Altithermal is marked by erosion, soil formation, and calcium carbonate formation (locally called *caliche*). Lakes dried up, salt was removed from the lake beds by wind deflation, dune fields formed, and glaciers disappeared completely from the mountains (Fig. 5–11).

During the Medithermal, dated from 4000 years ago to the present, climatic conditions were like those of today. Evidence for an amelioration of climates over the Altithermal is shown by valleys filled with flood plain sediment, soil formation, partial regeneration of lakes that had been dried up, stabilization of dune fields by vegetation cover, and tree-ring-dated droughts. During droughts in the American Southwest, streams dry up or cut deeper into the valley flood plain. At higher altitudes in the mountains, there was a minor resumption of glacier activity as illustrated by the Triple Lakes, Audubon, and Arapahoe Peaks glaciers in the Colorado Front range (Fig. 5-11). Although the history of Medithermal glaciation is not uniform over the earth, the pattern of global cooling is evident. However, the intensity of Medithermal glaciation was never as great as that recorded for the preceding Pleistocene epoch.

Environmental Reconstruction

Archaeologists reconstruct ancient environments as a basis for building geological and glacial calendars and as a background for studying past human adaptations. Adaptation is the process whereby a society wrests a living from the natural environment and buffers such environmental extremes as floods, droughts, cold waves, storms, and shortened growing seasons. Society adapts to these aspects of nature by devising technology, systems of human organization, and belief systems. To the materialist, adaptation is the crucial process explaining the evolution of culture.

The basic data for reconstructing prehistoric environments are called *ecofacts* (Binford 1964). This term was coined to parallel the archaeologist's use of the word *artifact*. Ecofacts are evidences of ancient environments, such as fossil plants, animals, soil, and sediment (Evans 1978; Butzer 1976).

In order to reconstruct past environments, the ecofactual data must be identified by a biological or geological specialist. These identifications are then converted into inferences about past habitats and climates based on analogy with contemporary ecological conditions, a form of reasoning that closely parallels the use of ethnographic analogy. These interpretations are subject to limitations such as: (1) the habitat requirements of the modern plant or animal may not be fully known; (2) environmental constraints for the contemporary plant or animal may have changed over those of the past; and (3) the death transformation of the ecofactual evidence may have distorted the evidence enough to make reliable interpretation impossible.

To circumvent these shortcomings, it is advisable for the archaeologist to cross-check the inferences for each component of the environment looking for examples of verification or refutation. For instance, since the natural environment is a system, ecofactual evidence for one component should match or be compatible with that of another. Thus, a reconstruction of an open woodland based on fossil land snails should match a reconstruction based on plant species taken from fossil pollen, macro-plant parts, and phytoliths (plant opals) (Fig. 5-12). Furthermore, the indicated climatic type should match the habitat requirements of the snail population. If even one aspect of the total environmental reconstruction, in this case an open woodland, is incompatible, then reasons for this discrepancy must be examined rigorously. Perhaps some environmental constraint has been altered, past-to-present, or the death transformation from living biological community to fossil assemblage shows

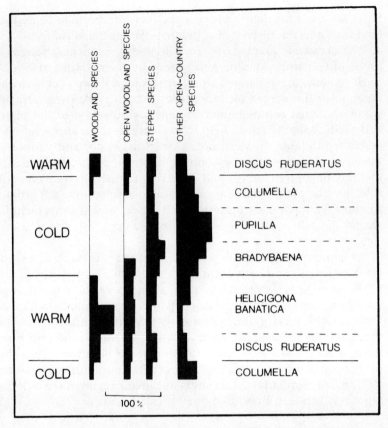

FIGURE 5-12   Histogram of fossil identifications (right column) taken from Germany. Warm/cold climatic interpretations reflect two glacial/interglacial stages of the Pleistocene epoch. Graph peaks indicate changing habitats along an ecological scale from closed woodland to open country.

Source: John G. Evans, *An Introduction to Environmental Archaeology,* courtesy of Granada Publishing Limited.

a serious and previously undetected bias. For the purpose of cross-checking, the archaeologist studies plant remains, animal remains, and soils and sediments from the past.

Plant Remains

Given favorable preservation, fossilized plant parts can be identified from pollen, macroscopic plant parts, charcoal, and impressions, to name just a few classes of plant fossils (Evans 1978). In Europe, assemblages of pollen types are used for dating purposes. Other interpretations are forest history, land use, and the history of cultivated plants, called *cultigens.*

Macroscopic plant parts, such as twigs, branches, stems, leaves, and roots, often can be identified to species by their characteristic cell structure. Such remains are separated from archaeological deposits by means of water flotation or fine-screening procedures. After drying these remains, the consulting botanist can make microscopic identification of the pieces of plants and seeds. Identifications help to explain the site's surrounding vegetation, edible wild plants, domesticated plants, firewood, and various organic materials employed in tools as handles, lashings, shafts, and other parts, not to mention fibers for cordage and timbering for architectural construction. As a rule, specific plant species were carefully selected for each artifact use. Macroscopic plant parts are preserved in a variety of situations including dry rock shelter deposits, water-logged soils (called *wet sites*), and as a result of charring.

Plant impressions form when some plant part, such as a seed, is treaded into soft, plastic soil such as mud or the clay of a pottery vessel. Identification of the plant species provides information about the natural vegetation surrounding a site as well as the useful plants carried home for food or materials. Particularly, cereal grain impressions have been used to interpret farming practices. Ratios of grain, such as wheat-to-barley, indicate how successful the agricultural strategy was. Drier climates of Southwest Asia show a higher proportion of wheat, while the damper climates of Europe favor barley (Evans 1976, p. 26). Similarly, subtle shifts in climatic regimen are reflected in changing ratios between these two domesticated cereals.

Animal Remains

Because of adverse factors of preservation, the flesh of animals decays and rots after death, leaving the more durable skeleton as a fossil relict. From the skeleton a paleontologist or zoologist can identify species, age, and sex by examining parts such as teeth, skull, and the articular ends of long bones. Some soft parts preserve, in particularly favorable circumstances, such as the freezing of flesh, hair, and hide in the arctic. Dry rock shelter deposits of the arid lands often yield soft-part anatomy preserved by desiccation.

Once the assemblage of animal species from a site has been identified, the information must be interpreted. Many questions surface at this stage of research because humans make selective use of their natural surroundings. For instance, hunters concentrate on particular game species and ignore other animals that live in the vicinity. Furthermore, of animals preferred as quarry, hunters may select particular age and sex categories according to the season of the hunt, the needs of society, and conservation ethics. Because hunting strategies are selective, it is not possible to interpret the natural environment surrounding an archaeological site directly. Some allowance must be made for cultural bias in the data.

Since Neolithic times, practices of animal husbandry also have distorted the faunal data. In these agrarian societies, the skeletal collection mirrors practices of selective breeding and slaughter by the farmer. Thus, the age-at-death and sex ratios reflect customs of human harvest rather than conditions in the wild.

To reconstruct the environment from fossil animal remains, the paleontologist observes habits of present-day animal species and assemblages of such species. Interpretations are drawn from knowledge of feeding habits, preferences for vegetation cover, tolerance of climatic extremes, and the mapped distribution of the geographical range of a species. Such reasoning by analogy works very well when animals of the past have modern counterparts. But when the biologist encounters the remains of extinct species or species such as the elephant-like mammoth of the Pleistocene, which has only a rough modern equivalent, problems of interpretation become apparent. For extinct species, the animal habits and habitat may have to be interpreted directly from the ancient environmental context in which the fossil form was found. But in general, a fossil animal assemblage reflects the vegetation cover and climatic regimen in which the animals once lived. (See Figure 5–12 for an example of such a reconstruction taken from the Pleistocene epoch of Germany.)

Furthermore, special interpretive problems result from the mobility of many hunting-and-gathering societies and nomadic pastoral tribes. The mobility of these economic types is usually based on a migratory pattern in which the community relocates on a schedule keyed to the seasonal availability of resources. In order to identify patterns of seasonal migration in the archaeological record, it is necessary to examine plant and animal remains that reflect some seasonal aspect of the organism's growth. Among plants, for example, flowers indicate spring and seeds indicate fall. Even more significant is the contribution of animal remains to seasonal interpretation, which includes: (1) age range of individuals, (2) ring studies of fish bones, called *otoliths*, (3) the condition of antlers (whether attached to the skull or shed), (4) oxygen isotope analysis of shells, and (5) insect evidence (Evans 1978, pp. 62–63).

Sediments and Soils

Sediments and soils are the matrix within which artifacts and ecofacts are buried and the mineral material of which archaeological and geological deposits are formed. Sediments result from the physical and chemical breakdown of parent bedrock, the hard rock crust of the earth. The actual process, called *weathering*, is the disintegration of the earth's rock crust into smaller particles of rock and mineral. Soils are a special class of sediment that has been zoned by vertical movement of organics and chemicals under the influence of a vegetation cover and the circulation of ground water.

To describe both sediments and soils, the geologist and the soil scientist (called a *pedologist*) note the various physical and chemical features of an exposure, such as the vertical wall of a test pit or a balk of a full-scale excavation. Physical observations include particle size, that is, the texture of the sediment with classification to clays, silts, sands, gravel, and cobbles (Evans 1978). Other physical attributes to be considered are shape, grain surface, and gross morphology (form) of the sediment particle. Chemical features to be observed include mineral composition, organic humus content, chemical compounds, color, and pH (hydrogen ion concentration).

From such observations, the nature of the environment of deposition can be inferred. For instance, the sediments may have formed into layers in aquatic environments such as streams, lakes, estuaries, or oceans. Other sediments may have deposited as layers on land to form slopewash deposits, cave deposits, precipitates, peat, swamp muds, glacial deposits, wind sediments, loess, lavas, and volcanic ash deposits. Each of these depositional types shows discrete physical and chemical attributes and internal structure because of the depositional processes involved.

Summary

Dating, chronology building, and environmental calendars are the outgrowth of temporal studies. Time is an important measure when the archaeologist is investigating the pace or rate of evolutionary change. Time, itself, is defined in astronomical terms as a measurement based on the year, or one revolution of the earth around the sun. Dating assigns a past event to a time scale, either relative or absolute. Relative dating, the first step in building a chronology, places events in a series so that the position of any one event can be specified in terms of all surrounding events. Thus, one event can be said to be younger or older than another. Examples of relative dating are stratigraphy, chronological seriation, paleontology, and terrace dating.

Absolute dating, on the other hand, upgrades relative chronology so that events can be placed on a time-in-years scale. By absolute dating it is possible to specify the length of an event, the elapsed time between and among events in series, and the duration of an event before the present. Examples of absolute dating are the radiometric techniques such as potassium/argon and radiocarbon dating. Other examples are tree-ring dating, used to recalibrate C–14 dating, and paleomagnetic dating.

As a principle, these dating techniques should not be used in isolation, but in sets that provide internal verification for the system of temporal units. Cross-checks on the validity of any given date result from the need for congruence with many other temporal assays. The time frame so established is called a *calendar*, or division of time into units. Calendars are useful in the study of human evolution, both biological and cultural. Four such calendars, in order of increasing specificity, are: (1) geological, (2) glacial, (3) paleomagnetic, (4) and Holocene calendars. The geological calendar is a subdivision of the history of the earth, which spans a vast sweep of time measured by uranium/lead (Ur/Pb) radioactivity as 4.6 billion years. Of this immense amount of time, only the last 2 million years are of direct relevance to the study of culture evolution since our earliest reliable dates for stone tools extend back only 2.5 million years. Thus, human adaptation to the changing environments of the earth is found only in the last great period of geological time, the period called the Quaternary and the very latest portion of the Tertiary.

On the glacial and paleomagnetic calendars, the Quaternary period is broken down into finer subdivisions, the Early, Middle, and Late Pleistocene epoch and the Holocene epoch. During the Early Pleistocene (1.9–0.7 mya), the earliest tool-using hominids appeared—the *Australopithecines* in multiple species. These were followed by the Middle Pleistocene (0.7–0.1 mya) *Homo erectus* fossils, who were pre-modern peoples using the fist-axe or biface industries of the Old World. By Late Pleistocene times (0.1–0.01 mya), the pace of cultural evolution had greatly accelerated and fully modern *Homo sapiens* were becoming sophisticated band hunters of the large Pleistocene fauna. During this time symbolic artifacts appeared in the archaeological record in the forms of formal burial, hunting cult fetishes, cave paintings and sculptures, and female (venus) fertility figurines.

The Holocene calendar subdivides postglacial times, the last 10,000 years. The environmental pattern is a progression of global warming that reached a temperature maximum about 6000 years ago, followed by a slight amelioration to modern conditions. Antevs (1955) has subdivided the Holocene epoch, or Neothermal period, into three periods: Anathermal, Altithermal, and Medithermal. The cool, moist Anathermal period saw the extinction of the Pleistocene fauna, which was replaced by modern wildlife. During this period mountain and continental glaciers shrank, leaving only the Greenland icecap and the polar ice sheets to persist to the present. With the extinction of the huge biomass of Pleistocene herd animals, particularly those adapted to the tundra or barren ground environments north of the arctic treeline, Paleolithic hunters were forced to readapt to the smaller game animals of the Altithermal forests and deserts. This process led to different human economies and cultural stages, called the *Mesolithic* in the Old World and the *Archaic stage* in the New World. As new game was hunted by techniques of stalk and ambush, so new food sources were utilized including a wide range of edible plants, marine resources, and freshwater aquatic life.

This short-lived stage of intensive food collecting was rapidly followed by the Neolithic revolution, which began 8000 to 9000 years ago in the Near East. The Mesolithic villagers evolved into food-producers at different rates in different parts of the world. By Medithermal times, the early civilizations had appeared. City living, which was an integral part of some but not all of the earliest civilizations and primitive states, most often evolved in arid lands in a zone that extends just north of the equator. Irrigation agriculture was the technology by which these peasant farmers adapted to semidesert lands such as the Nile valley, Mesopotamia, the Indus valley, the Yellow river valley, the arid basins of central Mexico, and the desert of coastal Peru. In each case, Medithermal climates facilitated the growth of irrigation agriculture, which feeds on seasonal runoff from mountainous snow pack. Notable exceptions to these geographical climatic trends are found in the few early tropical civilizations, such as those of the Olmec on the Vera Cruz coast of Mexico and early agricultural based high cultures in Southeast Asia.

Knowledge of ancient environments is essential for dating and calendar building. Furthermore, the study of adaptation, the causal mechanism for culture evolution, can be conducted only through knowledge about the prehistoric environment. Three lines of evidence contribute to environmental reconstruction: plant remains, animal remains, and sediment/soil types. Archaeologists attempt to verify the ages of prehistoric artifacts by crosschecking among these several kinds of remains.

References

AITKEN, M. J.
   1961   *Physics and Archaeology*. New York: Interscience.

ANTEVS, ERNEST
   1955   Geologic-Climatic Dating in the West. *American Antiquity* 22(4):317–35.

ARIAS, CLAUDIO, AUGUSTO AZZAROLI, GUILIO BIGAZZI, and FRANCESCOPAOLO BONADONNA
   1980   Magnetostratigraphy and Pliocene-Pleistocene Boundary in Italy. *Quaternary Research* 13(1):65–74.

BANNISTER, BRYANT
   1963   Dendrochronology. In *Science in Archaeology*. New York: Basic Books.

BANNISTER, BRYANT, and TERAH L. SMILEY
   1955   Dendrochronology. In *Geochronology*, Physical Science bulletin no. 2. Tucson: University of Arizona Press.

BENEDICT, JAMES B.
   1975   Prehistoric Man and Climate: The View from Timberline. In *Quaternary Studies*, edited by R. P. Suggate and M. M. Cresswell. Wellington: Royal Society of New Zealand.

BINFORD, LEWIS R.
   1964   A Consideration of Archaeological Research Design. *American Antiquity* 29(4):425–41.

BRACE, C. LORING, HARRY NELSON, NOEL KORN, and MARY L. BRACE
   1979   *Atlas of Human Evolution*. New York: Holt, Rinehart and Winston.

BROTHWELL, DON, and ERIC HIGGS, eds.
   1963   *Science in Archaeology*. New York: Basic Books.

BUTZER, KARL W.
   1976   *Environment and Archeology*. Chicago: Aldine.

BUTZER, KARL, and GLYNN ISAAC
  1974   Stratigraphy and Patterns of Cultural Change in the Middle Pleistocene. *Current Anthropology* 15(4):508–14.

COLES, J. M., and E. S. HIGGS
  1975   *The Archaeology of Early Man.* Middlesex: Penguin Books.

COOK, R. M.
  1963   Archaeomagnetism. In *Science in Archaeology.* New York: Basic Books.

COOKE, H. B. S.
  1973   Pleistocene Chronology: Long or Short? *Quaternary Research* 3:206–20.

COX, ALLAN
  1969   Geomagnetic Reversals. *Science* 163:237–45.

EVANS, JOHN G.
  1978   *An Introduction to Environmental Archaeology.* Ithaca, N.Y.: Cornell University Press.

FAGAN, BRIAN M.
  1977   *People of the Earth.* Boston: Little, Brown.

FRIEDMAN, IRVING, and ROBERT L. SMITH
  1963   Obsidian Dating. In *Science in Archaeology.* New York: Basic Books.

FRITTS, HAROLD C.
  1972   Tree Rings and Climate. *Scientific American* (May):93–100.

GENTNER, W., and H. J. LIPPOLT
  1963   The Potassium-Argon Dating of Upper Tertiary and Pleistocene Deposits. In *Science in Archaeology.* New York: Basic Books.

HALL, E. T.
  1963   Dating Pottery by Thermoluminescence. In *Science in Archaeology,* New York: Basic Books.

HAURY, EMIL W.
  1955   Archaeological Stratigraphy. In *Geochronology,* Physical Science bulletin no. 2. Tucson: University of Arizona Press.

HAY, RICHARD L.
  1976   *Geology of the Olduvai Gorge.* Berkeley: University of California Press.

HOWELL, F. CLARK
  1960   European and Northwestern African Middle Pleistocene Hominids. *Current Anthropology,* 1:195–232.

JOLLY, CLIFFORD J., and FRED PLOG
  1982   *Physical Anthropology and Archaeology.* New York: Alfred A. Knopf.

KURTZ, EDWIN B., JR., and ROGER Y. ANDERSON
  1955   Pollen Analysis. In *Geochronology,* Physical Science bulletin no. 2. Tucson: University of Arizona Press.

LANCE, JOHN F.
  1955   Paleontology. In *Geochronology,* Physical Science bulletin no. 2. Tucson: University of Arizona Press.

LAPORTE, LEO F.
  1968   *Ancient Environments.* Foundation of Earth Science series. Englewood Cliffs, N.J.: Prentice-Hall.

MICHELS, JOSEPH W.
  1973   *Dating Methods in Archaeology.* New York: Seminar Press.
RENFREW, COLIN
  1971   Carbon–14 and the Prehistory of Europe. *Scientific American* 225(4):63–72.
ROWE, JOHN HOWLAND
  1961   Stratigraphy and Seriation. *American Antiquity* 26(3):324–30.
  1962   The Law of Association. *American Antiquity* 28(2):129–37.
SMILEY, TERAH L.
  1955   *Geochronology.* Physical Science bulletin no. 2. Tucson: University of Arizona Press.
WILLIS, E. H.
  1963   Radiocarbon Dating. In *Science in Archaeology.* New York: Basic Books.
WILSON, DAVID
  1976   *The New Archaeology.* New York: New American Library.
ZIHLMAN, ADRIENNE
  1982   *The Human Coloring Book.* New York: Barnes & Noble Books.

6

Human Biological Evolution

To understand cultural evolution, it is first necessary to understand biological evolution and how it relates to the human capacity for culture, which has been the prime survival mechanism leading to success of the species.

Human beings are animals and as such are related to all other members of the animal kingdom. The Swedish systematist, Carolus Linnaeus, organized the animal world into a biological taxonomy around the middle of the eighteenth century (Howells 1966). In fact, this hierarchical classification became one of the important arguments against the prevailing theological view of that day, which saw humans as a special creation of God rather than as part of nature. But if the view of Linnaeus is correct and humankind is part of nature, which particular animals are we most related to? Linnaeus answered this question by classifying humans with the apes, lemurs, lorises, tarsiers, and monkeys to form the taxonomic order called *Primates*. One branch of the *Primates*, the family Hominidae, includes all living humans, regardless of their racial varieties, and two genera of extinct prehumans, *Ramapithecus* and *Australopithecus* (Table 6–1).

The Linnaean classification is a nomenclature in which higher groups such as kingdom, phylum, and class, are inclusive, while lower groups become progressively less inclusive moving downward through order, family, genus, and species toward the individual. A particular kind of animal is identified by a two-part Latin (binomial) name composed of the genus and spe-

TABLE 6-1.   The Linnaean classification of the Hominoidea including both living and extinct fossil forms

Taxonomic Levels	Linnaean Categories	Genera	Description
Order	Primate	—	Humans, apes, monkeys, prosimians
Superfamily	Hominoidea	—	Apes and humans
Family	Pongidae	—	Great apes
		Pongo	Orangutan
		Pan	Chimpanzee
		Gorilla	Gorilla
		Dryopithecus	Extinct great ape of the Miocene epoch
	Hominidae (hominid)	Ramapithecus	Early hominid of the late Miocene epoch
		Australopithecus	Fossil hominid of the Pliocene and early Pleistocene epoch
		Homo	Living humans with some fossil species

cies. Humans are assigned to the genus *Homo* and species *sapiens,* with these identifiers set in italics.

But what about the humans of the past? Do humans share common ancestors with other primates? The answers to these questions have long been sought by physical anthropologists, paleontologists, and anatomists. One of the first to discover actual evidence that prehumans of the past were anatomically different from ourselves was the Dutch anatomist Eugene Dubois, who discovered skeletal elements of a near-human creature popularly called *Java man* but more accurately classified to the genus of modern man, *Homo,* but in a different species, *erectus.* This find, made by Dubois in the Trinil district of central Java in 1890, was one of the first bits of evidence that the morphology of humans has evolved through time, and in particular, the brain has increased in size and complexity (Brace and others 1979, p. 59).

Dubois' find was preceded by a still earlier discovery, the Neanderthal skeleton, located by quarry workers and a high school teacher in western Germany as long ago as 1856. But the Neanderthal skeleton, although an important grade in fossil evolution, is currently placed in the same genus and species as modern humans (Brace and others 1979, p. 103).

Today there are hundreds of fossil finds that show how modern *Homo sapiens* evolved by slow but steady steps from simpler, prehuman primates. Furthermore, other fossil finds suggest that humans are linked to our nearest primate kinsmen by a series of apes whose anatomy displays an intermediate position between the pongids (great apes) and the hominids, which include ourselves and our nearest fossil ancestors such as *Homo erectus.*

Fossil Apes

During the Tertiary period, the entire order of Primates began evolving by adaptive radiation, that is, by adapting to a variety of habitats, each occupant transforming to a new species. One line of this evolutionary ascent is a lineage of fossil apes that includes such genera as *Aegyptopithecus*, *Dryopithecus*, *Sivapithecus*, and *Gigantopithecus*, all of which have been suggested as either direct ancestors or close collaterals to the human family tree (Brace and others 1979, p. 13). Of this set, the best known genus is the fossil ape called *Dryopithecus*, who can serve as an example of a common link between the pongid great apes and the hominids (Pilbeam 1972, p. 44).

There are six species of *Dryopithecus*, which are dated to the Miocene epoch of the Tertiary period, approximately 18 to 23 mya. Individual finds have occurred in Southern Europe, Africa, and Asia, but not in the New World. Based on geological sediments and associated fauna, these ancestral apes are inferred to have occupied habitats ranging from tropical rain forest to lowland woods and even wooded savannas. The likely form of locomotion was tree-swinging and most of the daily diet was leafy foliage in this arboreal existence. A distinctive Y–5 cusp pattern to the lower molar teeth is one of the most telling lines of evidence that this Miocene ape gave rise to the modern anthropoid apes, fossil hominids, and modern humans (Brace and others 1979, pp. 16–17).

The First Hominid: *Ramapithecus*

After the branching split with the pongids, the hominid line diverged its separate way. According to Simons (1977) and Pilbeam (1972), the first fossil member of the family Hominidae is the genus *Ramapithecus* who thereby becomes the earliest ancestor of humankind. This fossil hominid, then, illustrates an evolutionary grade just after the split with the ape line of ascent. *Ramapithecus* is represented by multiple species, abbreviated *spp.* in biological nomenclature. The various species, including *punjabicus* and *wickeri*, are dated to the late Miocene epoch, 10 to 14 mya. Examples have been discovered in northern India and east Africa and tentatively in Europe and China (Brace and others 1979, pp. 17–18). The reconstructed habitat is a forest fringe of wooded savanna and low-relief terrain drained by wide, sluggish rivers. The habits of the animal include ground feeding, a vegetarian diet obtained by browsing on leaves and fruit, and a bipedal gait—that is, a semiupright stance on two legs. It is thought that this earliest hominid continued to live in trees, however, with occasional forays to the ground for nuts or roots.

Pilbeam (1972) states that this hominid definitely did not make tools although Leakey (1971) claims evidence for the use of hammerstones to smash open animal skulls and long bones in order to extract and eat brains and bone marrow. Some controversy exists as to whether *Ramapithecus* belongs in the hominid line or in a generalized Dryopithecine grouping of prehominids, but most human paleontologists agree that it was an ancestor to the later ground-dwelling, bipedal, and tool-making true hominids (Brace and others 1979, p. 18).

Proto-Humans

The Australopithecines are the earliest tool-making hominids known, and as such they open the story of culture evolution. These proto-humans are dated by association with Villafranchian fauna and, more directly, by means of K/Ar radiometric assays on volcanic rocks and ash layers. By these determinations, the proto-humans are dated from the Pliocene to Early Pleistocene between 5 and 1.25 mya (Pilbeam 1972, p. 100).

FIGURE 6–1   The distribution of Australopithecine fossil finds and Oldowan chopper tools in the Lower Pleistocene.

Source: From *Atlas of Human Evolution,* 2nd edition, by C. Loring Brace, Harry Nelson, Noel Korn, and Mary L. Brace. Copyright © 1979 by Holt, Rinehart and Winston. Reprinted by permission of Holt, Rinehart and Winston, CBS College Publishing.

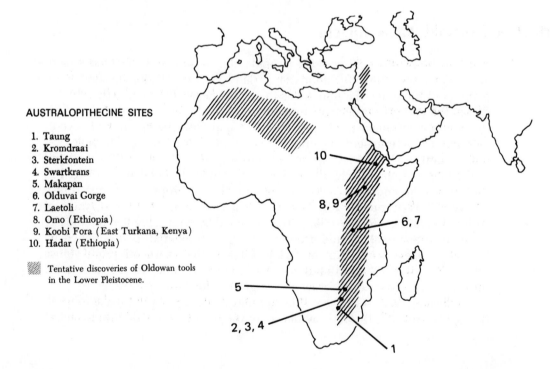

AUSTRALOPITHECINE SITES

1. Taung
2. Kromdraai
3. Sterkfontein
4. Swartkrans
5. Makapan
6. Olduvai Gorge
7. Laetoli
8. Omo (Ethiopia)
9. Koobi Fora (East Turkana, Kenya)
10. Hadar (Ethiopia)

Tentative discoveries of Oldowan tools in the Lower Pleistocene.

Australopithecus

Australopithecine sites are principally confined to east and south Africa although distribution of the Oldowan tool industry, of which they are the authors, also includes northwest Africa and the Near East (Fig. 6–1). Given this geographical spread, it is not unreasonable to characterize allegorically Africa as the Biblical Garden of Eden.

The first Australopithecine finds were made in limestone, or more properly dolomite, caves in south Africa. In 1924 quarry workers blasted an almost complete skull from a site at Taung. The skull was sent to the anatomist Raymond Dart in Johannesburg (Broom 1949). After cleaning and restoration, the fossil find was classified as *Australopithecus africanus*. This skull, said Dart, has many apelike characteristics but in fact is a fossil on the direct evolutionary line leading to modern humans. Although Dart's conclusion was not immediately accepted by the scientific community, continuing work at other lime quarries yielded additional finds, and the mass of evidence eventually won over the skeptics. Indeed a kind of "missing link" had been found. Darwin's postulation that humankind had evolved from "ape-men" or an apelike ancestor was essentially correct.

The first five Australopithecine sites shown in Figure 6–1 have one feature in common: They were caves that gradually filled from the ground surface with in-washing, fossil-rich sediment (Fig. 6–2a). After closure, the fill became cemented by carbonates and then the ground surface eroded to remove the vertical entrance shaft (Fig. 6–2b). The fossil contents of the filled cave make up what paleontologists call a *death assemblage*, that is, an assemblage derived from a number of contemporary animals. Sampson (1974) suggests that the Australopithecines and the Villafranchian fauna in the south African cave deposits may have come together from three sources: (1) rodent bones dropped by owls, (2) herbivore bones discarded by carnivorous cats such as leopards, and (3) the prey of the meat-eating Austalopithecines who camped around the vertical shaft opening of the cave. From time to time, the Australopithecines also fell into the shaft opening, or the dead were thrown in by their band members. Although the fossil hominids can be relative-dated to the Plio-Pleistocene boundary by association with the Villafranchian fauna, particularly fossil pigs, it is unfortunate that no volcanics are present in the cave sediments to allow absolute dating by radiometric techniques. For this reason, it is difficult to correlate the south African cave finds with the open-air living sites of east Africa, which are firmly located in time by K/Ar measurements.

The east African Australopithecines represent a more favorable set of finds made in Tanzania (Sites 6 and 7 on Fig. 6–1), Kenya (Site 9) and Ethiopia (Sites 8 and 10). In all cases they are open-air living sites representing camps near streams or lakes. The first Australopithecine finds from east Africa were discovered in 1931 in Olduvai Gorge by the late L. S. B. Leakey and Mary Leakey, whose research continues to the present (Leakey 1971). Here natural

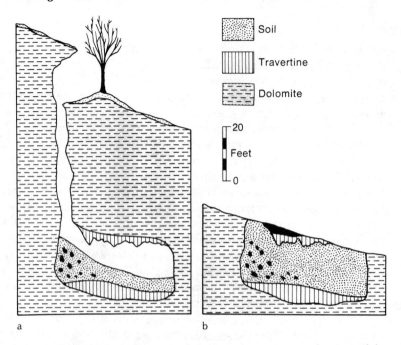

FIGURE 6-2   Diagrammatic drawings of the Swartkrans cave at the time of deposition (a), and just before excavation (b). After Brain 1967a.

Source: Reprinted with permission of Macmillan Publishing Co., Inc., from *The Ascent of Man* by David R. Pilbeam. Copyright © 1972 by David R. Pilbeam.

erosion has revealed a section of lake, shore-side, and fan deposits more than 200 feet thick. Within this depositional series, dating between 2.1 million and 15,000 years BP, are found many hominid sites formed by human activities.

The Australopithecine sites of Bed I, the oldest stratum in the stratified series, contain Oldowan cobble chopping tools, debris from tool manufacture, the broken food bones of the Villafranchian fauna hunted by the proto-humans, and in one case, a stone circle that may be the remains of a hut, hunting blind, or wind break. Directly on the occupation surface, called a *floor* by the Old World archaeologists, in association with the artifacts, are the fossil remains of two different species of Australopithecines, *boisei* and *habilis*. From nearby volcanoes there is a basal lava flow, and many airborne ash flows are stratified above and below the various sites of Early Pleistocene occupation. Consequently, it has been possible to K/Ar-date the tuff deposits and thereby bracket-date the hominid sites.

Elsewhere in east Africa, at locations in Kenya and northern Ethiopia, other field investigations are currently underway to reveal the biological and cultural habits of the Australopithecines. These studies are typically international and multidisciplinary. The project in the east Turkana, Kenya, area led by Richard Leakey is a good example (Walker and Leakey 1978). Here in the Koobi Fora district of Lake Turkana, a party of geologists, human paleontologists, archaeologists, and many other scientists are combing hundreds of square miles of arid landscape prospecting for early Pleistocene hominids and Villafranchian fauna. Finds to date number 150 individual hominids of three different species, *Australopithecus africanus*, *Homo habilis*,[1] and *Homo erectus*. The presence of five tuff marker beds lying above and below the hominid finds at archaeological sites such as Koobi Fora, has led to very precise K/Ar dating. Walker and Leakey (1978, pp. 10–11) indicate that three hominid specimens from the Koobi Fora district are stratigraphically older than the Tulu Bor tuff dated at 3.18 mya. In effect, the investigations of Richard Leakey have amply verified the earlier work of his father and mother at Olduvai even to the age of the occupation sites and oldest stone chopping tools, which is 1.8 million years.

Based on sediment study of the hominid-producing strata, coupled with the foraging requirements of the Villafranchian fauna, it is known that the Australopithecines occupied grassland country in east and south Africa not unlike that found there today. Open woodland was present but no true forest. The distributional pattern of Australopithecine sites entirely surrounds, but does not enter, the Congo Basin and its tropical rainforest. Furthermore, study by C. K. Bain of sediment grain size found in the south African caves suggests that the climate alternated between dry and wet, but always within a semiarid range (Clark 1970).

The biological taxonomy of the Australopithecines is open to considerable controversy. The position taken here is that of David Pilbeam (1972) who classifies the *Australopithecus* genus into multiple species (Fig. 6–3). In south Africa, he recognizes a slender form, *africanus*, as originally proposed by Raymond Dart, and a rugged species named *robustus*. Paralleling this dichotomy in east Africa are a light-framed form called *habilis* and a massive species named *boisei* (Tobias 1967). Alternative views are rampant. The Leakey family, for example, place the *habilis* species in the genus *Homo* and claim that this earliest member of our modern genus is the tool-maker who preyed on the cultureless Australopithecines. Other human paleontologists would combine the slender and rugged forms from south and east Africa, reducing the species diversity from four to two forms, called *africanus* and *robustus*.

More recently another Australopithecine species has been discovered and named *afarensis* (Johanson and Edey 1981a,b). This taxon is based on fossils recovered from late Tertiary deposits located in two districts: Hadar in northeastern Ethiopia (Locality 10) and Laetoli, Tanzania (Locality 7, in Fig. 6–1). The large collection of specimens found by human paleontologist Donald Johanson and geologist Maurice Taieb in the Hadar site provided the material to reconstruct a creature that is likely to have been ancestral to both the re-

[1]Pilbeam (1972) placed this fossil in the genus *Australopithecus*.

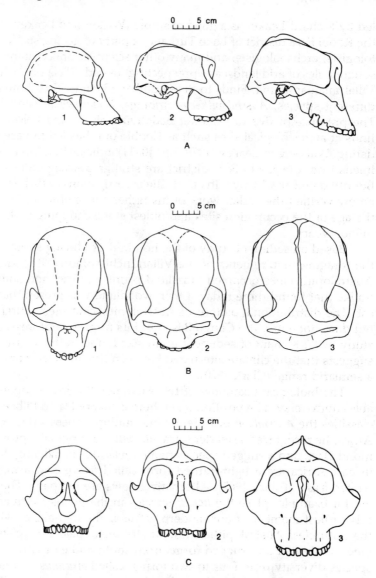

FIGURE 6-3   Lateral (A), superior (B), and frontal (C) views of *Australopithecus africanus* (1), *A. robustus* (2), and *A. boisei* (3). Of particular interest are the cranial characteristics that change with the increasing cheek-tooth size. (*A. africanus* having the smallest teeth, *A. boisei* the largest). Considered as a series, the face is flattest and deepest in *A. boisei,* crests and bony buttresses are better developed in *A. boisei,* and the temporal fossa (indicating temporal muscle bulk) is largest in *A. boisei.* All these features appear to be related to the size and mechanical efficiency of the posterior dentition. After Tobias 1967.

Source: Reprinted with permission of Macmillan Publishing Co., Inc. from *The Ascent of Man* by David R. Pilbeam. Copyright © 1972 by David R. Pilbeam.

mainder of the Australopithecines and the *Homo* genus. Several extraordinary fossils are included in the Hadar collections, among which are Lucy, an almost complete female, and a family of 13 individuals found together at one spot. Johanson and Edey (1981a, p. 51) describe the overall appearance of *A. afarensis*:

> smallish, essentially human bodies with heads that are more ape-shaped than human-shaped. Their jaws were large and forward-thrusting. They had no chins. The upper parts of their faces were small and chimplike. The crowns of their skulls were very low.

From the study of the Hadar bones, it is known that these earliest Australopithecines stood upright and walked with a two-legged gait. Startling confirmation of this bipedal locomotion was recovered from the Tanzanian site of Laetoli, where a trail of *afarensis* footprints was traced through the fallen ash of a 3.7 mya volcano (Johanson and Edey 1981b, pp. 244–51). Study of the impressions shows that the stride of this earliest ground-dwelling proto-human was remarkably similar to that of a modern human. The prints reveal a well-shaped heel, a strong arch, and a well-formed sole. The big toe does not stick out to the side like that of an ape.

Geological investigations of the Hadar stratigraphy has revealed a thick section of Pliocene deposits, which have been dated by K/Ar and paleomagnetic means. Within this context, the *afarensis* finds are placed between 3 and 4 mya (Johanson and Edey 1981b, p. 203). Stratigraphically higher are archaeological sites containing Oldowan stone tools dated between 2 and 2.5 mya (Kalb and others 1982). Although not associated with the pretool *afarensis*, these are the oldest human-made artifacts in the world. Since no hominids were found in direct association with the Upper Pliocene tools, archaeologists are left to speculate whether the implements were made by members of the *Australopithecus* or the *Homo* genus. Still higher in the stratigraphic section, in deposits dated to the Middle Pleistocene, the excavators found a *Homo sapiens* and burned animal bone fragments, early evidence of the use of fire for cooking (Kalb and others 1982, pp. 27–28).

By Plio-Pleistocene times, the brain had increased in size to 400 or 500 cubic centimeters, as indicated by the cranial vault of the Australopithecines (Fig. 6–3). It has been suggested that the brain was internally reorganized so that the hominid was capable of language and tool production (Pilbeam 1972). Instead of swinging through the trees, this hominid walked upright on the ground. The hand was now free to manipulate and carry objects, including food and tools. Study of a complete hand recovered from Bed I at Olduvai Gorge has led Napier (1962) to conclude that the Australopithecines had an opposable thumb and a grip adequate for tool handling, but not the fine precision grip of modern humans.

The following description of the *robustus* species illustrates the *Australopithecus* genus in general:

> Characteristically they are large of face and massive of jaw; the molar and pre-molar teeth are very large, although the incisors and canines are small, about the same size as the front teeth of modern man. Although the facial skeleton is large, the brain case is relatively small: the average cranial capacity is about 500 cubic centimeters, compared with the modern human average of 1360 cc. Because the chewing muscles were evidently of a size commensurate with the large cheek teeth and massive jaws, many *A. robustus* individuals have not only extremely wideflaring cheekbones but also a bony crest that runs fore and aft along the top of the brain case to provide a greater area for the attachment of chewing muscles. (Walker and Leakey 1978, pp. 10–11)

In terms of their reconstructed behavior, the Australopithecines were the first hominids to live as ground dwellers and feeders. Furthermore, they made and used chopping tools, the Oldowan industry, by 1.8 my. In this sense, they were cultural animals surviving by learned behavior rather than relying on instinct. Probably they maintained the vegetable diet of their pretool-making ancestors, but now supplemented it with meat obtained through hunting, as amply attested by tools and food bone refuse at their campsites. Analysis of the food bones, however, indicates that they were scavengers rather than hunters. They captured slow game (tortoise, lizards, insects), immature young (such as newborn antelope), and aged adult animals.

Homo habilis

The preceding discussion has placed the *habilis* species in the genus *Australopithecus* following the classificatory schemes of such human paleontologists as Pilbeam and Brace. This classification recognizes the large degree of morphological variation present during Plio-Pleistocene times and the need to simplify this variability by using fewer rather than more taxonomic labels.

Other paleontologists, such as the various members of the Leakey family and their co-workers, John Napier and Phillip Tobias, maintain a contrary opinion. They feel that the fossil hominid variability of Plio-Pleistocene times is simply too great to be classified properly as wholly *Australopithecus*. Instead, they feel that certain fossils of an age ranging between 1.5 and 1.8 mya belong to the *Homo* genus. This taxonomic step, of course, is not just the assignment of one label or another, but recognition that fully human ancestors had already developed at the very beginnings of the Pleistocene epoch and lived around the shores of such East African lakes as Olduvai and Turkana. The Leakeys contend that only the *habilis* were sufficiently advanced mentally to make tools, live in camps, and hunt game. In fact, they believe that part of the animal prey of *habilis* were the contemporary robust Australopithecines such as the *robustus* and *boisei* species.

By this reasoning, all of the various Australopithecine species are non-tool-makers, that is, proto-humans without culture who evolved to a dead end as shown by the position of *A. boisei* in Brace's human phylogeny. The tree diagram is based on one aspect of biological evolution, total average tooth size measured in square millimeters and plotted against time. The tree illustrates the evolutionary development of the Australopithecines as they gradually evolved into the *Homo* genus. The collateral branch of the *A. boisei* led to species extinction in the Lower Pleistocene.

In 1959 Mary and L. S. B. Leakey discovered the Zinjanthropus (meaning East African ape-like) type fossil of *Australopithecus boisei* in middle Bed I at Olduvai (Leakey 1971, pp. 49–50). This nearly complete skull was found in a geological context dated at 1.8 mya and on the occupational "floor" of Site FLK 1 in direct association with manufacturing debris and Oldowan tools. The first newspaper releases of this find, called the "nutcracker man" by the press, was that the origins of humankind had been discovered and this first "man" was not only a tool user but also a tool maker.

In 1962, additional hominid fossils were reported, which led Leakey to reconsider his original tool-making interpretation. These were four fossils given popular names such as Twiggy, Johnny's child, George, and Cindy. These four habilis type fossils were distributed stratigraphically through Beds I and II where they overlap the spread of both the *Australopithecus* genus and the Oldowan tool industry. Since the reconstructed cranial capacity averaged 642 cc and the teeth were much more modern than the contemporary Australopithecines, Leakey assigned the fossils to the genus *Homo* and a new species that he called *habilis* or handy man (Johanson and Edey 1981b, p. 102). Subsequently two leg bones found on the same occupational surface as the Zinjanthropus skull also were assigned to this new taxon so that the site of FLK 1 is now recognized as the context of both a massive robust Australopithecine and a *habilis*. Mary Leakey (1971, p. 49) states, "Whether Zinjanthropus or the co-existent *Homo habilis* was responsible for making the tools and occupying the floor is an open question although the balance of evidence favours *Homo habilis*." This assertion summarizes the position of the Leakey family. Critics of the newly described species contended that the four fragmentary skulls are too incomplete to define a new species and that they might better be retained as slender Australopithecines.

The debate continued until 1972 when Richard Leakey, then hard at work on the east bank of Lake Turkana, announced a dazzling and largely complete new find—a very human-like skull that he has labeled 1470, the field accession number for the hominid. Because of the many modern features of this 1.8 mya find, some scientists accept his claim that it should properly be placed in the genus *Homo* and is in fact a *habilis* species (Leakey and Lewin 1977). This specimen has a thin skull that is higher and rounder than the Australopithecines. Furthermore, and of utmost importance, the firm cranial capacity is 775 cc, which lends strong support to the concept of a species lying at a transitional position between the Australopithecines and *Homo erectus*. From the evidence, it can be seen that the gorilla-size brains of the Australopithecines (430–550 cc) were being replaced by a larger brain (500–800 cc) in a population called *habilis*—definitely an important first step in an evolutionary process that has continued until today, when modern humans have a very enlarged brain (1000–1800 cc) (Johanson and Edey 1981b, p. 100).

Modern Humans

Following the thesis of Pilbeam (1972, p. 157), *Homo erectus* represents the first appearance of *Homo* or the genus of modern humans. It is at this fossil grade that the morphological diversity noted in all earlier hominid forms is narrowed to one species rather than multiple as in earlier grades.

FIGURE 6-4   The distribution of *Homo erectus* fossil finds and Lower Paleolithic tools (bifaces and flakes) in the Lower and Middle Pleistocene.

Source: From *Atlas of Human Evolution,* 2nd edition, by C. Loring Brace, Harry Nelson, Noel Korn, and Mary L. Brace. Copyright © 1979 by Holt, Rinehart and Winston. Reprinted by permission of Holt, Rinehart and Winston, CBS College Publishing.

(Restricted to the most important and best preserved specimens).

1. Java	7. Ternifine (Algeria)
2. Choukoutien	8. Rabat (Morocco)
3. Lan-t'ien (China)	9. Koobi Fora (Kenya)
4. Heidelberg	10. Olduvai Gorge
5. Vertesszöllös (Hungary)	11. Swartkrans
6. Arago (France)	12. Saldanha

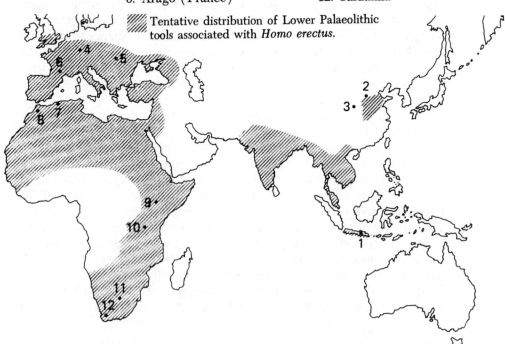

Tentative distribution of Lower Palaeolithic tools associated with *Homo erectus.*

Homo erectus

Outside of Africa, *Homo erectus* finds in Europe and Asia are dated to the Middle Pleistocene by faunal association, geology, and, in the case of the Java find, by K/Ar (Fig. 6–4). The latter specimen stratigraphically underlies meteoritic stones, called *tektites*, assayed at 710,000 years ago (Howells 1966). Within Africa, however, the situation is far more complicated. At east Turkana *H. erectus* specimens have been recovered from early Pleistocene strata in association with Australopithecines and underlying tuff K/Ar-dated at 1.57 mya. Furthermore, an upper time limit can probably be placed on the *H. erectus* finds by the associated tools, the Acheulean (biface) industry dated in Europe as late as 100,000 years ago. If we assume that *H. erectus* was the maker of this industry, then an inclusive age range of this fossil grade would be 0.1 to 1.57 my.

Howells (1966) describes *Homo erectus* as follows: From an accumulation of finds

> there emerges a picture of men with skeletons like ours but with brains much smaller, skulls much thicker and flatter and furnished with protruding brows in front and a marked angle in the rear, and with teeth somewhat larger and exhibiting a few slightly more primitive traits. (1966, p. 8)

In comparison with the Australopithecines, *Homo erectus* of the Middle Pleistocene times exhibited a stature increase with a postcranial skeleton fully adapted to upright walking. Furthermore, they had larger brains, reaching capacities around 700 to 1250 cc and relatively smaller faces and teeth (Fig. 6–5). These adaptive trends have led Pilbeam (1972) to conclude that *Homo erectus* was biologically capable of more complex forms of behavior than the earlier hominids. These behavioral traits include: (1) using language, (2) mak-

FIGURE 6–5   Composite restoration of *Homo erectus* finds taken from the upper member of the Koobi Fora formation, East Turkana, Africa. Lower jaw not shown.

Source: From "The Hominids of East Turkana" by Alan Walker and Richard E. F. Leakey. Copyright © 1978 by Scientific American, Inc. All rights reserved.

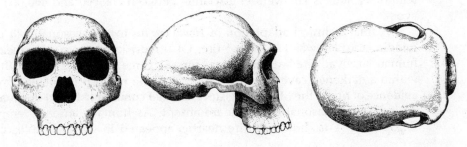

ing clothing, (3) building huts, (4) inhabiting seasonally cold areas, (5) hunting big game, and (6) using fire (Time-Life Books 1973, p. 9). The argument for the use of language is based on the flexure of the basicranium, a morphological evolution reflecting the dropping of the larynx and thereby improving the voice box (Issac 1974; Editors of Time-Life Books 1973). A supporting argument for the appearance of true language among the hominids is that for the first time the brain size was sufficiently developed for open symboling.

Evidence of clothing is largely speculative since no artifacts have been preserved. However, at least some form of wrap-around wearing apparel was likely because of the need for warmth during the snowy winter of the temperate latitudes. *Homo erectus* was capable of hunting big game, including fur bearing animals with hides suitable for winter wraps.

The earliest known hut architecture outside of Africa is a series of structures constructed at the French site of Terra Amata ("beloved land") on the Mediterranean coast at modern-day Nice. These structures, excavated by Henry de Lumley (1969), are dated to the Mindel glaciation some 300,000 years ago. The site consists of 21 separate occupation surfaces located on three fossil beaches. The huts were all oval in outline and constructed of saplings imbedded in the sand and bent to form an arched roof. The largest hut measures 26 by 49 feet. Each house has a fire hearth protected by a wind screen, and tool knapping work spaces (Fig. 6–6). The stratigraphic succession of huts strongly indicates that the same hunting band repeatedly returned to the coastal camp at Terra Amata for big game hunting, manufacture and repair of stone tools, and collection of shell fish. Perhaps these episodic camps are remains of seasonal occupancy. The finding of a lump of red ochre with ground facet is thought to be evidence of the use of body paint.

Evidence of big game hunting is well illustrated at two kill sites, Torralba and Ambrona, located in central Spain. The hunters ambushed a herd of elephants by driving them into a bog. It is thought that fire brands were used to stampede the animals, who then became mired in the bog mud. Immobilized in this fashion, the huge animals could be killed easily. After butchery, some of the bones were cracked open to extract the edible marrow. At Ambrona, one section of the site consists of a number of fire hearths, which must have served as a banqueting area. The dating of these two closely contemporary sites is late Mindel glaciation between 300,000 and 400,000 years ago.

A final technical adaptation of *Homo erectus* to the seasonal cold of the middle latitudes was the use of fire. Of utmost importance as a means of human survival, fire was employed for: (1) game drives, (2) heat, (3) light within a darkened cave at night, and (4) cooking meat. It is noteworthy that evidence of fire in the Middle Pleistocene is not commonly found in equatorial Africa where seasonal extremes are absent. As humans entered temperate Europe and Asia, however, fire hearths appeared in the archaeological re-

FIGURE 6-6   Oval huts, ranging from 26 to 49 feet in length and from 13 to 20 feet in width, were built at Terra Amata by visiting hunters. A reconstruction shows that the hut walls were made of stakes, about three inches in diameter, set as a palisade in the sand and braced on the outside by a ring of stones. Some larger posts were set up along the huts' long axes, but how these and the walls were joined to make roofs is unknown; the form shown is conjectural. The huts' hearths were protected from drafts by a small pebble windscreen.

Source: From "A Paleolithic Camp at Nice" by Henry de Lumley. Copyright © 1969 by Scientific American, Inc. All rights reserved.

cord. Some of the oldest of these are hearths found at Terra Amata, Vertes-szollos in Hungary, and Choukoutien in northern China. The Chinese site is a cave containing deposits of humanly derived wood ash up to 22 feet deep (Time-Life Books 1973). Since no strike-a-light kits or fire drills are known from *Homo erectus* sites, it is thought that fire was obtained from active volcanoes or lightning-struck forest fires. If the fire had been allowed to go out, it could not be rekindled at will. Thus, when the hunting band was on the move from one seasonal camp to another, they must have carried fire brands or smoldering embers to the new campsite.

At the time of the transition from *H. erectus* to *H. sapiens*, around 200,000 years ago, the brain became larger, reaching average population values between 1000 and 1400 cc. At the same time, the teeth, jaws, and face became relatively smaller with a reduction in the brow ridge area. Coupled with this larger brain, the cranial housing became more rounded and the facial plane pulled in under the skull to a more vertical profile (Pilbeam 1972). In conclusion, *erectus* evolved smoothly into *sapiens* without any noticeable break in continuity.

Homo sapiens

Biologically modern humans are classified to a single genus and species, *Homo sapiens*, with two sequential subspecies grades. These are called *Archaic H. sapiens* and *fully modern humans* by Pilbeam (1972). In addition to these Late

FIGURE 6-7   Distribution of archaic *Homo sapiens* and Middle Paleolithic tool industries during the Late Pleistocene.

Source: From *Atlas of Human Evolution,* 2nd edition, by C. Loring Brace, Harry Nelson, Noel Korn, and Mary L. Brace. Copyright © 1979 by Holt, Rinehart and Winston, CBS College Publishing.

1. Neanderthal
2. Spy
3. Ehringsdorf
4. La Chapelle-aux-Saints
5. Le Moustier

6. La Ferrassie
7. La Quina
8. Gibraltar
9. Saccopastore
10. Monte Circeo

11. Krapina
12. Teshik Tash (Uzbek S. S. R.)
13. Shanidar (Iraq)
14. Mount Carmel
15. Haua Fteah (Libya)

16. Jebel Irhoud (Morocco)
17. Diré Dawa (Ethiopia)
18. Cave of the Hearths (South Africa)
19. Mapa (China)

Distribution of cold-adapted Mousterian cultural elements in the early Upper Pleistocene.

Distribution of contemporary but less specialized "Mousterioid" or Middle Palaeolithic cultural remains.

Pleistocene fossils, there are several Middle Pleistocene *sapiens* that represent the transition from *H. erectus* to *H. sapiens*.

Individual fossil finds of transitional taxonomic status (Fig. 6–7) include those from (1) Steinheim, Germany; (2) Swanscombe, England; (3) Fontech-evade, France; and (4) Solo, Java (Brace and others 1979, pp. 86–99). Geologically, they date from the Riss glaciation and the end of the Holstein interglacial. In absolute age, all are dated between 100,000 and 200,000 years ago.

The Archaic *H. sapiens* are a taxon composed of multiple subspecies of racial or population levels of differentiation. The best known examples are called *Neanderthal* from a type site in Germany (Fig. 6–8). Examples of the *H. sapiens* neanderthalensis are distributed throughout Europe, north Africa, and southwest Asia (Fig. 6–7). Other contemporary Archaic *sapiens* are found in subsaharan Africa and the Far East. Archaic *sapiens* are noticeably absent from Australia, New Zealand, Oceania, or the New World, parts of the world that had not yet been colonized by *Homo sapiens* immigrants.

The Neanderthal populations of Europe are consistently found in association with the Mousterian culture of the Middle Paleolithic stage. Other Archaic *sapiens* populations were outfitted with comparable tool assemblages. Geologically, the Neanderthals are dated to the Eemian interglacial and the Würm I (first stadial) of the glacial calendar. In absolute time, this stage was between 100,000 and 35,000 years ago.

By 100,000 years ago, Archaic *sapiens* had successfully adapted to all of the world's latitudinal zones. Fossil examples have been recovered from the

FIGURE 6-8   Skulls of *Homo sapiens* (a) and Neanderthal man (b) are compared. The *Homo sapiens* skull is that of Cro-Magnon man, who lived in Europe during the latter part of the fourth glacial period. The Neanderthal skull is that of "classic" Neanderthal man.

Source: From "Neanderthal Man" by J. E. Weckler. Copyright © 1957 by Scientific American, Inc. All rights reserved.

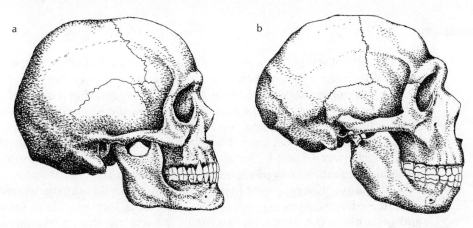

tropical low latitudes to the ice front and onto the tundra. In conclusion, Archaic *sapiens* had conquered all of the earth's major ecosystems including the rigorous arctic during the extremes of glacial advance of the late Pleistocene (Würm I). A number of cultural practices contributed to the adaptation of cold climates: (1) the use of wrap-around skin clothing, (2) use of the jabbing spear in hunting, (3) predation on herd animals such as reindeer, and (4) cliff drive of other herd animals such as horses and the ibex.

Fully modern *sapiens,* taxonomically designated *Homo sapiens sapiens,* is associated with the Upper Paleolithic and later evolutionary stages. At the end of the Pleistocene, these *sapiens* fossils are found in association with the late stadials of the Würm/Weichsel (Würm II and III) glaciation. These modern *sapiens* are separated from the Neanderthals of Europe by a named interstadial called the *Paudorf* (30,000–40,000 BP).

Some of the modern *sapiens* of the Upper Paleolithic in Europe are referred to as Cro-magnon, a population subspecies (Fig. 6–8). Elsewhere in the world equivalent local populations of people also were practicing an Upper Paleolithic way of life. Modern *sapiens* continued occupancy of all previously inhabited parts of the world and colonized new lands to fill up the world's geography. For instance, the New World was colonized by immigration from Siberia via the Bering Land Bridge sometime between 20,000 and 40,000 years ago. Similarly, Australia was colonized from New Guinea about 30,000 BP. And finally, the island world of the Pacific, called *Oceania,* was peopled by boat during the last 2000 to 5000 years.

Following the pattern first established by the Neanderthalers, modern *sapiens* adapted to all of the world's environmental zones. The severe arctic environment required ingenious inventions for survival. Upper Paleolithic hunters invented sewing and made tailored clothing to combat freezing temperatures, a technology revealed in rock art drawings, bone buckles, and the eyed sewing needle. Hunting efficiency was advanced through the use of spears that were hand-hurled or projected by a throwing board.

Summary

The 1890 discovery of "Java man," a fossil of the *Homo erectus* species, was important evidence that humans have evolved by slow but steady steps from simpler, prehuman ancestors. Other fossil finds suggest that a series of now-extinct great apes, who lived about 20 mya, were the common link between the ape lineage (pongids) and the human lineage (hominids). The archaeological field is divided between those who think that the Australopithecines, who lived between 5 and 1.25 mya, were the first tool makers, and those who attribute the first tools to members of the *Homo* genus.

At Olduvai Gorge in east Africa, Louis and Mary Leakey discovered important evidence of creatures who made stone tools, hunted animals for meat, and built huts. The oldest human-made artifacts are these Oldowan stone tools, dated around 2.5 million years BP. The Leakeys believe the tools were made by *Homo habilis*, the earliest *Homo* yet discovered, and contend that only the *habilis* was sufficiently advanced to make tools, live in camps, and hunt game. Pilbeam, however, believes that *Homo erectus* represents the first appearance of the genus of modern humans. According to Pilbeam, *erectus* was capable of using language, building huts, making clothing, and using fire—behaviors that were essential to species adaptation in cold climates.

Erectus evolved into *sapiens*, the species of modern humans. The Neanderthal man is a member of an archaic *H. sapiens* that populated the Old World 100,000 to 35,000 years ago but is not found in Australia, New Zealand, Oceania, or the New World. These regions were populated by the fully modern species, which scholars identify as *Homo sapiens sapiens*. Except for Oceania, all were populated by 20,000 BP.

FIGURE 6-9   The hominid family tree, or phylogeny, revealed by a graph of tooth size plotted against time.

Source: From *Atlas of Human Evolution,* 2nd edition, by C. Loring Brace, Harry Nelson, Noel Korn, and Mary L. Brace. Copyright © 1979 by Holt, Rinehart and Winston. Reprinted by permission of Holt, Rinehart and Winston, CBS College Publishing.

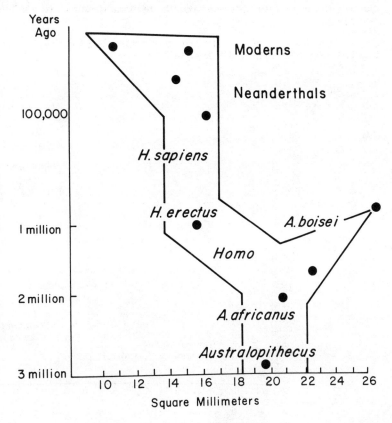

During biological evolution (1) the cranium was enlarged to accommodate a larger brain; (2) hominids began to live on the ground and walk on two legs; (3) hand and finger development improved so that the hominids could grip and manipulate tools; (4) general body build was enlarged, but the face, jaw, and teeth became relatively smaller; (5) the skull became less rugged and rounded out to house more brain per surface area. (Figs. 6–9, 6–10). Pilbeam (1972) has postulated that these changes have come about through adaptation to a changing environment, which in turn has led to selective pressures for biological and social change. Under the influence of a changing climate in Plio-Pleistocene times, the tropical forest cover of the Tertiary period gave way to open woodland mixed with savanna. As the forest thinned, the Miocene ape called *Ramapithecus* began to evolve under the effects of natural selection from a predominantly leafy diet to ground feeding on nuts and roots. Harder foods required dental changes including thickened and buttressed jaws, flattened molars, and reduced canines and incisors (Simons 1977). Increasingly, unwary small animals were attacked and con-

FIGURE 6-10   Relationship between brain volume and time in hominid evolution. The capacity of *Ramapithecus* is estimated; the temporal positions for the later species are approximate.

Source: Reprinted with permission of Macmillan Publishing Co., Inc. from *The Ascent of Man* by David R. Pilbeam. Copyright © 1972 by David R. Pilbeam.

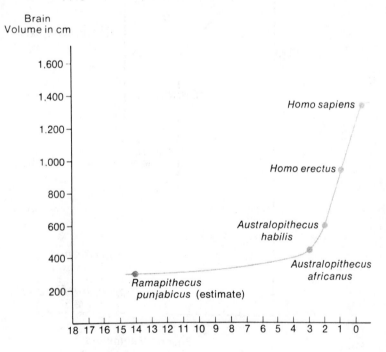

sumed. In the adaptation to ground living, the vegetable diet gave way to a mixed diet of plants and meat. The gradual change to an omnivorous diet created a need for tools and weapons and led to cultural changes including (1) a new social organization, the family; (2) a new form of communication, true language; and (3) learned behavior in general, the adaptive mechanism for survival and mastery of the world.

The most controversial element in Pilbeam's evolutionary scheme is the evolution of language. Pilbeam believes the Ramapithecine troop used call signals of fear, alarm, and location information, similar to modern-day infra-human primates. But signals were not adequate to support cooperative behavior in the hunt, the new subsistence activity. Pilbeam believes that an open symbol system—the beginning of true language—developed among the Australopithecines as a result of the need for cooperation. Opponents to this thesis point out that band hunters, such as the bushmen of South Africa, communicate with silent hand signals, rather than audible sounds that would frighten the game (Howell 1968, p. 184). Others argue that speech was not possible because the hominid brain was not sufficiently developed in size and neural organization until the Middle Pleistocene.

References

BRACE, C. LORING, HARRY NELSON, NOEL KORN, and MARY L. BRACE
   1979   *Atlas of Human Evolution.* New York: Holt, Rinehart and Winston.

BROOM, ROBERT
   1949   The Ape-Men. *Scientific American Offprints* 832:1–7.

CLARK, J. DESMOND
   1970   *The Prehistory of Africa.* New York: Praeger.

COLES, J. M., and E. S. HIGGS
   1975   *The Archaeology of Early Man.* Baltimore: Peregrine.

DE LUMLEY, HENRY
   1969   A Paleolithic Camp at Nice. In *Old World Archaeology: Foundations of Civilization.* Readings from Scientific American. San Francisco: W. H. Freeman ⑩ Company Publishers.

HOWELL, F. CLARK, and EDITORS OF TIME-LIFE BOOKS
   1968   *Early Man.* New York: Time-Life Books.

HOWELLS, WILLIAM W.
   1966   Homo Erectus. *Scientific American Offprints* 215(5):46–53.

ISSAC, GLYNN
   1974   Stratigraphy and Patterns of Cultural Change in the Middle Pleistocene. *Current Anthropology* 15(4):508–14.

JOHANSON, DONALD C., and MAITLAND A. EDEY
   1981a   Lucy: A 3.5 Million-Year-Old Woman Shakes Man's Family Tree. *Science* 81:48–55.
   1981b   *Lucy: The Beginnings of Humankind.* New York: Simon and Schuster.

KALB, JON E., C. J. JOLLY, ASSEFA MEBRATE, SLESHI TEBEDGE, CHARLES SMART, E. B. OSWALD, DOUG-
LAS CRAMER, PAUL WHITEHEAD, C. B. WOOD, G. C. CONCROY, TSRHA ADEFRIS, LOUISE SPERLING, and
BERHANE KANA
   1982   Fossil Mammals and Artifacts from the Middle Awash Valley, Ethiopia. *Nature* 298:25–
           29.

KALB, JON E., ELIZABETH B. OSWALD, SLESHI TEBEDGE, ASSEFA MEBRATE, EMMANUEL TOLA, and DEN-
NIS PEAK
   1982   Geology and Stratigraphy of Neogene Deposits, Middle Awash Valley, Ethiopia. *Na-
           ture* 298:17–25.

LEAKEY, L. S. B.
   1971   Bone Smashing by Late Miocene Hominidae. In *Adam or Ape*, edited by L. S. B. Leakey,
           Jack Prost, and Stephanie Prost. Cambridge, Mass.: Schenkman Publishing Co.

LEAKEY, M. D.
   1971   *Olduvai Gorge: Excavations in Beds I and II, 1960–1963*, vol. 3. Cambridge: Cambridge
           University Press.

LEAKEY, RICHARD E., and ROGER LEWIN
   1977   Origins: What New Discoveries Reveal about the Emergence of Our Species and Its
           Possible Future. New York: E. P. Dutton.

NAPIER, JOHN
   1962   The Evolution of the Hand. *Scientific American Offprints* 207(6):56–62.

PILBEAM, DAVID
   1972   *The Ascent of Man*. New York: Macmillan.

SAMPSON, C. GARTH
   1974   *The Stone Age Archaeology of Southern Africa*. New York: Academic Press.

SIMONS, ELWYN L.
   1977   Ramapithecus. *Scientific American Offprints* 236(5):28–35.

TIME-LIFE BOOKS
   1973   *The First Men*. New York: Time-Life Books.

TOBIAS P. V.
   1967   *The Cranium of Australopithecus (Zinjanthropus) boisei, Olduvai Gorge*, vol. 2. Cambridge:
           Cambridge University Press.

WALKER, ALAN, and RICHARD E. F. LEAKEY
   1978   The Hominids of East Turkana. *Scientific American Offprints* 239(2):54–66.

WECKLER, J. E.
   1957   Neanderthal. *Scientific American Offprints* 197(6):89–97.

7
The Old Stone Age

From the investigation of prehistory, archaeologists have uncovered the evidence for cultural evolution. Prehistory is defined as the human condition before the invention of writing, which occurred around 3000 BC in the Near East and at later times elsewhere in the world. In fact, the prehistoric period continues up to the present in certain remote parts of the world occupied by illiterate, primitive societies. Prehistory makes up approximately 99 percent of human existence and is the sole domain of the archaeologist, whose mission is to study the past through unwritten, material remains.

Christian Thomsen's classification of prehistoric artifacts by material type—stone, bronze, and iron—has been replaced by Sir John Lubbock's five-stage scheme based on the technical means of making tools: (1) the Paleolithic, (2) the Mesolithic, (3) the Neolithic, (4) the bronze age, and (5) the iron age. This chapter traces the beginnings of culture back to the Paleolithic stage in the Old World.

The Paleolithic stage is the stage of ice-age hunters. *Paleo* means "old," and *lithic* means "stone." World prehistory was originally organized according to the kinds of stone tools made by early humans. Some of the oldest tools discovered from the Early Pleistocene sites in south and east Africa are made of bone, antler, teeth, and hooves, but stone tools are the most durable and therefore the most numerous in the early archaeological record. By absolute dating, the Paleolithic begins 2.5 mya and ends 10,000 years ago. It covers the entire length of the Pleistocene geological epoch. If prehistory makes up 99 percent of the human condition, then the Paleolithic makes up 99 percent of prehistory.

By definition, a stage classification such as Lubbock's combines the most important characteristics of many different archaeological cultures or phases. Some of the major named industries and cultures of the Old World Paleolithic are shown in Figure 7–1. Recent reinterpretation of Lubbock's stage scheme by V. Gordon Childe (1961) and Willey and Phillips (1958) has shifted the emphasis from material and technical aspects to the productive economy. The Paleolithic, originally defined as the old stone age, has been redefined as the era of food collecting. Its subsistence economy included both the hunting of game and the gathering of edible plant parts.

FIGURE 7–1   Chronological chart of Paleolithic industries and cultures (phases) in the Old World.

Source: From Francois Bordes, *The Old Stone Age;* London: Weidenfeld & Nicolson Ltd.

Glacial Calendar	Europe		Africa		India	Asia S.E.	Asia S.W.
10,000 Würm III	Magdalenian Solutrean Gravettian Perigordian/Aurignatian Chatelperronian		Capsian Ibero-Maurusian Aterian	Egyptian up.pal. Dabban, etc. Lupembian	(?)		Upper Paleolithic
Würm I and II 80,000	Mousterian Final Acheulean		Mousterian Upper Acheulean	Sangoan	Late Soan	Final Anyathian	Mousterian Final Acheulean
Riss/ Würm 200,000	Upper Acheulean	Pre- Mousterian	Upper Acheulean		Upper Acheulean Upper Soan	Fenho Complex Anyathian	Acheulean
Riss	Upper Acheulean Middle Acheulean	'Tayacian' Clactonian	Acheulean		Acheulean Soan	Choukoutien loc. 15 ↑	Acheulean
Mindel/ Riss	Middle Acheulean Early Acheulean	Clactonian	Acheulean		Soan?	↑ OLD ANYATHIAN	Old Acheulean
Mindel 500,000?	Early Acheulean Abbevillian	Clactonian	'Old Acheulean'		Acheulean? Old Soan?	Choukoutien loc. 1 ↓ OLD ↑ Ubeidyia Choukoutien loc. 13	
Gunz/ Mindel	Flakes?		Oldowan				↓
Gunz	?		Oldowan				
Danube 1.9 million Biber	UPPER VILLAFRANCHIAN	Vallonet pebble tools	↑ Olduvai I.1 (Oldowan) ↓				

Lower Paleolithic

The Lower Paleolithic covers the Lower and Middle Pleistocene epoch, here dated between 1.9 and 0.1 mya. Based on the recent finding of 2.5 million-year-old stone tools in the Hadar region of Ethiopia, the last part of the Pliocene epoch must now be included in the time range of the Lower Paleolithic. At this time *Australopithecus* species and *Homo erectus* inhabited the Old World (Edey 1972; Time-Life 1973).

The artifact assemblage of the Lower Paleolithic consists of largely undifferentiated stone tools, each of which served a variety of purposes, such as cleaving, cutting, chopping, and pounding. The principal artifact types are the cobble chopper and later the fist axe or biface (Figs. 7–2, 7–3). The tools gradually became standardized so that recognizable patterns emerged by the Holsteinian interglacial.

FIGURE 7-2   Unifacial choppers of the Oldowan industry, upper Bed I and Olduvai Gorge, Tanzania.

Source: M. D. Leakey, *Olduvai Gorge, Volume 3,* Cambridge: Cambridge University Press, 1971.

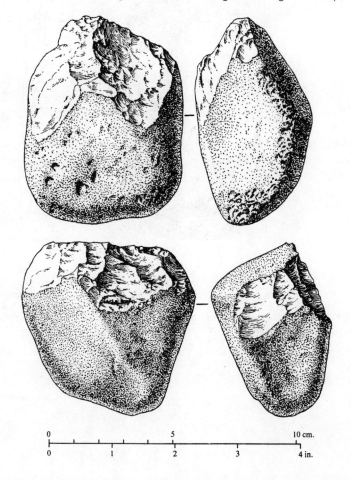

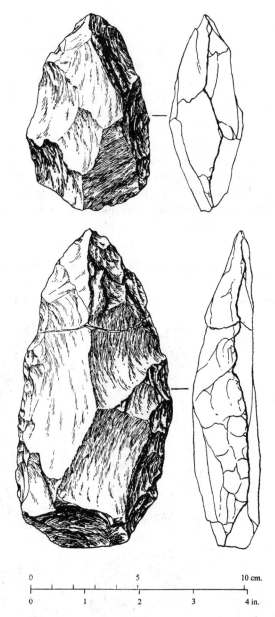

FIGURE 7-3   Fist axes (bifaces) of the Acheulean (Abbevillian) industry, upper Bed II at Olduvai Gorge, Tanzania.

Source: M. D. Leakey, *Olduvai Gorge, Volume 3,* Cambridge: Cambridge University Press, 1971.

Lower Paleolithic tools were manufactured by direct percussion techniques. In the earliest procedure, a stone hammer was used to pound and shape another stone, the core, out of which a chopper tool was fashioned by sculpturing (Fig. 7–4a). This stone-on-stone technique is recognized as early as the Australopithecine sites of Bed I at Olduvai Gorge, east Africa. As a minor variant, the anvil or Clactonian technique was utilized to produce sharp-edge flakes by swinging the core nodule against a stationary stone.

FIGURE 7-4   Stone working techniques of tool manufacture employed in the Paleolithic. (a) Direct percussion flaking with a hammerstone; (b) pressure chipping; (c) direct percussion with a soft or cylinder hammer.

Source: From Francois Bordes, *The Old Stone Age;* London: Weidenfeld & Nicolson Ltd.

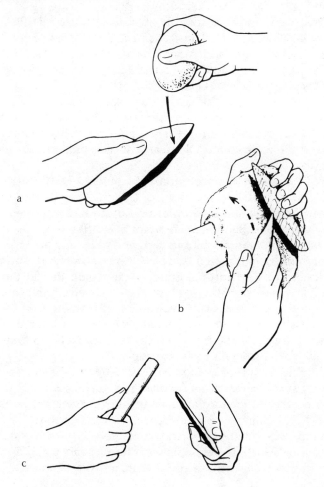

By Riss glacial times, a billet, sometimes called a *baton* or *cylinder hammer*, was used to finish the manufacture of fist axes (Fig. 7–4c). This baton was made of a material such as wood, bone, or antler, which was softer than the stone core but easier to control than the stone hammer. The finely made fist axes, with symmetrical teardrop outline and thin biconvex cross-sections, were used as skinning and butchering tools (Keeley 1977).

The Lower Paleolithic of the Plio-Pleistocene boundary was an age of considerable hominid diversity including both the Australopithecines and *Homo* genera. Sites have been found in Africa and adjacent portions of Asia as far east as Israel. In Africa, major finds of early hominids are located in South Africa, Tanzania, Kenya, and Ethiopia. In addition, the geographical spread of cobble chopping tools into northwest Africa indicates Plio-Pleistocene occupation throughout most of the dry tropical savanna country. The wet tropical rain forest of the Congo basin, however, was not entered by humans until late in the Pleistocene epoch.

One of the most thoroughly studied of these Plio-Pleistocene localities is Olduvai Gorge located in Tanzania, east Africa. Some 40 years of investigation by Louis and Mary Leakey revealed fossil lake deposits surrounded by early hominid sites, a stone hut circle, and two species of hominid fossils, *boisei* and *habilis* (Leakey 1971).

Recent erosion of the gorge has exposed a geological section approximately 225 feet in thickness over lava dated 2.1 mya. In fact, a stratified series of seven beds spans the entire Pleistocene epoch. The Australopithecine hominids and their associated Oldowan chopper industry are found only in the lower two, Beds I and II.

Bed I is one of the most thoroughy studied Early Pleistocene deposits in the world. Its absolute age span is 1.7 to 2.1 mya based on 57 K/Ar dates obtained from six stratified volcanic tuff deposits derived from a series of nearby volcanoes. Bed I is made up of five different kinds of sediments: lava flow, lake, lake margin, alluvial fan, and alluvial plain (Fig. 7–5). The Bed I environment has been reconstructed from sedimentary and faunal evidence. The climate was semiarid although wetter than that in the Olduvai region today (Hay 1976, p. 53). Open grasslands covered the plains and fan slopes leading up to the base of the volcanic highlands. Along the margins of the lake was a damp marsh. Archaeological sites are located where freshwater streams flowed into the lake from the highlands. Sand dunes along the lake shore suggest a sparse vegetation cover.

Wildlife recovered as food bone refuse from the hominid "living floors" is mostly small to medium-size creatures such as rodents, bats, lizards, turtles, and juvenile grazing animals including antelope. Some minnow-sized fish and crocodiles were taken from the lake. The lack of long-bone ossification indicates that the grassland animals were immature at the time of death. Large animals such as elephants were hunted rarely and only in the subadult stage. In conclusion, these proto-humans were scavengers who ran down

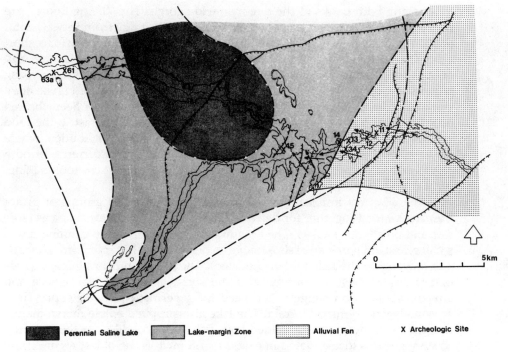

FIGURE 7-5   Paleogeography of Bed I showing the saline lake, the lake-margin zone, and the alluvial fan with Australopithecine sites on the eastern shore. The reconstructed landscape is superimposed upon the map of the modern-day Olduvai Gorge.

Source: From *Geology of Olduvai Gorge,* by Richard L. Hay; courtesy of University of California Press.

young, weak animals and occasionally fed on the carcasses of large animals killed by more adept predators such as lions and wild dogs.

The tool assemblage found on the Bed I living floors represents some of the world's earliest attempts at stone tool making. The artifact inventory includes (1) cobble choppers for heavy duty cleaving, (2) stone flakes for scraping and cutting, (3) hammerstones for knapping and opening food bone for marrow, (4) stones thrown as missiles in the hunt, and (5) rope-bound bolas stones thrown to bring down running game by entangling their feet. In addition, there are certain bone tools showing wear but whose function is largely unknown. One implement appears to have been used for rubbing, perhaps as a hide scraper. Otherwise no direct evidence of wooden or other perishable implements have been preserved, and no evidence of clothing or fire (Leakey 1971; Bordes 1970, p. 44).

The proto-human settlements of Bed I include 18 principal sites along the eastern shore of the 15-mile (25-km) diameter lake. They outcrop for 4.3

miles along both banks of the one-mile-wide gorge. The "living floors" are packed surfaces representing shore-side camps. To judge from the soil compaction and the density of artifact litter, they were occupied only for a short time. The camps are littered with tools, flaking debris from manufacture, and animal bones from prey butchered and consumed at home base. The long bones show spiral fractures and impact scars from being smashed on an anvil stone in order to extract the bone marrow. The bones have not been charred as if the meat had been cooked, however, a significant contrast to the food refuse bones obtained from the Middle Pleistocene site of Choukoutien, where *Homo erectus* cooked meat. Mary Leakey explains the co-occurrence of both *boisei* and *habilis* species on these sites by hypothesizing that the tool-making, meat-eating *habilis* preyed on the dull-witted *boisei* species.

The adaptive implications of this data are that small groups of proto-humans banded together for defense against natural predators such as large cats and poisonous snakes. The hominid group cooperated in running down small grassland game animals, stoning to death larger but immature animals, and scavenging the kill of other predators. The fixed campsites imply a sense of territory as well as continuity of the social group. The lake-shore and stream-side location suggests the need for a permanent water supply in a seasonally dry, semiarid terrain. The lake also supplied edible marsh plants, and the near-shore waters yielded both fish and crocodiles for food. A ring of stones at this locale, dated in excess of 1.8 mya, is the oldest architectural construction known, although its exact purpose is debated: windbreak, hunting blind, or night protective corral for sleeping.

During the later Lower Paleolithic, *Homo erectus* moved northward from the tropical savanna of Africa to occupy a variety of habitats in Europe and Asia. By the Middle Pleistocene, the temperate zone was inhabited as far north as 49 degrees latitude, as indicated by the Mauer jaw find recovered from a gravel quarry near Heidelberg, Germany (Brace and others 1979, pp. 74–75). At this time, *H. erectus* was occupying such Old World habitats as: (1) the shores of African savanna lakes and rivers, (2) Mediterranean sea-shores, (3) a riverside in the tropical rain forest of Java, and (4) temperate forests of France, Greece, and northern China.

Colonization of the seasonal, cool temperate zone is dated to the Brunhes-Matuyama paleomagnetic boundary, 700,000 years ago (Issac 1974, pp. 508–14). Relatively abundant fossil and artifactual evidence of humans in equatorial Africa extends far back into the Matuyama reversed epoch. The later occupancy of Europe and Asia is largely confined to sites of Brunhes age. The Mauer jaw, dated early in the Brunhes, came from one of the oldest Pleistocene hominids of Europe. Archaeological sites serving as exceptions to this generalization are Ubeidiya, Israel and Vallonet, France, both of late Matuyama age (Coles and Higgs 1975, p. 264). These sites are thought to be examples of pioneer stages in the expansion of the hominid ecological range from the equatorial tropics into the mid-latitude temperate zone (Issac 1974).

Hand axes and cleavers are the hallmarks of the Lower Paleolithic during the Pleistocene (Issac 1974). These tool types from the Acheulean industries began in the Matuyama epoch of Africa around 1.5 mya. In contrast, the Acheulean tools of Atlantic and Mediterranean Europe were rare until halfway through the Brunhes, when they are documented by such sites as Torre in Pietra, Italy; Terra Amata, France; and Torralba, Spain (Coles and Higgs 1975). On the other hand, flake and chopper tools replace bifaces as the principal industries at localities in central Europe, continental Asia, and east Asia. These nonbiface industries are characterized by the presence of scrapers, denticulates (toothed flake tools), small pointed tool forms, and other miscellaneous tool types made on flakes. As a rule, however, bifaces are not completely absent as members of the flake and chopper industries even in the Far East (Issac 1974). The significance of this pattern is not altogether apparent because of the rarity of excavated finds.

A variety of competing hypotheses have been offered to explain these industrial variations. Among these are hypotheses that the biface and nonbiface artifacts are (1) products of different cultural and ethnic groups, (2) products of separate and distinct species or subspecies of humans, and (3) products of the same makers but reflecting different seasonal activities (Issac 1974).

Middle Paleolithic

The Middle Paleolithic is assigned to the last interglacial, the Eemian, through the first part of the Würm glaciation (Würm stadial I). In absolute terms, this age range extends from more than 100,000 years ago to approximately 35,000 years ago as determined by radiocarbon dating. But in fact, most of the C–14 assays extend back no more than 50,000 to 55,000 years. The fossil form most common in Europe, Asia, and North Africa is the Neanderthal subspecies in the Mousterian phase of archaeological culture. Taxonomically, Neanderthal is an Archaic *Homo sapiens*.

Specialized Tools

The Middle Paleolithic is marked by the beginnings of specialized stone tools and tool kits (Constable and others 1973). For the first time, there were a variety of tools made for specific purposes such as reaming, boring, scraping, and cutting (Fig. 7–6). Manufacturing involved complex ways of making stone tools from a prepared core, such as the Levallois technique. The Levallois procedure is a particularly efficient means of removing many finished tools from one prepared core. One example of a finished tool is the Levallois point, which was hafted on a short jabbing spear for the killing of large, Late Pleistocene game.

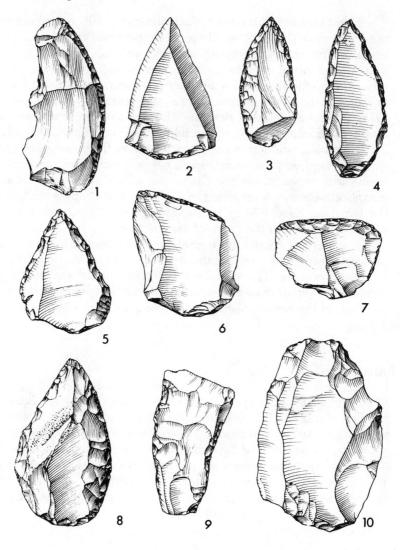

FIGURE 7-6   Flint implements of the typical Mousterian: (1) convex side-scraper; (2) Levallois point; (3, 4, 5) Mousterian points; (6) canted scraper; (7) transversal scraper; (8) convergent scraper; (9) double scraper; (10) Levallois flake. (Combe-Grenal, Dordogne, layer 29, except 2, from Houppeville, Normandy, and 10, from Corbiac, Dordogne.)

Source: From Francois Bordes, *The Old Stone Age;* London: Weidenfeld & Nicolson Ltd.

The Neanderthal hunted big game herd animals such as the woolly rhinoceros, reindeer, and horses. The particular foe of Neanderthal hunters was the large Pleistocene cave bear who competed with humans for the same natural limestone shelters. Game kill techniques included hunting in organized groups, driving animals over cliffs (a practice that was particularly effective in killing large herds of horses), and using fire to herd animals toward cliff edges. Once the herd had been stampeded over the edge, the individual animals would be killed instantly or immobilized by broken legs. The stricken herd could then be finished off with thrusting spears and clubs.

Neanderthal bands occupied natural limestone caves in southern Europe, particularly in southwestern France. They made sustained use of these natural shelters, as indicated by deeply accumulated refuse deposits. Post holes at the entrance to some of the rock shelters suggest that the cave mouth was sealed by a partition made of branches covered with hides. Such natural shelters, sealed and heated with small fires, would allow Neanderthal bands to withstand the rigorous climate of the Würm I stadial.

Open-air structures also were occupied by the Neanderthal. These consist of small, circular huts constructed of a wood or bone frame covered with hides. Small fire hearths were used for heating, light, and cooking. (Fig. 1–12). Judging from the season-at-death analysis of reindeer teeth, rock shelters were occupied temporarily by reindeer hunters tracking herds in northern Europe. Bands of constantly moving hunters preyed upon migrating reindeer that wintered in the boreal forest of the subarctic then moved northward onto the open tundra in the summer (Butzer 1976) (Fig. 2–1).

Evidence of Religion

Perhaps the appearance of religion is the single most significant development of the Middle Paleolithic times. This inference is derived from several observations of a ritual, symbolic nature. One line of evidence consists of arrangements of the bones of the cave bear, one of the more formidable enemies in the Neanderthal environment. These bone arrangements are often interpreted as shrines where cult followers gathered for magic rites. Evidence of the cave bear cult is most concentrated in caves located high in the mountains of Switzerland, southern Germany, and Yugoslavia (Coles and Higgs 1975, p. 220). In one such shrine found in Switzerland, a burial chamber contained stacked bear skulls. Other arrangements consisted of sorted long bones placed along the walls of the cave. Another pile of bones included a bear skull pierced by a leg bone. The skull of this heap rested on two other long bones. In Bavaria, ten skulls of cave bears were placed on a stone slab platform. In Yugoslavia, a natural crevice in the wall of a cave had been sealed off by stacked rocks. When opened, this crypt was found to contain a deposit of cave bear bones (Coles and Higgs 1975, pp. 286–87).

Another line of ritual evidence is the first appearance of formal human burials. All known finds of Lower Paleolithic hominids consist of bones thrown onto the garbage dump without ritual care. Many fractured skulls show evidence of cannibalism, because the cranium had been entered from the base to extract the brains, presumably for consumption. By Middle Paleolithic times, however, the human body was carefully interred in a pit dug into the floor of a habitation cave. Neanderthal burial arrangements often appear to be shrines.

The earliest Neanderthal burial discoveries were made in southwestern France at such well-known cave sites as La Chapelle-aux-Saints, Le Moustier, and La Ferrassie. The skeleton at the Chapelle cave is that of an old man whose molars had been missing for many years prior to death (Brace and others 1979, p. 116). This evidence supports the idea that some Middle Paleolithic societies were sufficiently well off economically that they could afford to support a few nonproductive members. The corpse of the old man was placed in a shallow trench. Grave offerings interred with the body include a bison leg, which was laid on his chest. Offerings of bones, tools, and other debris were thrown into the burial trench as it was filled (Wenke 1980, p. 184). The Le Moustier burial find is that of a late adolescent male associated with the Mousterian culture. This body was drawn up in a flexed position and lying on its right side. At Ferrassie, a small cemetery of Neanderthal skeletons were buried together (Brace and others 1979, p. 122). These consisted of an adult male, an adult female, three infants, and a possible fetus. The bodies had been laid out in a rather stylized manner. The adult male was covered with a stone slab. The woman was interred in a flexed position. At the back of the cave, the skull and body of one child had been buried in separate pits, with the skull covered by a limestone slab (Wenke 1980, p. 184). The front teeth of the two adults were worn from holding objects—a form of dental abrasion not observed in later Upper Paleolithic skeletal specimens.

Another example of Neanderthal burial has been reported from the cave site excavations of Shanidar, located in the Zagros Mountains of Iraq (Coles and Higgs 1975; Solecki 1979). From the basal layers of the shelter are Mousterian phase deposits dated to Würm I times, around 50,000 years ago. Here some seven Neanderthal skeletons were found. Many of these people had been killed by impact from large rocks fallen from the cave ceiling, but at least one skeleton had been interred. To judge from pollen samples taken from fill around the body, flowers had been placed with the deceased. These include pollen types such as grape hyacinth, bachelor's button, and hollyhock (Coles and Higgs 1975, p. 372; Wenke 1980, p. 184).

Usually the Neanderthal body was placed in a pit dug into the cave floor. Sometimes the deceased was covered with flowers and red ochre pigment (hematite). The presence of tools and food, as revealed by butchered animal bones, indicate a belief in the after-life of the human spirit—an important step in the direction of abstract thinking.

Other finds suggest that human skeletal parts were incorporated into religious shrines just as cave bear skulls were. At a small cave at Monte Circeo near Rome, a complete but badly encrusted adult male skull and the jaw of another individual were positioned in the center of a circle of rocks (Brace and others 1979, p. 114; Coles and Higgs 1975, p. 287). The bones of many wild animals had been heaped around the cave, perhaps as food offerings. The adult skull had a large hole in the right side and the base had been cut away, presumably to extract the brain. Among primitive peoples today, it is not uncommon to find evidence of ritual cannibalism in which some flesh is carved from a slain enemy and consumed in order to gain the power of that person by magic. The Neanderthal practice of breaking the skull open may well be an early form of this ritual practice.

Another Neanderthal burial shrine has been reported from the shores of the Caspian Sea in Russia. At the Teshik-Tash site, a Neanderthal child's skeleton was partly surrounded by a circle of five goat skulls, the horns of which had been pushed into the dirt floor of the cave (Coles and Higgs 1975, p. 329).

Upper Paleolithic

The Upper (Late or Advanced) Paleolithic of Europe is dated to the late part of the last or Würm/Weichsel glaciation (Würm II and III). In absolute terms, this age interval extends from 35,000 to 10,000 years ago. At this time the Neanderthal populations of Europe were replaced by the Cro-magnon race, fully modern humans taxonomically identified as *Homo sapiens sapiens*. Much debate centers around the process by which this subspecies change took place. Some physical anthropologists have assumed that the Neanderthals became extinct or were killed off by Cro-magnons invading Europe. Others believe that the Neanderthals became absorbed into the Cro-magnon population by intermarriage, and still others posit that the Archaic *Homo sapiens* simply evolved by natural selection and gene mutation into fully modern humans of the subspecies *sapiens*. The last hypothesis has been most favored by the archaeological evidence, which suggests a continuity between the late culture of the Neanderthal and the early culture of Cro-magnon. From this viewpoint it seems reasonable that continuity in the development of culture through time can best be explained by continuity in the corresponding biological populations (Coles and Higgs 1975, pp. 222, 332).

Tools and Weapons

During the Upper Paleolithic, workers invented tools for the manufacture and repair of other tools (Clark 1967). These include tools for working in wood, stone, bone, and antler. Bones and antlers were slotted, carved, and en-

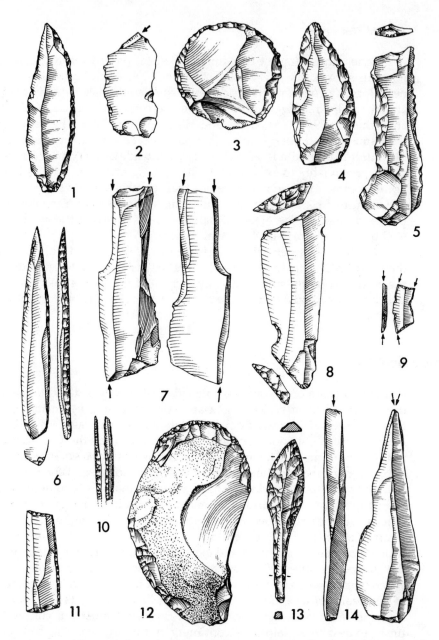

FIGURE 7-7 Flint tools from the Perigordian. *Lower Perigordian:* (1) Chatelperron knife; (2) burin; (3) scraper on a flake; (4) Mousterian point; (5) denticulated and truncated blade. *Upper Perigordian:* (6) Gravette point; (7) multiple burin on truncation; (8) bitruncated blade; (9) Noailles burin; (10) backed bladelet; (11) truncated element; (12) flake scraper; (13) Font-Robert point; (14) dihedral burin. (1–5, Arcy-sur-Cure; 6, 7, 8, 10, 14, Corbiac, Dordogne; 9, Noailles; 11, Oreille d'Enfer, Les Eyzies; 12, La Gravette; 13, Laussel.)

Source: From Francois Bordes, *The Old Stone Age;* London: Weidenfeld & Nicolson Ltd.

graved with a stone tool called a *burin*. Bone and antler harpoons are characteristic of some of the later Upper Paleolithic cultures of Europe, as are ivory and bone eyed needles, bone points, perforated animal teeth, bone and ivory beads, spear-throwers, and shaft straighteners.

Stone tools were manufactured from prismatic cores for the production of flake blades. The conical-shaped, fluted cores were reduced to flakes by the use of indirect percussion involving either a hand-held punch or a chest punch (Fig. 1–13). Once the flakes had been removed, they were shaped into finished tools by use of a pressure tool as shown in Figure 7–4b. The tool edges were shaped and finished by pressing off fine chips, a process called *retouch* by the French, to manufacture spear points, bifacial hafted knives, and the many other specialized forms illustrated in Figure 7–7.

The people of the Upper Paleolithic were advanced and highly specialized hunters of the large herd animals of the late Würm glaciation. During stadial times they tracked and killed tundra animals, and during interstadial times they sought forest animals. Hunting weapons included spears propelled by a spear-thrower board, harpoons, clubs, stone missiles, bow-and-arrow, boomerangs or throwing sticks, and bolas. The bola, which consists of rocks tied to a rope, was swung so as to entangle the feet of running game. By the end of the Upper Paleolithic, the Magdalenian culture had invented the bow-and-arrow, judging by the stone arrow tips found in their sites. Other hunting devices were snares and pitfalls, as interpreted from cave drawings. Sites consisting of piles of slaughtered and butchered animal bones indicate that herd animals were stampeded over a cliff or into a gorge.

The hunting economy of each European band was specialized on a certain animal. For instance, reindeer was the principal meat source in France and Germany, woolly mammoth in eastern Europe, and horses in various localities (Butzer 1976).

Fishing supplemented the hunting of large mammals. Implements utilized were the fish weir or trap, hand-held harpoons, and fish spears with barbed tips of carved ivory (Fig. 7–8b). Much of this technology was developed by the end of the Pleistocene during the Magdalenian phase between 20,000 and 12,800 BP (Coles and Higgs 1975, p. 252). Along the Dordogne River of southwestern France, where salmon fishing was particularly important, Upper Paleolithic sites are rich in fish scales and vertebrae. Fishing was a new subsistence development and one that led smoothly into the maritime economic practices of the succeeding Mesolithic stage.

Indirect evidence of Upper Paleolithic clothing consists of bone sewing needles and belt fasteners. Elaborate wearing apparel, presumably of tanned skins and furs, is pictured in cave art. Such form-fitting apparel was an important adaptive device for survival in the rigorous arctic environment of the times.

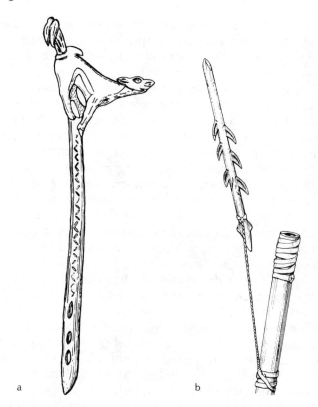

a   b

FIGURE 7-8   Upper Paleolithic artifacts from Europe. (a) Magdalenian spear-thrower carved from reindeer antler depicts a young ibex evacuating, so that the dropping forms a hook to engage the base of the spear shaft; (b) the hafting of a barbed harpoon head, typical of the late Magdalenian culture.

Source: Graham Clark, *The Stone Age Hunters.* London: Thames and Hudson Ltd., 1967.

Dwellings

Upper Paleolithic settlements consist of both open-air and cave habitations. Natural rock shelters were occupied when available and located near animal trails or grazing areas. Human mobility was dictated by the habits of the game. If the herd animals, such as reindeer, migrated seasonally, the predatory human hunting bands were required to follow the herd. On the other hand, settlement was semipermanent when gregarious herd animals were present in one area all year, as illustrated by the mammoths of the forest in eastern Europe.

Evidence of constructed dwellings is found in cave art and in the form of architectural remains. Construction types consist of round or rectangular skin tents, skin-covered huts framed in wood, or huts framed by mammoth tusks rammed into the ground. In Russia some of the Upper Paleolithic houses were sunk partly into pits to combat the extremely cold winters (Coles and Higgs 1975, p. 335).

Residence groups varied in size. Single families used the smaller tent structures while tracking migratory game. Multiple families lived in long houses composed of separate compartments of two to five rooms, each with its own fireplace. These spacious structures suggest an extended family or a small band of multiple families, as interpreted for long houses located on the Don River of Russia (Coles and Higgs 1975).

Art and Religion

Evidence for religious concepts is rich during the Upper Paleolithic. The presence of a fertility cult is revealed by small bone and ivory female sculptures called *Venuses*, which are thought to have served the function of magically insuring human reproductivity. The figurines typically have large breasts, protruding buttocks, and exaggerated sexual parts, although facial detail is minimal (Coles and Higgs 1975, p. 226).

Other aspects of fertility are found in cave art depicting animals deep in the inner chambers of natural limestone caverns (Fig. 7–9). The engravings, polychrome paintings, and sculptures in such hidden sanctuaries are thought to have played a magical role in the fertility and slaughter of wild game. This mural art, which is some of the earliest known art in the world, has been recognized since 1895. Although not always identifiable to a particular Upper Paleolithic culture, it is generally dated between 33,000 and 10,000 years ago. Most of the cave art is confined to southwestern France and adjacent portions of northern Spain although a few examples have been discovered in southern Spain, Sicily, and Russia (Coles and Higgs 1975, pp. 251, 341). Within the core area of western Europe, more than 100 cave sanctuaries contain several thousand paintings.

The animals are painted in mineral pigments of yellow, red, brown, and black. Other techniques include carving into the limestone wall of the cave using the burin tool or drawing on clay surfaces using sticks or fingers (Coles and Higgs 1975, p. 250). The bison and horse were the animals most commonly reproduced. Other figures also rendered included auroch, reindeer, red deer, mammoth, rhinoceros, ibex, chamois, boar, wolf, lion, bear, bird, fish, human hand, and various signs and symbols (Coles and Higgs 1975, pp. 250–51). Some murals show these figures superimposed upon one another.

Formal burials provide additional evidence of religious concepts. The Upper Paleolithic bodies were usually flexed with arms and legs pulled close to the body for easy insertion into a pit. Sometimes the corpse was covered with red ochre, an iron mineral pigment symbolizing life after death. Occasionally, the body was covered with a stone slab or surrounded by a ring

FIGURE 7-9   Upper Paleolithic cave art. Figures painted on the walls of limestone caves include snake-like scribbles, stencilled hands, engraved salmon with tally marks, elephant, woolly rhinoceros, horse, wounded bison, cave-lion, reindeer, and engraved wooly mammoth.

Source: Kenneth Oakley, *Man the Toolmaker;* courtesy of Trustees of the British Museum (Natural History).

of rocks. Body ornaments included stone, bone, ivory, or seashell beads arranged as a bonnet, crown, garter, necklace, pendant, bracelet, or anklet (Coles and Higgs 1975, p. 232). Some bodies were interred over a hearth that scorched the corpse, indicating that fire was part of a burial ceremony. Grave offerings were included with the deceased, either as status symbols or as tools to be used in the afterlife.

Although not directly tied to religion, Upper Paleolithic musical instruments must relate to an esthetic appreciation of sound and group participation in ceremony (Coles and Higgs 1975, pp. 226–27). Instruments include bone whistles, panpipes, and flutes, but no system of tones has been worked out for these wind instruments.

Paleolithic Evolution

During the Pleistocene epoch, tools evolved from simple to complex. This important trend in technical behavior is reflected by (1) an increasing standardization in the form of tools, (2) an increasing variety of tool types, and (3) an increasing specialization of tool uses. In comparison, the unspecialized Oldowan industry dated to the Early Pleistocene and Lower Paleolithic produced only a few basic tool types consisting of core choppers and flakes that served a variety of purposes. By the Middle Paleolithic of Late Pleistocene times, highly standardized tools and tool kits had been invented. Each tool played a specific role in the technical operations either of equipment manufacture and repair or of processing materials and foodstuffs.

A second significant regularity in Paleolithic evolution is that the rate of tool technology was accelerating rapidly, like the ramp model of evolution. This trend is particularly apparent during the Late Pleistocene when the growth curve is exponential in its upswing.

The importance of these two findings is that the evolving tool technology increased human control over the natural environment. The early history of the hominids was marked by successful adaptation to changing environmental conditions through biological evolution under the twin agents of natural selection and genetic mutation. By Late Pleistocene times, however, cultural evolution had replaced biological evolution as the primary adaptive mechanism. Advanced technology enabled humans to deal with changing Pleistocene environments and enter new environmental zones, including the arctic and subarctic, as well as the New World. The change from biological to cultural adaptation took place during Middle Pleistocene times when the *Homo erectus* hominids left the dry tropical savanna of Africa and colonized the mid-latitude, seasonal, deciduous forests of Europe and Asia.

The principal cultural means for adapting to both middle and high northern latitudes was the organized hunting of big game. This advance was effected by offense weapons, particularly projectiles, by cooperation of the hunting party, and through the psychological reassurance of hunting and fertility magic.

Projectiles were an important technical device for dealing with Pleistocene game because many of the most important quarry were naturally armed for combat with claws, tusks, sharp canines, thick skin, high running speed, and massive bulk. Relatively unspecialized humans were no match for this formidable array of defenses. Thus, it was only through culture that the gap could be closed. As early as Bed I times, the Australopithecines of Olduvai Gorge had the habit of collecting cobbles from stream beds while on their daily travels from camp in search of food. These stream-rounded rocks were systematically returned to base camp, where the Leakeys found them littering the occupation surface. Few if any of these collected rocks display any intentional marks of manufacture, although they are recognizable as imports because they are out of their natural stream-bed context. These rocks were named *manuports* by Louis Leakey to distinguish them as true artifacts, that is, objects of hominid use but not manufacture. The stones were used as missiles to hurl at any marauding carnivores that might prowl the Australopithecine camp at night. Carnivores were a particularly severe threat until humans were able to control fire, which could be used to hold such predators at bay. The manuport missile interpretation was confirmed by noncampsite finds called *butchering sites.* An example is reported by Mary Leakey (1971, pp. 64–66) from upper Bed I, Level 6, where the skeleton of a single elephant (*Elephas recki*) was found just below Tuff IF, which marks the top of the formation. Here an almost complete Villafranchian-age elephant lay on its left side. It is almost as big as a fully grown modern elephant, although this animal was immature, since the caps on the long bones had not fused to the shafts. From the largely articulated skeleton, shown in Figure 7–10, Leakey deduced that the find represents:

> a butchering site where an elephant was cut up by early man, who may have come upon it accidentally, or deliberately driven it into a swamp to be slaughtered. The tools found nearby would seem to represent those used for cutting the meat off the carcass. (1971, p. 64)

In all, 123 tools of the Oldowan industry were found with the skeleton, including choppers, a proto-biface, anvils, hammerstones, cobblestones, nodules or blocks, light-duty flakes and other fragments, waste flakes from tool manufacture or sharpening, and manuports. Because of the size of the animal and its relatively undisturbed condition, it seems likely that the animal was killed in place before butchering with the meat being stripped off of the skeleton. The seven manuports may be the thrown missiles that killed the beast in the swamp fringing the ancient lake at Olduvai Gorge.

The use of rock missiles to hunt mature big game is further documented for African Acheulean sites of the Middle Pleistocene (Clark 1970). These later missiles were often stockpiled at camps, ready for the chase should game be sighted or for defensive measures should carnivores approach camp.

The earliest evidence of shaft missiles appears at the end of the Middle Pleistocene times. At Clacton in England, excavators recovered portions of a shaped wooden spear shaft with a fire-hardened point, dated to interglacial deposits (Oakley 1956, p. 14). Corroborating evidence for missile shafts, this

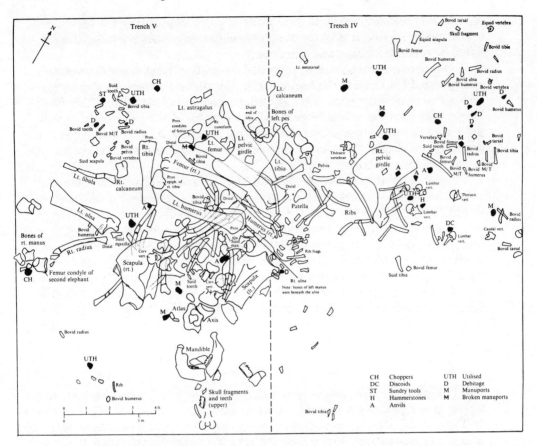

FIGURE 7-10   Plan of elephant skeleton and associated artifacts in a butchering site at Olduvai Gorge, Tanzania.

Source: M. D. Leakey, *Olduvai Gorge, Volume 3,* Cambridge: Cambridge University Press, 1971.

time with stone tips, has been obtained from Late Pleistocene sites of Middle and Late Paleolithic age.

Technical achievements that enabled humans to occupy severe winter environments included: (1) the controlled use of fire, (2) the construction of dwellings, (3) the use of natural rock shelters, and (4) the construction of clothing. Fire was in use by *Homo erectus* as long ago as Middle Pleistocene times. Formal fire hearths and charred animal bones found at Vertesszolles, Hungary, and in the Choukoutien caves of northern China suggest that meat was cooked, rather than simply eaten raw. These *Homo erectus* deposits are dated to late Mindel times around 0.5 mya. No evidence that fires were kindled by humans appears until thousands of years later during the Mesolithic (Clark 1954). Rather, it is likely that lightning or volcanoes provided the fire, which was carried home and cared for.

Architectural construction provided protection from natural predators and retained heat inside the house walls. The earliest architectural construction is the stone ring from Bed I at Olduvai Gorge in east Africa. This fixed facility may have been little more than a hunting blind or a hut erected against predatory cats. The first substantial housing is reported by de Lumley (1979) dating to the Middle Pleistocene. Subsequently, many such shelters are found in the Middle and Upper Paleolithic.

Another kind of shelter is the mouth of a cave. In spite of the popular belief that early humans lived in caves, there is no record of cave dwelling during the Early Pleistocene. Even the South African caves were natural traps into which the Australopithecines fell or were thrown after death, rather than abodes for the living. It is not until fire had been controlled to warm the cave interior during the Middle Pleistocene that rock shelters were fit for habitation. The problem of cold and dampness was further alleviated by the building of frame and skin houses within the cave, as was practiced in Riss glacial times at the French site of Lazaret, near the Mediterranean port of Nice.

Summary

The Paleolithic or "old stone age" can be divided into Lower, Middle, and Upper stages, each one identified by specific forms of adaptation to the natural and social environment. In the Lower Paleolithic, the Australopithecines adapted to ground dwelling within the savanna grasslands of Africa by using rudimentary hunting practices called *scavenging*. By Middle Paleolithic times, *Homo erectus* was using fire. The Neanderthal subspecies (Archaic *Homo sapiens*) inhabited regions of Europe and Asia, as well as Africa. Two cultural developments of the Middle stage were the invention of specialized tools and the beginnings of religion, which indicates the capacity for abstract thought. Neanderthal bands hunted big game herds.

During Upper Paleolithic times, the Cro-magnon race of fully modern *Homo sapiens* replaced the Neanderthals. New technology produced tools for the manufacture of other tools, and such weapons as spears, harpoons, bow-and-arrow, boomerangs, and bolas. Besides killing large herd animals for food, humans added fish to their diet. By using fire, clothing, and man-made shelters, they were able to adapt to cold climates of the arctic tundra. These early humans left a record of their culture in the cave art of southern Europe, including some paintings that date back 33,000 years. Their burial practices indicate belief in the afterlife.

References

BORDES, FRANCOIS
1973 *The Old Stone Age.* New York: McGraw-Hill.
BRACE, LORING C., HARRY NELSON, NOEL KORN, and MARY L. BRACE
1979 *Atlas of Human Evolution.* New York: Holt, Rinehart, and Winston.
BUTZER, KARL W.
1976 *Environment and Archaeology.* Chicago: Aldine.
CHILDE, V. GORDON
1961 *Man Makes Himself.* New York: New American Library.
COLES, J. M., and E. S. HIGGS
1975 *The Archaeology of Early Man.* Baltimore: Peregrine Books.
CONSTABLE, GEORGE, and EDITORS OF TIME-LIFE BOOKS
1973 *The Neanderthals.* New York: Time-Life Books.
DE LUMLEY, HENRY
1979 A Paleolithic Camp at Nice. In *Hunters, Farmers, and Civilizations.* San Francisco: W. H. Freeman and Company Publishers.
EDEY, MAITLAND A., and EDITORS OF TIME-LIFE BOOKS
1972 *The Missing Link.* New York: Time-Life Books.
HAY, RICHARD L.
1976 *Geology of the Olduvai Gorge.* Berkeley: University of California Press.
HOWELL, F. CLARK, and EDITORS OF TIME-LIFE BOOKS
1968 *Early Man.* New York: Time-Life Books.
ISSAC, GLYNN
1974 Stratigraphy and Patterns of Cultural Change in the Middle Pleistocene. *Current Anthropology* 15(4):508–14.
LEAKEY, M. D.
1971 *Olduvai Gorge: Excavations in Beds I and II, 1960–1963,* vol. 3. Cambridge: Cambridge University Press.
SOLECKI, RALPH S.
1979 Shanidar Cave. In *Hunters, Farmers, and Civilizations.* San Francisco: W. H. Freeman and Company Publishers.
TIME-LIFE BOOKS
1973 *The First Men.* New York: Time-Life Books.
WENKE, ROBERT J.
1980 *Patterns in Prehistory: Mankind's First Three Million Years.* New York: Oxford University Press.
WILLEY, GORDON R., and PHILIP PHILLIPS
1958 *Method and Theory in American Archaeology.* Chicago: University of Chicago Press.

8

Later Stone Ages and Civilizations of the Old World

Ten thousand years ago, in the early part of the Holocene epoch, the ice age ended, and as the glaciers slowly melted away, humans began their adaptation to a different world. Deciduous forests replaced subarctic boreal forest and tundra in northern Europe, and new plants and animals appeared. In arid lands, deserts expanded, pushing people into oases, perennial river valleys, and seacoasts. As the glaciers shrank, sea level rose and the oceans flooded shallow continental shelves, bays, and coastlines. Coastal submergence isolated many islands—such as Sumatra, Java, and Borneo—that were formerly linked to the mainland by land bridges.

Mesolithic Stage

The end of the ice age marks the beginning of the Mesolithic stage in the Old World: *meso-* meaning "in the middle" and *lithic* meaning "stone," hence the intermediate stone age. In Europe and the Near East, the Mesolithic ranges from 10,000 to 11,000 years ago to the beginning of the Neolithic stage around 9000 years ago. Elsewhere in the world the absolute dating may be quite different, but the Mesolithic always occurred between the Paleolithic and the Neolithic as a developmental step.

In economic terms, the Mesolithic is a stage of intensive food gathering. Wild food products, gathered by women, began to supplement the meat supplied by the stone age hunters. When people began to observe plant life and to think of plants as a source of food, they had taken the first essential step toward the development of agriculture and the beginning of civilization.

The characteristic technology of the Mesolithic was the manufacture of microlithic (small stone) tools, which were made by snapping long blades into segments. Blades, the hallmark of the Upper Paleolithic, are long, parallel-sided flakes removed from polyhedral (many-sided) fluted cores by direct or indirect percussion. When snapped into many individual pieces, the flake blade was converted into small bladelets, which could be set into wooden shafts to form composite tools such as knives, arrows, or sickles (Fig. 8–1). Microliths produced in this way were further modified by retouching with a pressure tool to yield geometric shapes such as crescents, triangles, trapezoids, and rectangles. These shaped microliths were then mounted in slots cut into the wooden shaft, cemented in place by a natural mastic such as asphaltum or tree resin, and sometimes tied to the shaft with animal sinew or twisted cordage made from fibrous plant material or hair.

These composite (multiple-part) Mesolithic tools are shown in murals on cliffs and in rock shelters of eastern Spain (Coles and Higgs 1975, p. 261). Murals painted in red, black, or white mineral pigments show scenes of hunting, tracking, chasing, and shooting of deer, goat, boar, and aurochs. Some of these painted or engraved scenes show human groups armed with bow and arrow. Other Mesolithic scenes depict the collection of honey, women clapping or dancing, and mother-and-child groups.

The economy of the Mesolithic represented a profound change from the specialized hunting of herd animals by Upper Paleolithic peoples to a broad-spectrum food quest. As the Pleistocene herd animals became extinct because of overhunting and/or climatic change, people adopted a mixed resource strategy involving plant collecting, hunting of modern game, gathering of stream, lake, and seashore shellfish, and deepwater fishing. Study of plant remains from Mesolithic sites indicates that nuts, berries, wild greens, and grass seeds were all collected intensely as they came into season. Many of the plant products were reduced to edible form by milling between two grinding stones. The mill consisted of a hand-held grinder that was run over a flat slab. Such implements first appeared along the Nile river of northeastern Africa in late glacial times and were an integral part of Mesolithic assemblages in northwestern Africa between 9000 and 14,000 years ago (Coles and Higgs 1975, p. 180).

Attention to the plant world was a significant precondition for the invention of agriculture because knowledge of plants and their habits was accumulated rapidly.

The bow-and-arrow was now commonly used to hunt individual deer, elk, aurochs, wild pig, and other medium-sized, modern animals of the forest. Hunting techniques included stalk and ambush by small groups or solitary hunters. Small hunting parties replaced the large game drives that had

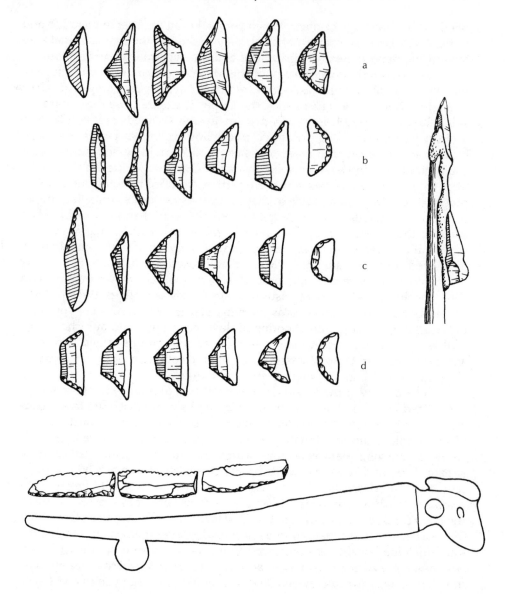

FIGURE 8-1   Microliths and microlithic tools. (*Left*) Microliths used to barb and tip projectile heads, from (a) Star Carr, England; (b) La Cocina, Spain; (c) Palegawra, Iraq; and (d) Jarmo, Iraq. (*Right*) Forepart of a Mesolithic arrow from Løshult, Sweden, showing a microlithic tip and barb held in position by resin. (*Lower*) A slotted reaping knife with flint insets from Mugharet el-Kebarah, Israel.

Source: Graham Clark, *The Stone Age Hunters*. London: Thames and Hudson Ltd., 1967.

been profitable on the tundra during Pleistocene times. Hunters used decoys and antlered headresses that mimicked the silhouette of game. Transportation and hunting in winter was made easier by the invention of skis and sleds (Fig. 8-2). In addition, traps and snares were invented to capture small game such as rabbits, birds, and rodents.

The gathering of shellfish along lakes, streams, and seacoasts reflects an intensive utilization of aquatic resources. Discarded shells of oysters, clams, and mussels accumulated in huge mounds, some covering 30 or more acres.

FIGURE 8-2   Mesolithic artifacts for transportation and fishing. (a) Three skiers with their sticks are depicted on a rock engraving in Carelia, on the river Vyg. (b) A wooden ski from the stone age of South Travastland, Finland. (c) Bone harpoon head found with the skeleton of a ringed seal in a clay deposit at Norrkoping, Sweden. (d) Maglemosian and Natufian barbless bone fishhooks.

Source: Graham Clark, *The Stone Age Hunters*. London: Thames and Hudson Ltd., 1967.

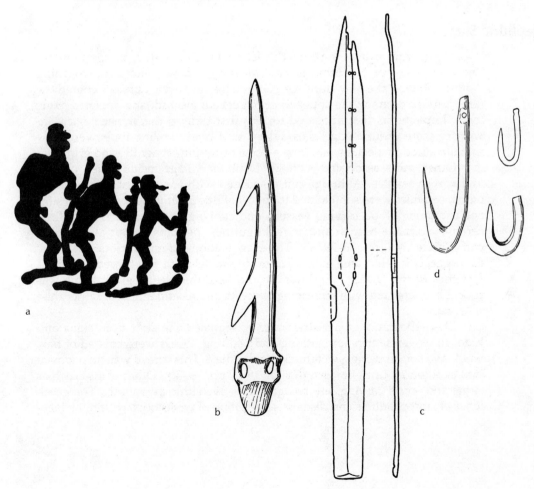

a

b

c

d

In addition to tidewater crustacea and inshore fish, the people caught deep-water fish. The presence of harpoons, fish bones, and carvings of salmon in Upper Paleolithic sites indicates that fishing was already underway late in Pleistocene times. Fishing increased during the Mesolithic with the use of bone hooks and line from small boats as depicted in rock art. Actual parts of boats include wooden paddles and dugout canoe fragments. The use of nets with floats and sinkers, fish traps, and weirs was greatly expanded in early postglacial times.

The new Mesolithic community was made up of small bands of kin-related people. Some of these bands were composed of no more than a half dozen families, judging from the number of houses present in certain semipermanent villages. In general the population was sparse and seasonally dispersed over the landscape. The broad-spectrum, scavenging existence necessitated a constant seasonal mobility in the quest for food except in those favored locales where the natural food supply was exceptionally bounteous. The Mesolithic, a transition stage in which humans adapted to a changing climate, led to an agricultural revolution in the Neolithic stage.

Neolithic Stage

In contemporary usage, the Neolithic is the stage of settled, village farming. The etymology of Neolithic is *neo-* meaning "new" and *lithic* meaning "stone," hence, the new stone age. Originally, however, Lubbock coined the term *Neolithic* to mark the appearance of pecked, ground, and polished stone tools. Implements that appeared for the first time in the archaeological inventory were ground-edge axes, adzes, and hoes. Milling tools were now manufactured by pecking (shaping a stone by tapping it lightly) and grinding.

Other crafts associated with the Neolithic village include fired pottery and woven textiles. Although not associated with the earliest domesticated crops, ceramics were soon added to the Neolithic assemblage to serve as storage containers, food serving vessels, and cooking pots. Artisans used fired ceramics to make human and animal figurines, perhaps as part of a fertility cult (Childe 1961, pp. 76–79, 85). The exaggeration of female sexual parts easily suggests fertility and reproduction, a parallel with the carved "Venus" figurines of the Upper Paleolithic. In the Neolithic the magical theme was probably connected with increasing domestic plants and animals, rather than wild game.

The appearance of a textile industry signaled the shift from skins and hides to woven fabrics for clothing and bedding. Fibers were twisted of flax, wool, and cotton using a weighted spindle shaft. This thread was then woven into cloth on an upright loom (Childe 1961, pp. 79–80). Other crafts, such as stone and wood carving, are recognized as Neolithic inventions. The excellence of craft products and discrete segregation of workshops within the Neolithic village suggests the beginnings of specialization, a period when crafts were at least part-time occupations.

In the Near East, the Neolithic began around 7000 BC and ended with the first appearance of bronze age civilization around 3000 BC. Elsewhere, however, village farming began at different times, and it still continues in various nonindustrial peasant societies today.

Mellaart (1970) divides the Near East Neolithic into three divisions: (1) a preceramic period, (2) a period of plain, unpainted or monochrome pottery followed by polychrome or multicolored painted pottery, and (3) a chalcolithic period that introduced cold-hammered copper. Mellaart dated the early Neolithic, a period before ceramics, between 6000 and 7000 BC. The middle Neolithic, marked by the invention of pottery, is bracket-dated between 5000 and 6000 BC. And finally the late Neolithic, an interval that included metalworking experiments, extends from 5000 to the beginning of the bronze age around 3000 BC. Although these time periods are not world-wide, they describe a technical progression seen in many Neolithic sequences that evolved out of a Mesolithic base.

Some authors employ the term *chalcolithic* as a synonym for the late Neolithic to recognize the beginnings of metal-working, a technical step that led smoothly into bronze age metallurgy. During the Neolithic, native copper was first worked by cold hammering. Later it was extracted from such ores as azurite and malachite by the smelting process. The metal was melted in kilns to a liquid state, then poured into one-piece molds to cast simple objects, most of which were ornaments. The word *chalcolithic* signifies this rudimentary metal-working technology in copper. The prefix *chalco-* is a combining form meaning ''copper,'' a word root taken from the Greek. With the suffix *lithic*, the term describes the copper-stone age, a transitional step between the Neolithic and the bronze age. Many scholars feel that the development of kiln-fired ceramic technology provided the necessary background for the evolution of metallurgy.

Food Production

In early Holocene times (7000–9000 BC) hunters began to bring home live animals. The newborn wild sheep and goats of the Near East were probably brought home as pets and cared for until, over a period of thousands of years, their offspring had developed a dependence on humans for food and protection. Braidwood (1960, p. 9) has suggested that some species may have become domesticated through the capture of young animals for use as decoys on the hunt. He also points to the fact that certain adult wild animals, such as goats and sheep, occasionally approach human beings when sufficiently hungry. Any or all of these practices would eventually lead to the domestication of certain tractable animals and the evolution of stock raising.

By a similar process, stone-age plant gatherers became agriculturalists. The planting of grain may have begun very early in certain parts of the Old World. Archaeologists have found evidence for the use of barley and einkorn wheat by Upper Paleolithic peoples living along the Nile river of Egypt (Wendorf and others 1979). Charred seeds found in several sites at Wadi Kubbaniya located just north of Aswan, indicate the preparation of ground grain. The barley may have been collected as wild cereal, but the einkorn wheat appears to show some of the genetic changes of domestication. That is, the wheat exhibits signs of plant selection, an early step in the domestication process, dated between 17,000 and 18,000 years ago.

The various domesticated cereals all have wild grassy ancestors that live outside of control by humankind. Wheat and barley propagate in the wild when the brittle spike holding the seed breaks. But certain plants, through genetic mutation, develop tough spikes and thus retain their seeds longer. And it was these rare plants that were amenable to harvest by stone-age gatherers. The tough-spiked plants that retained their seeds were more suitable for sickle reaping than plants that readily dropped their seeds on the ground. During late Paleolithic and Mesolithic times in the Middle East, the seeds of these wild cereal grasses were harvested for milling into flour and ultimately for consumption as cakes or gruel. In some cases, humans carried the harvested grass seeds out of their natural range, such as the mountains of the Near East, to a lower elevation in the foothills. Thus, mutations and recessive characteristics were not suppressed but encouraged, leading to genetic change such as that reported for Wadi Kubbaniya (Braidwood 1960, p. 8).

No doubt the food gatherers observed that seeds spilled on soft earth quickly took root. In time, such accidents were turned to profit so that slowly the old hunting and gathering economy was transformed to one of food production. As agriculture became a larger and larger part of the productive economy, the length of time spent at any one campsite lengthened. When people had become more sedentary, it was more profitable to invest in capital improvements such as more permanent housing, fragile clay pots for cooking and food storage, and larger fixed storage facilities for the burgeoning food supply. With the storage of food easing the lean winter months, farmers could now turn to leisure-time pursuits such as the decorative arts. They began to decorate their pottery containers, first with simple geometric lines to produce bichrome (two-color) patterns and then with polychrome (many-colored) patterns (Fig. 8–3).

Today the Neolithic is defined as the economic stage of food production, in contrast with the Paleolithic and Mesolithic in which food was collected rather than produced. The significance of this new food-producing era was that for the first time humans controlled the means of economic survival, rather than depending on "nature." Childe (1961) was so impressed with this new economy that he called the Neolithic an *agricultural revolution*. Many archaeologists have pointed out, however, that any event that requires 4000 years for completion is hardly revolutionary in the sense of sudden change

FIGURE 8-3   Mesopotamian painted pottery typology of the Neolithic. (a–g) Hassuna ware; (h–j) Samarra ware; (k–m) Hajji Muhammad ware.

Source: James Mellaart, *Earliest Civilizations of the Near East.* London: Thames and Hudson Ltd., 1970.

in the existing order. The real importance of the Neolithic stage lies not in the rate of social improvements, but rather in the far-reaching effects of the qualitative changes that took place. In this sense, agriculture was revolutionary.

The consequences of this new and more bountiful productive economy was a sharp rise in human population size and density. With more people to govern, more complex forms of human organization were developed. At the same time, the new food-producing economy yielded a surplus in food-stuffs so that farm workers could support nonfarmers in leadership roles and craft occupations. But unlike the hunter, the farmer was tied to the land. Now land was coveted and people lived near their fields year-round. Farmsteads evolved into villages, which in turn grew into towns and ultimately cities. The Neolithic revolution led directly into the second great step in culture evolution, a social transformation that Childe (1961) called the *urban revolution*.

To Childe, the explanation for this materialist cause-and-effect sequence was a Marxist belief that new means of production trigger social change. In the case of the Neolithic, food production was that prime cause. To the Neo-

FIGURE 8-4   Simplified diagrams of barley spikelets, showing some of the changes which took place after domestication.

Source: From "The Ecology of Early Food Production in Mesopotamia," Flannery, K. V., *Science* Vol. 147, pp. 1247–56, 12 March 1965. Copyright 1965 by American Association for the Advancement of Science.

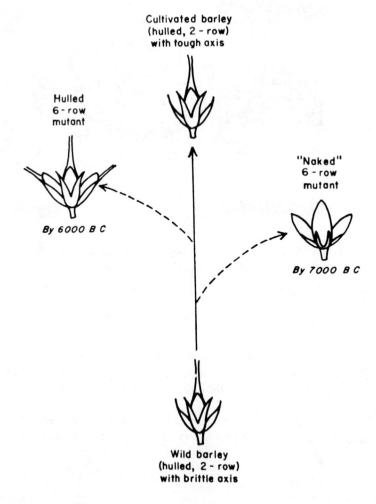

Cultivated barley
(hulled, 2 - row)
with tough axis

Hulled
6 - row
mutant

"Naked"
6 - row
mutant

By 6000 B C

By 7000 B C

Wild barley
(hulled, 2 - row)
with brittle axis

lithic farmer, the basic means of production were plant cultivation and animal husbandry, a mixed economy in contrast to that of the pastoral nomad who lived on the fringe of the agricultural world. Agriculture is the planned control of useful plant and animal products.

Each of the great independent Neolithic revolutions of the world built its economy around one or more cereal grains, such as wheat, barley, rye, oats, millet, rice, and maize (corn). The cereal proteins are supplemented by other plant domesticates such as orchard fruits, beans, peas, and edible roots, including taro and potatoes. These cereal, fruit, and vegetable cultigens were all improved upon by cross-pollination and seed selection so that subsequent generations of plants yielded more fruit during a shorter growing season while resisting disease and drought (Fig. 8–4).

Animal husbandry is the planned control of barnyard animals such as sheep, goats, cattle, horses, oxen, pigs, and chickens. All of these animals represent a resource that could be tapped at the farmer's convenience. Stock raising, then, provided a ready and assured supply of meat and such subsidiary products as milk, hides, wool, ligaments, and bone. Selective breeding amplified useful traits, such as above-average milk or wool production or a tendency for high weight gain per unit of forage (Fig. 8–5). Always the

FIGURE 8-5   Simplified diagram showing some of the steps in the evolution of domestic sheep. (a) Section, as seen through a microscope, of skin of wild sheep, showing the arrangement of primary (hair) and secondary (wool) follicles; (b) section, similarly enlarged, of skin of domestic sheep, showing the changed relationship and the change in the size of follicles that accompanied the development of wool.

Source: From "The Ecology of Early Food Production in Mesopotamia," Flannery, K. V., *Science* Vol. 147, pp. 1247–56, 12 March 1965. Copyright 1965 by American Association for the Advancement of Science.

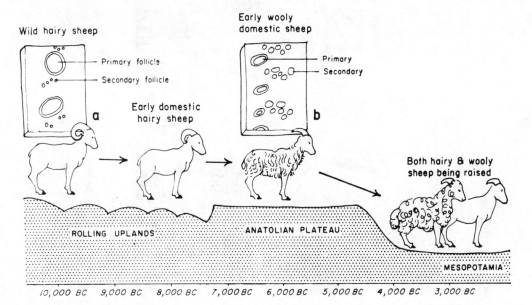

docile animals were retained as breeding stock while the more troublesome youngsters were slaughtered as yearlings.

In the Near East, sheep and goats appeared as domesticates early in the preceramic Neolithic, to be followed by the remaining domesticated stock higher in the stratigraphic column. The ubiquitous dog was domesticated in the Mesolithic in both the New and Old Worlds for use as a sentry and as an aid in hunting large game.

The revolution in human food sources resulted in technical inventions to plant, cultivate, and store the food supply. Some of these technical devices

FIGURE 8-6   Characteristic objects of the prepottery Neolithic culture from the site of Jarmo, Iraq. *Below left,* earliest pottery from the upper levels.

Source: James Mellaart, *Earliest Civilizations of the Near East.* London: Thames and Hudson Ltd., 1970.

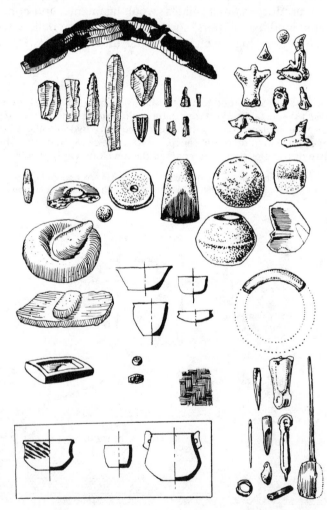

were actually invented during the preceding Mesolithic stage and thus have been characterized as examples of pre-adaptation, that is, preparation for a change before the change is needed. The old dibble, or digging stick, used in Mesolithic times to grub for wild tubers, for example, could be used also to make holes or furrows for seed planting or to cultivate seedlings after the seeds had sprouted. The dibble gradually evolved into the stone-bladed hoe of the Neolithic stage, the wooden plow of the bronze age, and the iron plow of the iron age. To harvest cereal grains, the Neolithic farmers used a stone sickle first invented during the Mesolithic to harvest wild grass seeds. By bronze age times this microlithic reaping-knife had evolved into the metal scythe. Once harvested, grain was carried to the farmyard where the seeds were removed from the straw by threshing. Early threshing was accomplished by driving cattle round and round over grain laid out on a prepared threshing floor. (This method is still used today in peasant populations of the world.) After the hooves broke the grain free, the chaff was winnowed out, or blown away. Once free of chaff, the grain was milled into flour or meal. In early Neolithic times milling was accomplished on a hand-operated mill of grinding stones (Fig. 8–6). Later milling was done with large circular grinding stones powered by water, wind, or animals. The milled flour was boiled as gruel in ceramic vessels, fried as cakes on flat griddles of stone or fired ceramics, or baked as bread in dome-shaped ovens. Flour or grain not needed for immediate consumption could be stored in slab-lined granaries or cylindrical silos. In general, then, the cereal grains provided a food supply that could be prepared in a variety of ways or stored for long periods as a buffer against uncertain times and nonproductive seasons.

Village Settlements

In the Neolithic, the population became sedentary because of the high capital investment of farmers in fixed facilities and equipment such as houses, barns, mills, ovens, storage silos, and arable land. Thus, one of the major consequences of the agricultural revolution was the invention of village architecture. By early Neolithic times permanent, all-weather housing had been designed to ameliorate the extremes of climate and to house large, extended families. Now even the very old and very young members of the household were useful in the new occupation of farming. Youngsters could tend herds of sheep and goats as their Bedouin descendants do today in the Near East. The grandparent generation preserved the oral tradition of farming lore and fertility magic, and served as guardians of the fields. Neolithic families, unlike those of the Paleolithic, were large and included three or more generations.

Houses designed in cubes of equal size could be extended on all sides or stacked like blocks to form communal dwellings of two or more stories. These modular communities, made of sun-dried mud brick in arid lands, are sometimes called *bee-hive villages* (Fig. 8–7). Typically they were rectilinear and

FIGURE 8-7   Two Neolithic villages from the Anatolian plain of Turkey. (a) Plan of building-level VIB at Catal Hüyük around 6000 BC. The letter *S* indicates a shrine. (b) Isometric drawing of a group of houses from Hacilar VI around 5600 BC. Note the horseshoe-shaped ovens in the back walls and small fireplaces in front.

Source: James Mellaart, *Earliest Civilizations of the Near East.* London: Thames and Hudson Ltd., 1970.

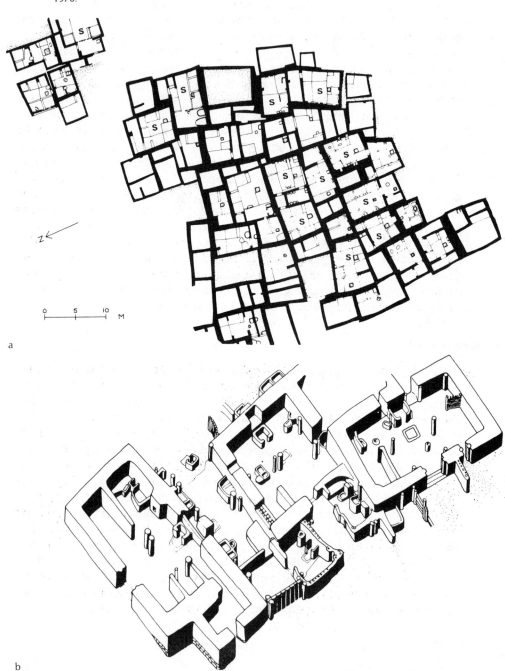

a

b

built around patios or courtyards. Even the earliest of these communities contained some evidence of public buildings, usually shrines. Each room housed a family that had its own food storage facilities, often within the cell-like residence. The family in residence was probably a monogamous, nuclear family that included grandparents (Flannery 1972).

Village life is not necessarily correlated with agriculture (Flannery 1972, p. 24). For instance, some Upper Paleolithic sites of eastern Europe and Russia have yielded evidence of small villages made up of permanent-looking houses but obviously supported by a nonagricultural economy. The persistence of these settlements year after year suggests that the food base was assured and predictable. But in the absence of agriculture, any storable food resource occurring in quantity provides the necessary economic base. Other subsistence activities are the hunting of herd animals, fishing, shellfish collecting, and intensive gathering of grass seeds.

An example of a semipermanent village supported by a nonagricultural subsistence economy is Dolni Vestonice, located in Czechoslovakia between 25,000 and 29,000 BP (Coles and Higgs 1975, pp. 296–98). This Upper Paleolithic hamlet consisted of at least five circular huts. Some were tentlike structures made of mammoth bones covered with skin and warmed by two hearths in the wintertime. Large size, unroofed summer huts also were found. The two kinds of architectural units were arranged around an open compound, with the entire settlement enclosed and protected by mammoth tusks stuck upright in the ground to form a palisade wall. Outside of the enclosed compound, another hut had been built on a hillside. This structure housed an accumulation of artifacts including bone musical instruments. At the center of the room was an oven consisting of a fire hearth covered by a mud dome. The oven contained 2000 fired clay lumps, some of which are small statues of animal heads, bodies, and feet. Identifiable animals include bears, foxes, lions, and mammoths. Other figurine carvings are human heads and Venuses. All of this data suggests that semisedentary village life was practiced in late glacial times and was based on mammoth hunting. The subsistence base of these sophisticated hunting bands was sufficiently stable to support both summer and winter occupancy year after year. Furthermore, the Dolni Vestonice people had sufficient leisure time to develop elaborate and artistically pleasing crafts in carved and modeled figurines that probably held ritual meaning in their lives.

From late Mesolithic times between 7000 and 9000 BC, other Near Eastern settlements of small, circular houses also represent the development of village architecture and sedentary life supported by the mere beginnings of agriculture. These settlers harvested wild wheat and barley, kept domesticated sheep, and hunted wild goats, cattle, and pigs (Higgs and Jarman 1972, pp. 3–4). By 7000 BC these animals and barley were undergoing domestication— the beginnings of true agriculture—in the early Neolithic stage. Thus, the archaeological records show that a sedentary lifestyle and village architecture began long before the appearance of agriculture.

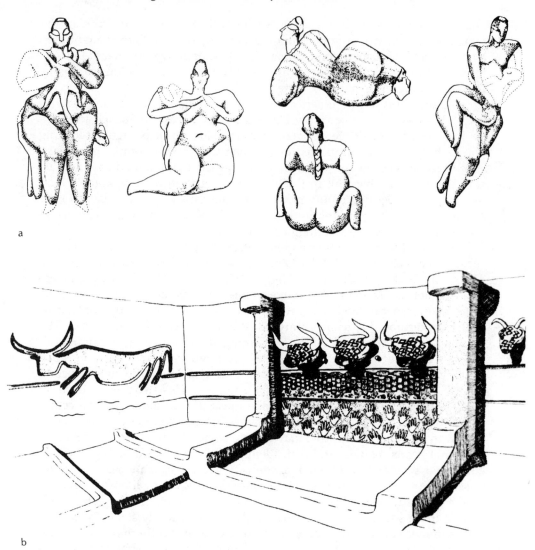

FIGURE 8-8   Ritual artifacts from Neolithic sites in Turkey. (a) A group of naturalistic baked-clay statuettes of the Mother Goddess found in houses in level VI at Hacilar. (b) At level VI, Catal Hüyük, walls of a shrine were decorated with a ram's head, bulls' heads, the cut-out figure of a bull, and paintings of human hands.

Source: James Mellaart, *Earliest Civilizations of the Near East.* London: Thames and Hudson Ltd., 1970.

Specialization

The Neolithic food-producing economy created new roles for some of its members and led to a restructuring of society. Presumably, informal leadership arose in the Paleolithic society through the need for someone skilled in animal lore to head the hunting party. The Neolithic settlers needed someone in authority to arbitrate squabbles involving land trespass and appropriation, theft of farm equipment, pilfering of produce, and other differences that arise both within and between small communities.

Another new role was that of the religious specialist. Cave art indicates that the religious role (shaman or magician) was already in existence late in the Paleolithic stage. During the Neolithic the religious role was formally defined and focused on plant and animal fertility. At Near Eastern sites, shrines with altars and painted wall murals attest to the evolving power of the religious individual, a role that culminated in formal priesthood and state-run religious institutions in the bronze-age civilizations of 3000 BC (Fig. 8–8).

Part-time artisans who appeared in the Neolithic community included the potter, stone mason, lapidary, weaver, brewer, and wood carver. Hand constructed pottery, which was invented by middle Neolithic times, is thought to have been made by women as a routine household task. After the potter's wheel was invented, however, men took over this craft and produced a variety of pots to barter with neighboring households. Increasing specialization in various crafts must have been necessary to equip homes and public buildings such as shrines.

Centers of Population

V. Gordon Childe (1961) felt that sudden spurts in the size of the human population signal important technological changes in food production. He had documented the relationship between far-reaching technological changes during the eighteenth-century industrialization of England and a sudden surge in the population of Great Britain. From this analog model, he concluded that similar growth spurts in the Neolithic and bronze ages must indicate similar revolutions in technology and social organization. The population explosion that he documented for the Neolithic was based on the assured, year-round food supply from mixed planting and stock breeding, which led to increased longevity and a drop in infant mortality. Both of these consequences were confirmed when human skeletons found in Neolithic cemeteries were analyzed for their age at death. Childe's conclusion is that during the Neolithic, the number of people in the world shot up sharply, and the

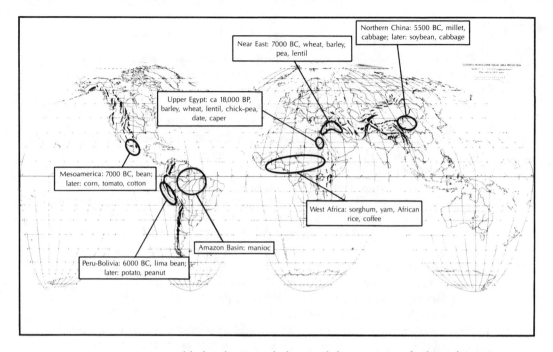

FIGURE 8-9   World distribution of the Neolithic centers of plant domestication. Primary centers are radiocarbon dated while the secondary centers of tropical agriculture are domestication areas of unknown time depth (data from Daniel 1970; Wendorf, Schild, and Close 1982).

Source: Base map © Rand McNally & Company, R.L. 83–5–35. Data from Glyn Daniel, *The First Civilizations,* New York: Thomas Y. Crowell, 1970; F. Wendorf, R. Schild, and A. E. Close, "An Ancient Harvest on the Nile," *Science 82* 3(9):68–73, 1982.

density of population increased because of the new form of adaptation, food production.

The archaeological record shows that the Neolithic revolution occurred independently in many places (Fig. 8–9). Examples of primary centers in the Old World include the Middle East, Southeast Asia, and northern China. Mesoamerica and Peru-Bolivia were two New World domestication centers. In each of these primary centers of domestication, however, the list of domesticated plants and animals varied according to the native wild species whose energy resources were captured.

In the Near East, for instance, the domesticable assemblage was barley and einkorn and emmer wheat, cereal grains that were cultivated by 7000 BC

(Higgs and Jarman 1972, pp. 3–4). As farming spread by migration into Europe (Fig. 8–9) rye and oats replaced wheat and barley. In southwestern Asia, the wheat-barley cereal grains were supplemented by vegetables and fruits such as beets, cabbage, onions, cucumbers, apples, pears, almonds, and somewhat later, grapes, figs, and dates. To these garden crops farmers added two kinds of flax for fiber and oil-rich seeds (Linton 1955). In the Middle East the brewing of beer eliminated the main dietary problem, a shortage of the B-complex vitamins (Linton 1955, p. 94). Along with the garden crops, farmers bred such domesticated animals as cattle, sheep, goats, and donkeys. Sheep (9000 BC) and goats (7500 BC) appear first in the archaeological record to be followed somewhat later by pigs (7000 BC), and cattle (6500 BC). Eventually dromedary camels, horses, and oxen were exploited for meat, transportation, and traction. But particularly important was the invention of milking, which apparently took place only once in the world (Linton 1955, p. 94).

Another primary center of domestication was southeastern Asia, where 12,000-year-old beans have been excavated from the lowest levels of Spirit Cave, Thailand. In younger levels of the cave excavators found pepper, butternut, almond, candlenut, betel nut, cucumber, water chestnut, and peas. Although the domestication of these edible plants is not definitely proven, their consumption by the cave occupants seems likely. Some archaeologists claim that the domestication of plants and the pig, chicken, and dog began in southeast Asia as far back as 13,000 BC (Solheim 1972, p. 6).

In this part of the world, domestication followed two independent paths, one in the lowlands and another in the hill country, both able to support dense populations. In the wet tropical lowlands farmers cultivated such crops as yam, taro, and banana. In addition, breadfruit may have been domesticated here—although it is better known in Oceania—along with the coconut palm and screw pine (Linton 1955, p. 96). The paper mulberry plant also is part of this tropical lowland complex.

Another domestication path is found in the hill country of southeast Asia. Upland crops include yams and several varieties of rice. Dry rice, grown by slash-and-burn agriculture, probably preceded wet rice, grown on irrigated terraces, which later became more common (Linton 1955, p. 101). As a companion trait to wet rice agriculture, farmers domesticated the water buffalo, which supplied milk, meat, and traction for pulling plows and wheeled carts.

Another primary center of Old World domestication arose in northern and central China. Some of the earliest farming communities along the Yellow river are dated to the late sixth millennium BC (Chang 1981, p. 152). Red pottery and villages of semisubterranean houses have been found in association with millet farming and pig raising. In the Yangtze valley, a village excavation has been dated to the late sixth and early fifth millennia BC. Within this early Neolithic context, excavators recovered plant remains identified as rice, bottle gourd, acorn, water chestnut, and sour jujube. Domestic animal bones identify water buffalo, dog, and pig. Other elements of the subsistence economy were hunting, fishing, and collecting shellfish.

All of these activities called for more efficient tools and weapons. Experiments with cold-hammered copper led to the invention of bronze and the end of the stone age.

Bronze Age

The use of metal actually began in the Near East where native copper and lead were cold-hammered around 6000 BC at the site of Catal Hüyük (Mellaart 1979, p. 129). But it was not until cities appeared in Mesopotamia between 3000 and 3500 BC that bronze, an alloy of tin and copper, was invented. The immediate advantages of bronze are that it is more durable than soft native copper and it could be cast in one-, two-, and multiple-piece molds of earth, clay, and stone to manufacture ornaments, vessels, axes, and military equipment like daggers, swords, shields, lances, helmets, and chariot parts.

Urban Civilization

The bronze age is an approximate horizon marker for the first appearance of urban civilization in its various centers of Old World development. Thus, bronze age civilization appears around 3000 BC in the Middle East (Mesopotamia, Egypt), 2500 BC in the Indus valley of Pakistan, and 2000 BC in northern China.

Today the bronze age of Thomsen has been redefined in terms of the new organizational structure of society, state government and stratification of social classes, coupled with intensive agriculture, the adaptive technology on which this social hierarchy rests. This evolution occurred from a Neolithic base at least six different times and in six different places: (1) the Pharaonic society of Egypt, located along the lower Nile river of northeast Africa; (2) the Sumerians of Mesopotamia, between the twin rivers of the Tigris and Euphrates in Iraq; (3) the Indus or Harappan civilization of the Indus valley, Pakistan and India; (4) the Shang dynasty of the Huango Ho (Yellow) river in northern China; (5) Mesoamerica of ancient Mexico, Guatemala, and contiguous parts of Central America; and (6) the Andean civilization of Peru and Bolivia, South America (Fig. 8–10).

Despite this diversity of cultural heritage, Steward (1955) posited a strong convergence in structural form resulting from a common adaptation to arid-land river valleys: Large scale irrigation farming calls for strong, authoritative leadership. Carl Wittfogel (1970) has pointed to these irrigation economies as the source of "oriental despotic societies."

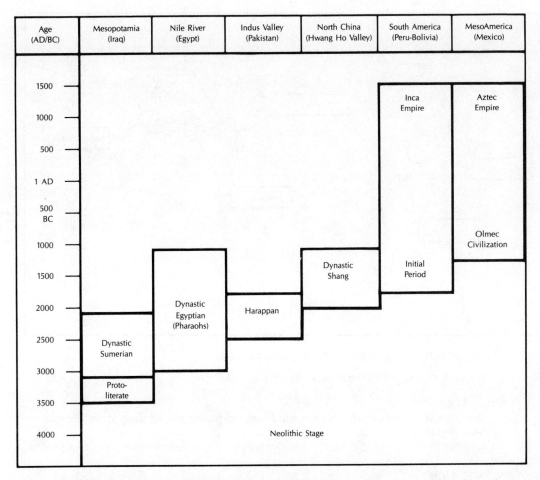

Age (AD/BC)	Mesopotamia (Iraq)	Nile River (Egypt)	Indus Valley (Pakistan)	North China (Hwang Ho Valley)	South America (Peru-Bolivia)	MesoAmerica (Mexico)

FIGURE 8-10 Comparative chronology of early civilizations in the Old and New Worlds.

Certain generalizations apply to the six early civilizations. All occupied a subtropical zone near but not on the equator (Fig. 8–11). Most of these lay in the northern hemisphere and were situated in large, fertile alluvial valleys with a high agricultural potential. All were limited by natural boundaries so that expanding human populations soon found themselves tightly packed and in severe competition for agricultural lands to feed their citizens. Most of the civilizations grew up along rivers and developed economies based on intensive irrigation agriculture. A history of this form of agriculture reveals

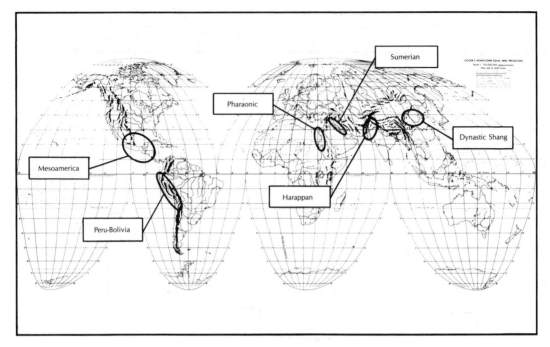

FIGURE 8-11   World distribution of early civilizations.

Source: Base map © Rand McNally & Company, R.L. 83–5–35.

the manner in which this technology has led to the rise of despotic state governments.

Irrigation Agriculture

Agriculture of the Early Neolithic was an outgrowth of Mesolithic practices involving the harvest by microlithic sickle of natural stands of wild grasses or those stands that had sprung up around camp as a result of human intervention. Probably agriculture began 9000 years ago with the intentional sowing of wild grass seeds, which once germinated, were given a minimum of attention and grew at the whim of natural rainfall. During the anathermal climatic period, however, many arid lands were better watered than those same areas are today, especially in the hill country where agriculture began (Braidwood 1975).

But after 5500 BC, as the altithermal climate began to warm and become increasingly more arid in many parts of the world, upland dry farming became so risky that farmers began to plant their crops in the valley bottoms in the rich alluvial soils of major rivers (Lamberg-Karlovsky 1979, p. 165). Since many of these flood plains were marshlands with water-logged soils, often the problem was too much rather than too little water. But through a combination of drainage canals to drain off water and other canals to lead water to the well-drained, arable plots, small-scale irrigation agriculture began. At first these irrigation systems were probably constructed by a farmer and his kinsmen for one or two fields. Of course, reciprocity called for one kinsman to help another. As the ditch systems were expanded and joined, single farm canals were merged with others until water conduits were village-wide. The system expanded until it covered the entire river valley supporting a Late Neolithic town and ultimately to control by a state capital. The medithermal climate after 2500 BC amplified this process. As rainfall increased, snow accumulated in the high mountains and provided the spring runoff needed for planting.

The basic elements of a gravity-flow irrigation system are simple, but each part must be carefully fitted to every other part for a smooth and successful operation (Fig. 8–12). Upstream, a dam impounds sufficient water to feed the headgate of the master canal. Usually the dam is not of solid construction but rather porous so that excess water can pass through it without the need for spillway or bypass structures. Once in the master canal, the water is led at a low gradient away from the river and toward the side of the valley (Fig. 8–12b). In this manner a hydrostatic head is built up as the canal waters are gradually raised above the river gradient. From this elevated position, the irrigation waters can be dumped onto floodplain fields from small lateral ditches, which are controlled by gates or simply by breaking and refilling the earthen walls of the master canal. The fields, themselves, are furrowed lengthwise to lead the irrigation waters back to the lowest, central portion of the valley where the waste water tailings re-enter the river.

Several technical problems may arise in such gravity-fed waterworks. Breaks and washouts frequently occur in the dirt-excavated canals if the gradient in the master canal is too steep or if natural gullies cross the canal line on their way to the river. Or conversely, the canals may silt up if their gradient is too shallow and there is heavy input of silt from the headgate. A more serious problem is salt contamination in the fields. Irrigation waters leach salt from the fields and dump it into the river. When the water is picked up for reuse by downstream irrigation systems, the salt contaminates the next lower field. As downstream fields become contaminated, their productivity drops off and salt-intolerant crops such as wheat may have to be replaced by less useful crops such as barley (Jacobsen and Adams 1974, p. 285). Eventually old fields may have to be abandoned altogether until an entire river valley has been exhausted of farming potential.

Other problems of a social nature had far-reaching consequences for the rise of leadership, authority, and preferential treatment among citizens of a bronze-age town or city. Any given irrigation system tends to favor upstream farmers with fields located near the headgate. The downstream fields are often shorted in their water needs. When strife built up between favored and un-

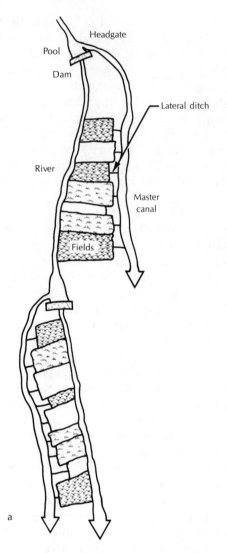

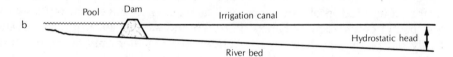

FIGURE 8-12   Schematic diagram of two irrigation systems in a single river valley. (a) A dam impounds water and diverts it into a canal; water flows through irrigation ditches and back into the river; (b) a longitudinal section compares the level of the canal with the level of the natural river bed.

favored water users, one man was appointed as ditch boss or manager to arbitrate disputes and measure water flow through laterals in a fair and equitable manner. A measuring device might be a pan with a hole in the bottom. The ditch boss floated this pan in the canal and timed the flow of field-diverted water until the measuring pan eventually sank. As the ditch boss measured the flow of lateral diversion for each villager, an equitable apportionment was effected. But if a drought occurred during any given year, the downstream fields were shorted and produced a meager crop. The result was hard feelings within the community of water users, all of whom had invested in the construction and maintenance of the waterworks. In addition, the ditch boss might favor his kinsmen not only in water allocation but also in assignment to upstream field locations. Slowly over the years, the egalitarian social relations that characterized a Neolithic farming village were replaced by nonegalitarian relations dividing the rich and the poor. Imperceptibly, the social dynamics shifted in the direction of a class-structured society of ''haves'' and ''have-nots'' as citizens became unequal in their socioeconomic standing within the community.

When two or more irrigation systems occupy the same valley and compete for the same finite amount of river discharge, as shown in Figure 8–12, an intercommunity conflict arises. The downstream irrigation system is shorted of water because of upstream use, and the waters it receives are polluted by silt and noxious salt. The downstream community complains to the upstream community, and if a compromise is not reached, or compensation not offered, then intervillage warfare may result. Irrigation systems are particularly vulnerable to vandalism since damage to the dam, master canal, head gate, or valves on lateral ditches will cause the system to break down. Retaliation by the victimized community might lead to a valley-wide collapse in productivity.

Several obvious solutions to such intercommunity strife are possible: (1) An engineering solution would merge the systems by building one integrated, valley-wide waterworks with the capacity to serve more fields by pushing the master canal to a higher level along the rim of the valley; (2) in a military solution, one community would conquer the neighboring communities and dictate water allocation thereafter. In either case, Steward (1955) has pointed to the tendency for irrigation systems to expand and integrate until they fill entire valleys with administration in the hands of a single water-managing bureaucracy. This development was associated with elitism and the rise of bronze age cities. The new elite included both water managers and military leaders, since what is once gained must be defended for the profit of the upper class, which eventually controls and directs a vast population of peasant farmers.

This new form of technical adaptation increased the crop yield compared to the yield from dry farming by individual villages. Furthermore, unlike upland dry fields that were relocated every few years because of soil exhaustion, irrigated fields were freshly fertilized by new silt and soil nutrients from the irrigation waters passing over them. Large-scale irrigation led to more sedentary existence and the build-up of local population.

State Government

The economic effects of increased food production intensified the trend that in Neolithic times had already begun to differentiate specialists from the common agrarian citizens. Specialized roles developed when part of the population had been released from direct involvement in food production. The new specialists lived off the labor of the peasant farmer, who contributed to the new form of political institution, the state government, through taxes paid in goods and raw labor. The new elite were administrators such as priests, princes, scribes, and bureaucratic officials. Craftsmen, who had been part-time specialists in Neolithic village society, now became full-time specialists in the bronze age town and city. Professional soldiers and a standing army led by an aristocratic officer corps replaced the voluntary citizens' militia of the Neolithic town. All of these nonfarming members of society occupied a privileged position as the upper class in a new social form, the class-stratified social organization. From the democratic Neolithic village, where every male head of household voted in community-wide decision making, control shifted to a few top administrators, who decided the fate of thousands of underlings, peasant freemen, serfs, and slaves.

Laborers were needed for all kinds of public works. Canals had to be constructed and maintained. City defensive works must be built and manned at the cost of thousands of lives. Years of off-season labor poured into erecting the moats, walls, and battle towers that ringed the urban capital of every city-state. In those rare early bronze age civilizations that were run by a dispersed, rural aristocracy, central fortified points of refuge were constructed on high, commanding hilltops as points of retreat should armies of a neighboring valley invade.

Because of the efficiency of irrigation farming, intense farm labor during the summer months produced enough food to support large masses of people and fill the state granaries. Workers had idle time during the off-farming season, and it was this idleness that the state feared (Mendelssohn 1974). For this reason, when all other forms of public works had been completed—water projects, defense battlements, roads, bridges, civic and religious buildings—then the enslaved agrarian populace was turned to the construction of such monumental works as gigantic tombs and the sculptured likenesses of the maximum leader, which advertised the ruthless power of the king, the ruling house, and the state government (Fig. 8–13). Nationalism, or at least civic consciousness, had begun to play a prominent role in the mind of the citizen.

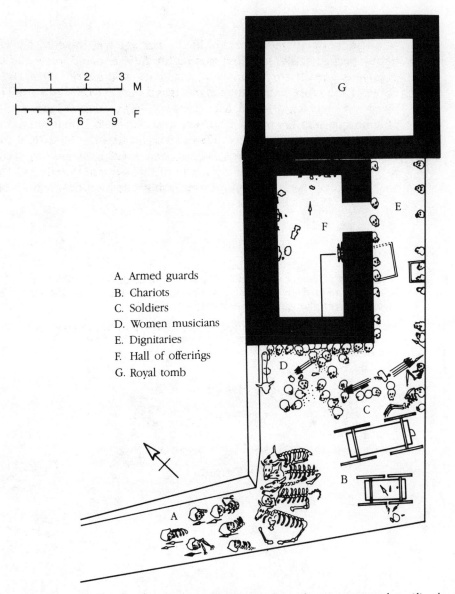

A. Armed guards
B. Chariots
C. Soldiers
D. Women musicians
E. Dignitaries
F. Hall of offerings
G. Royal tomb

FIGURE 8-13   The Royal tomb of Queen Shubad (Puabi) with arrangement of sacrificed victims, 2400 BC, Sumerian civilization.

Source: C. C. Lamberg-Karlovsky and Jeremy A. Sabloff, *Ancient Civilizations: The Near East and Mesopotamia,* Figure 3.8, Menlo Park, CA: The Benjamin/Cummings Publishing Company, Inc., 1979.

THE CITY

The new settlement form of the bronze age was the city. The city was a tightly packed settlement that was highly differentiated internally and competitive externally for labor, food, materials, and energy (Figs. 8–14, 8–15). Some of the more important differentiated parts of the city were (1) palace, (2) sacred precinct, (3) industrial quarter(s), (4) market or bazaar, (5) a fringe of slum quarters for peasant farmers and displaced urban immigrants. The palace was the living quarters of the secular leader—the king—and his family, concubines, servants, guards, slaves, and royal hostages from conquered neighboring city-states. The opulence of these quarters reflected the power and wealth of the kingdom in terms of both its own economic productivity

FIGURE 8-14   Map of the city of Nippur inscribed on a clay tablet dating from about 1500 BC, Sumerian civilization. The writing on the map gives the names of various buildings, rivers, and gates in Sumerian and Akkadian.

Source: Reprinted from *The Sumerians* by Samuel N. Kramer by permission of The University of Chicago Press. Copyright © 1973 by The University of Chicago Press.

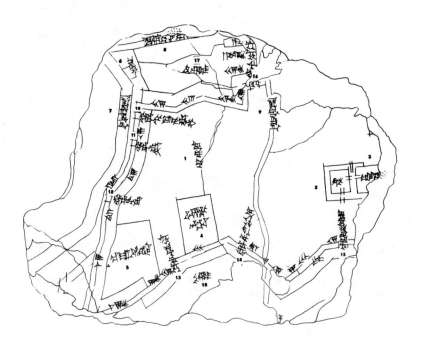

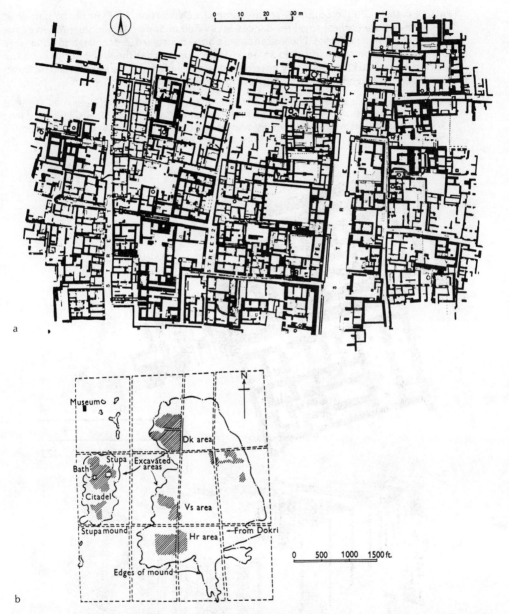

FIGURE 8-15 Gridded street plan of Mohenjo-daro, a bronze age city of the Indus civilization. (a) The HR residential quarter of the city; (b) overall plan of the city showing the location of the HR quarter and also the citadel or civic center.

Source: Mortimer Wheeler, *Civilizations of the Indus Valley.* London: Thames and Hudson Ltd., 1972.

FIGURE 8-16   Public buildings of the Sumerian civilization. (a) Plan of the palace at Kish—one of the earliest royal residences excavated in Sumer; (b) reconstruction of the temple at Harmal (1900 BC). The entrance vestibule, courtyard, antecella, and cella were arranged with communicating doors on a single axis, so that the niche in the cella, on which the statue of the deity may have rested, was visible from the street when all doors were open. Life-sized terra-cotta lions guarded the doorways.

Source: (a) From C. C. Lamberg-Karlovsky and Jeremy A. Sabloff, *Ancient Civilizations: The Near East and Mesopotamia,* Figure 3.9, Menlo Park, CA: The Benjamin/Cummings Publishing Company, Inc., 1979. (b) Reprinted from *The Sumerians* by Samuel N. Kramer by permission of The University of Chicago Press. Copyright © 1973 by The University of Chicago Press.

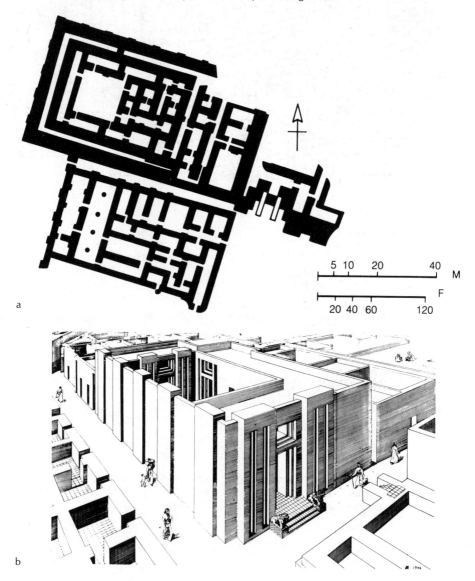

and the booty it had obtained by plundering neighboring city-states (Fig. 8–16a).

The sacred precinct was a temple area set aside for the rites of polytheistic religion. Often a wall separated the sacred ground from the profane portion of the city to symbolize prevention of secular contamination. But on special religious holidays, the citizens were allowed into the precinct to observe pageantry by the priesthood, including animal and human sacrifices. The sacred precinct usually housed one or more temples, often elevated on truncated pyramids, which served as a stage for religious ritual. The priesthood, dedicated to a large number of nature, agriculture, and war gods, collected tribute in the name of these gods. Taxes were paid in goods, services, and sacrifices (even of infants). Dry goods were kept in storehouses for the city gods. In addition, the walled precinct surrounded residential buildings for the priests and priestesses, novices, scribes, and sacrificial victims waiting their slaughter to the gods on a feast day (Fig. 8–16b).

Industrial quarters of the city included workshops and residences for the various artisans. Often each craft was segregated in one district, run by a guild that might be kinship based.

The city market(s) were large, open courts where merchants, craftsmen, and peasant farmers assembled to exchange goods. By the iron age coinage had been invented but even in the bronze age mediums of exchange or standard value commodities were in use. The market was an exchange point for the products of specialists and the foodstuffs of the farmer. Markets were rotated by region and day of the week on a schedule so that farmers and outlying villagers could journey into town on the assigned day.

Merchants, as a separate and privileged class, were often housed near the marketplace. They conducted the import and export trade and often traveled under military escort when passing through foreign lands. In addition, they operated ports-of-trade at intermediate points between two cities or took up residency in a foreign city to supervise export of goods to their hometowns. Goods that moved over these state-sponsored trade networks included both raw materials not found in the alluvial valleys and luxury items, such as gold, silver, or gems, for status display of the elite. Trade was an important factor in the spread of civilization from primary to secondary points of development.

SOCIAL CLASSES

The decision-making regulator in the bronze age city was the state government. Although autocratically run by a king or supreme ruler, the government was made up of a hierarchy of officials. Two sets of rules governed the behavior and well-being of the state citizen: (1) a set of codified laws, and (2) the bribe used to pay off the avarice and greed of individual bureaucrats. Archival records tell of courts of law staffed by one or more judges who heard cases involving disputes between litigants (Kramer 1963). These judges had

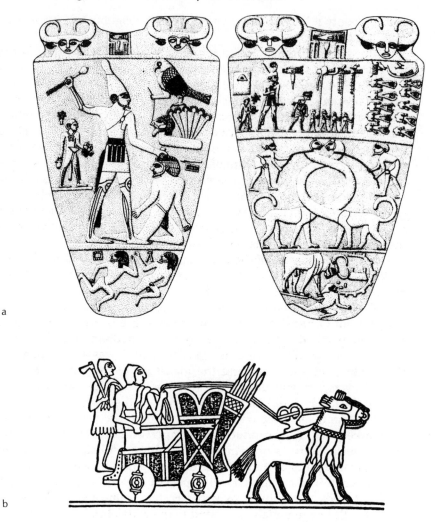

FIGURE 8-17   Military scenes from two early civilizations. (a) One side of this carved stone votive plaque (3200 BC) depicts a man wearing the crown of Upper Egypt and subjugating an individual. The other side shows a man wearing the combined crowns of Upper and Lower Egypt marching behind standard bearers and rows of decapitated individuals. (b) Early Sumerian war chariot.

Source: (a) From C. C. Lamberg-Karlovsky and Jeremy A. Sabloff, *Ancient Civilizations: The Near East and Mesopotamia,* Figure 3.3, Menlo Park, CA: The Benjamin/Cummings Publishing Company, Inc., 1979. (b) V. Gordon Childe, 1961, *Man Makes Himself,* p. 102, by permission of Pitman Books Ltd., London.

the power to fine, incarcerate, or execute those who were found guilty, or to sell them into bondage. Often fines were in the form of lost land, withheld irrigation waters, or repayment to the claimant. To insure compliance, a police force was at hand.

The civil bureaucracy included scribes for record keeping, tax collecting, and letter writing. Also the historical documents mention governmental inspectors for roads, warehouses, and craft production. Often merchants who traveled abroad were spies seeking information on the military preparedness of neighboring states. Civil administration included the technocrats who managed and engineered the construction of public works such as the irrigation projects. They also designed and built catapults and battering rams that were engines of destruction in siege warfare.

The third branch of the bronze age city government was the standing army, which dealt with neighboring city-states by threat and exploitation. A trained officer class of landholding aristocrats stood ready at all times to lead the peasant farmers into battle (Fig. 8–17). Each farmer brigade was a kinship unit that fought under their clan banner. Military service during time of war was part of their obligation to the king and the state. The strategy of the army included use of the infantry phalanx, chariot attack, siege warfare, and frontal attacks on fixed positions using scaling ladders, battering rams, and catapults. Specialized military equipment was kept in a state armory until needed. Individual weapons included swords, bow and arrow, slings, and burning oil. Armor included shields, helmets, and mail.

Another important arm of the government was the state granary. This building served as a bank repository for the taxes and tribute used to finance public works such as canals, city walls, sculptural likenesses of the megalomaniacal king, and royal tombs. The state also used these goods and produce stored in the granary as a source of capital in foreign trade and to feed troops while engaged in siege warfare. Foodstuffs in the granary were redistributed to peasants in times of famine, enemy attack, pestilence, or drought (Adams 1973).

Writing

Because of the large size of the city-state, the face-to-face communication of the Neolithic village had long ago broken down. Now communication involved written edicts from persons in authority, announcements by the town crier, and letters delivered by messengers traveling over state roads in relays.

A civilization, as a complex social system, must have a memory unit. Simple, band-organized societies utilize the memory of the grandparent generation and myth and legend as bodies of information concerning the solutions to adaptive problems. The heterogeneous nature of civilization, however, precludes reliance solely on individual memory or myth. For this reason, written records are essential to the running of urban societies. And, in fact, nearly all of the early, pristine civilizations invented some form of writing early in their history. At first these systems were largely picture writing but they gradually evolved so that the pictures took on a symbolic quality. The ultimate development was the invention of an alphabet in which groups of letters could express the phonetics of the language.

But each early civilization had its own system of writing. The Sumerians wrote on tablets of wet clay with a triangular-shaped stylus, using cuneiform writing (Fig. 8–18). The Egyptians used hieroglyphic writing painted on papyrus paper scrolls, while the Shang Chinese used a pictographic writing cast on bronze vessels and scratched on divining bones. All of these writing systems served the purpose of recording important state statistics such as size of population in each region, tax rolls, tribute owed, or labor levy.

The bronze age civilizations, then, are marked by the rise of a literate tradition. The literate specialists, called *literati*, were the priests and scribes, who kept records for the church and state, ran schools to educate the sons and daughters of the aristocratic class, and developed related symbol systems such as mathematics, calendars, and astronomy-astrology lore. Both church

FIGURE 8-18   Early form of Egyptian hieroglyphics from Abydos (3000 BC) and Mesopotamian pictographs and cuneiform from Uruk (3300 BC).

Source: From C. C. Lamberg-Karlovsky and Jeremy A. Sabloff, *Ancient Civilizations: The Near East and Mesopotamia,* Figure 3.4, Menlo Park, CA: The Benjamin/Cummings Publishing Company, Inc., 1979.

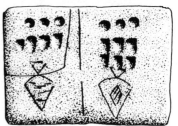

and state kept archives for commercial records such as taxes, bills of sale, deeds, census, and inventory of holdings. The priests kept libraries for religious books so that many of the myths and legends of Neolithic times were written down to preserve the oral literature of an earlier age, an example being the Epic of Gilgamesh (Mason 1972).

Bronze age civilizations were a new structural form of society in which functional cohesiveness was achieved through differentiation of social status organized into stratified classes. Whereas all earlier forms of society—band, tribe, and chiefdom—had been organized according to increasingly more complex kinship systems, in the primitive state, kinship remained important only within a class or occupational group. Classes were based on (1) differential access to wealth and resources, (2) social prestige as publicly displayed through status symbols such as jewelry, clothing, mannerisms, and speech, and (3) birth, so that status in society was acquired through one's parents rather than by individual achievement. The aristocratic rulers directed secular matters such as the agricultural economy, diplomacy with neighboring states, foreign trade, and the standing, professional army (Fig. 8–19). This same aris-

FIGURE 8-19   A composite picture of Sumerian city-state social organization.

Source: Adapted from Robert McAdams, *The Evolution of Urban Society.* Chicago: Aldine, 1966.

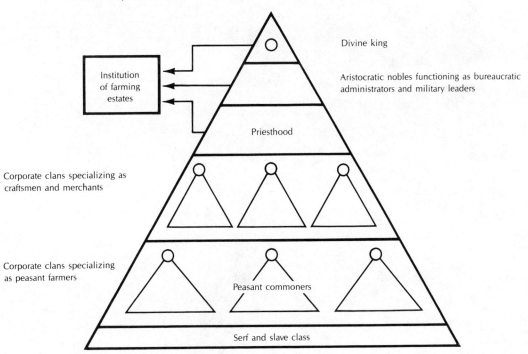

tocratic segment of society provided sons and daughters for the priesthood to conduct worship of the many city gods on feast days.

The middle class was made up of government bureaucrats, advisors to the king, merchants, and artisans. And finally, the lower class was comprised of free peasant farmers, slaves captured in war, and serfs sold into bondage as a result of debt. The peasant class provided labor for public works construction, paid taxes based on farm goods and labor levy, and served as foot soldiers in the army during wars. One's relative standing in the urban community could be defined quite accurately according to the kinds of taxes paid to the state. The lower class provided both physical labor and produce; the middle class paid in nonphysical service and craft products, and the upper class paid only in loyalty to the king.

FIGURE 8-20   The limits of iron working in the eastern Mediterranean world at 1000 BC.

Source: Colin McEvedy, *The Penguin Atlas of Ancient History,* drawn by John Woodcock (Penguin Books 1967), p. 41. Copyright © Colin McEvedy, 1967. All rights reserved. Reprinted by permission of Penguin Books Ltd.

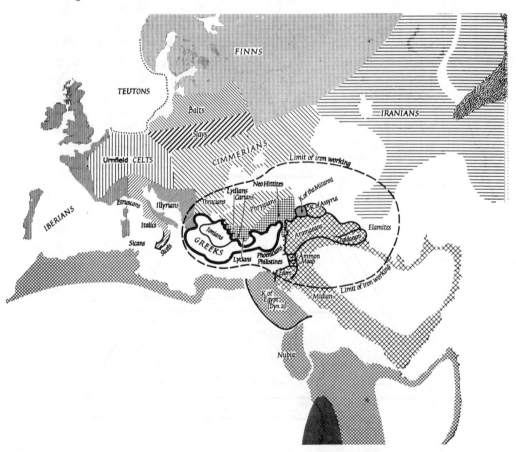

Iron Age

Although some ornamental use of iron was known throughout the bronze age, it was not until sometime between 1200 and 1000 BC that the use of iron began to replace the use of copper and its alloys (Maddin and others 1977; McEvedy 1970). The transition from one metallurgy to the other began in the Near East and gradually spread by diffusion, trade, and ethnic migration in ever wider circles thoughout Europe, Asia, and Africa (Fig. 8–20) (McEvedy 1970, p. 49).

Iron, unlike copper, does not occur in pure nugget form in sufficient quantities to supply the military needs of the conquest empires of the last millennium BC. For this reason, the early ironsmiths needed access to metallic ore bodies. The process of reducing ore to pure iron by smelting had been invented by the bronze age metalworkers, who filled a stone furnace with alternating layers of charcoal and ore combined with a flux (Fig. 8–21). When the charcoal was ignited and aerated with a bellows or a flue, the ore melted into a puddle of pure metal at the bottom of the furnace. In the case of iron, the smelted ore had to be treated by forging (hammering) to remove impurities and shape the metal into finished form. The early ironworkers of the Mediterranean world could not achieve sufficiently high temperatures to cast iron into useful objects; this process was accomplished much later by the Chinese (Maddin and others 1977). Iron did not replace bronze until several additional metallurgical processes had been invented: quenching, tempering,

FIGURE 8-21   Iron smelter, seen here in a speculative reconstruction based on the remains of European iron age furnaces, was first filled with a mixed charge of ore, usually hematite or magnetite, and charcoal (a). The charge was ignited and the furnace temperature was raised to about 1200 degrees Celsius by a draft. Because iron does not melt below 1537 degrees C. the product of the smelting process (b) was the spongy mixture of nonmetallic wastes and iron known as a *bloom*. The blacksmith reheated the bloom on a forge to above 1170 degrees C., making the wastes viscous. The smith then removed the wastes from the iron by hammering. What remained was soft iron.

Source: From "How the Iron Age Began" by Robert Maddin, James D. Muhly, and Tamara S. Wheeler. Copyright © 1977 by Scientific American, Inc. All rights reserved.

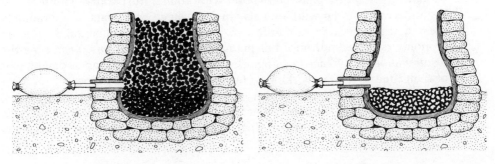

and steeling. Quenching involves plunging the glowing metal object into cold water to achieve brittleness. Tempering is the further forging of the object by pounding it on an anvil, and steeling involves smelting in the presence of an abundance of carbon, which penetrates the metal and adds superior strength (Maddin and others 1977). All of these processes, which make iron objects superior to bronze, were invented and commonly used by the fourth century BC. By 900 BC, documents referred to a large inventory of iron objects including axes, hoes, picks, saws, arrowheads, scissors, fetters, and iron furniture and lamps. Iron had replaced bronze in military weapons also. Iron served not only the ruling elite, the warrior class of bronze age society, but also the common peasant farmer. With it forest lands of Europe and Africa were cleared for crops and heavy clay soils were tilled to open up vast new areas for agrarian colonization.

The social consequences of the iron age were an intensification of the warfare begun by the bronze age city-states and the growth of ever larger conquest empires. Such imperial states controlled vast populations, exacted tribute from conquered peoples, and controlled far-flung trade networks, both overland and maritime. Clearly the new form of human adaptation was warfare by means of standing armies employing iron weapons.

Summary

Cultural evolution can be traced through the Mesolithic, Neolithic, bronze, and iron ages as progressive steps in human adaptation to the natural and social environments of the times. The adaptive practices of the early postglacial Mesolithic hunters involved a reorientation from the large Pleistocene herd animals to the smaller, solitary forest game. Instead of hunting in large parties, individual hunters stalked their prey with bow and arrow, shooting from ambush. Food gathering by women led to the knowledge of plants as food sources and set humankind on the path to agriculture and food production. After Mesolithic economies were expanded to include fish, shellfish, and water fowl, a seasonal shortage in one food source could be made up by increased reliance on another.

The new form of adaptation, sometimes called the *Neolithic* or *agricultural revolution*, combined plant cultivation with animal husbandry. Hunters had begun to bring home wild animals, such as sheep and goats, and gradually these animals became domesticated. This significant transition in human economy occurred not once but many times in many places. Each time the result was settled village farming. The Neolithic peoples began to devote part of their time to crafts, working in textiles, ceramics, and copper.

The farming villages, which grew up in the flood plains along rivers, became the cities of the bronze age. Most of these early civilizations employed irrigation agriculture as the principal adaptive technology to feed increasingly large numbers of sedentary populations. With the advent of intensive agriculture, only part of the manpower was needed to produce food. Some workers began to specialize in crafts, while others contributed administrative skills. As the flood plains became overcrowded, competition developed. A strong, authoritative leadership was needed to mediate disputes about water and property rights. Nevertheless, some farmers became rich and others became poor. During the bronze age, the Old World was stratified into lower, middle, and upper classes, under the control of a despotic ruler. The bronze age marks the beginning of urban civilization, but it also marks the beginning of serfdom and of warfare between neighboring city-states.

Warfare was a means of capturing ever larger supplies of energy to fuel the needs of the predatory state, now evolving into the conquest empire. The development of iron age technology provided the necessary weapons.

References

ADAMS, ROBERT McC.
  1973   *The Evolution of Urban Society.* Chicago: Aldine.

BRAIDWOOD, ROBERT J.
  1975   *Prehistoric Men.* Chicago: Scott, Foresman.

CHANG, K. C.
  1981   In Search of China's Beginnings: New Light on an Old Civilization. *American Scientist* 69:148–60.

CHILDE, V. GORDON
  1961   *Man Makes Himself.* New York: New American Library.

CLARK, GRAHAM
  1977   *World Prehistory.* Cambridge: Cambridge University Press.

COLES, J. M., and E. S. HIGGS
  1975   *The Archaeology of Early Man.* Baltimore: Peregrine.

DANIEL, GLYN
  1970   *The First Civilizations.* New York: Thomas Y. Crowell.

FAGAN, BRIAN M.
  1977   *People of the Earth.* Boston: Little, Brown.

FLANNERY, KENT V.
  1973   The Ecology of Early Food Production in Mesopotamia. In *In Search of Man,* edited by Ernestene L. Green. Boston: Little, Brown.

HIGGS, E. S., and M. R. JARMAN
  1972   The Origins of Animal and Plant Husbandry. In *Papers in Economic Prehistory,* edited by E. S. Higgs. Cambridge: Cambridge University Press.

HOWELL, F. CLARK, and EDITORS OF TIME-LIFE BOOKS
  1968   *Early Man.* New York: Time-Life Books.

ISSAC, GLYNN
  1974   Stratigraphy and Patterns of Cultural Change in the Middle Pleistocene. *Current Anthropology* 15(4):508–14.

JACOBSEN, THORKILD, and ROBERT M. ADAMS
  1974   Salt and Silt in Ancient Mesopotamian Agriculture. In *The Rise and Fall of Civilizations*, edited by C. C. Lamberg-Karlovsky and Jeremy A. Sabloff. Menlo Park, Calif.: Cummings, pp. 282–94.

KRAMER, SAMUEL NOAH
  1963   *The Sumerians.* Chicago: University of Chicago Press.

LAMBERG-KARLOVSKY, C. C., and JEREMY A. SABLOFF
  1979   *Ancient Civilizations.* Menlo Park, Calif.: Benjamin/Cummings.

LINTON, RALPH
  1955   *The Tree of Culture.* New York: Alfred A. Knopf.

MADDIN, ROBERT, JAMES D. MUHLY, and TAMARA S. WHEELER
  1977   How the Iron Age Began. *Scientific American* 237(4):122–31.

MASON, HERBERT
  1972   *Gilgamesh: A Verse Narrative.* New York: New American Library.

MCEVEDY, COLIN
  1970   *The Penguin Atlas of Ancient History.* Manchester, England: Jesse Broad.

MELLAART, JAMES
  1970   *Earliest Civilizations of the Near East.* New York: McGraw-Hill.

  1979   A Neolithic City in Turkey. In *Hunters, Farmers, and Civilizations*. San Francisco: W. H. Freeman and Company Publishers.

MENDELSSOHN, KURT
  1974   A Scientist Looks at the Pyramids. In *The Rise and Fall of Civilizations*, edited by Jeremy A. Sabloff and C. C. Lamberg-Karlovsky. Menlo Park, Calif.: Cummings.

SOLHEIM, WILHELM G. III
  1972   An Earlier Agricultural Revolution. *Scientific American* 226(4):2–9.

STEWARD, JULIAN H.
  1955   Development of Complex Societies: Cultural Causality and Law. In *Theory of Culture Change*. Urbana: University of Illinois Press.

WHEELER, MORTIMER
  1972   *Civilizations of the Indus Valley and Beyond.* New York: McGraw-Hill.

9
Settlement of the New World

New World prehistory demonstrates many striking evolutionary parallels with Old World prehistory despite the lack of convincing evidence for historic contact. Thus, the New World serves as a powerful test case for a theory of world evolution in which the same principles of growth and development lead to the same end—civilized society.

Compared to Old World civilization, the human society of the New World is a relatively recent phenomenon. Archaeological evidence shows that early sites in the New World are no more than 16,000 to 20,000 years old. Other evidence supports the idea that humans are a recent arrival in the New World. For instance, no known early fossil hominids comparable to the Australopithecines, *Homo erectus*, or Neanderthal grades have been found in the New World. Instead, all known early skeletal finds in the New World are classified *Homo sapiens sapiens*. Furthermore, the nonhominid primates are all New World monkeys rather than apes, which suggests that no proto-hominids, such as the Dryopithecines, were present in the New World to provide the evolutionary springboard for hominid evolution. The earliest inhabitants of North and South America probably immigrated from Asia via the Bering straits, a narrow neck of arctic waters separating Siberian Asia from Alaska (Fig. 9-1). This route is postulated because the 60-mile-wide strait, with its stepping stones of islands called the *Diomedes*, represents the shortest passage for *Homo sapiens* immigrants. During glacial episodes when world sea levels were lower, a land bridge may have linked Asia and America. A second hy-

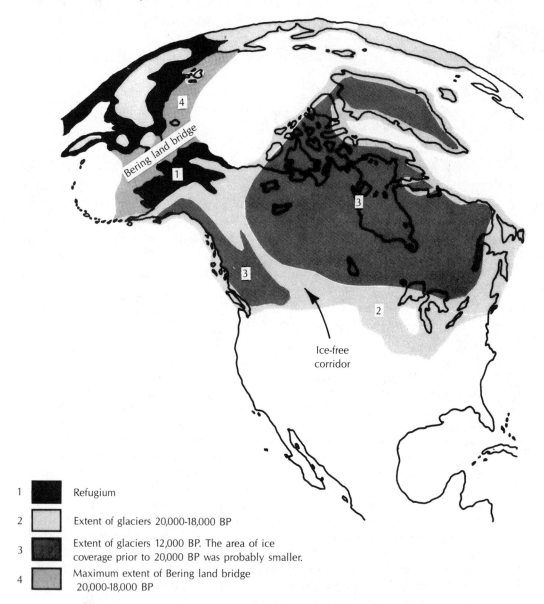

1	Refugium
2	Extent of glaciers 20,000-18,000 BP
3	Extent of glaciers 12,000 BP. The area of ice coverage prior to 20,000 BP was probably smaller.
4	Maximum extent of Bering land bridge 20,000-18,000 BP

FIGURE 9-1   Distribution of the Bering land bridge (4), ice-free areas (1), and extent of glaciers.

Source: From *Ancient Native Americans*, edited by Jesse D. Jennings. Copyright © 1978 by W. H. Freeman and Company. All rights reserved.

pothesis is that the immigrants used canoe-type boats, a not impossible technical development despite the lack of any actual boat remains from an Old World Upper Paleolithic assemblage. And finally, it may have been possible to walk across the strait during the winter when the Bering sea was frozen solid. The last two possibilities have been accomplished by Eskimos during recent times.

It seems reasonable that Upper Paleolithic hunting bands from glacier-free Siberia reached Alaska during the late Pleistocene epoch. Perhaps they were stalking large herbivores such as bison or mammoth. Once in ice-free Alaska, however, these earliest immigrants would have been hemmed in on the south by continental ice sheets that extended from the Great Lakes westward to the Cascade range of Oregon. Study by geologists of the late Pleistocene glacial history has indicated that these sheets parted before 20,000 BP and again after 12,000 BP to form an ice-free corridor toward the close of the last New World glaciation, the Wisconsin, which is equivalent to the Würm/Weichsel of Europe. Paleontologists believe that herds of Pleistocene herbivores grazed southward through this corridor with predatory humans in close attendance. Of course, once they reached the southern front of the continental ice, the animals and human hunting bands were free to disperse southward, ultimately settling in North, Central, and South America. That this process was completed by at least 11,000 years ago is demonstrated by the finding of radiocarbon-dated tools and stemmed projectile points in Fell's and Palli Aike caves located on the straits of Magellan at the southern tip of South America (Lynch 1978). Otherwise, direct evidence for this hypothesized peopling of the New World is sparse and the immigration hypotheses are largely untested. The strongest arguments are those provided by geography and glacial history. The supporting evidence of Upper Paleolithic archaeology, in particular the core-blade technology of stone tool manufacture, points to a Siberian heartland for dispersal into the New World. Linguistic evidence is lacking since New World aboriginal languages have few counterparts with those of Asia.

Certainly the C–14 age of the earliest archaeological sites indicates considerable antiquity, but these are minimal ages since the actual immigration must have taken place some time before hunting bands actually reached the tip of South America. Furthermore, the rate of movement is not easy to calculate because a southward shift by any particular hunting band would have occurred only in the pursuit of seasonally migrating game or as a result of dispersal of a hunting community to relieve human population pressure— both necessarily slow processes (Haynes 1966).

Some writers speculate that the New World was settled as the result of transoceanic voyages. These hypotheses usually favor a Pacific ocean route with boats island hopping from Asia (Jett 1978). Hypothetical boat crossings of the Atlantic are less favored in the archaeological literature. Of course, popular writings and movies depicting the experimental raft trips of Thor Heyerdahl and his party support the reverse hypothesis, that South American indians peopled the eastern Pacific (Heyerdahl 1962). All of these maritime hypotheses suggest that civilizations or high (socially complex) cultures were introduced to the New World by small boatloads of Old World immigrants. None of these historical explanations is generally accepted by anthropological archaeologists. The prevailing opinion is that native Americans held the same genius as peoples of the Old World to carry out the agricultural and urban revolutions independently. Stories of lost continents, such as Mu and Atlantis, are considered folklore—not to mention the landings of extraterrestrial space ships as advocated by Von Dainiken (1969).

Thus, human occupation of the New World appears to have been a comparatively late phenomenon made by Asiatic hunting bands using the only feasible land bridge—the Bering straits route—to enter the New World at the close of the ice ages. Although the exact age of this immigration is not known, it must have occurred more than 20,000 years ago, judging from the oldest archaeological sites now known. This postulation is supported by other lines of evidence, such as human morphology, since all American indians and their excavated fossil ancestors are fully *Homo sapiens* in taxonomy. Furthermore, the earliest well-documented archaeological phase, the Clovis culture of the High Plains,* shows similarities with the Old World Upper Paleolithic in the core-blade technology and big-game hunting subsistence. On the other hand, no New World early archaeological assemblage shows an exact identity with an Old World culture. Therefore, it is apparent that sufficient time had elapsed after the migration of humans to the New World so that entirely distinctive languages and cultures evolved. Direct evidence of the first Americans is yet to be discovered.

The cultural stage formulation of the New World departs from Lubbock's Old World scheme. Although a number of such stage classifications have been presented, that of Gordon Willey and Philip Phillips (1958) is most generally in use. These developmental steps—Lithic, Archaic, Formative, Classic, and Postclassic—are roughly parallel to those of Lubbock's Old World scheme with some important differences. In general, Willey and Phillips used artifact types and traditions of technology to distinguish the earlier, preagricultural stages, such as Lithic and Archaic, and employed human organizational principles to identify the food producing stages such as Formative, Classic, and Postclassic. Specifically, criteria of these latter stages are: (1) social and political institutions, (2) religious institutions, and (3) aesthetic developments such as great art styles. The shift in emphasis is in large part due to the increase through time in the richness of the archaeological record.

---

*A physiographical province that extends from west Texas (Llano Estacado) to southern Canada. This is a high (ca 5000 ft elevation) plains country characterized by short grass and a semiarid climate.

Because human occupation of the New World is a comparatively late event in the Pleistocene epoch, Willey and Phillips labeled the New World Paleolithic as the Lithic stage. The New World Archaic stage, besides representing postglacial adaptation to essentially modern plant and animal subsistence, has long been recognized as the context in which agriculture first arose. This chapter describes the Lithic and Archaic stages.

Lithic (Paleo-Indian) Stage

The Lithic stage is variously called the Paleo-Indian, Paleo-American (Krieger 1964), Early Hunters (Coe 1967), Early Man, or Big Game Hunters (Willey 1966). All of these synonyms refer to the same stage concept, that of the New World Upper Paleolithic. The Lithic hunters were descendants of the earliest Asiatic hunting bands to enter the New World and as such are representative of the first Mongoloid peoples to occupy the new continent. The definitive criteria of Lithic sites are percussion and pressure stone technology without pottery. The distinctive artifacts that identify Lithic sites are narrow, tapering dart points, called *lanceolates*, which once tipped hand-hurled or throwing-board propelled shaft missiles. The herbivores hunted by these projectiles were herds of Pleistocene fauna including bison of several species, mammoth, and lesser numbers of horse, sloth, camel, wolf, and four-horned antelope. According to the geological calendar, Lithic sites are dated to the Late Pleistocene and early Holocene (anathermal period) epochs.

The Lithic stage is an area of New World research in which opinions are varied and new finds frequently change the scope of archaeological thinking. New evidence of the earliest ancestors of the American indian demand constant revision of chronology. At present, it is convenient to divide the Lithic into three time periods: (1) 30,000 to 50,000 years ago, (2) 12,000 to 20,000 years ago, and (3) 7000 to 12,000 years ago.

Period 1

The earliest period of 30,000 to 50,000 years ago is largely speculative because of questionable data. Each site lacks one of the elements needed to validate a Lithic stage site: early artifact typology, association of artifacts and Pleistocene fauna, Pleistocene geological context, and undisputed early radiometric dates. Of the proposed sites, most controversy revolves around a location called the Old Crow site (Morlan 1978). The Old Crow exposures are found along the Porcupine river in the Yukon province of Canada just east of the Alaskan border. This site is actually a district made up of many localities where Pleistocene bones exhibit spiral fractures reputed to be of human manufacture. This area was part of the unglaciated (ice-free) subarctic refuge suitable as settlements for Siberian immigrants first arriving from Asia during Middle Wisconsin times. No stone tools have been found, but the 100 bones of mammoth and caribou are said to be humanly modified on a stone anvil by stone hammer, which spirally fractured the bones. Fracturing of the bones would provide edible bone marrow and produce sharp ends suitable as butchering tools. One other tool is more convincing evidence: a toothed fleshing tool for removing hides from a slain animal in the butchering process. Most of these bones were removed from their original geological context by river erosion. Radiocarbon dating on the bone yields an age range between 25,000 and 29,000 years ago. Although field work is continuing, the data seem suspect because of the lack of confirmed geological context and validation that the bones were fractured by humans. Wild carnivores such as cats and bears could have fractured the green bones, yielding pseudo-artifacts that mimic human tools. If the full technical report on Old Crow overcomes these reservations, it will date the first Old World migrants sometime before 30,000 years ago. Two stadials of the Wisconsin glaciation would have provided a land bridge for entry on foot from Siberia, one at 30,000 BP and a second between 40,000 and 50,000 BP.

Other recent claims of extreme antiquity for humans in the New World have come from eastern Colorado (Stanford 1979), the state of Puebla, Mexico (Steen-McIntyre, Fryxell, and Malde 1981), and the Old Crow drainage basin (Jopling, Irving, and Beebe 1981). The site of Hueyatlaco in Mexico, the oldest, is variously dated between 180,000 and 600,000 years ago depending on which dating procedure is employed (Steen-McIntyre, Fryxell, and Malde 1981, p. 1). Like the other Period 1 data, these Middle Pleistocene claims call for further documentation.

Period 2

Lithic Period 2, dated between 12,000 and 20,000 years ago, attests to the fact that humans were not only present in the New World but had populated both North and South America. Human presence in North America south of the continental ice-sheet during late Wisconsin times is demonstrated by a carefully excavated rock shelter named Meadowcroft (Adovasio, Gunn, Donahue, and Stuckenrath 1978). This shelter is located in the Ohio river valley in Pennsylvania not far from the West Virginia line. The shelter has yielded many stratified components of human occupation, of which the next to lowest, Stratum IIa, contains the earliest evidence of culture. Some 40 artifacts include tools reminiscent of an Old World Upper Paleolithic assemblage: biface thinning flakes, denticulates (toothed tools), micro-engraver, Mungai knife (bifacially retouched flake knives), and one bifacial lanceolate projectile point without fluting. In addition, a fragment of a basket was recovered. The artifacts of Stratum IIa were sealed by a massive rock fall when the shelter's roof collapsed, and thus there is no possibility that these specimens intruded from later and stratigraphically higher layers. Eight radiocarbon assays date Stratum IIa and its artifactual contents between 12,000 and 16,000 years ago.

Only two criticisms can be leveled at the Pleistocene dating of Stratum IIa. One is that the radiocarbon dates may have been distorted by contamination by dead carbon from coal seams eroded from the limestone bedrock within which the Meadowcroft shelter is formed. Second, the presence of modern animal fossils and absence of any extinct Pleistocene animal bone is curious. Modern animal bones would be expected in a Holocene rather than a Pleistocene context. Similar evidence has been obtained from caves in Oregon and Idaho (Jennings 1978).

Period 2 occupancy of South America is evidenced by excavations in Pikimachay or Flea Cave located at 9000 feet in the Ayacucho valley of the Peruvian Andes (MacNeish 1971). Here the lowest layers revealed an extinct ground sloth in association with stone tools. These tools form an assemblage called the *Paccaicasa complex,* recovered from Layers *i* through *k*. Associated radiocarbon dates range from over 14,000 to just under 20,000 years ago. If accepted as evidence, this artifact complex is the oldest evidence of humans in South America. However, Lynch (1978) has questioned the validity of the artifacts since most are made of volcanic tuff and may have been natural breaks from the roof of the cave. Even if this is so, the *Ayacucho complex* recovered from overlying layers is radiocarbon dated around 14,000 years ago, which would qualify this completely acceptable assemblage for inclusion in Lithic period 2.

Period 3

Period 3 of the Lithic stage is based on firm, uncontested data spanning the millennia from 12,000 to 7,000 BP. In North America, three phases are recognized in the time series of Clovis, Folsom, and Plano, the latter being subdivided into many named subphases. These units are identifiable by the presence of stylistically distinctive dart or spear points used in the hunting of extinct Pleistocene herd animals of which the mammoth and various species of bison formed the staple subsistence prey.

CLOVIS PHASE

The Clovis hunters, dated between 11,000 and 12,000 BP, during the Two Creeks interstadial of the Wisconsin glaciation, focused their predation on mammoth but their kill sites also display minor occurrences of camel, horse, and an early long-horned bison (Fig. 9–2a). Clovis sites were located throughout North America south of the continental ice sheet. They are principally found in the High Plains but have been identified also in the eastern woodlands of Virginia (Gardner 1974) and in southern Arizona (Haury 1953). The Clovis tool assemblage is made up of fluted points (called *Clovis points*), scrapers, knives, hammerstones, blades, and bone points (Fig. 9–2b). At the Murray Springs site in Arizona, Haynes and Hemmings (1968) have reported a mammoth ivory wrench used to straighten wooden spear shafts.

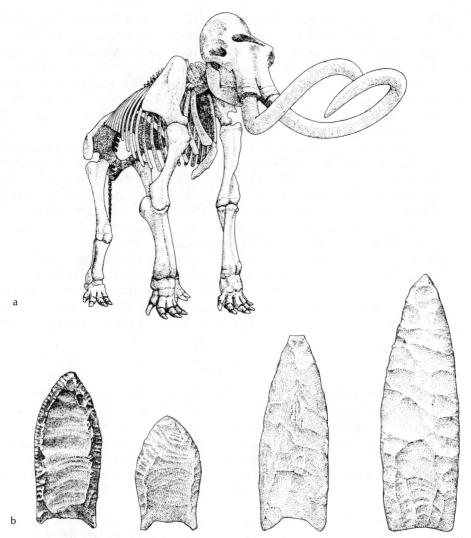

a

b

FIGURE 9–2   (a) American elephants were all of the genus *Mammuthus*. They included the woolly mammoth, which also ranged the Old World, and the imperial, confined to North America. This skeleton of one imperial variety, the Columbian, is 12 feet tall at the shoulder. (b) Characteristic differences between Folsom (*left*) and Clovis (*center and right*) projectile points. The Folsom's long, neat flute scar was produced by the detachment of a single flake. Clovis points tend to be coarser and larger; flute scars are shorter and often show the detachment of more than one flake.

Source: From "Elephant Hunting in North America" by C. Vance Haynes. Copyright © 1966 by Scientific American, Inc. All rights reserved.

Most sites are not campsites but places where Columbian mammoths were killed and butchered, so that the life-way reconstruction is skewed toward this specialized activity. The one possible exception is the basal layer at Ventana cave, southwestern Arizona, which contains a small tool inventory including one unfluted bifacial point. Associated extinct Pleistocene fauna includes horse, bison, tapir, jaguar, ground sloth, and four-pronged antelope. Originally the excavator, Emil W. Haury (1950), thought that this tool assemblage was of Folsom age but a recent radiocarbon assay of 11,290 ± 1000 years clearly places the basal volcanic rock layer of Ventana cave in Clovis times (Haynes 1970). The cave was a natural shelter to which Clovis hunters returned after a kill. Mammoth bones have not been identified from this site although mammoth kill sites are well documented from the nearby San Pedro valley of southeast Arizona.

The most commonly recorded Clovis site is the mammoth kill and butchering location. These kill sites consist of beds of butchered bones usually at the site of the animal kill. Butchering has somewhat disarticulated the skeletons. Tools, such as butchering knives, scrapers, and fluted projectile tips, were distributed among the rib bones where the implements were lost in the gore of the slain and butchered animals. Based on the geological setting of the kill, the techniques of attack have been reconstructed to show a surprising diversity of hunting strategies. At Dent, Colorado, for instance, the mammoths were stampeded over a cliff and then stoned to death. At Blackwater Draw, New Mexico, the mammoths were driven into a shallow lake where they became mired in mud, and then were killed with hurled spears (Hester 1972). At the Lehner ranch site, Arizona, young mammoth babies were separated from their adult parents, held at bay by a bend in a stream, and killed by spears (Haury, Sayles, and Wasley 1959). Many of these kills took place at or near a watering spot. At the Murray Springs site in southeastern Arizona, a Clovis kill took place at a spring, where mammoth tracks were fossilized in the mud as evidence of the long-ago event.

FOLSOM PHASE

At the close of Clovis times, most of the Pleistocene megafauna became extinct. This extermination of the mammoth, horse, camel, and other big game may have happened because of climate change or as a result of overkill by early hunters. The overkill thesis has been championed by Paul S. Martin, who points to hunting pressure exerted by Upper Paleolithic humans to explain the disappearance of Pleistocene herd animals in Africa, Europe, Asia, and the New World. In North America, only the extinct bison, *Bison antiguus*, remained to form the prey of Folsom hunters.

The Folsom assemblage is dated between 10,000 and 11,000 radiocarbon years ago. In geological terms, this cultural unit correlates with the Valders stadial, the last ice readvance at the end of the Wisconsin glaciation.

Although the principal center of distribution for Folsom sites is the High Plains, the Folsom point, a distinctive fluted spear tip, has been found as far south as South America (Lynch 1978).

The tool assemblage found in association with the fluted Folsom point includes prismatic blades, burins, snub-nosed scrapers, retouched flakes, drills, and spokeshaves (concave scrapers for shaping wooden spear shafts). Tools such as the scrapers, flakes, and points are found in bison kill sites where they were used to kill, skin, and butcher the herd animals. Other tools such as drills, spokeshaves, and burins are most common in base camps where they were used to manufacture and repair hunting gear.

In contrast to the Clovis phase, Folsom base camps, such as the famous Lindenmeir site of northern Colorado, are well documented (Wilmsen 1974; Wilmsen and Roberts 1978). Kill sites are far more common, however, particularly on the High Plains. These data illustrate several hunting strategies in which the bison herds were driven over a cliff (Bonfire shelter, Texas) or into a ravine (Folsom type site, New Mexico). In each case, the animals suffered broken legs from falling, after which the hunters finished off the animals by spear thrusts.

PLANO PHASE

During the Plano phase between 10,000 and 7000 radiocarbon years ago, a series of subphases are recognized in terms of named, stylistically distinct lance points. Geologically, these Plano phases are dated to the anathermal period in the early Holocene epoch following the close of the Wisconsin glaciation. This cool, moist climatic period is marked by the last of the Pleistocene megafauna, *Bison occidentalis*, which was hunted by Plano man until its extermination in the altithermal period.

Remains of Plano cultures are found almost exclusively on the High Plains and adjacent portions of the western United States where they are contemporaries of early Archaic cultures found in California and the Great Basin of Utah and Nevada. On the High Plains, Plano sites are distributed from Mexico north to Canada. The distinctive fossils of the Plano phase are parallel-flaked lanceolate points, which lack the distinctive fluting attribute of Clovis and Folsom times. Two series of Plano points have been defined: Plainview and parallel-flaked (Fig. 9–3). The remainder of the tool assemblage is similar to that described for the Folsom phase.

Like the earlier Folsom-age bison hunters, Plano hunters used driving techniques in which the stampeded herd was run into a ravine (Olsen-Chubbuck site, Colorado) or a natural trap (Wheat 1967; Frisen, Wilson, and Wilson 1974). With the bison herd empounded within a natural trap, or partially immobilized by a fall, Plano hunters could make the kill with spear thrusts. At the Olsen-Chubbuck site, the herd was stampeded across a ravine. As the animals jumped for and missed the opposite wall, the impact upon landing snapped necks, broke legs, and ruptured internal organs. After the fallen

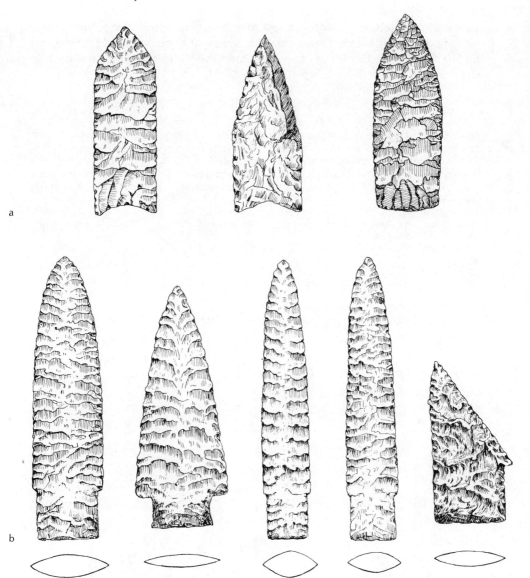

a

b

FIGURE 9-3 Lanceolate points of the Plano phase. (a) Plainview point, Meserve point, and Milnesand point; (b) artifacts of the Cody complex including the Scottsbluff Type I, Scottsbluff Type II, Eden with collateral flaking, Eden with transverse flaking, Cody knife.

Source: From H. M. Wormington, *Ancient Man in North America*, Popular Series, no. 4. Denver: Denver Museum of Natural History, 1957.

animals had filled the ravine, the last members thundered across their strug-gling bodies to freedom. Thin strips of bison meat were removed and stacked for "jerking" (air drying) in order to lighten the weight for transport back to the hunting band's base camp (Fig. 9–4).

FIGURE 9–4   Butchering methods used by the Paleo-indians have been reconstructed on the dual basis of bone stratification at the Olsen-Chubbuck site and the practices of the Plains indians in recent times. Once the carcass of the bison (*skeleton at top*) had been propped up and skinned down the back, a series of "butchering units" probably were removed in the order shown on the numbered outline figures. The hunters ate as they worked.

Source: From "A Paleo-Indian Bison Kill" by Joe Ben Wheat. Copyright © 1967 by Scientific American, Inc. All rights reserved.

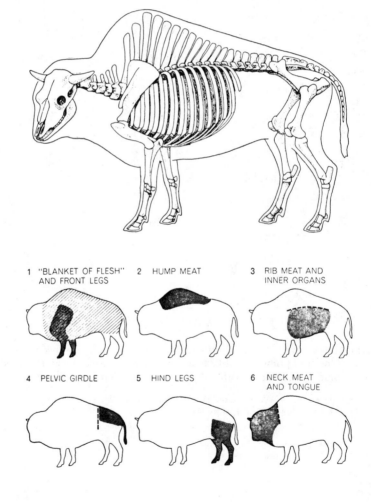

1 "BLANKET OF FLESH"
   AND FRONT LEGS

2 HUMP MEAT

3 RIB MEAT AND
   INNER ORGANS

4 PELVIC GIRDLE

5 HIND LEGS

6 NECK MEAT
   AND TONGUE

FISH-TAIL POINT HORIZON

The Fish-Tail point horizon, of which the Huanta complex of Pepper cave in the Ayacucho valley is a local example, is dated between 10,000 and 12,000 BP (Lynch 1978). This South American point style horizon is temporally and typologically equivalent to the Period 3 Clovis and Folsom assemblages of North America. The Fish-Tail points are dated geologically to the El Abra stadial, the South American equivalent of the Valders stadial of the north.

Like other Period 3 Paleo-Indians, the Fish-Tail hunting bands of South America subsisted on large game such as mammoth, horse, ground sloth, a Pleistocene deer, and camelids that were the ancestors of the modern llama, alpaca, and vicuña.

Sites with stylistically distinctive Fish-Tail points are found in the high Andes mountains from Venezuela south to the Straits of Magellan at the tip of the continent. Several sites are found on the Brazilian highlands but none have been located in the South American lowlands. This distributional pattern indicates that Period 3 Lithic stage hunters favored the open savanna country of the high altitude Andean mountain chains but avoided the dense wet tropics of the Amazon and Orinoco drainage basins as unfit for large-game hunters. It seems likely that the large Pleistocene megafauna foraged on grassland savanna vegetation found in the uplands, thereby influencing the human geography. It was not until around 7000 BP that Archaic stage humans made a successful adaptation to the wet tropics and then only along the seacoast of South America (Argentina, Brazil, and Venezuela) through shellfish collecting.

Tools associated with the large, primary stemmed and fluted Fish-Tail points (Fig. 9–5) include snub-nosed scrapers, thumbnail scrapers, gravers,

FIGURE 9–5   Fish-Tail points from the site of El Inga, Ecuador.

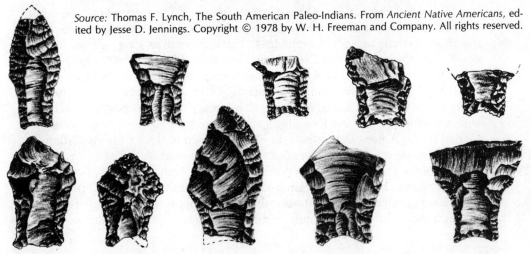

notched tools (denticulates), bifacial knives and scrapers, and flake scrapers with retouch from alternate sides. Lynch (1978) thinks that the double pointed El Jobo points and the Paijan points with triangular blades and long stems may also have been associates of the Fish-Tail assemblage.

By the beginning of the altithermal period, 7000 years ago, ancient hunters had begun to readapt to a subsistence focused on modern game and plant foraging, an adaptive pattern characterizing the Archaic stage.

Archaic Stage

The Archaic societies of the New World are the functional equivalents of the Old World Mesolithic. Both stages represent postglacial societies with subsistence economies based on hunting of modern game and intensive foraging of plant foods. Other significant developments were attention to aquatic resources such as water fowl, fishing, and shellfish collecting. The latter practice produced one of the most distinctive Archaic site types, the shell midden. The focus of Archaic peoples on wild vegetable foods yielded the knowledge from which agriculture developed. But in contrast to the early dates for Old World plant domestication, the earliest cereal cultigens of the New World are dated no older than 7000 years ago. The New World agricultural revolution focused mostly on plants, rather than the mixed plant-animal combinations of the Old World, and lacked many significant Old World traction animals. The Archaic societies of the New World represented a readaptation to a broad-spectrum food quest after the gregarious megafauna herds of the Pleistocene had become extinct as a result of hunting pressures of early humans and worldwide climate changes that took place between 10,000 and 7000 years ago.

Dating of the earliest Archaic is variable for different parts of the continent depending on the extinction rates of the Pleistocene herd animals. For instance, Archaic artifact assemblages first appeared as long ago as 10,000 years at Danger cave in the Great Basin (Jennings 1957), but late Paleo-Indian remains of the High Plains of North America are radiocarbon-dated to around 7000 BP. The end of the Archaic is variable in time depending upon the effective appearance of the agricultural revolution, true fired pottery, and village settlements. The Archaic stage ended around 2000 years ago (time of Christ) in the American southwest, 3000 years ago in the eastern woodlands of North America, and 4000 years ago in Mesoamerica.

In other parts of the New World, however, Archaic life-ways continue in the present. These are marginal areas where hunting and gathering peoples either survive today or whose cultures have become extinct only recently through the influence of modern industrial societies. Such Archaic societies exist in environments unsuitable for agriculture and therefore are not in competition with the agro-business concerns of modern nation states. Some examples are the Eskimo and Aleuts of the Arctic, the Athabascan and Algonkin indian tribes of the subarctic boreal Canadian forests, and desert dwellers such as the Paiute, Shoshone, and Ute (Wissler 1950; National Geographic Society 1968).

Subsistence Economy

Subsistence pursuits such as hunting, collecting, fishing, fowling, and incipient agriculture varied with the environmental habitat from one part of the continent to another.

Hunting provided meat protein and materials (bone, antler, ligament, hide, furs, claws, feathers) from a wide range of modern fauna. Many kinds of animals required very specialized hunting technology. Deer, elk, and moose were taken by stalk and ambush from hunting blinds. Antelope were driven by groups of hunters into chute and compound structures, where they were speared. Bison were stampeded through drive lines and over cliffs, while bear were taken by dead-fall and pit trap. Rabbits and rodents were either obtained by net or spring trap or, in the case of jackrabbits, surrounded by club-swinging hunting parties. Although much of this technical reconstruction is based on the ethnographic literature of North American indians, strong support for these hunting practices is provided by the excavation of the pertinent hunting gear from dry rock shelters of Archaic age, for instance, those of the Basketmaker II culture of the American southwest, dated between AD 1 and 450. Although this culture practiced corn agriculture and lived in houses, its foraging strategy indicates that it was late Archaic in its subsistence practices.

Aquatic resources, both marine and freshwater, became important during the Archaic. Fish were secured by weirs, a kind of trap made up of thousands of wooden pilings driven into tidal flats to catch fish schools on the receding tide. An example, radiocarbon-dated to 2500 BC, has been found in the backwaters of Boston bay. Other fishing gear included barbed spears, hook-and-line from dugout boats, nets, cylinder-shaped box traps, and toggle harpoons, the latter dating as far back as 7500 BC in Belle Isle and southern Labrador (Griffen 1978, p. 230). In addition, sea mammals, such as whales, seals, and walrus, were harpooned. In arctic waters these were either hunted down from boats or caught by ice fishing at blow holes.

Water fowl could be secured with propelled darts or simply grabbed from underwater after first being decoyed by floats similar to a modern duck decoy. At Lovelock cave, Nevada, dry rock shelter excavations have uncovered actual decoys made of wrapped cattail leaves covered by the feathered skins of real ducks (Aikens 1978, p. 157).

As a complement to modern wild game, Archaic people intensely gathered and collected plant and animal products. The so-called slow game, such reptiles as turtles, lizards, and frogs, provided a kind of buffer against starvation during the lean seasons in the annual round of subsistence activities. Sedentary shellfish, including mussels, clams, and oysters, provided huge quantities of food for people adapted to waterside habitats. Vegetable products added an important dietary complement that included roots, tubers, seeds, leafy greens, fruits, nuts, and berries. The greens were available in the spring to carry Archaic consumers over a lean season of the year.

It was in adaptation to the seasonal periodicity of edible wild plants that agriculture, or purposeful cultivation, evolved. The earliest agriculture consisted of tending wild plants at their natural growth site. But the disturbed ground of a campsite, particularly around garbage dumps, also provided a favorable setting for any seeds purposefully or accidentally brought home.

In the New World, the single most important cereal was corn. In the eastern United States, indians grew hard flint corn and pulverized it with mortar and pestle. Softer varieties, called *flour corn,* were developed in the American southwest, and these were milled with hand-held milling stones. The corn meal was used in cakes and gruel. A refinement in the eastern woodlands was soaking the corn in a lye mixture to produce hominy.

Coupled with corn are two other crops of considerable antiquity, beans and squash, each of which has evolved into many species and varieties. In addition, indians cultivated bottle gourds, chili peppers, and cotton.

Improvements in these preceramic cultigens led to increasing yield, shorter growing seasons, resistance to drought and disease, and more varieties. For instance, seed selection and cross-breeding, or intentional hybridization, with two related wild grasses improved corn by increasing the size of kernels, number of rows, and size of cob (Wilkes 1977). Corn was an especially important staple crop because the ears could be dried and stored in cists and pits for wintertime use, thereby distributing the annual food supply more evenly (Fig. 9–6). No longer was there such disparity between the bountiful summer and the lean winter. But experimentation with corn genetics did not have an immediate effect on human settlements and population size. Corn productivity improved from early Archaic times onward, but it is not until early Formative times that marked social effects of this agricultural revolution are commonly noted in the archaeological record.

In addition to the food triad of corn, beans, and squash, which were staples of the aboriginal diet, other crops were regionally important. For instance, in the eastern woodlands of North America, sunflowers were much more important than corn in Archaic times. In highland Peru, potatoes were locally important. Sweet and bitter manioc, a root crop, was significant in the Amazon and Orinoco basins of lowland tropical South America (Wissler 1950).

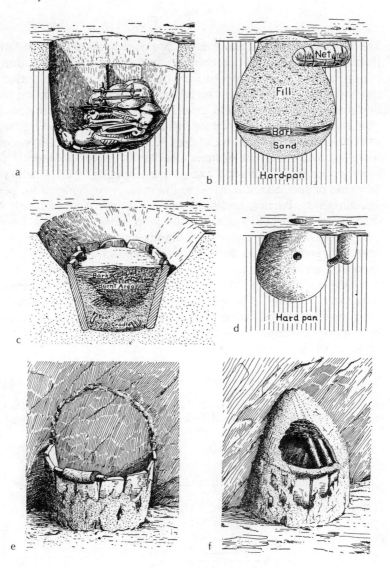

FIGURE 9–6   Slab lined cists and dug pits used for burial (a), sleeping (b), cooking ovens (c), and food storage (d, e, f), Basketmaker II culture, northeastern Arizona.

Source: Reprinted from *Basket-Maker Caves of Northeastern Arizona* (Guernsey and Kidder 1921, Peabody Museum Papers vol. 8, no. 2) with permission from the Peabody Museum of Archaeology and Ethnology, Harvard University.

Tool Technology

The tool technology of the Archaic is a continuation of some Lithic stage artifacts and manufacturing techniques but with considerable additions reflecting specialized adaptations to local habitats. For instance, Lithic stage stone
tools were made by direct percussion and pressure chipping techniques as
described for the Old World Upper Paleolithic. To this technology were added
new manufacturing procedures including pecking, grinding, and polishing
as described for the Neolithic of the Old World. Tools and sets of tools became
more specialized. In the eastern woodlands of North America, for instance,
woodworking kits included axes, adzes, gouges, chisels, and wedges. Another set of specialized tools were the milling implements for pounding and
grinding nuts, berries, and seeds. In the desert West of North America, indians used hand-held stones to mill wild grass seeds and, later, cultivated
corn (Fig. 9–7). In the eastern woodlands, mortars and pestles, made of stone
or wood, were used to pound and pulverize nuts, berries, and corn. Also
used in the east was a special kind of crushing device called a *nutting stone*,
a flat stone with many pecked holes that held nuts, which were then cracked
to remove the shell. Carved stone vessels made of a soft stone called *soap
stone* were employed for boiling liquid directly over a flame. These pots were
an important substitute for fired clay pots, which were not yet in use in Archaic times.

FIGURE 9–7   Developmental chart showing the principal traits of the Cochise culture,
an Archaic stage sequence found in southern Arizona: Sulphur Springs, early Archaic;
Chiricahua, middle Archaic; San Pedro, late Archaic.

Source: From E. B. Sayles and Ernst Antevs, *The Cochise Culture*, Figure 11; Globe, Arizona: Gila
Pueblo, 1941.

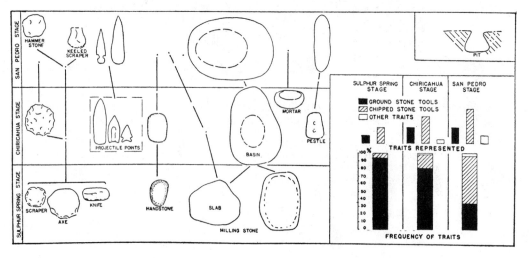

The stone tool industry always makes up the most prominent part of any archaeological assemblage simply because stone is a durable material. However, archaeologists have some knowledge of the Archaic wood and fiber industry. Excavators have found these perishables in preserved dry rock shelters and in muds at the bottom of lakes and rivers. From these finds, it is known that Archaic peoples had invented a rich array of containers and devices for exploiting their natural environments, although most of this evidence is missing from the archaeological record of open, dry-land sites.

From the east coast of North America, archaeologists have found evidence of boats. In the southeast, these are usually dugout canoes shaped from a tree trunk by axe, adze, and fire. In the northeast, however, evidence of the elm or birchbark canoe is to be found.

Baskets woven in a loose weave were used for dry storage of foods and materials or as containers during traveling (Fig. 9–8). For instance, Archaic

FIGURE 9–8   Baskets from the Basketmaker II culture, northeastern Arizona.

Source: Reprinted from *Basket-Maker Caves of Northeastern Arizona* (Guernsey and Kidder 1921, Peabody Museum Papers vol. 8, no. 2) with permission from the Peabody Museum of Archaeology and Ethnology, Harvard University.

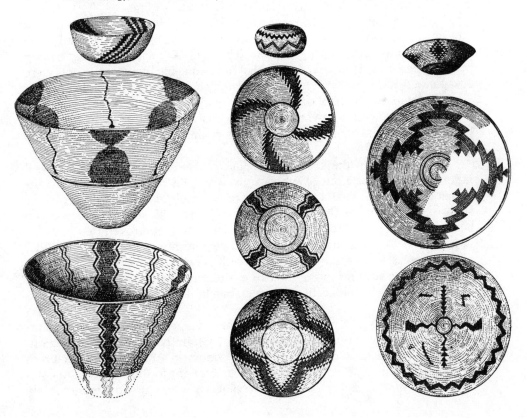

seed collectors in the desert West of the United States and northern Mexico used cone-shaped baskets, slung over the back with a tumpline, in collecting quantities of grass seeds for transport back to base camp. Loose-woven baskets for parching seeds were made in the shape of flat plates or trays with low sides. Hot embers were placed in the parching basket, along with edible seeds, and the contents swirled to cook the seeds without scorching them. Other baskets were woven tightly in a necked-jar shape for storage, transport, and pouring of liquids. These water jars and canteens were made watertight by a covering of pitch or resin. Other waterproof baskets were used to cook soups and gruels by stone boiling, in which heated rock was dropped into the container with tongs to bring the liquid to a boil. Such a preceramic cooking technology produced huge Archaic stone dumps in Texas and elsewhere. The resulting site type is called a *burnt rock midden,* essentially an immense pile of heat-fractured rock, the discarded residue of stone boiling and other hot-rock techniques of cooking meat and vegetal foodstuffs.

Other perishable gear and equipment of Archaic age include leather bags, pouches, moccasins, and cordage in considerable quantities (Fig. 9–9). Cordage is made of hair and plant fibers spun by Z– and S–twist into strong rope. Rope and cords were then manufactured into nets, spring traps and snares, lashing for hafted knives and spears, and fish line.

The bone and antler industry of Archaic age includes a large array of tools made from the skeletons of hunted animals. The bone was worked while still green, either by grooving out bone splinters with a graver, or by flaking by direct percussion and abrading with a sandstone file. Bone ornaments were also painted and perforated for suspension by drilling. Examples of bone and antler tools are: bone fishhooks, awls for working leather and weaving baskets, eyed needles for sewing, throwing board parts such as handles and hooks, bone chisels, antler tine pressure tools, and cylinder hammers for direct percussion.

Particularly on the seacoast, Archaic refuse sites yield a marine shell industry. Items made out of whole univalve shells include strung bead ornaments and conch shell trumpets and cups. The broad segments of bivalve shells could be cut or flaked to make shell fishhooks and disc beads. The beads are often scored, drilled for suspension, and then broken free from the larger valve. Disc and whole-shell beads were strung as anklets, armbands, and necklaces, either alone or mixed with other kinds of stone and bone beads. Archaic sites far in the interior of the continent yield marine shell artifacts, which were traded there over elaborate, long-distance exchange networks.

Archaeologists have found a most unexpected technical industry founded on native copper (Griffen 1978, p. 238). In the Lake Superior region, indians mined natural deposits of native copper in Archaic and later times by tunnel diggings. The native copper was brought to the surface and cold-hammered into a variety of utilitarian objects, which in turn were widely

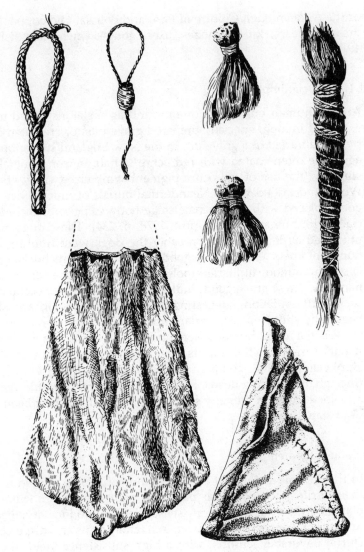

FIGURE 9-9 Snares, human hair, and skin bags from the Basketmaker II culture, northeastern Arizona.

Source: Reprinted from *Basket-Maker Caves of Northeastern Arizona* (Guernsey and Kidder 1921, Peabody Museum Papers vol. 8, no. 2) with permission from the Peabody Museum of Archaeology and Ethnology, Harvard University.

traded. The profusion of these hand-beaten metal items formed a copper industry called the *old copper culture* of late Archaic age. It is significant that this copper technology never developed into a true metallurgy involving smelting of ores or casting of objects as did the metallurgy of Postclassic Mesoamerica or the Andean High Culture of Peru and Bolivia. Old copper culture artifacts include spears, knives, adzes, axes, gouges, awls, and fishhooks (Griffin 1978).

Burials and Their Social Implications

Archaic human burials are often found as skeletons flexed in a storage pit, extended in long, specially prepared grave pits, or cremated over a funerary pyre and buried in a grave pit. In the New England states, burials of Archaic age were often coated with red ochre, a natural iron mineral pigment. Presumably, the use of red ochre pigment symbolized vitality both in the New World and in Old World Neanderthal burials of much older vintage. Grave goods placed with the Archaic stage body sometimes included dogs, especially with human males (Griffin 1978, p. 234). These dogs may be whole or mutilated as if sacrificed. Probably the dogs were hunting companions or household pets. Other grave goods found with some but not all Archaic burials include food, utilitarian tools including copper artifacts, and various ornaments. These grave goods indicate the beginnings of occupational and even social differentiation, suggesting that some, but not all, Archaic societies had begun the shift from egalitarian tribal organization to ranked chiefdoms. Because some infant humans were buried with exotic artifacts obtained by long-distance trade, archaeologists infer that social status in some lower Mississippi valley Archaic communities was ascribed by birth rather than achieved through outstanding deeds. Since a newborn infant would not have achieved a major success in life, any status distinction must have been inherited from high status parents.

Architecture and Settlement

In the Archaic settlement pattern, bands of people shifted from one part of their territory to another as particular plants came into fruit or animal populations were available. During seasons of low productivity, these bands broke up into smaller segments or even into family units and dispersed for foraging. During favorable seasons, with a high subsistence yield, the entire macro-band could reassemble with an assured food supply and remain semisedentary for some limited period of time. Settlements are found in rock shelters where deep refuse deposits formed. Other signs of early settlements appear primarily in late Archaic times with small clusters of houses that gradually grew into villages (Fig. 9–10). The social effects of agriculture and the technical efficiency of intensive foraging were beginning to generate larger human populations, village life, some social differentiation, and in a few cases, the beginnings of elitist control.

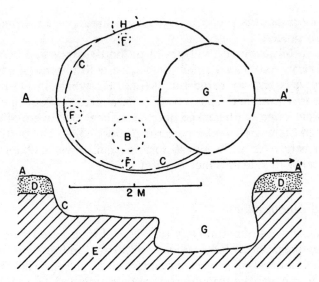

FIGURE 9–10   A late Archaic pit house of the San Pedro phase, Cochise culture, southeastern Arizona. (B) Irregular depression .35 m. deep (fire area); (C) slope at edge of floor; (D) sand containing artifacts, burnt stone, charcoal to floor level; no pottery beneath the surface; (E) native soil; (F) poorly defined, shallow holes (roof supports?); (G) storage pit; (H) wall step entry.

Source: From E. B. Sayles, *The San Simon Branch Excavations at Cave Creek and in the San Simon Valley. I. Material Culture,* Figure 2; Globe, Arizona: Gila Pueblo, 1945.

Everywhere house architecture was simple. One form of Archaic residence, called a *pit house,* is probably a diffusion from the Old World, where it first appeared in Upper Paleolithic times. In Europe, pit houses date back some 20,000 or 25,000 years. To construct a pit house, the builders dug a large circular hole with a flat-bladed digging stick. They hauled the dirt away in basket loads and dumped it around the perimeter of the excavation. They leveled the bottom of the pit and outfitted it with a fire hearth for cooking, light, and warmth. Upright posts were raised from the floor, usually in a rectangular pattern, to support a horizontal frame. Leaners from ground surface to these horizontal cross-timbers completed the roof. The pit sides became the lower walls of the structure. Smoke from the hearth fire escaped through a roof hole, which often served as the entryway with inhabitants coming and going over a log ladder. Although the house was simple in construction, it represented a capital investment in time and effort because of the amount of earth that was hauled away. Thus, the larger the house and the more houses present in a village, the more advanced was the settling-down process.

In Mesoamerica, villages of pit houses appeared before 2300 BC. In the American southwest, small pit houses with interior storage pits and lateral entryways had appeared by 1000 BC. Elsewhere in North America simpler houses without a deep excavation for a recessed floor had appeared by 2300 BC. Pole lodges with packed floors have been documented in the northeastern United States by circular patterns of post holes. The vertical poles were forcibly bent over at the top to form a hemispherical-shaped, brush-and-mud shelter with side entrance (Griffin 1978).

Chronology and Periodization

Establishment of chronology for the Archaic is based on conventional dating techniques, particularly radiocarbon dating and relative dating derived from stylistic analysis of projectile points. During the Archaic, the customary hunting device was the throwing board that projected a dart with a stone tip (Fig. 9–11). This dart point was lashed to a notched wooden projectile shaft (Fig. 9–12). Dating is based on systematic changes over time in the style of the base of the dart point, the most useful guide fossil found on Archaic sites. Using these two dating techniques, archaeologists have divided the Archaic stage into three intervals, called *Early, Middle,* and *Late.*

EARLY ARCHAIC

In the eastern woodlands and in the Great Basin of Utah and Nevada, the Pleistocene megafauna became extinct at the end of the Pleistocene epoch some 10,000 years ago. Therefore, the earliest Archaic assemblages appeared immediately following the end of the ice ages. Elsewhere and particularly on the High Plains of North America, however, bison (*B. occidentalis,* now extinct) lingered into the anathermal period. For this reason, Archaic assemblages with distinctive notched and stemmed points did not appear on the High Plains much earlier than 7000 BP at the start of the altithermal climatic period. In the periodization used here, the early Archaic ends around 5000 BP with the close of the long drought.

MIDDLE ARCHAIC

In the American west, the Middle Archaic is dated to the early medithermal period and marked by dart points that are stemmed and indented at the base. These serve as a convenient horizon marker expressed as many local point types extending from California into Texas and dated between 5000 and 3000 BP. In Wyoming, Frison, Wilson, and Wilson (1974) have called these horizon markers the *McKean technocomplex,* which is made up of three point

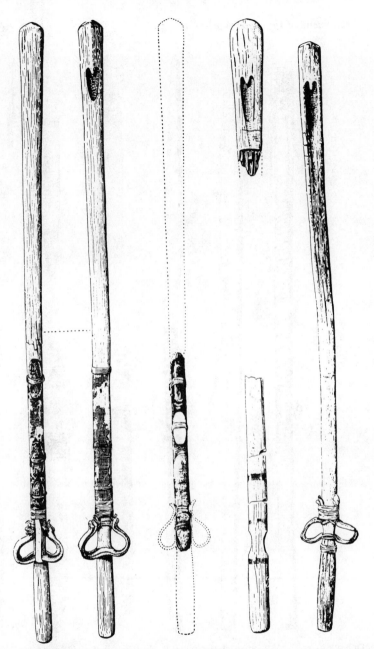

FIGURE 9–11   Wooden throwing boards from the Basketmaker II culture, northeastern Arizona. Note the finger grips, weights, and recessed notches to engage the concave end of the dart shaft.

Source: Reprinted from *Basket-Maker Caves of Northeastern Arizona* (Guernsey and Kidder 1921, Peabody Museum Papers vol. 8, no. 2) with permission from the Peabody Museum of Archaeology and Ethnology, Harvard University.

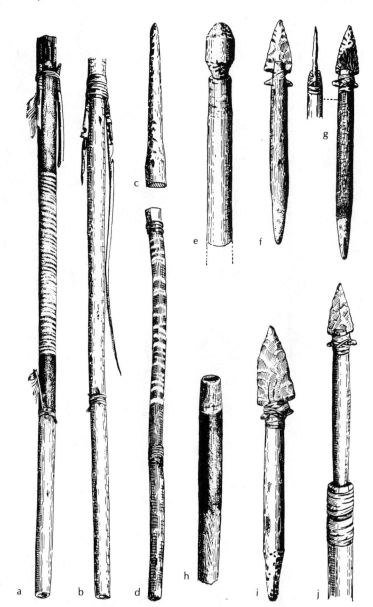

FIGURE 9-12   Wooden shafts from Basketmaker II culture, northeastern Arizona: (a, b, d) lower portion of darts showing method of feathering; (c) point of dart; (e) upper portion of dart showing blunt head; (h) upper portion of shaft showing socket for fore-shaft; (f, g, i) foreshafts with chipped stone points; (j) foreshaft in position, and upper part of shaft.

Source: Reprinted from *Basket-Maker Caves of Northeastern Arizona* (Guernsey and Kidder 1921), Peabody Museum Papers vol. 8, no. 2) with permission from the Peabody Museum of Archaeology and Ethnology, Harvard University.

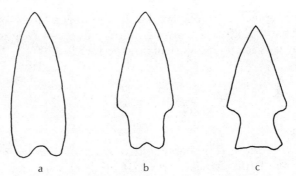

a   b   c

FIGURE 9–13   Outline drawings of points in the McKean technocomplexes. (a) McKean lanceolate point; (b) Duncan point; (c) Hanna point.

Source: From George C. Frison, Michael Wilson, and Diane H. Wilson, "The Holocene Stratigraphic Archaeology of Wyoming: An Introduction," Figure 2. In *Applied Geology and Archaeology: The Holocene History of Wyoming,* edited by Michael Wilson; Laramie: The Geological Survey of Wyoming, 1974, Report of Investigations No. 10.

types: McKean lanceolate, Duncan, and Hannah (Fig. 9–13). In the northeastern United States, Griffin (1978) defines the bannerstone, a throwing-board weight, as the middle Archaic guide fossil.

The Early and Middle Archaic are significant for the first appearance of agriculture. In Bat cave, New Mexico, corn has been radiocarbon-dated to 2500 BC (Dick 1965). Even older cultigens have been documented from the Tehuacan valley of southcentral Mexico, where MacNeish (1971) obtained dates between 5200 and 3400 BC on corn, squash, chili, avocados, bottle gourds, amaranth, and five kinds of beans. Comparable early dates have been reported on cultigens from coastal Peru (Patterson 1971), including bottle gourd and squash. Still older radiocarbon dates were obtained from highland Peru on lima and common beans, which range in age from 8500 to 5500 BC.

LATE ARCHAIC

The last period of the Archaic stage begins between 3000 BP and the first appearance of the village farming, or early Formative, stage. This end date, of course, is variable depending upon the first appearance of Formative guide fossils such as village architecture, fired pottery, and the bow and arrow. The principal guide fossil for the late Archaic is the large, corner-notched dart point. These points are found over most of North America, where they gradually evolved into much smaller arrow points around the time of Christ.

Noteworthy developments in the Late Archaic times are houses, villages, and fiber-tempered pottery in the southeastern United States, the latter dated back to 2000 BC. At about the same time in the Great Lakes region the Late Archaic is marked by hand-beaten copper implements (Griffin 1978). One of the most significant architectural and settlement developments is the first appearance of public works. In the lower Mississippi valley, crescent-shaped earth platforms are thought to have served as substructures for houses and perhaps for religious structures, dated to 1300 BC.

Summary

The New World was probably settled by Asiatic immigrants who crossed what is now the Bering straits from ice-free Siberia into an unglaciated Alaskan refuge. A number of hypotheses have been advanced for this migration, including the use of small boats or crossing on foot over winter ice. The most favored hypothesis, however, is that the Upper Paleolithic immigrants walked over a land bridge that formed as the sea level was lowered by water stored in continental ice sheets during Middle Wisconsin (Würm/Weichsel) glaciation around 30,000 to 42,000 years ago.

Evidence of this migration is not directly recorded in the archaeological record except by the questionable Old Crow site of Period 1 times. The more acceptable Lithic sites of Period 2 times demonstrate that humans had spread out over North America, South America, and Mesoamerica by 20,000 years ago. By late glacial times, 7000 to 12,000 years ago, Period 3 peoples had reached a climax hunting adaptation preying on the Pleistocene grazing animals such as mammoth, horse, camel, and bison. Eventually they hunted these herd animals to extinction.

The Archaic is the stage of hunting and gathering societies immediately following the extinction of the Pleistocene megafauna—although some primitive societies still follow this life-way today. When Europeans reached America in the fifteenth and sixteenth centuries, they found these band-organized peoples living in environments in which agriculture was marginal.

Throughout the Western Hemisphere, the Archaic was the base for a wide variety of environmental and social adaptations, including (1) agriculture, (2) sedentary village life, (3) the beginnings of social differentiation, and (4) long-distance trade in exotic materials used for ornaments and other status symbols.

References

AIKENS, C. MELVIN
 1978   The Far West. In *Ancient Native Americans,* edited by Jesse D. Jennings. San Francisco: W. H. Freeman and Company Publishers.
ADOVASIO, J. M., J. D. GUNN, J. DONAHUE, and R. STUCKENRATH
 1978   Meadowcroft Rockshelter, 1977: An Overview. *American Antiquity* 43:632–51.

COE, MICHAEL D.
   1964   The Chinampas of Mexico. In *New World Archaeology: Readings from Scientific American,* assembled by Ezra B. W. Zubrow, Margaret C. Fritz, and John M. Fritz. San Francisco: W. H. Freeman and Company Publishers.

DICK, HERBERT W.
   1965   Bat Cave. *Monographs of the School of American Research,* no. 27, Santa Fe: The School of American Research.

FRISON, GEORGE C., MICHAEL WILSON, and DIANE J. WILSON
   1974   The Holocene Stratigraphic Archaeology of Wyoming: An Introduction. In *Applied Geology and Archaeology: The Holocene History of Wyoming,* edited by Michael Wilson. Report of Investigations, no. 10. Laramie: Geological Survey of Wyoming.

GARDNER, WILLIAM M., ed.
   1974   *The Flint Run Paleo-Indian Complex: A Preliminary Report 1971–73 Seasons.* Department of Anthropology. Occasional Publication, no. 1. Washington, D.C.: Catholic University of America.

GRIFFIN, JAMES B.
   1978   The Midlands and Northeastern United States. In *Ancient Native Americans,* edited by Jesse D. Jennings. San Francisco: W. H. Freeman and Company Publishers.

GUERNSEY, SAMUEL JAMES, and ALFRED VINCENT KIDDER
   1921   Basket-Maker Caves of Northeastern Arizona. *Papers of the Peabody Museum of American Archaeology and Ethnology,* vol. 8. Cambridge, Mass.: Harvard University Press.

HAURY, EMIL W.
   1950   *The Stratigraphy and Archaeology of Ventana Cave, Arizona.* Tucson: University of Arizona Press.

   1953   Artifacts with Mammoth Remains, Naco, Arizona. *American Antiquity* 19:1–17.

HAURY, E. W., E. B. SAYLES, and W. W. WASLEY
   1959   The Lehner Mammoth Site, Southeastern Arizona. *American Antiquity* 25:1–30.

HAYNES, C. VANCE, JR.
   1970   Geochronology of Man-Mammoth Sites and Their Bearing on the Origin of the Llano Complex. In *Pleistocene and Recent Environments of the Great Central Plains,* edited by D. Wakefield and J. K. Jones, Jr. Department of Geology. Special Publication no. 3. Lawrence: University of Kansas Press.

HAYNES, C. VANCE, JR., and E. THOMAS HEMMINGS
   1968   Mammoth-Bone Shaft Wrench from Murray Springs, Arizona. *Science* 159:186–87.

HESTER, JAMES J.
   1972   *Blackwater Locality No. 1.* Dallas: Fort Burgwin Research Center.

HEYERDAHL, THOR
   1962   *Kon-Tiki: Across the Pacific by Raft.* New York: Permabooks.

JENNINGS, JESSE D.
   1957   Danger Cave. *Memoirs of the Society for American Archaeology,* no. 14. Salt Lake City: University of Utah Press.

   1978   Origins. In *Ancient Native Americans,* edited by Jesse D. Jennings. San Francisco: W. H. Freeman and Company Publishers.

JETT, STEVEN C.
   1978   Pre-Columbian Transoceanic Contacts. In *Ancient Native Americans,* edited by Jesse D. Jennings. San Francisco: W. H. Freeman and Company Publishers.

JOPLING, A. V., W. M. IRVING, and B. F. BEEDE
  1981   Stratigraphic, Sedimentological and Faunal Evidence for the Occurrence of Pre-Sangamonian Artifacts in Northern Yukon. *Arctic* 34:3–33.

KRIEGER, ALEX
  1964   Early Man in the New World. In *Prehistoric Man in the New World*, edited by J. Jennings and E. Norbeck. Chicago: University of Chicago Press.

LYNCH, THOMAS F.
  1978   The South American Paleo-Indians. In *Ancient Native Americans*, edited by Jesse D. Jennings. San Francisco: W. H. Freeman and Company Publishers.

MACNEISH, RICHARD S.
  1971   Ancient Mesoamerican Civilization. In *Prehistoric Agriculture*, edited by Stuart Strueger. Garden City, N.Y.: Natural History Press.

MORLAN, RICHARD E.
  1978   Early Man in Northern Yukon Territory: Perspectives as of 1977. In *Early Man in America*, edited by Alan Lyle Bryan. Department of Anthropology. Occasional Papers, no. 1. Edmonton: University of Alberta.

NATIONAL GEOGRAPHIC SOCIETY
  1968   *Vanishing Peoples of the Earth*. Washington, D.C.: National Geographic Society.

PATTERSON, THOMAS C.
  1971   The Emergence of Food Production in Central Peru. In *Prehistoric Agriculture*, edited by Stuart Struever. Garden City, N.Y.: Natural History Press.

SAYLES, E. B., and ERNST ANTEVS
  1941   The Cochise Culture. *Medallion Papers*, vol. 29. Globe, Ariz.: Gila Pueblo.

STANFORD, DENNIS
  1979   The Selby and Dutton Sites: Evidence for a Possible Pre-Clovis Occupation of the High Plains. In *Pre-Llano Cultures of the Americas: Paradoxes and Possibilities*, edited by Robert L. Humphrey and Dennis Stanford. Washington, D.C.: The Anthropological Society of Washington.

STEEN-MCINTYRE, VIRGINIA, RONALD FRYXELL, and HAROLD E. MALDE
  1981   Geological Evidence for Age of Deposits at Hueyatlaco Archaeological Site, Valsequillo, Mexico. *Quaternary Research* 16:1–17.

VON DAINIKEN, ERICH
  1969   *Chariots of the Gods?* New York: Bantam Books.

WHEAT, JOE BEN
  1974   A Paleo-Indian Bison Kill. In *New World Archaeology*, edited by Ezra B. W. Zubrow, Margaret Fritz, and John M. Fritz. Readings from Scientific American. San Francisco: W. H. Freeman and Company Publishers.

WILKES, GARRISON
  1977   The Origin of Corn—Studies of the Last Hundred Years. *Crop Resources*, edited by David S. Seigler. New York: Academic Press.

WILLEY, GORDON R.
  1966   *An Introduction to American Archaeology*, vol. 1. North and Middle America. Englewood Cliffs, N.J.: Prentice-Hall.

WILLEY, GORDON R., and PHILIP PHILLIPS
  1958   *Method and Theory in American Archaeology*. Chicago: University of Chicago Press.

WILMSEN, EDWIN N.
   1974   *Lindenmeir: A Pleistocene Hunting Society.* New York: Harper and Row.
WILMSEN, EDWIN N., and FRANK H. H. ROBERTS, JR.
   1978   *Lindenmeir, 1934-1974: Concluding Report on Investigations.* Smithsonian Contributions to Anthropology, no. 24. Washington, D.C.: Smithsonian Institution Press.
WISSLER, CLARK
   1950   *The American Indian: An Introduction to the Anthropology of the New World.* New York: Peter Smith.
WORMINGTON, H. M.
   1957   *Ancient Man in North America,* Popular Series, no. 4. Denver: Denver Museum of Natural History.

10 New World Civilization

Civilization of the New World began in the Formative stage. In fact, the word *formative* refers to formation—the formation of civilization. Formative societies are based on food-producing economies, usually involving agriculture, but sometimes involving fishing. Although food production is the definitive criterion, the presence of sedentary village settlements is another important characteristic.

The Formative stage of the New World spans two Old World stages, the Neolithic and the bronze age. Early Formative is defined as the stage of village agriculture equivalent to the Neolithic. Middle and Late Formative societies parallel the bronze age civilizations of the Old World, but without metallurgy or wheeled vehicles. During the New World Formative stage, social organization did not advance beyond chiefdoms. Prehistoric civilization of the New World did not reach its peak until the Postclassic stage.

The Classic stage of the New World is marked by the appearance of theocratic states and urbanism, growth trends that parallel the beginnings of bronze age civilization in the Old World. These developments were followed in the Postclassic by secular empires based on the conquest of many individual civilized societies, which were taxed to support the conquering elite. Outstanding examples were the Toltec and Aztec empires of Mesoamerica and the Hauri-Tiahuanaco and Inca empires of the Andean high culture. These societies show striking analogies to their Old World counterparts of the late bronze and iron ages.

Formative Stage

In addition to agriculture and village settlements, some secondary criteria identify Formative sites in the archaeological record: (1) true fired ceramics for cooking, storing, and serving food and liquids, (2) weaving of textiles on upright looms, (3) stone carving, and (4) specialized ceremonial architecture.

Incipient civilization appears during Middle Formative times (1000 to 300 BC) in Mesoamerica, where it is recognizable by monumental religious architecture in the form of earthen pyramids topped by small thatch temples. Religious priests presided over ceremonial centers surrounded and supported economically by villages of peasant farmers. In the New World, these Middle Formative theocratic societies represent the first common example of social differentiation and the rise of elite authority. Examples in the civilized world called *Nuclear America*—Mexico, Central America, and Peru—are the Olmec civilization of the Mexican gulf coast and the Chavin civilization of the north highlands of Peru.

Several ethnographic examples of Formative cultures are still living in the twentieth century (Forde 1963). These food producing cultures include tribally organized Pueblo indians of the American southwest whose economy is largely focused on corn agriculture in a semiarid region. Another example is the northwest coastal chiefdom society (British Columbia) with surplus production based on marine sea mammal hunting by boat and riverine salmon spearing.

The evolution of the village Formative resulted from the food surplus created by agricultural and other food-producing revolutions. Food production led to human population increases, expressed not only as communities made up of larger and larger numbers of people, but also as the increased density of human populations throughout the hemisphere. Another result of the food-production revolution was the increase in social complexity needed to control and regulate these large communities. A spin-off was the rise of elitism with more and more power concentrated in the hands of political administrators. Of course, these trends, which were begun in the late Archaic, were not completed until many millennia later in the Classic and Postclassic stages of Nuclear American civilization. The Formative stage merely represents a waypoint in these long-term developmental regularities.

Surplus Economy

Food surplus became increasingly effective in promoting evolutionary change as agriculture shifted from a minor to a major role in the productive economy, essentially between the late Archaic and the early Formative stages. But other food stuffs provide the same effect when these are fixed in location and highly productive. Examples are salmon in coastal rivers, shellfish in marine estuaries, and certain plentiful plant resources such as acorns in California or mesquite beans in the American southwest.

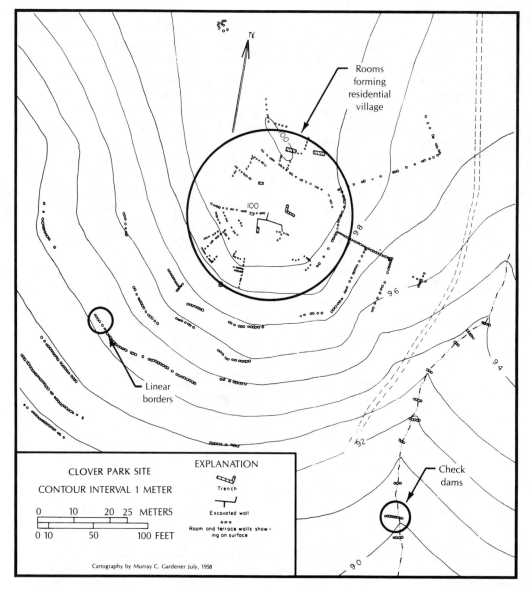

FIGURE 10-1   Contour map of the Clover Park site, east central Arizona, showing the site exposed on the ridge top with linear border fields on the slope and check dams in the nearby gulley.

Source: Richard B. Woodbury, Prehistoric Agriculture at Point of Pines, Arizona. Reproduced by permission of Society for American Archaeology from *American Antiquity*, Memoir No. 17, 1961.

But cereal cropping was always the most efficient form of surplus production with the greatest potential for social evolution. The principal cereal was corn (*Zea mays*). The early Formative saw the development of improved varieties based on seed selection and hybrid cross-breeding with related grasses (Wilkes 1977).

Many farming techniques were invented, including dry cropping, slope runoff agriculture, floodwater farming, and irrigation agriculture. In dry farming, the crops rely on rainfall. The earliest form was slash-and-burn land clearance, which added potash fertilizer to the soil and led to shifting settlements. Ethnographic examples from the New World are the Maya indians, who called slash-and-burn *milpa* farming, and indians of the Amazon basin, who cleared forest areas in order to grow manioc and bananas. Dry farming dates to the Late Archaic and especially to the very earliest Formative stage.

Another form of agriculture is based on slope runoff. Rainfall that collects at the bottom of a hill is controlled by features such as check dams, linear borders, or spreader devices (Woodbury 1961). Runoff farming of this sort, which is particularly well adapted to arid lands, concentrates the rainfall from a large region precisely where it is needed, at the field site. Check dams are low masonry retaining walls built in the bottom of a V-shaped gulley. The dam catches and holds fine agricultural soils on which small garden plots are grown. The dam not only conserves and restrains soil erosion, but also slows down the runoff following a shower; the restrained waters moisten the dammed-up soil to water the garden crops. Linear borders maintain the same soil conservation principles by using lines of rock to contour mildly sloping topography or to grid level stretches of arable land (Fig. 10–1). The Hopi indians of northeast Arizona still practice slope runoff agriculture with water control features (Forde 1963).

Floodwater farming can be practiced in many different natural environments of the Old and New Worlds. Such farming is conducted in fields on the alluvial flood plain next to the river channel, where the crops tap a high water table and take advantage of annual spring flooding.

Irrigation farming is another technique well adapted to arid lands. In this method of farming, canals lead water to the fields from a perennial source such as a river, spring, area of hillside runoff, or a reservoir storage basin (Fig. 10–2). In the New World as in the Old, such water control systems often expanded to incorporate many small-scale canals so that ultimately an entire valley came under one water management. On the north coast of Peru, in Postclassic times, adjacent river valleys were integrated under the direction of imperial bureaucrats.

Both Steward (1955) and Wittfogel (1970) have pointed to the role of irrigation in centralizing authority and generating early civilizations. Recent discoveries of Formative irrigation systems support their theory that arid land irrigation began sufficiently early to account for the rise of civilization in central Mexico and Peru (Flannery and Schoenwetter 1970).

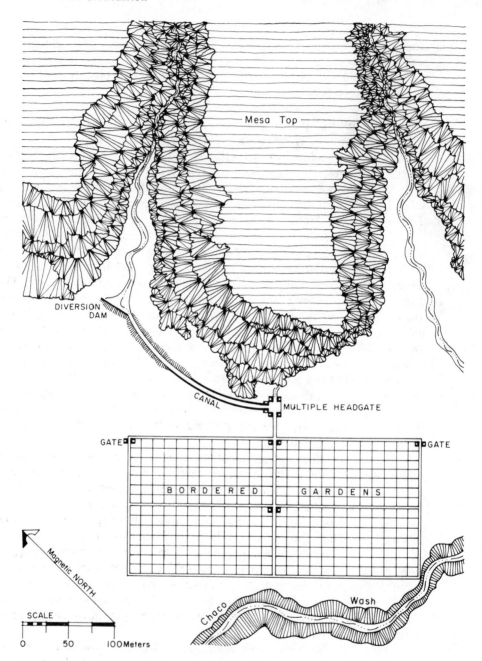

FIGURE 10–2   Plan of irrigated gardens fed by diversion from a side canyon, Chaco Canyon National Monument, New Mexico.

Source: By permission, from R. Gwinn Vivian, ''Conservation and Diversion: Water-Control Systems in the Anasazi Southwest,'' Figure 9–4, In *Irrigation's Impact on Society*, T. E. Downing and McGuire Gibson, editors; Tucson: University of Arizona Press, copyright 1974.

While the above farming methods were applied in dry sections of the continent, elsewhere two other techniques, ridged fields and chinampa farming, were used to control surplus water. In both cases, fields were constructed around lakes or rivers in rich, marshy soils. Prime examples have been documented around the southern perimeter of Lake Texcoco, now a largely filled-in lake in the Valley of Mexico surrounding modern-day Mexico City (Coe 1964). Other examples of marsh-side farming or farming in the wet tropics have been recorded by aerial photography in the Yucatan, Mexico, and in the jungles of South America, particularly around Lake Titicaca located on the border of Peru and Bolivia (Lennon 1982; Parsons and Denevan 1974). In chinampa farming, a grid of canals drained off surplus water. The lake mud was piled in the resulting grid squares to form raised garden plots. Vertical pole pilings and tree rows held the rich soil in place. Farmers grew multiple garden crops and transported their produce to market in dugout canoes. They unloaded vegetable crops at central villages, towns, and even cities in Postclassic times. Coe, who has studied the chinampa field systems of the Xochimilco region of the Valley of Mexico, has found evidence that chinampa farming extends back to Formative times and that it provided the economic support for urbanism and the conquest empire of the Aztecs.

The ridged field system of farming is another technique to drain waterlogged soils in the tropics. In this system, farmers dug long furrows, piled up the excavated marsh muds in parallel ridges, and grew crops upon each raised ridge. The artificial elevation above the level of the water table provided the necessary drainage to grow crops successfully.

By Formative times, crops could be consumed directly by the agrarian producer with enough left over for storage or exchange for exotic products. Storage facilities, many of which were first invented during Archaic times, consist of covered pits, cists (slab-lined pits), and silos. These containers were invented to hold preservable food surplus for use during the winter, or until the surplus could be exchanged by barter with neighboring communities. By Middle Formative times, farmers used their surplus crops to pay taxes to elite theocratic priests who in turn obtained status symbols such as marine shell and turquoise ornaments, copper implements, stingray spines, and decorated pottery by means of barter exchange with neighboring people. The storage containers, themselves, were designed to be mouse-proof, moisture-proof, and theft-proof. Many early domestic residences contained storage pits dug directly into the house floor, but because of crowding, outside storage containers also were constructed. Like housing, the number and volume of storage facilities is a handy index of surplus production and the success of Formative economies.

Religion

Formative religion centered on several themes that reflected economic practices. The dominance of agriculture in the economy led to worship of the forces of nature. Many ideological symbols that appear in religious structures, such as kivas, pyramids, and temples, relate to rain, snow, lightning, wind, and flood, which affect the germination, growth, and harvest of field crops.

Other ritual symbols focused on the control of game through magic and animal fertility rites. Hunting, of course, was not dropped from the repertoire of food-getting practices but was retained from Archaic times. In Formative times, however, farming had a higher priority whenever the hunting schedule conflicted with the agricultural cycle (Flannery 1968).

These ritual themes invoked a pantheon of nature deities, including a corn god, and various weather gods. The rain god of the Maya, called *Tlaloc*, appeared in stone carvings on the facade of temples in ancient Yucatan.

During the rise of Formative religion, the elite priest appeared as one of the earliest occupational specialists. In tribal Archaic and early Formative societies, the ritual practitioner was the shaman or magician. This part-time religious specialist made a living for himself like everyone else did but, in addition, practiced magic to cure the sick and guarantee success in hunting for those who sought him out. But by Middle Formative times, this shaman status had evolved into a full-time specialty amplified in numbers to form a priesthood. These religious leaders were organized into a hierarchy with statuses of high priest, rank and file members, and apprentices. The priests not only served as leaders in public rituals propitiating the nature gods, but also began to develop writing, astronomy, mathematics, astrology, and a calendar. They supported themselves by taxing the peasants in food, crafts, and labor. Priests also planned and directed the construction, maintenance, and use of such public ceremonial architecture as temples and pyramids. These priest-dominated societies of Nuclear America were well on their way to becoming civilized.

Climax Village Societies

Outside of civilized Nuclear America, the village Formative stage represents the climax condition, the high point of development, in New World cultural evolution. Three examples illustrate the range of evolutionary possibilities: the eastern woodlands and southwestern deserts of North America and the tropical rain forest of South America.

EASTERN WOODLANDS

The village Formative of the eastern woodlands of North America, called the *woodland cultural tradition*, is divided into early, middle, and late Woodland periods. The early Woodland period is bracket-dated between 1000 BC and 100 BC. The best known local example is the Adena phase of the Ohio valley (Griffin 1978, p. 242). Sedentary village life and an elaborate burial complex were supported by surplus production based on the growing of sunflower seeds and squash. Other economic aspects of forest adaptation were the intensive collecting of nuts and berries, a subsistence pattern first established during the Archaic.

Another early Woodland trait was the use of true ceramics, which were cord-roughened with the paddle and anvil technique before firing. Indians of the Ohio valley hunted forest game and constructed sizable burial mounds.

The Adena mortuary complex consists of mounds of earth heaped up to cover one or more human burials. Sometimes these burial mounds were surrounded by a circular earth enclosure. The burial mounds, themselves, cover circular log dwellings or tombs. The bodies were interred in a variety of ways: flexed, bundled, multilated, cremated, or decapitated (Griffin 1978, p. 242). Adult male graves often contain exotic offerings indicating status ranking. Some children also were buried with grave goods, indicating ascribed or inherited status, a pattern first noted for some lower Mississippi, late Archaic societies. Grave offerings found in Adena burials include mica and copper artifacts such as bracelets, beads, collars, crescents, celts, and adzes, and carved stone pipes of which some are effigy forms. Another type of grave offering was an engraved stone tablet.

The middle Woodland period ranges in age between 100 BC and AD 500. In the Ohio valley and in Illinois, this period is called the *Hopewell phase*. Hopewell is distinctive for earthworks and mounds (Griffin 1978, p. 246). The burial mounds often cover either single or multiple mortuary structures called *charnel houses*. These contain basins or altars with cremated human bones and offerings. Geometric earthworks also are associated with village sites (Griffin 1978, p. 248).

The middle Woodland Hopewell is noted for its long-distance trade, stimulated and managed by the elite members of society. Imports into the Ohio valley include six species of marine shells, barracuda jaws, ocean turtle shells, shark and alligator teeth. Mica for ornaments was obtained from North Carolina. Other imports were meteoric iron and galena (lead crystals). Copper was obtained from the Lake Superior region and silver from Ontario, Canada. Knife river chalcedony was imported from North Dakota. This huge trade network is a reflection of the degree of surplus food production and development of ranked elite that typify the Hopewellian culture.

The late Woodland period is dated between AD 500 and 1650, the time of initial European contact. It was not until late Woodland times that corn agriculture became dominant in the food producing economy. Concommitant with corn agriculture was the increase in human population size and marked social stratification signaling a shift to full chiefdom societies.

The climax Formative had shifted its center from the upper to the lower Mississippi valley. The most widespread and best known late Woodland phase is the Mississippian culture. Associated cultural traits characterizing the Mississippian are high-status burials as well as temple and effigy mounds (Fig. 10–3). The flat-topped temple mounds were the North American equivalent of the pyramid-temple complex that is distinctive of Mesoamerica. Ef-

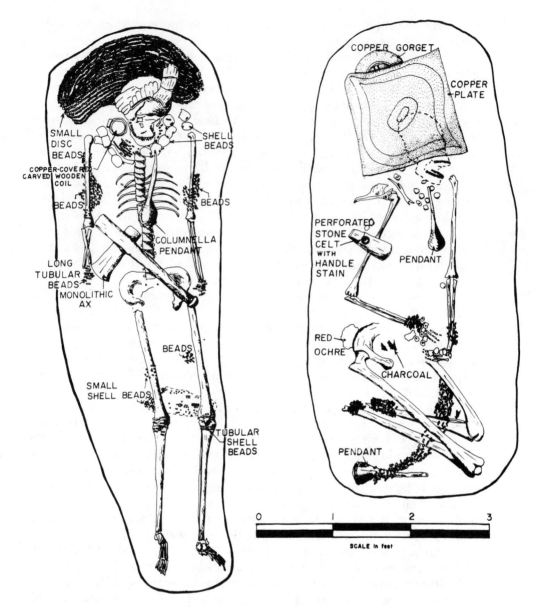

FIGURE 10–3   High status burials from the Mississippian site of Etowah, Georgia.

Source: Lewis H. Larson, Jr., Archaeological Implications of Social Stratification at the Etowah Site, Georgia. Reproduced by permission of Society for American Archaeology from *Memoirs of the SAA* No. 25, 1971.

figy mounds are earthen sculptured figures of humans and animals. During the late Woodland times the bow and arrow replaced the throwing board for use in hunting and in war. Invention of the bow and arrow was correlated with increased warfare. Offensive raids for harvested crops and the capture of women were countered by such defensive measures as the construction of stockades. These stockade-surrounded, late Woodland village sites contained groups of light frame houses surrounding an open, central plaza. Within the plaza were one or more temple mounds.

SOUTHWESTERN DESERT

In the southwestern United States, there were three village Formative cultural traditions: Hohokam, Anasazi, and Mogollon (Lipe 1978). The Hohokam culture was located in the southern Arizona desert where it endured from 300 BC to AD 1400. Influences from the Pueblo Salado peoples modified the Hohokam tradition between AD 1100 and Spanish contact in the sixteenth century. It is likely that the modern descendants of the Hohokam are the Pima and Papago indians who live on reservations in southern Arizona today.

Some of the distinctive cultural traits of the Hohokam are red-on-buff fired pottery constructed by the paddle and anvil technique, cremation of the dead, village settlements made up of haphazardly arranged frame houses, a ceremonial game played in a ball court, pyramids or temple mounds, and canal irrigation agriculture with crops of corn, beans, squash, and cotton.

The Anasazi, sometimes called the *Pueblo* cultural tradition, were found on the Colorado plateau centering on the Four Corners region of Utah, Colorado, New Mexico, and Arizona. This tradition evolved from an Archaic base about AD 1 and continues today among Pueblo indian tribes such as the Hopi, Zuni, Keresan-speakers, and Tanoan peoples of the Rio Grande valley. A few of the traits that identify the Anasazi-Pueblo Formative are black-on-white and corrugated true-fired pottery, gridded masonry, and mud-walled, apartment-house type villages and towns. The multiple-story, tiered buildings were called *Pueblos,* meaning ''towns,'' by the early sixteenth-century Spanish to distinguish these people from their nomadic neighbors, the Apache and Navajo indians (Fig. 10–4). The Anasazi-Pueblo peoples used a special religious chamber, called a *kiva,* that reflected a rich pantheon of nature gods. The Pueblo indians grew corn, beans, and squash by dry and floodwater farming.

The third southwestern tradition is the Mogollon. These village Formative peoples were located in the mountainous country lying between the Colorado plateau and the southern desert. The Mogollon tradition endured from 150 BC to approximately AD 1000, after which it changed dramatically under the influence of the Anasazi-Pueblo peoples. Subsistence of the Mo-

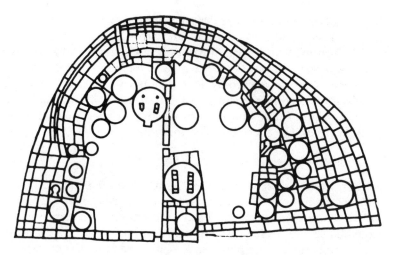

FIGURE 10-4   Plan of Pueblo Bonito, a large, gridded, multiple-story Anasazi town located at Chaco Canyon National Monument, New Mexico. Rectangular masonry rooms were for residence and storage, while the circular rooms were kivas or ceremonial structures.

Source: Alden C. Hayes, David M. Brugge, and W. James Judge, Archaeological Surveys of Chaco Canyon, New Mexico. National Park Service.

gollon was based on dry farming, hunting mountain game, and collecting edible greens. Settlements were unstructured villages of pit houses, often with one great kiva, a large religious meeting hall. Burials were flexed and pottery was a polished red-on-brown.

TROPICAL RAIN FOREST

The village Formative of lowland South America, which developed out of a semisedentary Archaic, is characterized by shell mounds distributed along the Atlantic coast (Meggers and Evans 1978). Some of these shell midden sites, dated between 5000 BC and AD 1, contain pottery made as early as 3000 BC, some of the earliest fired ceramics found in the New World. In Venezuela and the islands of the Antilles, the Formative economy was based on maize agriculture. Other lowland tropical regions, such as the Orinoco and Amazon river basins, developed surplus food production on bitter manioc, as indicated by tropical rain forest sites containing ceramic cooking griddles. The tropical rain forest was the scene of shifting villages supported by slash-and-burn agriculture. Houses were often built on high ground or raised on artificially constructed mounds in order to elevate them above standing water. The circular or oval houses were arranged around an open plaza, sometimes in a street layout. Humans were buried in large, ornate pottery urns, placed under or near the houses, in the plaza, or in an isolated position away from the village (Meggers and Evans 1978).

Nuclear America

Two independent New World civilizations form Nuclear America. These high cultures are the Mesoamerican and Andean (Sanders and Price 1968). In both of these areas, the Formative rapidly evolved into many individual civilizations, which were local theocratic states run by a priesthood (Fig. 10-5). By

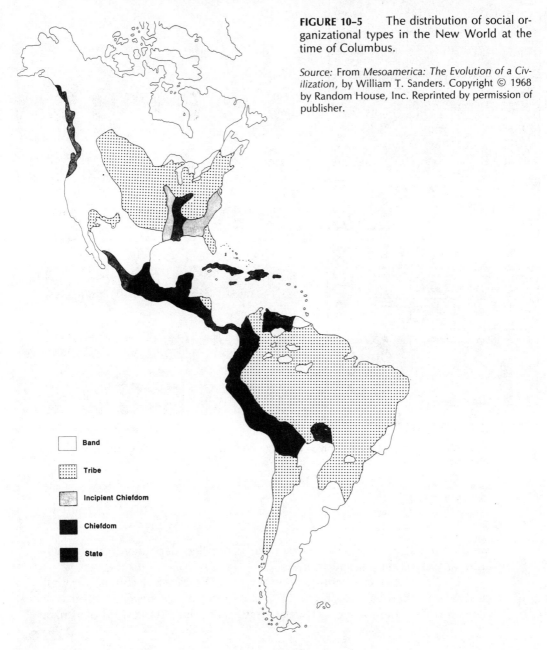

FIGURE 10-5   The distribution of social organizational types in the New World at the time of Columbus.

Source: From *Mesoamerica: The Evolution of a Civilization*, by William T. Sanders. Copyright © 1968 by Random House, Inc. Reprinted by permission of publisher.

Band

Tribe

Incipient Chiefdom

Chiefdom

State

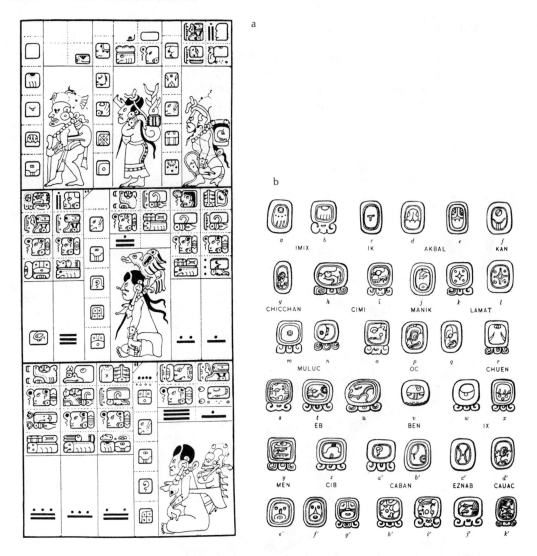

FIGURE 10–6   Maya hieroglyphs: (a) a page from the Dresden Codex; (b) the day signs taken from stelae inscriptions.

Source: Gordon R. Willey, 1966, *An Introduction to American Archaeology*, Vol. 1. Englewood Cliffs, N.J.: Prentice Hall.

middle Formative times, the elite priests controlled dependent satellite villages of tax-paying peasant farmers.

In general, we can define a New World civilization as a complex or high culture with the following traits: (1) a state form of government, (2) use of religion rather than magic, (3) social stratification into classes, (4) urbanism and large populations, and (5) science and literature. Not all of these indicative traits were fully developed by Formative times. Government, for instance, was run by the priesthood without benefit of a civil bureaucracy or a ruling military class; these developments did not appear until Postclassic times. Religion in Formative times was focused on a pantheon of agriculture and nature gods. War gods did not become prominent until Postclassic times. Social stratification had evolved in a rudimentary form; the classes were the elite priesthood and the peasant agricultural workers. Urbanism and large, dense populations were present only in a few favored locales within Nuclear America (Sanders and Price 1968).

Formative science and literature developed unequally between the two centers of civilization. In Mesoamerica, the Middle Formative Olmec civilization was making calendars and writing, as indicated by glyph notations for numbers and words appearing on stelae and ceramic vessels. However, these notational systems have never been deciphered. From Classic times in Mesoamerica, the calendars are decipherable, so that a few written symbols for gods, days, and leaders' names can be read (Schele 1981, p. 68). A few actual books, called *codices*, are preserved from Postclassic times and these can be read because of the pictographic quality of the writing (Fig. 10–6). Unlike all other early civilizations, the Andean high culture lacked a formal system of writing. A set of color-coded, knotted ropes served to record quantitative information.

Mesoamerican Civilization

The term Mesoamerica applies to those civilized cultures located in ancient Mexico and adjacent portions of Central America including Belize, Guatemala, Honduras, and El Salvador. Mesoamerica is not one civilization but a series of civilized primitive states forming a sphere of cultural interaction so that all evolved simultaneously (Culbert 1978).

Mesoamerica is a land of great geographical diversity, which probably helped to stimulate the growth and development of civilization. The varied topography ranges from coastal lowlands to the central and southern highlands of Mexico where mountains rise to 18,500 feet. Vegetation and climate are zoned by elevation. Tropical rainforests along the coast are systematically replaced by semiarid to desert conditions in the interior highlands. Early civilizations appeared in both the wet tropics and the arid, interior highland basins—unlike the Old World early civilizations, which have been found exclusively along major rivers that flow through arid lands. The rich contrast in Mesoamerican ecological zones stimulated the exchange of raw materials and manufactured products. Goods were transported over long distances to market centers located in another zone. Thus, bartering expanded the total resources available to any given civilization or community.

Trade is an important key to understanding the growth history of Mesoamerican civilization. The elite rulers evolved a system of concentrating

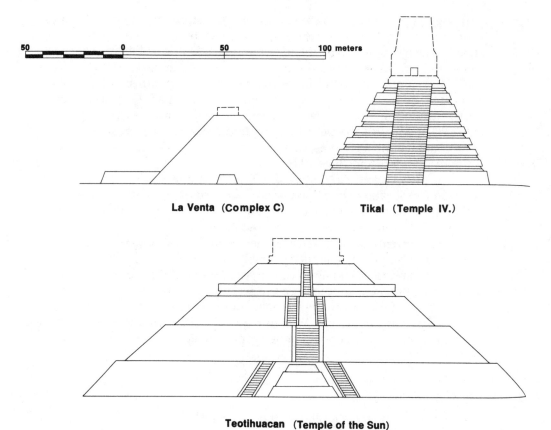

FIGURE 10–7   Architectural elevations of the three principal temple mounds at La Venta, Tikal, and Teotihuacan drawn to the same scale. La Venta is of middle Formative age, while the other two are Classic pyramid-temples.

Source: From *Mesoamerica: The Evolution of a Civilization*, by William T. Sanders. Copyright © 1968 by Random House, Inc. Reprinted by permission of publisher.

food surplus in their own hands by taxing peasants and conquered neighbors. The rulers were able to convert this wealth of food stuffs into more durable ornaments and status symbols by trading with neighboring elite during productive years. During lean years, the durable ornaments and exotic materials could be reconverted into food through trade with adjacent elevation zones where productivity had not suffered. In this way the elite rulers buffered their existence against adversity, even though the exploited peasant worker still suffered shortages on a periodic basis (Flannery and Schoenwetter 1970).

The early Formative of Mesoamerica is dated roughly between 2000 and 1000 BC. It is characterized by the first appearance of true fired pottery and sedentary village life (Culbert 1978). In the dry interior highlands of Mexico, farming was carried out by both dry and irrigation techniques. Coastal sites give evidence of a marine adaptation by the aquatic resources that they contain. Large shell mounds are located at many sites, particularly along the Pacific coast. These early Formative societies were simple, self-sufficient, egalitarian villages (Culbert 1978, p. 414). The middle Formative saw the rise of social complexity marked by ceremonial, pyramid-temple architecture in central places, which served to integrate the dependent peasants from remote villages (Fig. 10–7).

The first widely recognized Mesoamerican civilization is the Olmec, dated between 1250 and 500 BC (Culbert 1978, p. 414). The Olmec, which covers parts of both the early and middle Formative, is sometimes called the *mother civilization* of Mesoamerica. Geographically it was distributed over the Mexican states of Veracruz and Tabasco in the wet tropics on the Caribbean coast. In this swampy coastal lowland, the best known sites are two ceremonial centers, San Lorenzo and La Venta. The Olmec is known for its distinctive art motifs featuring the jaguar cat and infantile humans (Fig. 10–8). Olmec archaeology reflects an organized, formal leadership and incipient class stratification. The complexity of the culture is expressed by monumental religious enterprises such as pyramids faced with adobe (clay) and huge, helmeted human heads carved out of basalt. The heads seem to be sculptures

FIGURE 10–8   Olmec statuary: (a) jadeite celt with anthropomorphic jaguar face; (b) two views of a jadeite human figurine showing infantile features; (c) figurine of a seated woman from La Venta, Tabasco. A small polished hematite mirror or ornament has been fastened to the breast. The figurine was carved from whitish, mottled jadeite and was found covered with red cinnabar powder.

Source: Gordon R. Willey, 1966, *An Introduction to American Archaeology*, Vol. 1. Englewood Cliffs, N.J.: Prentice-Hall.

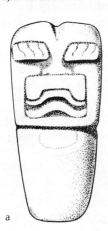
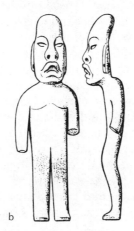

a   b   c

of individual religious leaders. The helmet is thought to identify a ball court player. Another social implication is the rise of craft specialists, who produced art objects for trade and home consumption. Long-distance exchange was conducted by the Olmec who exported objects made of obsidian, jade, and magnetite carved in the distinctive Olmec art style.

The late Formative of Mesoamerica ranged from 300 BC to AD 250. Its characteristics are regional growth, rise in cultural complexity, population increase, and the first development of great cities (Culbert 1978, p. 420). An outstanding example of urbanism is the city of Teotihuacan located some 25 miles north of modern-day Mexico City (Millon 1970). Teotihuacan was founded as a ceremonial center but rapidly drew artisans, occupational guilds, and foreign merchants to become the foremost city of Mesoamerica by the early Classic stage. The economic basis of Teotihuacan's urban growth was spring irrigation farming within walking distance of the city. But the major source of economic wealth for the city was the production and export of obsidian objects, which were widely traded throughout Mesoamerica. Between 150 BC and the time of Christ, the city grew to a population estimated at 30,000 people, many of whom had immigrated from the surrounding valley. At its heyday, Teotihuacan covered some 21 km² of territory.

Andean Civilization

A second great complex of civilized cultures lies in the Andean culture area of Peru and Bolivia, South America (Moseley 1978). This is the only early civilization of the southern hemisphere for which copious archaeological documentation is available. Although Mesoamerica and the Andean civilization were two separate entities, some interchange of goods and ideas occurred, probably by way of maritime traffic along the Pacific coast (Moseley 1975a).

Civilization in Peru climaxed a long developmental history beginning with nomadic hunting in the Lithic stage followed by agricultural experimentation during the Archaic. These developments, in turn, led to settled villages and eventually to towns and cities, and ultimately climaxed in great conquest empires such as that of the Inca.

The Andean civilization developed within two great topographic zones located along the western margin of South America facing the Pacific ocean. The interior zone is the high Andes, chains of parallel mountains. The exterior zone is the narrow coastal shelf lying between the mountains and the ocean. The Andes of Peru and Bolivia consist of three principal ranges with peaks ranging between 15,000 and 20,000 feet high. These chains, in turn, are separated by interior plateaus about 10,000 feet high, which become the high plains (altiplano) on the Peruvian-Bolivian border in the vicinity of Lake Titicaca. Characteristically, the Andes have very little vegetation below 5500 feet and only bleak shrubs and grass above this elevation. Cultivated high-altitude crops are potatoes and quinoa, a grain cereal. Wild game includes guanaco, vicuña, and deer. In addition, the Andes is known for its domesticated camelids, the llama and alpaca.

Although winter fog is common on the Peruvian coast, there is literally no rainfall in the area, one of the world's most complete deserts. The desert, however, is bisected by some 40 rivers which run from their headwaters in the highest, snow-capped Andes down to the ocean. Each of these rivers empties into the Pacific at roughly right angles to the coast so that each valley parallels its neighboring valleys to form many little, green Nile-like oases surrounded by total desert. The valley margins have virtually no vegetation. Each of these valleys was the home of a civilized state in Classic times.

When watered by natural flooding or canal irrigation, the rich, deep alluvial soils of the valley flood plains are highly productive farmlands. Crops grown here in prehistoric times included maize, beans, manioc, squashes, peanuts, cotton, avocados, and fruits. Because of aridity and lack of grass for grazing, there are few land mammals, but marine resources include fish, shellfish, sea birds, and sea mammals. Crops were fertilized by guano (bird droppings) mined from thick deposits on island rookeries and brought ashore in prehistoric times.

Edward P. Lanning and John H. Rowe divided Peruvian prehistory into six preceramic periods, three horizons, and two intermediate periods. In keeping with the evolutionary theme of this textbook, however, these time periods can be converted into cultural stages, actually an older system of classification developed by Steward and Faron (1959) and others (Bushnell 1963). A correlation of stages and periods is shown in Table 10–1 (Willey 1971).

Like the pristine Old World civilizations, the civilization of Peru evolved along parallel rivers that crossed the desert. Unlike the rest of the world, however, the springboard for Peru's civilization lay not in an interior farming adaptation but rather in a marine economy featuring agricultural experimentation. The coastal Archaic of Peru, dated between 4200 and 1800 BC, is climaxed by the development of sedentary village life and the beginnings of monumental religious architecture in preceramic times. Coastal sites expressing public architecture are dated to Period VI, sometimes called the *cotton preceramic* because of the widespread preservation of cotton textiles. Around 1800 BC, however, a marked shift in settlement and economy took place in which the Archaic marine adaptation was replaced quite rapidly by a Formative riverine adaptation. Coastal villages were relocated along the many interior rivers at the time when true fired ceramics and evidence of irrigation agriculture appear in the archaeological record.

By 900 BC, there is evidence of a widespread religious cult spreading through the Andean culture area. This cult is indicated in the fossil record by an art style named the *Chavin* after a north highland site, the Chavin de Huantar. The pan-Peruvian nature of this style, the principal art motif of which was a stylized cat, has been interpreted as indicating considerable uniformity in religious beliefs, perhaps stimulated by pilgrimages to the religious

TABLE 10-1.　Prehistoric Peruvian chronology correlating cultural stages and temporal periods

Cultural Stages (Bushnell 1963; Steward and Faron 1959)	Temporal Periods (Lanning and Rowe in Willey 1971)	Age Range	Cultural Characteristics
Postclassic	Late Horizon	AD 1476–1532	Artistic style continuity; Inca militarism and the Inca imperial state
	Late Intermediate period	AD 1000–1476	Style diversity; series of states and small kingdoms such as the Chimor (Chimu)
	Middle Horizon	AD 600–1000	Style continuity; Hauri and Tiahuanaco empires
Classic	Early intermediate period	200 BC–AD 600	Diversification of ceramic art styles; regional states such as Moche; urbanism underway
Formative	Early Horizon	900–200 BC	Art style of Chavin religious cult spread throughout most of culture area; uniformity in religious beliefs
	Initial period	1800–900 BC	Beginnings of civilization; first appearance of true fired plain pottery; irrigation agriculture; theocratic states
Archaic	Preceramic period VI (cotton preceramic)	2500–1800 BC	Large habitation sites; sizable public ceremonial constructions; first population increase; appearance of maize cultivation
	Preceramic period V	4200–2500 BC	Coastal shell midden sites; subsistence focused on marine resources; domestic plants: squashes, chili peppers, guavas, and cotton; agricultural experimentation
Lithic	Preceramic periods I–IV	9500–4200 BC	Subsistence based on hunting land mammals and collecting wild plant foods

capital at the north highland site. The Chavin cult with its ideological uniformity expressed in feline figures marks the Early Horizon of Peruvian prehistory.

The entire Formative stage, dated in Peru between 1800 and 200 BC, shows evidence of settlement organization parallel to the middle Formative of Mesoamerica, that is, theocratic states were made up of ceremonial centers surrounded by satellite farming villages. The peasant farmers paid homage to the gods of the elite priests and deferred to the supernatural power of the priests by payments of surplus food stuffs at times of annual religious festivals. The priests, in turn, preserved a balanced harmony between man and gods. The elite priests also managed the construction and maintenance of irrigation systems, thereby controlling the lives of the untutored peasants through water allocation, a source of considerable authority. By late Formative times, people with different occupational specialties were beginning to settle in the cities of the New World. The beginnings of social differentiation led to the Classic stage.

Classic Stage

The term *classic* means prosperous, cosmopolitan, and achieving great heights. In New World prehistory, the term refers to the climax in the developmental history of Nuclear America, the civilization of the theocratic state societies.

Willey and Phillips (1958) list five definitive criteria of the Classic: (1) qualitative and relative advancement over the Formative, (2) excellence in the great arts produced by artisans, (3) a climax in religious architecture, (4) a general florescence in material culture, and (5) the beginnings of urbanism. Today, of course, the appearance of cities has been pushed further back in time to the late Formative.

Formerly the Classic stage was thought to be composed of peaceful societies because symbols of military organizations and trappings of warfare seemed to be lacking in the archaeological record. Now it is recognized that the distinction between the "peaceful" Classic and the "militaristic" Postclassic is relative, rather than absolute. The Bonampak murals of the Mayas provide evidence of interstate warfare and the capturing of prisoners for religious sacrifice. Murals of the Mayan civilization have tended to refute the notion that Classic societies were completely peaceful (Fig. 1–3).

Mesoamerican Classic

The Classic of Mesoamerica is dated between AD 250 (or 300) and 900. It is subdivided into early and late periods with a time boundary at AD 600, actually the beginning point for the collapse of many Classic political centers between AD 700 and 1000 (Culbert 1978). Some of these important regional states are found in the lowland Mayan area of the Peten, Guatemala, and at Oaxaca and Teotihuacan in the Valley of Mexico. Collapse of political centers at the close of the Classic stage prepared the way for the formation of new political forms—the Postclassic conquest empires.

The preeminent urban center in the early Classic was the city of Teotihuacan, founded in Formative times. The site, now part of the parks and monuments system of Mexico, lies 25 miles northeast of modern Mexico City tucked away in a side pocket of the Valley of Mexico. Teotihuacan was founded as a ceremonial center but rapidly grew to an urban agglomeration of people ranging from resident peasant farmers to elite priests, artisans, and foreign merchants. By early Classic times, it may have been the political cap-

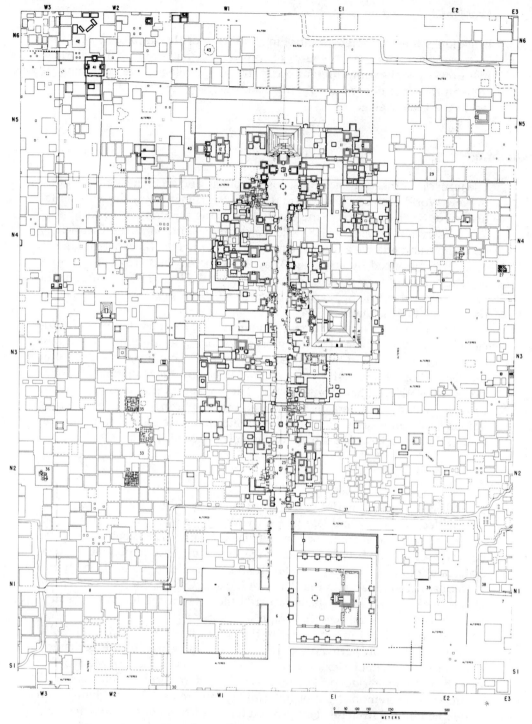

FIGURE 10-9   Map of Teotihuacan, an early Classic stage city of Mesoamerica (AD 600).

Source: © 1968 by René Millon.

ital of a widespread state, perhaps even an early empire, stretching south-ward to Kaminaljuyu (Willey 1966). Whether a political empire or simply a powerful exporting commercial center, Teotihuacan exercised widespread influence on the surrounding cultures and civilizations of Classic times.

In the first half of the Classic stage Teotihuacan was one of the largest pre-industrial cities in the world (Millon 1970, 1973). After AD 600 it was destroyed by invading barbarians, called *Chichimecs,* who sacked the city and then camped in the ruins during late Classic times. These Chichimec peoples were uncivilized, tribal barbarians who lived in the arid interior central plateau country of northern Mexico and periodically invaded the civilized world. Each time this happened in Mesoamerican prehistory, the intruders lost their tribal identities through acculturation, which converted them to civilization. Many of these tribal invaders subsequently rose to prominence after a tutorial period of learning civilized ways from their more advanced neighbors.

The layout of Teotihuacan, as shown in Figure 10-9, was a grid pattern of streets and blocks of buildings (Millon, Drewitt, and Cowgill 1973). The city was divided into quadrants by its north-south Street of the Dead and its East and West Avenues. Near the end of its life, around AD 600, the city covered some 30 km^2. As shown on the map prepared by Millon and his co-workers, Teotihuacan had a crowded center with a more sparsely settled periphery.

Architectural features include room complexes, platforms, temples, open plazas, walls, and thoroughfares (Millon 1973). One of the more prominent kinds of architectural units is called an *apartment compound.* Millon mapped more than 2000 of these one-story, rectangular structures (Fig. 10-10). The Ciudadela (citadel) and the Great Compound are located in the center of the city at the point where the major bisecting avenues intersect. Based on their large size, physical shape, and associated artifact classes, it is thought that these enclosures served as the religious, bureaucratic, and commercial center of the city.

The most sparsely settled section of the city was the southwest quadrant. Located at the extreme southern extension of the Street of the Dead, this sector forms a continuous and integral part of the city bordering the richest cultivated lands. Probably it housed the farmers who tilled spring-fed, irrigated fields just beyond the city limits.

The northwest quadrant of the city was the most densely settled. Artifactual evidence suggests that occupational specialists were concentrated here in associated apartment compounds. Supporting evidence for this interpretation is the fact that the northwest quadrant borders the poorest arable land. This quadrant, first settled around the time of Christ during the late Formative stage, is called the *Old City.*

Between the quadrant level of organization and that of the individual building blocks, is an intermediate level of settlement organization, the neighborhood, or barrio. These local organizational cells are defined by distinctive architecture. Often groups of buildings housed workers practicing the same

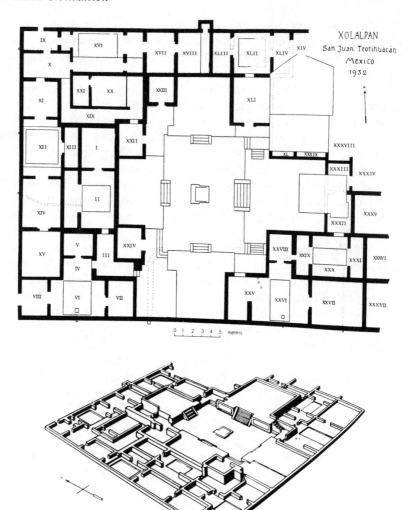

FIGURE 10-10   Plan and oblique view of the apartment compound of Xolalpan, city of Teotihuacan, Mexico.

Source: Gordon R. Willey, 1966, *An Introduction to American Archaeology*, Vol. 1. Englewood Cliffs, N.J.: Prentice-Hall.

craft, such as obsidian working, pottery making, or lapidary work. Some barrios were occupied by foreigners from the same place, as indicated by their exotic painted pottery. These foreigners included resident traders from the Gulf Coast, Yucatan, and Guatemala.

Millon (1970) characterizes Teotihuacan as a planned city. In support of this contention he points out that the major north-south axis, the Street of the Dead with its giant Pyramids of the Sun and Moon, was built in its entirety by the second century AD, before many permanent buildings had been constructed. He describes the role of this avenue in shaping the future growth of the city by saying that it was a five-kilometer-long street staked out as a claim for the future.

Based on the numbers and sizes of the apartment compounds in the barrios of craft specialists, it has been estimated that Teotihuacan housed between 75,000 and 200,000 people. The probable population was 125,000.

The apartment compound, which has a communal kitchen, a small pyramid for resident worship, and evidence of a specific craft industry, is the living, worshiping, and manufacturing place of a craft guild. Of more than 500 such resident workshops, the vast majority were for the manufacture of obsidian objects to support the export trade. At least 100 other craft workshops were distributed among specialists working in ceramics, basalt, slate, and unknown materials that have left no trace. In addition, a considerable number of other artisans, including masons, plasterers, and carpenters, must have been involved in building the city itself.

Millon (1970) points out that the city was intended to serve as an elite ceremonial center like many other civic-administrative sites of Formative times. But at Teotihuacan, manufacturing and trading functions were added by early Classic times. All three of these functions, then, created a powerful urban center of vast influence on the neighboring early Classic city states.

Andean Classic

The Classic stage of the Andean culture area is dated to the Early Intermediate period between 200 BC and AD 600, according to Willey (1971). Rowe and Menzell (1967) date the Classic even earlier, beginning at 400 BC. This age range is much earlier than that of the Classic of Mesoamerica, which overlaps only 300 years of the Andean sequence.

The Classic Andean civilizations are marked by theocratic regional states. Many of these named archaeological cultures or phases are confined to individual river valleys or several adjacent valleys where small-scale conquest took place. Warfare was endemic. Society was stratified by class and occupation, and authority rested in the hands of powerful, elite priest-rulers. The urbanization trend that began in the late Formative continued during Classic times (Rowe and Menzell 1967).

Some of the more distinctive traits of the Classic are metallurgy and massive adobe architecture, constructed of rectangular, mold-made and sundried clay bricks called *adobes*. Mud constructions are common on the totally arid Pacific coastal plain, whereas massive stone masonry buildings and monuments are found more frequently in the slightly wetter interior highlands.

The state planned and directed the construction of public structures such as palaces, pyramids (called *huacas*), forts, town walls, irrigation ditches, aqueducts, roads, and bridges. Surplus food production was based on intercommunity irrigation agriculture, also directed by the state. However, there is no evidence of writing or a calendar (Bennett 1947).

As an example of the many Early Intermediate theocratic states, the Moche state is well documented through excavation and museum pottery collections. The Moche, otherwise known as *Mochica*, was a Classic stage civilization and regional state located on the north coast of Peru. As its name implies, this Early Intermediate civilization is named for the Moche valley where most of its archaeological remains were found. But the Moche phase is also recognized in neighboring valleys to the north and south, indicating limited conquest.

The Moche or Mochica phase is dated between AD 1 and 650, after which time the people were subjugated by the first of the Postclassic pan-Peruvian empires, that of the Huari-Tiahuanaco (Rowe and Menzell 1967). Relative dating of the Moche site was first based on chronological seriation of decorated ceramics, in particular a special kind of jar with a stirrup spout (Fig. 10–11). Gradual changes in the form of the jar spout led Larco Hoyle (1948) to divide the Moche phase into five ceramic subphases identified by Roman numerals (I–V). This stylistic dating was verified through stratigraphic study of the Moche site (Kroeber 1926, Hastings and Moseley 1975). Next this relative chronology was transformed into an absolute chronology by radiocarbon dating. According to this dating, the Moche phase was contemporary to the urban state of Teotihuacan.

Modeled and painted ceramic vessels, some of which are pornographic in subject matter, have been recovered in very large quantities from Moche phase sites. Many that were obtained from the looting of graves now reside as large collections in the great museums of the world. From the pictorial quality of this art work, much of the everyday life of Mochica society has been reconstructed in very fine detail by Larco Hoyle (1947).

The economy of the Moche state was based on surplus production provided by gravity flow irrigation agriculture. In the Moche Valley, this form of agriculture dates back at least to 1500 BC but reached its peak during the Early Intermediate period (Moseley 1977). At first single ditches led water from the Moche river out on to the alluvial flood plain, where it fed garden plots. Gradually this system was expanded until it covered the entire valley. By Late Intermediate times, the master canals serviced an area some 40 percent greater than the modern-day irrigation of the Moche valley (Moseley 1977). At this same time, the Chimu kingdom connected the Moche with a ditch system originating in the Chicama valley to the north. In this way, additional waters were brought into the Moche valley through a canal system that crossed the intervalley divide, utilizing aqueducts to bridge ravines and other obstructions. During Moche times, the chief crops were corn, beans,

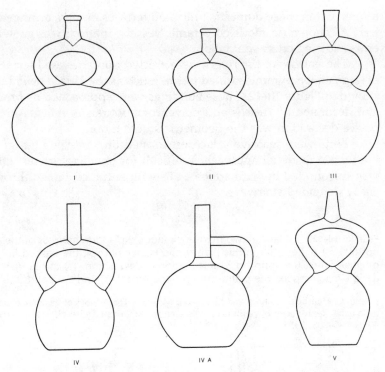

FIGURE 10–11   Chronological seriation of stirrup-spout water jars from the Moche phase, north coast of Peru.

Source: Gordon R. Willey, 1971, *An Introduction to American Archaeology*, Vol. 2. Englewood Cliffs, N.J.: Prentice-Hall.

peanuts, potatoes, manioc, sweet potatoes, pumpkins, gourds, apples, coca, and cotton (Larco Hoyle 1947).

Hunting supplemented farming. Deer, which browsed along the riverside, were taken with nets and spears. Birds, such as doves and wild ducks, were shot down with a blowgun or spear thrower, and sea lions were clubbed with a mace. In addition to this wild game, the Mochica hunters ate domesticated llama and guinea pig (Larco Hoyle 1947).

The ceramic art depicts a high dependence on seafood. Deep-sea fishing was conducted using nets and gourd floats from two kinds of balsa or reed boats. The larger type is like boats still used on Lake Titicaca, while the smaller type is similar to reed boats presently employed on the Peruvian coast. In addition to marine fish, the Moche people exploited shellfish from the intertidal zone.

Moche architecture includes both domestic dwellings and such public buildings as palaces, forts, temples, and roads (Larco Hoyle 1947, p. 164). Peasant dwellings were small and made up of a number of interconnected

rooms. Often these domestic units had terraces or were arranged around patios. As shown on modeled ceramic vessels, the roof was gabled with open
ends allowing cross-ventilation.

The palaces of the rulers were erected upon elevated terrain or on tops
of large adobe pyramids called *huacas,* such as the Huaca de la Luna complex
shown in Figure 10–12. These buildings were approached by broad stairways
and decorated by frescos and polychrome murals in relief. Another form of
palace decoration was the geometric stucco motif.

Forts were massive structures located on strategic high ground where
the terrain made all approaches difficult for invading armies. Often the fort
was surrounded by high adobe walls with entrance gained through narrow,
easily defended stairways.

FIGURE 10–12   Plans of two mud brick (adobe) platform mounds of the Moche phase,
north coast of Peru. (a) In this plan of the Huaca del Sol, the dashed line indicates the
original dimensions prior to Spanish colonial destruction; (b) in the plan of the Huaca
de la Luna complex, the platforms are numbered 1–3, and the courts are lettered A–D.

Source: C. Mansfield Hastings and M. Edward Moseley, The Adobes of the Huaca del Sol and Huaca
de la Luna. Reproduced by permission of Society for American Archaeology from *American Antiquity*
40(2): 196–203, 1975.

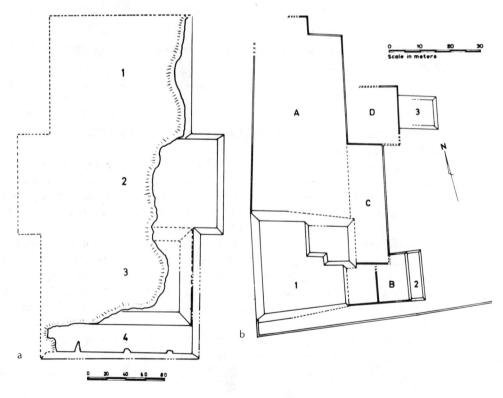

Temples were built upon huge mud brick pyramids. These religious buildings were decorated with intricate polychrome friezes depicting supernatural subjects.

The roads that traversed the entire state territory provided ready transportation for messengers, armies, and goods for exchange and distribution. The main roads had a standard width of 33 feet, with narrower roads branching into the interior. Small houses at intervals along the road system served as relay stations for messengers and check points through which the government controlled movement within the realm. Goods were transported by human backpacking or carried by llama, the only domesticated beast of burden. Ceramics show the llama carrying cargo in bags, saddlebags, and large baskets. Large state-regulated balsa boats carried goods along the Pacific coast (Larco Hoyle 1947, p. 166).

The most outstanding examples of Mochica architecture are two huacas, or mud brick platforms, found at the Moche site, an Early Intermediate city located near modern Trujillo in the Moche valley. Probably this Classic city was the capital of a Moche state and perhaps even a regional empire. One of these platforms, the Huaca del Sol, is characterized as the largest mud brick structure in South America. Although this structure was cross-shaped, as reconstructed by Hastings and Moseley, much of the original shape was destroyed during the Spanish colonial period. Figure 10–12a shows that the platform mound was constructed in four sections during eight construction stages extending over 100 years of use during the latter part of the Moche phase (Moche III and IV). The Sol or sun pyramid measures more than 342 by 159 m and is thought to have stood 41 m in height (Hastings and Moseley 1975, p. 196). It has been estimated that its construction required more than 143 million adobes. These sun dried, mud bricks were made in rectangular molds open at the top and bottom. The findings of more than 100 different kinds of maker's marks on these bricks, coupled with variations in mold characteristics, brick size, soil composition, and segmented construction, all point to episodic periods of building in which many different communities of Moche valley residents participated as a form of labor tax (Fig. 10–13). Hastings and Moseley (1975, pp. 202–3) conclude that:

> Moche adobes lack standardized dimensions. This may relate to the hypothesis that the Sol and Luna huacas were built with a mit'a-like labor tax and organizational system. In theory, a community met its tax obligations by sending a work party to build a particular section of construction designated by the governing body of authority. The party made its own bricks, marked them, transported the adobes to the building site, and then laid the bricks up in the assigned skin or construction segment. Presumably, skins and segments were the units by which the tax was measured. The central authority was interested in these finished products and not in the constituent bricks. This left the size and characteristics of the bricks to vary according to predilections of the different groups meeting their tax obligations.

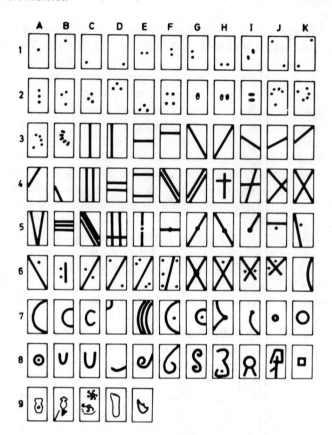

FIGURE 10-13   Index of maker's marks recorded at the Huaca del Sol, Moche phase, north coast of Peru.

Source: C. Mansfield Hastings and M. Edward Moseley, The Adobes of the Huaca del Sol and Huaca de la Luna. Reproduced by permission of Society for American Archaeology from *American Antiquity* 40 (2):196–203, 1975.

The *mit'a* term in the above quote is the Inca word for labor tax. This ancient system of paying taxes by community labor was still in effect during the colonial period, when Spanish authorities required a tax in labor by native indian communities.

The Huaca del Sol is a truncated pyramid thought to have supported adobe temples on its flat top. These buildings were decorated with polychrome murals with religious themes. As the Huaca was enlarged periodically, the earlier temples were filled in, thereby preserving some of the religious architecture (Willey 1971, p. 138).

The Luna (or moon) complex, situated nearby Sol, consists of three solid-fill adobe brick platforms with four courts attached (Fig. 10-12b). The pyramid platforms were capped with flagstone pavings, palace rooms, and other walled structures, some decorated with murals dating to the end of ceramic Phase IV or the opening of Phase V. One of these murals depicts anthropomorphized weapons and utensils revolting against their human masters (Willey 1971, p. 138). Although it is difficult to measure the maximum size of the Luna platforms accurately, it is estimated that they are filled with more than 50 million adobe bricks. Willey (1971, p. 138) believes that the Luna complex, with its many summit palaces, housed the aristocractic leaders of the state.

Metallurgy was one of the outstanding industries of the Mochica. Larco Hoyle (1947, p. 167) reports that they worked gold, silver, copper, and lead. Silver and copper were alloyed with gold or gilded with a gold amalgam. Silver was soldered with silver-gold alloy and gold was soldered with alloys of copper and gold. Gold sheeting as thin as paper has been found in Moche phase graves. Metal rattles were made on stone molds and burnished with a polishing stone.

A number of lines of evidence lead to the conclusion that the Mochica state was a complex organization under the direction of a central authority. The engineering and administrative direction required of huge state projects, such as the valley-wide irrigation systems, monumental public architecture, and a road network with controlled travel, all point to this finding. This conclusion is further supported in great detail by the ceramic pictorial art, which illustrates governmental dignitaries, artisans, and peasant farmers, the social classes making up an authoritarian society.

The society was organized in the form of a pyramid in which the elite rulers at the apex directed and controlled a vast citizenry of commoners at the base. A supreme ruler, of divine origin, is shown on funerary pottery as a human with feline teeth. He is sometimes young and sometimes mature. His many ceramic depictions indicate that he served as a civil ruler, military chief, and high priest, probably as a result of his aristocratic background. In his high priest role, the supreme ruler was portrayed as a semidivine cat-god. He received human sacrifices, which were thrown from a high cliff (Fig. 10–14). This supreme divinity is shown in other guises as an agriculturalist, fisherman, doctor, musician, and hunter. The high priest is often surrounded by a court of lesser animal gods, indicating nature worship. Burial offerings that reflect status indicate ancestor worship also.

Lesser royalty who served as regional governors are shown on effigy pots distributed in a single valley or sector of a valley. The supposition is that governmental position was inherited by birth rather than achieved through upward social mobility. The exalted status of both kinds of ranked officials is indicated by painted scenes showing elaborate clothing, body painting, hair style, bearing, and deference paid by underlings.

Lower ranks of the state government were made up of such bureaucrats as tax collectors, messengers, hydraulic engineers, civil engineers, water managers, and army officers.

FIGURE 10–14   Mochica life scenes taken from ceramic paintings, north coast of Peru: (a) battle scene with dog; (b) warriors with nude captives; (c) prisoners being thrown from cliffs.

Source: Raphael Larco Hoyle, 1947, A Cultural Sequence for the North Coast of Peru, in *Handbook of South American Indians*, Smithsonian Institution.

Various craftsmen served the elite aristocracy. These artisans included specialists in such major industries as pottery, weaving, and metallurgy, and workers in minor materials such as skins and gourds.

Commoners included both farmers and fishermen. Besides irrigating and tilling their fields, farmers had important labor obligations that included construction and maintenance of the various kinds of public works. They served as foot soldiers during times of war, labored in the mines, and contributed a percentage of their farm produce to support the ruling elite. Like the farmer, the fishermen provided food surplus and labor tax. In addition, fishermen hauled guano from island rookeries for use as agricultural fertilizers and transported goods along the coast.

Evidence of both defensive and offensive warfare indicates that the Mochica and other regional states of the Classic stage often conquered neighboring peoples. To the victor came booty, new territories, and additional taxable communities. In this fashion, the Classic stage regional states were built up or torn down. At the beginning of the Early Intermediate period, towns were fortified with surrounding walls. But by Mochica times, forts were built as points of refuge where people of the surrounding communities could defend themselves against attacks. The marauding armies could cut irrigation ditches to effect maximum disruption. With sustained invasion, a state would be forced to capitulate, particularly if its rulers were seized or killed.

Offensive warfare is well documented from painted scenes recorded on ceramic vessels (Larco Hoyle 1947). These scenes show warriors going into battle with harnessed dogs, leading nude captives from the battle field, and sacrificing prisoners by throwing them from the tops of peaks and then dismembering the bodies. In these battle scenes, the war chiefs, sometimes riding in hand-carried litters, are outfitted with sumptuous attire and quilted helmets or headdresses. Military rank was indicated by large ear ornaments. Rank and file soldiers wore breechclout, skirt, shirt, metal bracelets for wrist protection, and thick helmets to protect the head. The warrior carried a mace with a sharp metal point on the handle end. Circular or quadrangular shields, fastened to the left arm, were used to ward off blows from the mace. In addition to this hand-to-hand armament, the warrior carried a spear thrower that enabled him to hurl spears at the enemy from a long distance.

Scouts kept the armies informed of the movements of enemy troops. These observers took up hilltop positions where they could spy down on the enemy. The call to battle was announced with trumpets made of marine shells or pottery.

A number of trends that began in the Classic stage led to the disintegration of regional states and the beginning of the Postclassic stage: (1) secularism, (2) mature urbanism, (3) military conquest, (4) class stratification, and (5) rule by a military aristocracy.

Postclassic Stage

The Postclassic stage of both Mesoamerica and Peru was marked by the fall of many regional Classic states and the rise of a new order, large scale conquest empires. The measure of political disintegration is found in the breakdown of the old regional art styles. The new form of integration through military conquest is reflected in the sudden spread of Postclassic art styles across most if not all of the civilized world of Nuclear America.

In the conquest empire secularism began to replace ritualism. Willey and Phillips (1958) describe the reduction in the importance of religion by its effect on religious architecture. The number and size of pyramid-temples decreased between the Classic and Postclassic stages. Another indication of secularism was the rise of a military aristocracy, which became the preeminent social class by replacing the theocratic rulers of the Classic. Furthermore, this new class of nobility held much private property in the form of slaves, farm manors, and other property holdings. The church, with its war god and priesthood, was still an important institution, but now it was subservient to the new elite, the military aristocracy.

Although conquest of neighboring city-states had been a practice of the Classic, the resulting kingdoms were never very large. But in Postclassic times the scale of conquest increased dramatically until entire culture areas were under the political domination of single governments.

Urbanism reached a climax in the Postclassic. The number of Classic cities was relatively small and most theocratic states, especially in Mesoamerica, were administered from nonurban ceremonial centers. In Postclassic times mature, densely populated cities housed large numbers of people. Furthermore, the socioeconomic classes were segregated in barrios of the imperial capital, a pattern amply demonstrated through Millon's (1970) work on the precocious development of early Classic Teotihuacan. By Postclassic times, nearly all imperial capitals were cities rather than simply ceremonial centers, and many of these settlements were planned in advance as grids of streets and blocks.

Postclassic Mesoamerica

The Postclassic of Mesoamerica is divided into an early and a late half. The early Postclassic is assigned an age range of AD 900 to 1200, roughly the time of the Toltec empire. The late Postclassic is dated between AD 1200 and 1520, the period of the Aztecs. The terminal date of 1520 marks the conquest of the Aztecs by the Spaniard, Hernando Cortez (Prescott 1843).

Despite the presence of hieroglyphic inscriptions appearing on pottery, statuary, temples, and stelae since late Formative times, the lack of full translation makes it impossible to refer to a historical period before the advent of the Aztecs. From early Postclassic times, however, certain codices have been preserved so that a few brief sketches of rulers, their lives, dates, and times are available (Leonard 1967).

Other sources of historical data relating to the early Postclassic are myths and legends of early times as told to the Spanish by the Aztec nobility. One such set of stories claimed that the Toltecs, the heroic predecessors of the Aztecs, were originally wild barbarians or "chichimecs" inhabiting the northern interior plateau beyond the frontier of Mesoamerica. These Nahuatl-speaking tribes pushed southward into the Valley of Mexico where they became civilized. Led by the war chief Mixcoatl (Cloud Snake), the invading chichimecs were a motley amalgamation of disparate tribes who only later took on the identity of a specific ethnic people, the Toltecs. The Toltecs helped to precipitate the fall of Teotihuacan in the early Classic times around the seventh century.

By the tenth century, the Toltecs were sufficiently civilized to found a capital city, called *Tula* and located in the modern Mexican state of Hidalgo. Various dates are given for the founding; Willey (1966) uses AD 968 while Dutton (1955) uses 856. Around AD 960, a power struggle took place among four city-states, and the Toltecs of Tula survived as the preeminent power (Culbert 1978). The actual process of imperial expansion involved military conquest of some 40 formerly independent, neighboring city-states. This first well-documented conquest empire stretched from Michoacan in northern Mexico south to the Mayan city of Chichen-Itza in Yucatan and into the highlands of Guatemala to include the ancient city of Kaminaljuyu, now located under the modern-day Guatemala City.

Not long after the founding of Tula, factionalism broke out among the Toltecs. The two competing groups were symbolized by the gods they worshipped. Basically the issues at stake were the desire for peaceful rule championed by the faction of the Topiltzin Quetzalcoatl or "feathered serpent" god versus the demand for conquest as symbolized by the Tazcatlipoca or "smoking mirror" deity, the god of war. The tribal war god's followers won the power struggle and drove the Topiltzin followers out of the city of Tula in AD 987 (Coe 1967, p. 136).

At least three different legends purport to tell the tale of Topiltzin's fate after leaving Tula. The first states that he traveled to the Gulf Coast of Mexico, where he immolated himself on a burning pyre. A second myth says that he went by sea to conquer the Mayans on the Yucatan peninsula, where he founded the city of Chichen-Itza. The third myth states that he sailed away, promising to return in time of need by the Toltec peoples. This legend proved useful to the invading Spaniards of the sixteenth century. Since Quetzalcoatl was depicted in legend as a fair god with beard and blue eyes, it was a simple matter for Cortez to pose as the returning Quetzalcoatl, thereby striking great fear in the hearts of the Aztec warriors—an early form of psychological warfare.

Following the fall of the Toltecs in AD 1160, central Mexico was rent by warring rivalries among petty city-states. Out of this sociopolitical chaos, the

Aztecs rose as the last great native power. Thus the late Postclassic of Mesoamerica is a period full of history, recorded in pictures and the rebus writing (pictures pronounced as sounds) of the Aztec manuscripts. These, in turn, are supplemented by the eye-witness accounts of Aztec society provided by a Spanish soldier named Bernal Diaz del Castillo (Diaz 1963) and a priest named Bernardino Sahagun (Willey 1966).

From these sources, it is known that the Atzecs were the last of the Chichimec peoples to enter the Valley of Mexico. At first, they were vassals to people of the more civilized city-states, such as the Colhuacans. By the fourteenth century, they were residing on a small island, now called *Chapultepec Hill* (meaning grasshopper hill) in the marshy Lake Texcoco.

The political history of the Aztecs is set within a framework of 11 Aztec monarchs who reigned from AD 1367 to 1524 (Coe 1967, p. 179). To begin their political career, the Aztecs allied themselves with the Tepanecs of Atzcapotzalco. After a short affiliation in a secondary position of power, they turned on the Tepanecs and subjugated them in AD 1428. Military expansion began in earnest under the rule of Moctezuma I (AD 1440–1468), when for the first time Aztec troops pushed their attacks beyond the perimeter of the Valley of Mexico. Consolidation of the conquest empire began under Ahuitzotl (AD 1486–1502), who welded together diverse peoples from the Atlantic to the Pacific and from the Valley of Mexico to Guatemala. Despite the scope of the Aztec empire, a few peoples maintained their independence through strong military resistance. These were the Tarascans of Michoacan, some of the Mixtec peoples of Oaxaca, and the Tlaxcalans. The latter were the first and most numerous of the native peoples to join the conquering Spaniards during the siege and subjugation of the Aztecs between AD 1519 and 1521.

The first-hand account by Diaz, translated into English in 1963, provides a detailed description of the Aztec capital city, Tenochtitlan, founded in AD 1345 on the Chapultepec island in Lake Texcoco. The island city was connected to the mainland by three causeways that were easily defended from attack. A grid of canals that laced the city led Diaz to compare Tenochtitlan to the sixteenth-century Italian city of Venice. A flotilla of dugout canoes provided transportation of goods and people on the lake and the street-like canals. In this manner, the Aztec populace was daily supplied with fresh vegetables from the chinampa farms of nearby Xochimilco (Diaz 1963).

Tenochtitlan was composed of an estimated 60,000 dwellings housing 300,000 people. The city surrounded a religious compound containing a great pyramid topped by twin temples dedicated to the Aztec war god (Huitzilopochtli) and rain god (Tlaloc). Lesser pyramid-temple structures were clustered nearby along with a skull rack (Tzompantli) with its exhibit of sacrificed victims. This entire ceremonial precinct was enclosed by a wall to separate the sacred area from the profane civic, craft, industrial, and residential sectors of the city. The palaces of the Aztec emperors stood just outside this sacred precinct (Willey 1966).

Along streets and canals, each house stood on a stone-faced platform.

Rooms for cooking, sleeping, eating, and storage were arranged around a central courtyard. Houses were built of stone and adobe with flat roofs formed of wooden beams and poles. The exterior adobe walls were whitewashed so that they glittered in the sunlight, according to the Diaz account.

Superimposed upon the block pattern of canals and streets was a larger layout that divided Tenochtitlan into 20 barrios, each with its own plaza, temple, and marketplace. Each barrio was occupied by an Aztec clan. The clans were assigned guild craft specialties, in addition to farming, and these were localized by neighborhood. These barrios were grouped into four large city quarters, each of which had a large-scale plaza, ceremonial center, and market. The craft products included jewelry, feather work, and metal work of which the principal products were luxury articles for the aristocracy.

Tribute in food stuffs and materials supplied by conquered neighbors played an important part in supporting the urbanization of the Aztecs. The city's primary economic support, however, was always chinampa farming on garden plots built up by dredging marshland. The residents of Tenochtitlan farmed reclaimed marshland around the perimeter of the city. These fertile chinampa gardens produced bumper crops with ease. The resulting surplus was quickly and conveniently shipped to market by water transportation.

The social and political organization of Aztec society has long been a subject of controversy among scholars. Was Aztec society organized as a socially stratified despotism or as a clan-based tribal democracy? The truth probably lies between these two extremes. The egalitarian clan organization reflected the Chichimec tribal origins, while the despotic authoritarian behavior was the social form toward which Aztec society was evolving (Willey 1966).

At the head of the social pyramid was the emperor, who was selected from a single royal lineage by a council of senior nobles, high priests, and warriors. His status was semidivine, and he was treated with great reverence. Since top administrators also were chosen from the royal house, the Aztec government and aristocracy were the same. These royal administrators were supported by revenue from their private land holdings and thus were independently wealthy (Willey 1966).

Among the commoners who formed the lower class, peasant farmers were organized socially into some 20 clans called *calpulli*, each occupying a designated sector of the city. The clan owned the farm lands and allocated a portion to each family for as long as the land was kept in production. Certain aristocratic families in each clan held more land and thereby wielded more authority and influence.

Near the bottom of the social scale were the serfs or bondsmen. These people were dispossessed of their civil rights because of bankruptcy and were forced to work on private lands of the high nobility in order to pay off debts. Once they became solvent again, they regained their lost civil rights as free men. At a still lower level on the social scale were slaves who were prisoners of war (Adams 1971; Soustelle 1961).

The principal theme of Aztec society was war. Military service was an honorable profession and the only major avenue for upward social mobility. For brave deeds on the battlefields, a commoner might be given lands and elevated to a position of royalty. The aristocracy, which formed the officer corps of the military establishment, was organized into two orders of knighthood, the eagles and the jaguars. Otherwise commoners were called up for military duty as conscripts. They fought under their respective clan banners and were led by the aristocratic knights (Adams 1971).

Andean Postclassic

The Postclassic stage of the Andeans is marked by two cycles of empire building in which regional states were integrated by military conquest. These periods of imperial power were divided by a period of disintegration into a condition of regional states much like the Moche civilization of the preceding Classic stage.

The first of these imperial integrations, the Middle Horizon in the Andean sequence, is dated between AD 600 and 1000. The pan-Peruvian spread of certain ceramic styles is evidence of political unification. At least two great centers of development have been identified: Tiahuanaco and Huari. Tiahuanaco is located on the southern tip of Lake Titicaca in Bolivia. Although only a small part of the site has been excavated, it appears to be an immense city with imposing public monuments and megalithic masonry (Moseley 1975, p. 527). At one time archaeologists thought that Tiahuanaco was the imperial capital from which conquest spread by military might over most of the Andean culture area. More recently, however, it has been argued that the southern highland site of Huari was the actual center from which conquest originated. Even less detailed study has been performed here, but a sketch map indicates that the capital city of Huari covered an area somewhere between 1.2 and 1.5 km. The principal architecture is composed of cobbles and unfinished stone forming multistory masonry. The buildings consist of rectilinear enclosures with internal courts and rooms (Moseley 1975, p. 530).

Around AD 1000, the political organization of the Huari-Tiahuanaco empire collapsed. Regional states reasserted themselves at this time to form the Late Intermediate period of Peruvian prehistory, dated between AD 1000 and 1476. Although a half dozen states flourished, the principal example was the Chimu, sometimes called the *Chimor*, state of the Moche valley on the north coast of Peru. The Chimu was a local empire, founded on conquest of neighboring valleys and covering an area more than 1000 km extending from the Ecuadorian border southward along the Peruvian coast. The state capital was the immense urban site of Chan Chan situated in the lower end of the Moche valley. Monumental architecture covers 6 km^2 and residential housing an area three times as large. Public architecture in the nucleus of the capital city is dominated by ten large rectangular enclosures, called *ciudadelas*, which contain courts, corridors, and rooms (Fig. 10–15). A citadel served as an administrative palace during the life of an emperor and functioned as his mausoleum

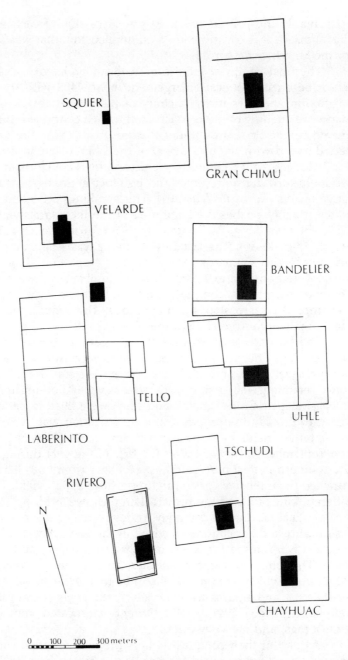

SQUIER

GRAN CHIMU

VELARDE

BANDELIER

TELLO

UHLE

LABERINTO

TSCHUDI

RIVERO

N

CHAYHUAC

0   100   200   300 meters

FIGURE 10–15 Simplified plan of the ciudadelas of Chan Chan, Moche valley, Peru. Burial platforms are indicated in solid black.

Source: Geoffrey W. Conrad, Cultural Materialism, Split Inheritance, and the Expansion of Ancient Peruvian Empires. Reproduced by permission of Society for American Archaeology from *American Antiquity* 46(1): 3–26, 1981.

upon his death (Conrad 1981). At the succession of each new king, a new citadel palace was constructed—a cultural custom that was documented also for the later Inca emperors.

The final conquest empire of Andean prehistory was the Inca state, which began its political enlargement in AD 1438 with the defeat of some neighboring peoples in the vicinity of the capital city of Cuzco. This date marks the opening of the Late Horizon, which continued until Peru was conquered by the Spaniards under Pizarro in AD 1532. The Late Intermediate period ended with the Inca defeat of the Chimu state in AD 1476.

Although still technically prehistory, the Late Horizon is enriched with certain historic dates preserved through Inca genealogical traditions and narrative poems (Rowe 1947, p. 201). Thirteen kings ascended the Inca throne, which roughly pushes the beginning of the Inca dynasty as far back as AD 1200. The ninth king, Pachacuti, who was crowned in AD 1438, expanded the empire (Fig. 10–16). The last Inca emperor was Atahualpa, who was taken prisoner by the Spaniards. At the close of empire building, the Inca dominions covered an area extending from Columbia southward to central Chile. On an east-west axis, conquest extended from the Pacific coast inland to the wet tropical eastern slopes of the Andes. This empire was the largest and most highly organized state in the New World.

The Inca economy was based on a combination of terrace agriculture and herding. The people terraced the sides of Andean mountains to farm narrow, level strips of land. The terraces were constructed of faced dry-masonry retaining walls rising in tiers from valley bottom up the sides of the steepest slopes. Stone, gravel, and earth were filled in behind this masonry facing to provide the proper drainage. Irrigation waters were then brought to the terrace fields by stone water channels. Crops were planted in August and September for harvest after the first of the year during the wet season, the southern hemisphere summer. Fertilizer from both llamas and humans enriched the intensive agriculture to produce a high yield. Potatoes of many different kinds formed the principal crop (Rowe 1947, pp. 210–16).

Animal herding in the high Andes is one of the few examples of prehistorical mixed agriculture practiced in the New World. Llamas, camel-like animals, were raised for wool, meat, ritual sacrifice, and transporting light loads. The companion alpaca, another cameloid herd animal, was raised only for its wool, which is of finer quality than that of the llama. During Inca times, most llamas and alpacas were owned by the government rather than by private citizens (Rowe 1947, p. 219). Other domesticated animals included dogs, guinea pigs, and moscovy ducks.

As part of their conquest policy, the Inca resettled conquered peoples in new towns far removed from their old hilltop forts and near their agricultural lands. Cuzco, the south highland Inca capital, consisted of a nuclear ceremonial center surrounded by a circle of satellite villages populated by relocated peoples from all over the kingdom. The civic center was inhabited

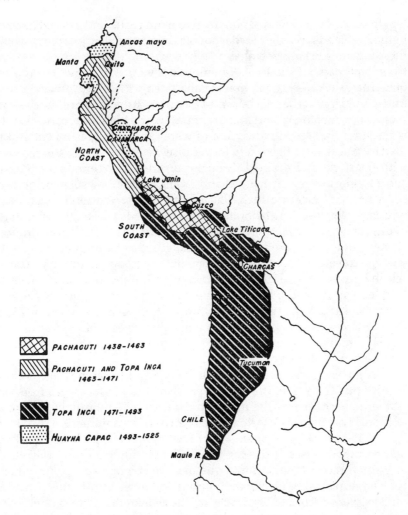

FIGURE 10-16 The expansion of the Inca empire between AD 1438 and 1525, west coast of South America.

Source: John Howland Rowe, Inca Culture at the Time of the Spanish Conquest, in *Handbook of South American Indians*, Smithsonian Institution, 1947.

exclusively by nobles, priests, government officials, and their servants. This center was planned as a grid of streets and five or six large squares. Estimates for the population of Cuzco exceed 100,000 people. The Inca program of planned settlements, however, did not approach the urban concentrations in Europe (Rowe 1947, p. 229).

The success of the Inca empire was based in large part on a magnificent system of roads that interconnected the entire realm (Von Hagen 1955). The length of the empire was served by two main roads, one coastal and the other in the highlands. Smaller feeder routes connected all important towns so that messengers, running between post houses, could carry administrative directives to all parts of the Inca dominion in a very short time. On the coast the main roadway was 3 to 4.5 m wide and lined with either low walls or upright posts. In places a channel of water ran along its course and trees shaded the messenger, merchant, and military traveler. The highland road was fitted with stone steps for steep grades. Slopes were made passable by cut and fill, and marshy places were filled in to form causeways. Any soggy surface was paved with flagstone and drained through culverts. In exceptional circumstances, short tunnels were constructed and rivers spanned by suspension bridges or balsa ferries. Since the Inca, like all other New World civilizations, lacked wheeled vehicles, this elaborate network of roads was engineered entirely for pedestrians and llama trains of 100 or fewer pack animals. In addition to the checkpoints that housed relay runners, groups of storehouses were built for feeding travelers and provisioning military troops in transit. The runners relayed governmental dispatches. Shifts of runners and storehouse supplies were all contributed by local villagers as part of their mit'a or service tax to the Inca. The average speed of a runner has been estimated at 150 miles a day. Not only were urgent governmental directives rapidly transmitted in this fashion, but the emperor had fresh fish shipped from the coast to 11,000 feet high Cuzco in two days (Rowe 1947, pp. 229–33).

A government dispatch was usually a short oral message accompanied by a quipu. The key to the accurate transmission of messages from one relay runner to another was the mnemonic device called the *quipu*. In the absence of formal writing, this knotted-rope record covered numerical counts in a decimal system and aided memory in reciting genealogies, liturgical material, and narrative verse. Thus, the Inca had accounting services despite the lack of written records. The quipu was made of a main cord from which many smaller strings were suspended. Numerical entries and other kinds of information were recorded by knots in these hanging strings, by color-coded strings, and by various methods of twisting (Fig. 10–17). Rowe (1947, p. 326) makes the point that:

> The quipu is excellently adapted for recording numbers, but would be an exceedingly clumsy instrument with which to calculate. The [Spanish] chroniclers make it quite clear that calculation was done with piles of pebbles or grains, or by means of an abacus consisting of a tray with rows of compartments in which counters could be moved. The results of the calculation could then be recorded on the quipu.

Bronze metallurgy appeared in the New World during the Postclassic empires, which was late compared to its invention in the Old World civilizations of Sumer, Egypt, Indus valley, and Shang China. By Classic times in both Mesoamerica and Peru, metallurgy was well underway. In Postclassic

FIGURE 10–17   Inca accountant with abacus and quipu, Peru.

Source: John Howland Rowe, Inca Culture at the Time of the Spanish Conquest, in *Handbook of South American Indians*, Smithsonian Institution, 1947.

Inca times, metallurgy was an urban craft specialization. Mining was the occupation of particular villages, where miners worked for the few short months of each southern hemisphere summer to supply metals to the Inca government as part of their mit'a tax. Metals mined in the Andean sierra include copper, gold, silver, tin, and lead. In addition, platinum was obtained from mines located in Ecuador within the Inca dominion. The metallurgists worked these metals by bronze alloying, casting, hammering, repoussé, incrustation, inlay, soldering, riveting, and cloisonné. Both native and pure metals were removed from veins. Ores were reduced to metallic form by smelting (Rowe 1947, pp. 245–48).

The Inca political system was organized as a monarchy with successive classes of citizens stratified in descending order beneath the divine ruler. Descent of the imperial Inca was traced to the Sun, the supreme deity; thus his word had the authority of supernatural as well as secular sanction.

Since the god-king could marry only a woman of equal divinity, his primary marriage was to his own sister. In fact, however, the emperor was wedded also to an entire harem of secondary wives, who were the daughters of neighboring rulers and young girls especially selected for their beauty and trained in schools for courtly etiquette. The offspring of this polygynous marriage constituted the royal ayllu, or clan. Upon the death of the emperor, his ayllu cared for the royal palace, which became the emperor's mausoleum.

The ayllu also maintained a cult to worship their founding ancestor. One of the principal customs was maintenance of the royal mummy, which was worshipped and brought out for public display upon occasions of state festivities. During the emperor's reign, members of his ayllu staffed the main governmental positions. Given the great number of claimants to the throne, an orderly succession of emperors was not always possible. Such a dispute was underway at the time of the Spanish conquest, and the ensuing civil war between two half-brothers (Huascar and Atahualpa) greatly contributed to the ease with which Pizarro conquered the Inca empire (Rowe 1947, pp. 257–60).

Beneath the reigning emperor was a class of nobility made up of hereditary aristocracy. It was this stratum of society that supplied personnel for government posts. Such political status was inherited by succession from father to son using the principle of primogeniture, or first born. If this individual was considered unqualified to govern, then a more competent son was invested with the administrative office. The class of nobles was comprised of two groups: members of the 11 royal Inca ayllus and members of upper-class families of conquered neighboring peoples. The latter became Incas by privilege. Of whatever origin, all of the Inca nobility were recognizable by such distinctive status symbols as head bands, braids, and especially large earplugs. This aristocratic elite was exempt from taxation and supported by the labor of commoners in the state agricultural fields. Like the emperor, nobles had the privilege of being borne on a litter or using a parasol (Rowe 1947).

Below the elite noble class was a stratum of commoners who paid no taxes. These hereditary government servants were specially trained in accounting, metalworking, tapestry weaving, and other luxury handicrafts. They were supported from government storehouses stocked from the mit'a labor tax. The craft products of this artisan class, especially objects made of gold, were manufactured solely for the emperor, who in turn might redistribute the luxury items as gifts to the nobility.

The base of society was the remaining commoners, free citizens who constituted the laboring class. It is this class that provided agricultural labor, foot-soldiery, and manual labor for all state construction projects. Commoners also performed the labor service of mit'a in various occupations, including messengers and miners (Rowe 1947, p. 268).

The religion of the Inca was primarily concerned with the food supply and curing illness. Basically a practical religion concerned with economic well-being, it stressed ritual at the expense of mysticism. A priesthood carried out the special duties of religious ritual, particularly divination, or the foretelling of the future. Nearly every rite was accompanied by a sacrifice of either specially chosen young girls or llamas. The pantheon of Inca deities consisted of a culture hero called *Viracocha* by the Spaniards and a host of nature gods including the sun, thunder, moon, stars, earth, and sea (Rowe 1947, pp. 293–314).

Much has been made of the lack of wheeled vehicles in the New World, but in fact this lack is more apparent than real. Wheeled toys pulled by strings were known from the Postclassic of western Mexico and thus the concept of wheeled vehicles was available for application (Kroeber 1948, p. 357). Furthermore, rollers and sledges were employed to move monumental stone blocks weighing many tons for the construction of state architectural projects. Other uses of the wheel were in flywheels for weighting rotating shafts, such as drills and spindles for twining thread. Still other arguments are that the New World terrain was unsuitable for wheeled vehicles, but in fact foot traffic in civilized Nuclear America moved very efficiently over level causeways and road systems, such as those of the Maya, Aztec, and Inca.

Summary

Formative societies in the New World, like their Neolithic counterparts in the Old World, were based on surplus food production as a consequence of the agricultural revolution. Although other forms of economic production often led to sedentary village life, the major thrust of cultural evolution was in the hands of farmers. In the New World, the most productive yields came from corn agriculture, which produced surplus that could be stored for future use and for barter with neighboring peoples.

The Formative encompasses two cultural patterns: Sedentary village agriculture was the stepping stone to incipient civilizations in Nuclear America, whereas elsewhere in the Americas it became the climax evolutionary condition. Three noncivilized culture areas that illustrate this village Formative climax are the eastern woodlands and the southwest of North America, and the tropical rain forests of South America.

In the New World, the term *Formative*, meaning beginnings, is applied to the first appearance of chiefdom-organized societies run by priest-rulers. These earliest states appear for the first time in Mesoamerica and Peru, dating between the first and second millennia BC. They are characterized by ceremonial centers run by the elite priests, who provided religious services to satellite and dependent village communities of peasant farmers. In Peru, this peasant class also included maritime fishermen. Both groups of commoners provided tax support in labor, crafts, and food stuffs in support of the religious elite. By late Formative times, the large agglomerations of peoples with different occupational specialties had begun to form the first cities in the New World. These conditions of beginning social differentiation led to the Classic stage, the appearance of mature civilization, in Mesoamerica and in the Andes.

The Classic stage is distinguished by the development of priest-run state societies. These authoritarian states were completely organized as stratified classes of elite rulers, bureaucrats, artisans, and commoners. Regional warfare was pervasive although not at a scale leading to large conquest empires. The urban revolution, first noted in the late Formative, was in full force in both areas of civilization. Writing, mathematics, and a formal calendar were characteristic of Mesoamerica but not of Peru.

The Postclassic stage is marked by the successive rise of large-scale conquest empires in Mesoamerica and the Andean culture area. In Mesoamerica, the successive empires were those of the proto-historic Toltecs and the Aztecs. In Peru-Bolivia, the Huari-Tiahuanaco empire was ultimately succeeded by the empire of the Incas. Although these two culture areas were independent of one another, the timing was very similar, both evolutionary developments beginning after AD 900 or 1000 and ending within a decade of one another; the Aztecs were defeated by the Spaniards around AD 1520 and the Inca in 1532. Other parallel trends between the two great centers of Postclassic civilization include the rise of secularism, urban maturity, military conquest, solidification of stratified classes, and rule by a hereditary military class.

Nuclear America, that part of the New World made up of Mexico, Central America, and Peru, was the scene of domestication of such cultigens as corn (*Zea mays*), beans, squash, cotton, chili peppers, tobacco, potatoes, and probably other root crops by 5000 BC (MacNeish 1971). Unlike the Old World, however, the New World had few animals suitable for either transportation or traction, and consequently animal power never replaced human portage in the New World as it did in the Old. Domestic animals in the New World included bees, guinea pigs, and two camel-like species, the llama and the alpaca. The llama provided pack transport but not traction or human transport comparable to the ox or horse of the Old World. Wheeled carts were not used in the New World, although native civilizations of the Americas used a flywheel on drills and rotating shafts for making fire, the wheel roulette for imprinting design, and the true wheel and shaft for ceramic toy animals pulled by string (Kroeber 1948, p. 357).

References

ADAMS, ROBERT McC.
  1971   The Evolution of Urban Society: Early Mesopotamia and Prehispanic Mexico. Chicago: Aldine-Atherton.
BENNETT, WENDELL C.
  1947   The Archeology of the Central Andes, Part 2. In *Handbook of South American Indians*. vol. 2, The Andean Civilizations, edited by Julian H. Steward. Smithsonian Institution, Bureau of American Ethnology, bulletin 143. Washington, D.C.: U.S. Government Printing Office.
BUSHNELL, G. H. S.
  1963   *Peru*. Ancient Peoples and Places Series, rev. ed., edited by G. Daniel. New York: Praeger.

COE, MICHAEL D.
  1967   *Mexico.* Ancient Peoples and Places Series. New York: Praeger.
  1974   The Chinampas of Mexico. In *New World Archaeology.* Readings from Scientific American, assembled by Ezra B. W. Zubrow, Margaret C. Fritz, and John M. Fritz. San Francisco: W. H. Freeman and Company Publishers.

CONRAD, GEOFFREY W.
  1981   Cultural Materialism, Split Inheritance, and the Expansion of Ancient Peruvian Empires. *American Antiquity* 46:3–26.

CULBERT, T. PATRICK
  1978   Mesoamerica. In *Ancient Native Americans,* edited by Jesse D. Jennings. San Francisco: W. H. Freeman and Company Publishers.

DIAZ, BERNAL
  1963   *The Conquest of New Spain.* Middlesex, England: Penguin.

DUTTON, BERTHA P.
  1955   Tula of the Toltecs. *El Palacio* 62 (7–8):195–251.

FLANNERY, KENT V.
  1968   Archeological Systems Theory and Early Mesoamerica. In *Anthropological Archeology in the Americas.* Anthropological Society of Washington. Brooklyn: Theo Gaus' Sons.

FLANNERY, KENT V., ed.
  1976   *The Early Mesoamerican Village.* New York: Academic Press.

FLANNERY, KENT V., and JAMES SCHOENWETTER
  1970   Climate and Man in Formative Oaxaca. *Archaeology.* 23:144–52.

FORDE, C. DARYLL
  1963   *Habitat, Economy and Society.* New York: E. P. Dutton.

GRIFFIN, JAMES B.
  1978   The Midlands and Northeastern United States. In *Ancient Native Americans,* edited by Jesse D. Jennings. San Francisco: W. H. Freeman and Company Publishers.

HASTINGS, MANSFIELD, and M. EDWARD MOSELEY
  1975   The Adobes of the Huaca del Sol and Huaca de la Luna. *American Antiquity* 40:196–203.

HAYES, ALDEN C., DAVID M. BRUGGE, and W. JAMES JUDGE
  1981   *Archaeological Surveys of Chaco Canyon, New Mexico.* Publications in Archaeology 18A, Chaco Canyon Studies. Washington, D.C.: National Park Service.

JENNINGS, JESSE D.
  1978   Origins. In *Ancient Native Americans,* edited by Jesse D. Jennings. W. H. Freeman and Company Publishers.

KROEBER, ALFRED L.
  1926   Archaeological Explorations in Peru. Part 1, Ancient Pottery from Trujillo, Field Museum of Natural History. *Anthropological Memoir* 2 (1):12–14.

LARCO HOYLE, RAFAEL
  1947   A Cultural Sequence for the North Coast of Peru. In *Handbook of South American Indians.* Vol. 2, The Andean Civilization, edited by Julian H. Steward. Smithsonian Institution, Bureau of American Ethnology, Bulletin 143. Washington, D.C.: U.S. Government Printing Office.

LARSON, LEWIS, H., JR.

1971   Archaeological Implications of Social Stratification at the Etowah Site, Georgia. In *Approaches to the Social Dimensions of Mortuary Practices,* edited by James A. Brown. Memoirs of the Society for American Archaeology, 25:58–67.

LENNON, THOMAS J.

1982   Raised Fields of Lake Titicaca, Peru: A Pre-Hispanic Water Management System. Unpublished Ph.D. dissertation on file with the Department of Anthropology, University of Colorado, Boulder.

LEONARD, JONATHAN NORTH, and EDITORS OF TIME-LIFE BOOKS

1967   *Ancient America.* New York: Time Incorporated.

LIPE, WILLIAM D.

1978   The Southwest. In *Ancient Native Americans,* edited by Jesse D. Jennings. San Francisco: W. H. Freeman and Company Publishers.

MACNEISH, RICHARD S.

1971   Ancient Mesoamerican Civilization. In *Prehistoric Agriculture,* edited by Stuart Struever. American Museum Sourcebooks in Anthropology. Garden City, N.Y.: Natural History Press.

1974   Early Man in the Andes. *New World Archaeology.* Readings from Scientific American, edited by Ezra B. W. Zubrow, Margaret C. Fritz, and John M. Fritz. San Francisco: W. H. Freeman and Company Publishers.

MEGGERS, BETTY J., and CLIFFORD EVANS

1978   Lowland South America and the Antilles. In *Ancient Native Americans,* edited by Jesse D. Jennings. San Francisco: W. H. Freeman and Company Publishers.

MILLON, RENE

1970   Teotihuacan: Completion of Map of Giant Ancient City in the Valley of Mexico. *Science* 170:1077–82.

1973   *Urbanization at Teotihuacan, Mexico,* vol. 1, Part One. Austin: University of Texas Press.

MILLON, RENE, R. BRUCE DREWITT, and GEORGE L. COWGILL

1973   *Urbanization at Teotihuacan, Mexico,* vol. 1. Part 2, The Teotihuacan Map. Austin: University of Texas Press.

MOSELEY, M. EDWARD

1975a   *The Maritime Foundations of Andean Civilization.* Menlo Park: Cummings Publishing Company.

1975b   Prehistoric Principles of Labor Organization in the Moche Valley of Peru. *American Antiquity* 40:191–96.

1977   Waterways of Ancient Peru. *Field Museum of Natural History Bulletin* 48 (3):10–15.

1978   The Evolution of Andean Civilization. In *Ancient Native Americans,* edited by Jesse D. Jennings. San Francisco: W. H. Freeman and Company Publishers.

PARSONS, JAMES J., and WILLIAM M. DENEVAN

1974   Pre-Columbian Ridged Fields. In *New World Archaeology.* Readings from Scientific American, assembled by Ezra B. W. Zubrow, Margaret C. Fritz, and John M. Fritz. San Francisco: W. H. Freeman and Company Publishers.

PRESCOTT, WILLIAM H.

1843   *History of the Conquest of Mexico* and *History of the Conquest of Peru.* New York: Random House, Inc.

ROWE, JOHN HOLLAND
1947   Inca Culture at the Time of the Spanish Conquest. *Handbook of South American Indians*, edited by Julian H. Steward. Bureau of American Ethnology, Bulletin 143. Vol. 2, The Andean Civilizations. Washington, D.C.: U.S. Government Printing Office.

ROWE, JOHN HOLLAND, and DOROTHY MENZELL
1967   *Peruvian Archaeology: Selected Readings.* Palo Alto, Calif.: Peek Publications.

SANDERS, WILLIAM T., and BARBARA J. PRICE
1968   *Mesoamerica: The Evolution of a Civilization.* New York: Random House.

SCHELE, LINDA
1981   What's in a Name? *Odyssey.* Boston: Public Broadcasting Associates.

SOUSTELLE, JACQUES
1961   *Daily Life of the Aztecs on the Eve of the Spanish Conquest.* Middlesex, England: Penguin.

STEWARD, JULIAN H.
1955   *Theory of Culture Change.* Urbana: University of Illinois Press.

VIVIAN, R. GRINN
1974   Conservation and Diversion Water-Control Systems in the Anasazi Southwest. In *Irrigation's Impact on Society*, edited by T. E. Downing and McGuire Gibson. Tucson: The University of Arizona Press.

VON HAGEN, VICTOR
1974   America's Oldest Roads. In *New World Archaeology*. Readings from Scientific American, assembled by Ezra B. W. Zubrow, Margaret C. Fritz, and John M. Fritz. San Francisco: W. H. Freeman and Company Publishers.

WILKES, GARRISON
1977   The Origin of Corn: Studies of the Last Hundred Years. In *Crop Resources*, edited by David S. Seigler. New York: Academic Press.

WILLEY, GORDON R.
1966   *An Introduction to American Archaeology*, vol. 1. North and Middle America. Englewood Cliffs, N.J.: Prentice-Hall.

1971   *An Introduction to American Archaeology*, vol. 2. South America. Englewood Cliffs, N.J.: Prentice-Hall.

WILLEY, GORDON R., and PHILIP PHILLIPS
1958   *Method and Theory in American Archaeology.* Chicago: The University of Chicago Press.

WOODBURY, RICHARD B.
1974   Prehistoric Agriculture at Point of Pines, Arizona. *Memoirs of the Society for American Archaeology*, no. 17. Salt Lake City: Society for American Archaeology.

11

Cultural Materialism

A comparison of Old World and New World prehistory provides a convincing demonstration that the course of cultural evolution, despite the historical independence of the Old and New Worlds, is much the same between the two land masses. Early civilization grew from a condition of hunting and gathering band societies in both hemispheres.

Despite the similarities in the course of cultural evolution, certain differences are apparent in the prehistoric evidence. First, the New World cultural history covers only some 20,000 years, compared to more than 2 million years in the Old World. Sedentary village life appeared much later in the New World, where agriculture was based on corn instead of wheat, barley, and rice, the chief cereal crops of the Old World. The cultivation of corn began around 5000 BC, although other grains had been domesticated 2000 years earlier in parts of the Old World.

Technical differences include the late appearance of bronze and metallurgy in the New World and the fact that iron metallurgy was never invented there. Especially significant was the absence of traction animals to pull wheeled farm carts and war machines such as chariots. The llama of the Andes, suitable only for carrying light loads, never equalled the horse, ox, yak, and camel of the Old World. This New World deficiency pushed the responsibility for moving loads onto the backs of human beings and somewhat limited the engineering feats of this hemisphere.

But despite these differences, the course of organizational complexity was much the same in both worlds. Parallel achievements included the basics of civilization: writing, mathematics, astronomy, and the calendar. And in both hemispheres, incipient agriculture produced a food surplus that led to growth spurts in population. Increasing numbers of people, more densely packed, require increasingly more complex forms of control to regulate social interaction. Thus, human population size is directly related to the complexity of social organization (Sanders and Price 1968). The critical turning points were the population upsurges that took place world-over during the Neolithic, bronze, and iron ages.

Social Organization

Initially the Neolithic population growth was offset by what Childe (1961) called a "budding-off process," the fissioning of the small agrarian community. When a critical size limit was reached, factionalism arose, causing a schism in the social structure of the community. Through this process, a daughter community broke away to colonize new lands and establish a new community, a replica of the parent community. In this way the Neolithic form of village social life spread outward from its various centers of origin until the arable land of the world had been settled. The farmer held a competitive advantage over the hunting and gathering Mesolithic bands now hemmed in and confined to agriculturally marginal lands and habitats—deserts, marshes, mountains, tropical forests, and arctic barrens (Breeden 1968). Nomadic herders, survivors of the Neolithic revolution, were increasingly shoved into less useful and marginal grasslands,where the sod could not be broken to agriculture prior to the invention of the iron plowshare, or else to semiarid regions of short grass that did not offer the herds sufficient forage. The fisher folk of the maritime villages flourished because they were not in direct competition with the highly competitive Neolithic farmer of mixed crop and stock economy.

The population increase of the bronze age was qualitatively different from that of the Neolithic. Since it was based on intensive rather than extensive agriculture, populations did not fission but expanded in place. Most of the bronze age civilizations developed in arid land river valleys where they were confined to the alluvial flood plain and circumscribed by the surrounding mountains. The density of people in each valley increased to the point of saturation as determined by the ability of the water managers to design valley-wide gravity flow irrigation systems and operate them efficiently. But as the human populations of each valley exceeded the food supply, there was an increase in warfare leading to conquest empires made up of many formerly independent city-states. This process was initially confined to the arid land river valleys where the bronze age civilizations arose; but by iron age times the conquest empires had expanded from regional to continental size. Comparable macro-organizations of the New World were the Inca empire of Peru and Bolivia and the Aztec empire of Mexico and Central America.

Another evolutionary theory demonstrates the relationship between human population parameters and their effects—complex social systems and standing armies. Elman R. Service (1962) used ethnographic data to classify contemporary primitive peoples and cultures into these organizational types: band, tribe, chiefdom, and primitive state. Service asserted that this simple-to-complex organizational scale reflects an actual evolutionary progression. Logical as it appears, however, the theory holds no validity without proof within some body of archaeological or historical data. Sanders and Price (1968) have provided the data for the specific evolution of Mesoamerica. This chapter will perform a world-wide test to complete the major review of the theory of culture materialism.

Bands

Today bands are small groups of primitive hunting and gathering peoples representing the simplest and most egalitarian organization known within the ethnographic literature (Service 1962, 1966; Sanders and Price 1968; Beardsley 1956; Lee and De Vore 1968). Some contemporary examples are: (1) the Arunta of Australia, (2) the Yahgan of South America, (3) the Andaman Islanders, and (4) the Canadian Eskimo (Service 1958).

SIMPLE BANDS

Simple bands are communities of 30 to 100 people. Bands of less than 100 individuals are typical, and the population density ranges from fewer than 0.2 to 1.0 persons per km². If resources are seasonal there will be a continual relocation of camp to form a predictable seasonal circle (Fig. 11–1a). If the territory is simply low in useful resources relative to the band size, however, erratic settlement mobility will result (Fig. 11–1b). Members may travel together as a group or disperse into family units, depending upon the productivity of the landscape in any given season or area.

The economy of simple bands is usually based on hunting and gathering without surplus production. Subsistence is some combination of hunting, fishing, and gathering. Community mobility is dictated by the seasonal nature of the food resources or by the low productivity of the territory. Most property is food-getting equipment such as the bow and arrow, spear, burden basket, and digging stick. Cultural rules for sharing (norms) dictate an equitable division of the food along kinship lines. The survival value of such a norm lies in the fact that the band prospers as a unit; either all eat well or all starve, but there is little possibility that some band members will starve while others grow fat from a game kill (Beardsley 1956).

The simple band is a local group that owns its territory, which may be defined by available resources as well as by area. The composition of the band may be a series of 10 to 30 families related by kinship or friendly alliance. Although the band has continuity, recent studies of living bands, such as the

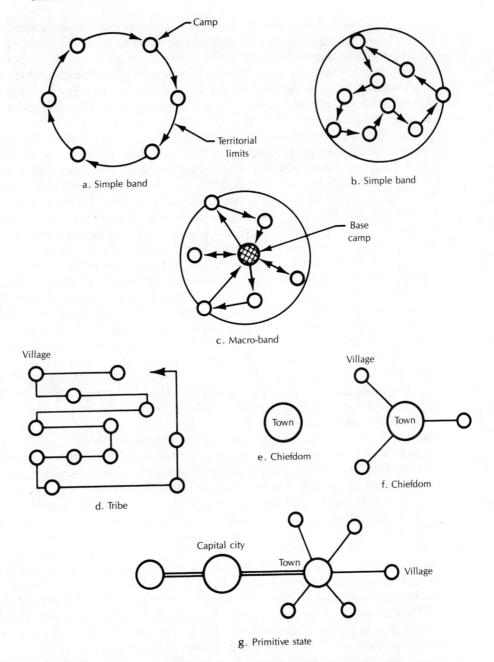

FIGURE 11–1   Network diagrams showing the evolution of settlement types: (a) predictable seasonal round; (b) erratic movement; (c) radial pattern with base camp hub; (d) continuous relocation of village; (e) village without satellites; (f) village center with satellites; (g) richly networked city-state with capital and satellite towns and villages.

bushmen of the Kalahari desert, South Africa, show that personnel and individual families shift membership from one band to another according to their own advantage in the food quest or the charisma of some temporary leader (Lee and De Vore 1968). If there is a group leader, this individual has little or no coercive power but serves in an advisory capacity, drawing on individual knowledge and wisdom in settling disputes and leading the hunt for game.

Commonly marriage is monogamous, that is, limited to one spouse at a time. Marital rules require each person to marry beyond the confines of the band. Usually the men remain with the band, because of their special knowledge of game trails and water holes, while the women marry into neighboring bands, where they join other females in digging for roots or harvesting wild seeds (Murdock 1949). The new couple may set up a light frame hut near the husband's relatives. Status differences among individual band members usually relate to age and sex differences. Considerable respect is accorded the grandparent generation because of the special knowledge of life, myth, ritual curing, and dance that they have accumulated over a lifetime. Work tasks are assigned so that men do the strenuous hunting while women perform the lighter tasks of caring for the young, preparing and serving food, and mending clothes. Such societies, in which everyone has equal status in decision making, are called *egalitarian*. Since personal property is rarely inherited, sons and daughters do not accrue wealth from their parents. Instead, at the death of an individual, personal property is buried with the body (Beardsley 1956).

Ceremonialism of the simple band is based on vaguely defined beliefs. Spirits are thought to inhabit animals, rocks, trees, and streams so that nature is permeated with supernatural forces. Magic is used to bring luck in hunting game and curing disease. Primitive people often believe that disease is the work of some evil person who has hired a magician to "shoot some foreign object" into the patient. A good wizard must undo the mischief by ritual means, such as sucking through a tube to remove the intrusive object.

If simple bands were the organizational type for the first appearance of society, the following test implications should apply to the oldest archaeological record: First, because of high settlement mobility, extensive accumulations of camp refuse will be lacking. If movement is erratic because of low food productivity in the territory, each camp will be occupied on a single occasion. On the other hand, if the band moves in response to a continuous and predictable seasonal fruition of plant products, then camp sites should show a pattern of repeated occupation at about the same time each year. A second test implication for the simple band is the presence of specialized tools invented to deal with intensive exploitation of the habitat.

The conditions of high settlement mobility are found in the Lower Paleolithic of the Old World during the Early and Middle Pleistocene epoch. Thus, it seems likely that the first organizational type of society, that practiced by the Australopithecines of the African savanna and the *Homo erectus* of the middle latitude woodlands of Europe and Asia, were band organized. Supporting evidence for simple band organization is provided by the long houses of Terra Amate, southern France, and the cave occupation of Choukoutien, northern China. Thus, simple hunting bands were probably in existence from about 2.0 million years ago up until 100,000 years ago.

MACRO-BANDS

A macro-band is a community that spends part of each year wandering and the remainder at a settlement or central base, to which it returns in subsequent years (Beardsley 1956). The settlement shifts to a radial pattern and away from the circular or erratic settlement pattern of the simple band (Fig. 11–1c). The radial settlement of the macro-band is made up of a hub, the central base camp, with seasonal dispersal to temporary camps occupied for the exploitation of some specific food resource. Dispersal from the base camp splits the band, a macro-unit, into many smaller units or micro-bands (MacNeish 1964).

Macro-bands are caused by any one of the three forms of subsistence adaptation: (1) a storable or preservable wild food harvest such as acorns or mesquite beans, (2) a locally abundant food, such as shellfish, and (3) incipient agriculture producing a small harvest (Beardsley 1956). Characteristic of this form of community is a slightly higher population density ranging from 0.6 to 1.0 persons per km^2 while the size of the local group is at the upper limit for the band organization, between 100 and 500 people. Because of this increase in population and density, the macro-band needs significantly more territory than the simple band requires.

The semi-sedentary camp is supported by some seasonally assured food supply that can be stored in pits or other structures. As the productivity of this staple food increases, for instance with the shift from intensive plant collection to cultivation, the amount of seasonal time spent at the base camp also increases. The dispersed macro-band occupies satellite camps during lean months of the year or when some particularly bountiful game, fish, or plant can be harvested and returned to the base camp for storage. The most important advancement in ceremonialism is increased concern for the dead, who are returned from the mobile camp to base camp for burial.

The hypothesis that macro-bands followed simple bands in an evolutionary progression can be tested through the following list of logical implications: (1) evidence of occupation at the different kinds of sites comprising the seasonal dispersal, (2) base camps exhibiting thick midden accumulations with evidence of repeated occupations, (3) storage pits in the base camp containing discarded food and material refuse from satellite camp exploitation, (4) abandoned storage pits containing formal burials of individual deaths, (5) evidence of more permanent housing at the base camp, and (6) religious shrines signifying hunting magic and an attachment to a fixed territory.

Base camps with thick accumulations of refuse are found from at least the Middle Paleolithic through the Mesolithic. By Mesolithic times, huge mounds of shellfish remains also distinguish the base camp settlement from outlying special activity sites. In the Near East, there are incipient villages composed of clusters of pit houses with storage pits from the Natufian phase of the Mesolithic. Upon abandonment, some of these storage facilities were converted to burial chambers. On the lower reach of the Nile river in Africa, the Quadan culture has base camp sites with formal cemeteries meeting the requirements of test implication 4 (Wendorf 1968). Evidence of hunting magic and territorial attachment can be found in Upper Paleolithic cave sanctuaries decorated with painted, engraved, and sculptured animal pictures that suggest ritual killings. Thus, the hypothesis of Old World macro-bands dated from 100,000 to about 9000 years ago can be tested successfully. The correlative cultural stages in the New World would be the Paleo-indian and Archaic, variously dated between 10,000 BC and AD 1.

Tribes

According to Service (1962), tribes are organizational types that evolved from bands. Some ethnographic examples are: (1) the reindeer Tungus of Siberia, (2) the Cheyenne of the North American plains, (3) the Nuer of the Upper Nile river, (4) the Navajo of the American southwest, and (5) the Jivaro of the Amazon Basin, South America (Service 1958). A tribe is a village community that establishes itself in successive locations, occupying each location for a period of years before moving on (Beardsley 1956). The resulting settlement pattern is diagrammed in Figure 11–1d.

Several explanations have been offered for this pattern of wandering relocation. One is based on soil fertility, which requires the agrarian society to relocate as the soil nutrients are depleted (Beardsley 1956). This kind of short-term farming is variously called *slash-and-burn, swidden,* or *milpa* (a Maya term). Prime examples are village farmers of the wet tropics who follow a cycle: (1) forest clearance and wood ash fertilization, (2) farming for a few years with successive declines in yield, (3) shifting to a new field location to begin the cycle again. Among the tribal examples given above, other causal factors, such as seasonal availability of forage, also contribute to the systematic wanderings of pastoral nomads.

Characteristic of tribal communities is a low population density ranging from less than 0.2 to 3.0 persons per km². Individual villages may range in size between 500 and 1000 persons. Although each village is independent and self-sufficient in the ethnographic examples, multiple villages may consist of members of a single tribe ranging in size between 300 and 3000 people.

The economy of many tribal groups is agricultural with some surplus production. Labor is divided on the criterion of sex, with men clearing and planting the fields and hunting game to supplement the diet, and women harvesting and preparing foods for the family. Surplus food is disposed of in community ceremonies or festivals called *give-away feasts* (Harris 1971). Prestige, then, accrues from the distribution or conspicuous destruction of goods and food stuffs rather than from accumulation by individuals—a mechanism that prevents the rise of marked differences in wealth (Beardsley 1956).

The social organization of the tribe is founded on descent groups and sodalities, or voluntary organizations (Sanders and Price 1968). Together, these groups provide the integration or social cohesiveness that binds the tribal community together. Common descent groups are the lineage and clan. A lineage is a family extended to three or more generations. The eldest member of the family is the spokeman with preeminence in decision making. Several lineages recognizing common descent from a mythical ancestor constitute a clan (Schusky 1965). Cohesiveness among the clan members rests on the fiction of descent from an animal ancestor, such as a wolf, snake, eagle, or puma totem. Lineage and clan units are exogamous, that is, out-marrying. They may be confined exclusively to the community (local) or cross-cut many communities (nonlocal). If descent groups are the vertical or warp elements in tribal integration, then sodalities are the horizontal or weft elements (Service 1962; Sanders and Price 1968). Examples of sodalities that cross-cut descent groups are age-grade clubs, secret associations, warrior groups, and religious organizations.

Politically, the tribal society often has a headman whose power depends on personal charisma rather than social sanctions vested in leadership status. Tribal warfare and shamanism are the primary means for gaining social prestige. Marriage is usually monogamous, although polygyny is permissible, and puberty rites signal the transition to adult status for one or both sexes (Beardsley 1956). Thus, social relations are still largely egalitarian although the ''germs'' of social differentiation are present as small deviations from the band pattern, which are amplified in succeeding evolutionary steps.

Tribal religion rests on belief in forest spirits and ghosts of the dead. Ceremonies featuring masked dances to promote success in agriculture are common. The shamans are involved in curing illness, and the dead are often buried under the house floor, after which the structure may be abandoned.

Social customs such as markets, organized trade, or craft guilds are lacking in the tribal organization.

Test implications for the hypothesis that the earliest agricultural societies were tribally organized are as follows: (1) Villages should leave thin refuse deposits because of their short-term use; (2) most characteristic artifacts of the tribal village would be a scatter of potsherds; (3) the village plan is marked by uniform house arrangements, some with subfloor burials; and (4) formal human burials should show little social differentiation in terms of grave offerings. These expectations are met by the archaeological data of the Early and Middle Neolithic stage of the Old World and the Early Formative stage of the New World. In fact, tribally organized communities survive today, not only as isolated primitive societies, but also as the peasant class in some non-industrialized Third World countries.

Chiefdoms

Chiefdoms are ranked societies in which the local group is organized into a cone-shaped hierarchy. Communities organized in this manner inhabit a permanent settlement, with or without satellites. This kind of settlement may be a self-supporting town (Fig. 11–1e) or a central market or ceremonial place that serves surrounding villages (Fig. 11–1f). Examples taken from the ethnographic literature are the Nootka of British Columbia, the Trobriand islanders of Melanesia, and the Tahitians of Polynesia (Service 1958).

Factors that produce this organizational form of community are: (1) a center maintained by intensive agricultural techniques, and (2) food surplus that allows some community members to be released from production for specialized roles (Beardsley 1956).

The agricultural subsistence of the chiefdom allows permanency of settlement and also promotes a much higher population density (2–4 per km^2) than is found in the tribal community. In fact, maximum numbers reach 2500 to 20,000 persons per chiefdom. The nuclear settlement may be a planned city.

The surplus production of the chiefdom allows specialization by full-time craftsmen, administrators, and priests, all of which become hereditary positions in society. Trade is now intense both within and between communities as a result of the excellence of craft products in ornaments and other symbols of high status. Private ownership has begun, so that the "haves" and "have-nots" are markedly segregated (Beardsley 1956).

Like tribes, chiefdoms are organized according to principles of descent reckoned through lineage and clan. In the chiefdom, however, these descent groups are ranked so that some are superordinate to others. The preeminent descent group is the lineage of the chief. Kinsmen are ranked within each lineage or clan so that each has obligations to those above and privileges with regard to those below (Service 1962).

Although the chief lacks police or judicial power, his authority is considerable, resting on social custom and taboo (Sanders and Price 1968). At the chiefdom level, for the first time, social relations are strongly nonegalitarian although sharply defined socioeconomic classes are absent.

The religion of chiefdoms is markedly formal. There are ritual sacrifices of animals and occasionally humans to appease the gods. Public ceremonies are directed toward successful harvests, rainfall, and victory over enemies.

In the archaeological record, chiefdom-organized societies meet the following criteria: (1) the presence of ceremonial structures such as earthworks and small temples, (2) ceremonial as well as utilitarian pottery, (3) elaborately stocked graves reflecting the few high-ranking individuals of society, (4) luxury items of local manufacture, (5) permanent village and town architecture of stone or mud brick construction, and (6) planned ceremonial areas (Beardsley 1956). In fact, the hypothesis of chiefdom-organized societies is met by late Neolithic settlements of southwest Asia dated between 5000 and 3000 BC. In the New World, the late Formative stage of both Mesoamerica and the Andean high culture meets these same requirements.

Primitive States

Primitive states are societies organized into sharply delimited classes or castes and administered by governments. Some examples are the Kalinga of the Philippine Islands, the Maya of Mexico, and the Ashanti of West Africa (Service 1958). In terms of its settlement organization, a state is a community differentiated into an administrative center, the capital city, and surrounding satellites consisting of towns, villages, hamlets, and scattered homesteads to form the network diagrammed as Figure 11–1g. The city administrative center contains the largest single population, although most of the people live in dependent satellites (Beardsley 1956). Sanders and Price (1968) found that primitive states range in density between 4 and 100 persons per km^2 with a total human population between 5000 and 100,000 persons. Urban states do not appear in the ethnographic literature until a density of more than 100 persons per km^2 has been reached.

The economy of the state is clearly marked by the distribution of goods and materials through the mechanism of the market. In some early civilizations, this redistributive function was handled directly by the state by means of the granary, as illustrated by the Harappan civilization of the Indus valley. Primitive states are organized so that there is a flow of goods, materials, and services from the broad base of society upward into the hands of the ruling elite. This concentration of wealth in the hands of the ruling class is performed by tax and labor levy, which extracts the food surplus of the peasant to run society. Primitive states are characterized also by full-time specialists in craft production and pronounced distinctions in wealth and property, which lead to the rise of socioeconomic classes.

The prime social integration of the state is effected by legal mechanisms whereby the government mediates disputes between individuals and corporate groups, a function formerly carried out by the kinship groups of tribally organized societies. Adams (1971), in a comparative study of the Sumerians and Aztecs, found that archival documents indicate that both societies were undergoing a transition from kinship organization to one founded on rule of law and government. Self-determination by the corporate clans, which were task-specialized and class-ranked, was being replaced by the sanctions of governmental bureaucracy. Thus, there is actual evidence for the evolution from a kinship to a class-organized social stage. Other attributes of the primitive state society include: (1) Administration is carried out by a hierarchy of officials forming a government; (2) the head of the state is a king; (3) social classes are marked; (4) the upper class is formally educated in schools run by the priesthood; and (5) writing and a literate tradition exist (Beardsley 1956).

The polytheistic religion is served by a hierarchy of ranked priests to form a church. Furthermore, there are impressive temples in the ceremonial centers of the capital city and principal towns. A recorded calendar serves as the basis for timing public ceremonies. The people worship a pantheon of gods and goddesses, each with its own idol and sometimes its own temple. Human and other sacrifices are made daily to influence powerful deities.

Test implications for the archaeological presence of a primitive state include the following: (1) The wealth of artifacts found in the capital city is lacking in the simple village satellites; (2) public buildings at the capital are one evidence of this richness; (3) fine craftsmanship and the segregation of craft production by city quarter evidence full-time specialists; and (4) social stratification is reflected in the rich burials of the proportionately few elite members of society. Elitism is marked by status symbols, human sacrifice of retainers, and sumptuous royal tombs. These conditions are first met in the bronze age of the Old World after 3000 BC and in the Classic stage of both Mesoamerica and Peru.

Conquest Empires

The conquest empire is an organization type recognized by Steward (1955) as a recurrent evolutionary phenomenon. Ancient history provides many examples.

Beardsley (1956) has outlined the needs responsible for conquest-integrated empires: (1) food to feed expanding populations, (2) commodities to fulfill the prestige requirements of the elite ruling class, (3) raw materials for craft industries, and (4) additional manpower, including slaves and sacrificial victims. But once established, empires founded on conquest tend to dissolve only to be followed by others in a cyclical fashion to form what Steward (1955, p. 204) has called the *era of cyclical conquest*. The rise and fall of civilizations has long intrigued historians such as Arnold Toynbee (1971). Causal factors for the collapse of imperial states include: (1) predation by pastoral nomads or savages who envy the civilized society's standard of living, (2) social revolt of the exploited peasant masses, (3) overexpansion of the state bureaucracy, and (4) natural disasters such as flood, famine, and pestilence. After the collapse, however, there is a strong positive push to form a new civilized empire.

In a conquest empire the capital of the reigning dynasty is typically the largest city. Populations of such imperial communities are quite variable but generally range into the tens of thousands. To control and suppress the conquered people, the government manipulates the subjugated populations by resettlement, colonization, and the forced founding of new communities for special purposes such as mining, commerce, or border defense (Beardsley 1956).

The imperial government and the elite ruling class are supported by taxes and tribute levied in produce (craftsmen), food stuffs (peasant farmers), and labor (peasants also). A labor levy is called *corvée tax* and may take various forms including military service and construction of public works such as roads, canals, city walls, tombs, and statues. Commerce is facilitated by the use of a medium of exchange, such as coinage. Indebtedness is punishable by a form of slavery called *serfdom*. To pay off debts to a landlord, families may sell their children into slavery, to be indentured for a designated period of time until the debt is worked off. Individuals may grow up and marry in bondage but usually children of such unions are born free (Adams 1971). As a generalization, goods, land, and slaves tend to be concentrated in the hands of the ruling class. Another aspect of economics is the keeping of records, such as accounts, deeds, bills of sale, and other documents that accompany business transactions (Beardsley 1956).

In social organization, imperial states are similar to city states with several additional attributes. The empire's military organization consists of a standing army instead of a militia or conscript army of free men, and the ruler is identified with the gods as a "divine king." This king wields absolute power with supernatural sanction.

The state religion of the conqueror is imposed upon the conquered. The priesthood represents a separate class whose interest is sometimes at odds with interests of the ruling, military aristocracy. Eventually scientific knowledge, including astronomy, mathematics, and calendrics, gradually replaces supernaturalism as a force in social control (Beardsley 1956).

There are only a few overt manifestations that allow archaeological differentiation of the conquest empire from the city-state. Some test implications for the conquest empire hypothesis are: (1) the presence of roads between centers, such as the Inca or Mayan road systems, (2) regional irrigation works, such as that of the Old Babylonian period (Fig. 11–2), (3) construction of forts in the characteristic style of the conqueror, and (4) abrupt termination of local art traditions (Beardsley 1956). These implications are found in the classical iron age empires of the Mediterranean, Near East, India, and Far East. They are also present in the New World during the Postclassic stage of Mesoamerica (Toltec and Aztec empires) and the Inca empire of South America.

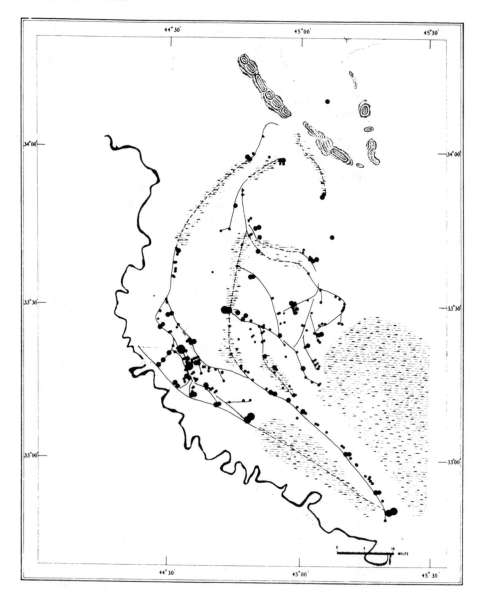

FIGURE 11-2   Early watercourses and settlements in the Diyala region, Iraq. The system shown in grey was in use during the Early Dynastic period, about 3000–2400 BC. Sites and watercourses shown in black, slightly displaced so that the earlier period remains visible, were occupied during the Old Babylonian period, about 1800–1700 BC. The size of the circle marking an ancient settlement is roughly proportional to the area of its ruins. Modern river courses are shown in grey.

Source: From Thorkild Jacobsen and Robert M. Adams, "Salt and Silt in Ancient Mesopotamian Agriculture," Figure 1. In *The Rise and Fall of Civilizations*, compiled by C. C. Lamberg-Karlovsky and Jeremy A. Sabloff; Menlo Park, California: Cummings Publishing Company, 1974.

Cultural Evolution

The growth and development of culture provide a means of organizing the seemingly great diversity of human behavioral customs into an orderly progression from savagery through barbarism to civilization. Although temporarily out of favor during the 1930s and 1940s, the study of cultural evolution returned to prominence during the 1950s through the research of such neoevolutionists as Childe, Steward, and White, each of whom has contributed to the macro-theory of evolution called *cultural materialism* (Harris 1969).

Materialist Theories

The major parts and contributors of the materialist theory are shown in Figure 11-3, a revision of the model presented in Chapter 2.

The materialist thesis of Julian H. Steward (1955) related the adaptation of the techno-economic base of society to the surrounding natural and social environments. The irrigation agriculture and warfare of the bronze and iron ages are causative factors in the rise of elitism and the state form of government.

FIGURE 11-3   A materialist model of society showing the source and direction of culture change and indicating the individual theorists who have contributed the separate parts of Harris' (1969) macro-theory of cultural materialism. Arrows indicate direction of change.

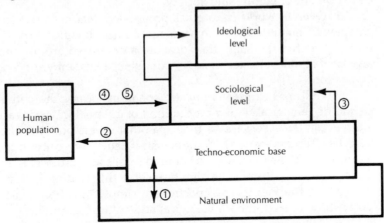

Legend: ◄───── direction of change

① Julian H. Steward (1955)
② V. Gordon Childe (1961)
③ Leslie White (1949)
④ William Sanders and Barbara Price (1968)
⑤ Robert Carneiro (1970)

V. Gordon Childe (1961) presented a variant of the materialist thesis that relates the appearance of new food-producing technologies to the sudden rise in human population size. Childe saw these revolutionary changes in society at two points in prehistory: the Neolithic stage and the bronze age. He attributed the Neolithic agricultural revolution to extensive dry farming and the bronze age urban revolution to intensive irrigation agriculture.

White (1949) saw the capture of energy as a causative factor in generating more advanced forms of human organization.

Sanders and Price (1968) provided yet another variant on the materialist thesis by showing empirically that increases in both size and density of human populations increase the complexity of social organization in the evolutionary progression of band, tribe, chiefdom, and primitive state. Their thesis is that more complex forms of human relations are needed to control larger populations.

And finally, Carneiro (1970) postulated that the physical or social restriction of expanding populations leads to warfare and ultimately to the rise of the state form of government. In this theory warfare is the result of overcrowding and competition for scarce resources.

The Archaeological Evidence

The pragmatic contribution of the archaeologist to the test of materialist theory consists of demonstrating the following regularities in the growth and development of culture and society:

1. Overall, world culture has progressed *unidirectionally* from simple to complex as illustrated in all archaeological stage classifications. This regularity is true whether the stage classification is organized around the criterion of artifact material, tool technology, subsistence economy, or institutional organization.

2. Culture has great *antiquity*, spanning nearly the entire Quaternary period of geological time for a duration of 2.5 million years based on potassium-argon (K-Ar) assays—a time span that covers both the Quaternary and very late Tertiary periods. To demonstrate such longevity, it is necessary to assume that the association of hominid fossils and artifacts is a proper index of society and culture. The significance of this finding is that earlier chronologies of the Pleistocene epoch were simply too short to account for the great strides taken in both biological and cultural evolution.

3. The growth of culture through time, particularly throughout the late Pleistocene, has *accelerated* in a continuous fashion. This generalization is well demonstrated when the subdivisions of the Paleolithic stage are plotted on an absolute time scale, particularly as measured by the C–14 time scale covering the last 50,000 years (Fig. 11–4).

4. Culture has promoted the *survival and success* of the human species, as recorded by the continuous growth of world populations and gradual geographical spread of the human species over the face of the earth. Population

Stage Subdivisions

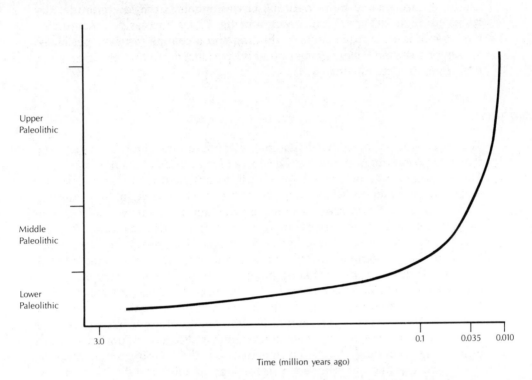

Upper
Paleolithic

Middle
Paleolithic

Lower
Paleolithic

3.0   0.1   0.035 0.010

Time (million years ago)

FIGURE 11-4   Curvilinear graph showing the acceleration of Paleolithic evolution during the Pleistocene epoch.

growth is expressed indirectly by the increasing number and density of archaeological sites through time. Spatial spread of the human species is revealed in the gradual peopling of every continent in an orderly outflow from a dry tropical homeland in Africa (Table 11-1).

TABLE 11-1.   The progressive geographical spread of humankind.

Time	Environmental Zones	Spatial Spread
Late Pleistocene (0.1–0.01 mya)	Arctic and subarctic	Australia and the New World; high latitudes of Europe and Asia
Middle Pleistocene (0.7–0.1 mya)	Temperate zone and wet tropics	Mid-latitude Europe and Asia
Early Pleistocene and Late Pliocene (2.5–0.7 mya)	Dry tropics and subtropics (savanna habitat)	Africa and adjacent portions of eastern Mediterranean

5. Evolution of culture is *adaptive* as shown by the progressive colonization of successively more rigorous environments, from low latitude, dry tropics to high latitude, arctic environments. These successively new adaptations required improvements in hunting and a change from unspecialized scavenging of small, slow game to highly specialized hunting of big game by fire drives and stampedes.

Summary

The macro-theory of cultural materialism stresses the interaction between technology and environment as the source of evolutionary change in society. The expanding role of technology is well documented in the archaeological record by ever more efficient adaptive practices: (1) scavenging, (2) hunting, (3) intensive food collecting, (4) food production by extensive, shifting cultivation, (5) food production by intensive irrigation agriculture, and (6) predatory warfare. While the exploitive technology was progressively improving, the natural environment was changing in a manner that stimulated cultural growth: (1) through the oscillating pattern of world climates, changing from glacial to interglacial episodes at high and mid-latitudes, (2) by expanding colonization in an orderly progression from dry tropical savanna to high arctic tundra, and (3) by the orderly migration into new continents from an African homeland. Thus, the environment limited human distribution until new forms of adaptive technology had been invented, but the environmental variation stimulated creative tinkering with technology to solve the dilemma of new environmental challenges.

Advances in food production, the result of successful new adaptations, led to an ever increasing number of people. As the numbers and density of people increased on the face of the earth, so did the need for ever tighter forms of social control. Organizational types shifted from egalitarian to elitist in the progression through band, tribe, chiefdom, primitive state, and conquest empire. From a primitive democracy based on kinship relations, the systems of social integration moved in the direction of autocratic control by early state and imperial governments.

And finally, a brief review of the relationship between economic type and ideology shows that religious practices are a direct reflection and justification of adaptive technologies and social organization. As each new economic adaptation appeared in the evolution of society, it was followed closely by a functional shift to new religious views. Thus Paleolithic and Mesolithic sites yield symbolic artifacts that are interpreted as evidence of hunting magic and animal fertility. With the appearance of Neolithic societies, artifactual symbols indicate the functional change to plant fertility magic and a concern with weather control. By the chiefdom stage of cultural evolution, magic is being replaced by religion and the beginning of a formal church run by a priesthood. Gods of war became preeminent with the intensive agriculture of the preindustrial state and conquest empire. In the empire stage of evolution, Willey and Phillips (1958) have recognized the change from sacred to secular values, a trend that appeared in New World civilizations between the Classic and Postclassic stages. Adams (1971) has documented a similar shift in Sumerian society. He believes that the earliest Mesopotamian civilization was a theocratic state run by the priesthood which was followed by a militaristic state with a secular war leader. Thus the ritual focus of each cultural stage is a functional realignment of the sociological and ideological levels of society to conform to the newly evolved material base.

From this review, it is apparent that cultural materialism is a powerful theory useful to explain and understand much of the general evolution of our own species. That it also has relevance to our own times is illustrated by the present energy crisis. But beyond our concern for petroleum fuels, a larger inventory of crises faces the globe: (1) environmental deterioration including pollution and resource depletion, (2) overexpansion of population, (3) governmental organizations that have become despotic, (4) the role of women in society, and (5) ideologies that are slow to respond to the contemporary needs and practical belief systems of their adherents. The techno-environmental and techno-economic sources of these and other pressing modern issues may be clearer when illuminated by over two million years of our own cultural heritage. Certainly these adaptive problem areas within modern industrial societies of the world must be addressed before global culture can proceed to even more advanced stages of organizational complexity.

References

ADAMS, ROBERT McC.
   1971   *The Evolution of Urban Society.* Chicago: Aldine.
BEARDSLEY, R. K.
   1956   Functional and Evolutionary Implications of Community Patterning. *American Antiquity* 22:129–57.
BREEDEN, ROBERT L., ed.
   1968   *Vanishing Peoples of the Earth.* Washington, D.C.: The National Geographic Society.
CARNEIRO, ROBERT L.
   1970   A Theory of the Origin of the State. *Science* 169:733–69.
CHILDE, V. GORDON
   1961   *Man Makes Himself.* New York: New American Library.
HARRIS, MARVIN
   1969   *The Rise of Anthropological Theory.* New York: Thomas Y. Crowell.
   1971   *Culture, Man and Nature.* New York: Thomas Y. Crowell.
JACOBSEN, THORKILD, and ROBERT McC. ADAMS
   1974   Salt and Silt in Ancient Mesopotamian Agriculture. In *The Rise and Fall of Civilizations,*

    edited by Jeremy A. Sabloff and C. C. Lamberg-Karlovsky. Menlo Park, Calif.: Cummings.

LEE, RICHARD B., and IRVEN DE VORE, eds.
1968   *Man the Hunter.* Chicago: Aldine.

MACNEISH, RICHARD S.
1964   The Origins of New World Civilization. *Scientific American* 211(5):29–37.

MURDOCK, GEORGE PETER
1949   *Social Structure.* New York: Free Press.

PRESCOTT, WILLIAM H.
1843   *History of the Conquest of Mexico and History of the Conquest of Peru.* New York: Modern Library.

SANDERS, WILLIAM T., and BARBARA J. PRICE
1968   *Mesoamerica: The Evolution of a Civilization.* New York: Random House.

SCHUSKY, ERNEST L.
1965   *Manual for Kinship Analysis.* New York: Holt, Rinehart and Winston.

SERVICE, ELMAN R.
1958   *A Profile of Primitive Culture.* New York: Harper and Brothers.
1962   *Primitive Social Organization: An Evolutionary Perspective.* New York: Random House.
1966   *The Hunters.* Englewood Cliffs, N.J.: Prentice-Hall.

STEWARD, JULIAN H.
1955   *Theory of Culture Change.* Urbana: University of Illinois Press.

TOYNBEE, ARNOLD J.
1971   *A Study of History*, vols. 1 and 2. New York: Dell.

WENDORF, FRED
1968   Site 117: A Nubian Final Paleolithic Graveyard near Jebel Sahaba, Sudan. In *The Prehistory of Nubia*, vol. 2, edited by Fred Wendorf. Dallas: Fort Burgwin Research Center and Southern Methodist University Press.

WHITE, LESLIE A.
1949   Energy and the Evolution of Culture. In *The Science of Culture.* New York: Farrar, Straus.

WILLEY, GORDON R., and PHILIP PHILLIPS
1958   *Method and Theory in American Archaeology.* Chicago: University of Chicago Press.

Glossary

Absolute Dating—Assignment of an event to an age-in-years scale.

Acculturation—A special case of diffusion that occurs when a dominant society forces a subordinate society to change.

Adaptation—The adjustment of a society to both its surrounding natural environment and its social neighbors.

Adaptive Radiation—An evolutionary process in which a subpopulation adapts to a unique habitat by transforming into a new species.

Adena Phase—The early Woodland archaeological culture of the Ohio valley that dates between 1000 and 100 BC.

Adobe—Sun-dried clay used as floor paving, wall construction, and plaster in architectural construction. A technical term employed throughout South and Central America, Mexico, and the American Southwest.

Adze—A woodworking tool with a check-shaped blade that is hafted at right angles to a wooden handle.

Afarensis—A nontool-using Pliocene age species of the *Australopithecus* genus.

Africanus—A fossil species of the *Australopithecus* genus marked by its slender bone structure. Found in South African caves.

Agricultural Revolution—A synonym for *Neolithic revolution*.

Agriculture—The planned control of useful plant and animal products.

Ahitzotl—The Emperor (AD 1468–1502) who consolidated the Aztec conquests.

Alluvium—Water-laid deposits such as stream gravels or floodplain silts.

311

Alternate Hypothesis—A hypothesis that predicts a causal relationship between two or more attribute variables.

Altiplano—The high interior plateau located on the international border of Peru and Bolivia in the vicinity of Lake Titicaca.

Altithermal—A climatic period of high (*alti-*) temperatures (*-thermal*) between 7500 and 4000 years ago.

Ambrona—*See* Torralba.

Anasazi-Pueblo Tradition—A village farming tradition of the Colorado plateau that evolved from the Archaic stage about AD 1 and continues in the various modern Pueblo indian tribes that live in north central New Mexico and northeastern Arizona.

Anathermal Period—Period of cool, moist climates dating between 10,000 and 7500 BP.

Anatomist—One who studies the form or morphology of both human soft parts and skeleton.

Ancestor Worship—A religious belief in which the deceased members of a family are worshipped for the aid they can supply in communicating with higher supernatural beings.

Andean High Culture—Ancient civilization found both on the Pacific coast and in the mountainous highlands of Peru and Bolivia.

Animal Husbandry—The planned control of domestic herd animals.

Anthropology—The study of human culture and society over the entire world throughout the last two million years.

Anvil—A stone work surface upon which other stone tools or materials can be manufactured.

Arboreal Living—Life in the trees, including locomotion, feeding, and sleeping.

Archaeology—The study of human existence through unwritten, material remains; sometimes referred to as the ethnology of the past.

Archaic Homo Sapiens—Primitive modern humans, such as the Neanderthal population, dating to the early part of the late Pleistocene—between 100,000 and 35,000 years ago.

Archaic Stage—Post-glacial hunters and gatherers who subsisted on essentially modern animals and plants. Sometimes referred to as New World Mesolithic.

Artifact—An object of human manufacture or use.

Assemblage—All of the artifact types of the same age from the same locality, regardless of materials industry.

Association Principle—A premise that all artifacts or ecofacts found in the same stratum or layer are of the same age. Thus association (meaning "togetherness") is a measure of contemporaneity in time as well as functional relatedness.

Atahualpa—The last Inca emperor, who was taken prisoner by the sixteenth-century Spanish conquerors of Peru.

Atlantis—Mythic, supposedly now submerged, continent that once supported an ancient civilization. Said to have been located in the Atlantic Ocean.

Atomic Clock—A popular term for the entire family of radiometric dating techniques.

Attribute—A particular characteristic of an artifact. Usually ascribed to a single or short run of actions by the original artisan or user.

Atzcapotzalco—The capital city of the Tepanec state located on the banks of Lake Texcoco, prehistoric Mexico, during the fifteenth century.

Australopithecine—Anglicized term for the fossil genus *Australopithecus*.

Australopithecus—A hominid genus of the Pliocene and early Pleistocene epochs.

Ayacucho Complex—An assemblage of tools found by Richard MacNeish in Flea Cave of the Ayacucho valley. Dated to 14,000 years ago.

Ayllu—A Quechua term meaning ''clan.''

Balk—An unexcavated block of site fill from which both vertical and horizontal stratigraphy can be ''read.''

Balsa Boat—A boat constructed of tied bundles of reeds. These boats were used in fishing both on the Pacific coast of Peru and on Lake Titicaca in the southern highlands.

Band—A small group of primitive hunting and gathering peoples organized according to egalitarian principles.

Bannerstone—A weight attached to a throwing board to provide momentum in hurling it in hunting and warfare.

Barrio—A neighborhood or section of a prehistoric city in ancient Mexico.

Basketmaker II—A cultural stage of the Anasazi-Pueblo tradition dated between AD 1 and 400. Although much of the hunting and gathering subsistence economy indicates Archaic stage development, the rise of village agriculture suggests that a transition to the Formative stage was in progress.

Baton—A synonym for *billet*.

Battleship Curve—A double convex graph pattern.

Bee-Hive Village—Cube-shaped rooms attached end-to-end and stacked to several stories.

Before Present (BP)—Form of a radiometric date that measures time from the present into the past.

Bell-Shaped Curve—A normal frequency distribution in which attribute measurements tend to imitate the shape of a bell.

Bichrome—Two-color painting on decorated ceramics.

Biface—*See* Fist Axe.

Billet—A soft hammer made of wood, bone, or antler, which was used to finish fist axes by bifacial flaking.

Binomial—A two-part name made up of genus and species that designates a particular kind of plant or animal.

Biomass—The biological amount of animals present on a specific landscape at one point in time.

Bipedal Gait—Upright stance on two legs.

Bison Antiguus—An oversize, extinct species of long-horn buffalo dating to the Valders stadial of the Wisconsin glaciation. Hunted by Folsom man.

Bison Occidentalis—The last pre-modern species of buffalo hunted to extinction by Plano hunters on the high plains of the western United States during the Anathermal climatic period.

Blackwater Draw—A Clovis and Folsom age site located in eastern New Mexico.

Blade—A long, parallel-sided flake removed from a polyhedral core by direct or indirect percussion.

Blow Gun—A weapon made of a long, hollow tube through which a dart is blown. Blow guns probably were invented in the Amazon basin and were diffused into the Andean High Culture area.

Blow Hole—A breathing hole in the pack ice of arctic seas and oceans. Used to hunt seals and fish during the winter.

Boisei—A massive species of the *Australopithecus* genus found in east Africa dating to early Pleistocene times.

Bolas Stone—Rope bound weight used to entangle the feet of running game and bring them down in hunting.

Bonampak—A Classic stage Maya ceremonial site where polychrome painted murals depicting warfare and human sacrifice were found.

Bonfire Shelter—A Plano age bison kill site located in southern Texas.

Boreal Forest—The subarctic coniferous forest of Canada, Siberia, and Scandinavia.

Bronze—An alloy of tin and copper in a ratio of approximately 1:9.

Burial Mound—An earthen mound heaped up over the dead body of one or more Woodland peoples.

Burin—A characteristic implement used to make other tools of bone, antler, or ivory during the Upper Paleolithic. From the French word for *engraving tool*.

Burnt Rock Midden—A discard pile of heat-fractured rock which had been used in stone boiling or pit roasting.

Bushmen—Band organized societies who practice a hunting and gathering subsistence in the Kalahari Desert of southern Africa.

Butchering Site—An archaeological site where animals were killed and butchered.

Cache—A group of artifacts stored or hidden in a hole.

Calendar—A system of fixing divisions of time.

Caliche—A regional term of the American Southwest referring to a hard, white, calcium carbonate soil formation.

Calpulli—Aztec clan.

Carrying Capacity—The ability of an environment to support a human population given a particular exploitive technology.

Cave Bear Cult—A middle Paleolithic religious ritual in which the skulls and long bones of an extinct Pleistocene age bear were stacked to form shrines.

Cenote—A natural sinkhole in the limestone bedrock of the Yucatan peninsula, Mexico. Used by the Mayan indians as a natural well and also as a shrine into which human sacrifices and religious fetishes were thrown.

Cenozoic Era—The latest geological subdivision of the earth's history including the rise of modern forms of life.

Census—The collection of all data making up a population of artifacts or all sites in a universe. A 100 percent sample.

Chacs—Rain gods of the prehistoric Mayan indians.

Chalcolithic—The late Neolithic of the Near East, which saw the beginnings of metal-working in the form of cold-hammering and simple casting of copper.

Chan Chan Site—The capital city of the Chimu state. Located in the lower Moche valley on the north coast of Peru.

Chapultepec Hill—A hill, called *grasshopper hill* by the Aztecs, around which the capital city of Tenochtitlan grew.

Charnel House—A tomb placed within a burial mound, containing basins or altars with cremated human bones and offerings.

Chavin de Huantar—A type site for the Chavin phase and the pan-Peruvian feline style of the same name. The culture and horizon style date between 900 and 200 BC.

Check Dam—Low masonry retaining wall built in the bottom of a V-shaped gulley.

Checkerboard Digging—Strategy of digging alternate excavation units to reveal the site stratigraphy and its horizontal variations throughout the site without digging up the entire site.

Chichen-Itza—A Mayan ceremonial site located on the Yucatan peninsula, Mexico. Occupied during the early Postclassic; also exhibits evidence of Toltec presence.

Chichimecs—A barbarian people who periodically raided and conquered civilized states of Mesoamerica. The Toltecs and Aztecs were some of the latest chichimecs to invade central Mexico from northern Mexico.

Chiefdom—A ranked society organized into a cone-shaped hierarchy of social statuses.

Chimor State—*See* Chimu State.

Chimu (Chimor) State—A late Postclassic regional empire located on the north coast of Peru.

Chinampa Farming—Marsh land reclaimed by a rectangular grid of canals for garden plots.

Chi-Square Test—A statistic employed to check for associations between pairs of discrete attributes.

Choukoutien—An archaeological site, dating to the middle Pleistocene and located near Beijing, China, where many *Homo erectus* fossils and fire hearths were found in caves.

Chronological Seriation—A relative dating technique based on systematic changes in the frequency or shape of different stylistically distinctive artifact types.

Circumscription Theory—A theory posited by Robert Carneiro (1970) that natural and social constraints to population expansion generate warfare and the rise of military elitism.

Cirque—A glacially sculptured mountain basin that fills with water following the melting and retreat of a valley glacier.

Cist—A slab-lined storage pit.

Ciudadela—A large compound enclosure found at pre-Columbian cities in Mesoamerica. Spanish term meaning "citadel."

Clacton Technique—A stone manufacturing procedure named for the Clacton site in

England where it was first recognized. A core is reduced to make flakes by swinging the nodule against a stationary anvil.

Clan—Several lineages recognizing common descent from a mythic ancestor symbolized by a totemic animal.

Classic Stage—The cultural climax of New World civilizations. A cultural development marked by the rise of theocratic urban states in both Mesoamerica and Peru.

Classification—A laboratory method in archaeology whose goal is to draw generalizations about the nature of an artifact collection by sorting the members into discrete subgroupings called *types*.

Class-Stratified Society—A society in which the citizens are organized into two or more superordinate-subordinate tiers based on birth and economic wealth.

Clovis Phase—A Lithic Period 3 archaeological culture characterized by a distinctive fluted spear point, the Clovis point. Dated between 11,000 and 12,000 radiocarbon years ago.

Cluster Strategy—A sampling procedure in which one artifact or site is collected by means of a random numbers table with a specified number of nearby neighbors also collected or observed in order to gather an associated set of data.

Cobble Chopper—A stone tool with a crude, blunt, heavy-duty cutting edge made on stream-rounded cobble rocks.

Codex—A Mesoamerican book dating from the Postclassic stage. Plural: *codices*.

Colluvium—Sediments washed down a slope such as a hillside.

Confidence Interval—Plus and minus one standard deviation, called a sigma by statisticians. Calculated as the root sum of the mean departures squared, divided by the number of assays.

Conquest Empire—Iron age societies amalgamated by war and held together by coercion.

Context—The relationship between an artifact and its physical setting. Examples of context might be a geological stratum, architectural unit, or activity area.

Co-Phase—An archaeological phase found in two or more contiguous localities.

Coprolite—Fossil feces of an animal or insect. A kind of ecofactual data from which the archaeologist can derive useful information about diet.

Core—A block of parent material out of which a stone tool was sculptured or from which stone flakes were removed for further tool manufacture.

Corn—A New World cereal crop technically labeled *Zea mays* and referred to as *maize*.

Corvée Tax—A tax to be paid in forced labor.

Cotton Preceramic—Preceramic Period VI dating between 2500 and 1800 BC in the Peruvian coastal sequence.

Cro-Magnon—A population subspecies of *Homo sapiens* dating between 35,000 and 10,000 years ago in Europe. Practiced an Upper Paleolithic culture.

Cross-Dating—Building a composite sequence by matching many individual sites.

Cultigen—A domesticated and cultivated plant such as the various cereals, vegetables, root crops, berries, and nuts.

Culture—Beliefs, values, and ideas held in common by a local community of people and leading to predictable behavior on the part of the group members.

Culture Area—A region occupied by contemporary societies sharing a similar culture.

Culture History—The sequences of human cultures examined over time and space.

Cuneiform—Ancient writing of the Sumerian civilization found in modern Iraq. Inscribed into a clay tablet by a triangular-shaped stylus.

Cuzco—The capital city of the Inca empire. Located in the south highlands of Peru.

Cyclical Conquest, Era of—A condition during the iron age in which successive imperial states dissolved only to be replaced by newly formed empires.

Cylinder Hammer—A baton-shaped precursor hammer, made of such soft materials as wood, bone, or antler, used to manufacture a stone tool by direct percussion.

Danger Cave—A cave site containing a long stratified series of archaeological cultures the lowest of which dates back 10,000 years. Located on the edge of the Great Salt Lake of north central Utah.

Dart—A stone-tipped shaft missile hurled by means of a throwing board. Sometimes called by its Aztec name, *atlatl*.

Dating—An assignment of a past event to the time scale.

Death Assemblage—A fauna or assemblage of fossil animals composed of contemporary bones derived from many different natural habitats.

Death Transformation—The steps by which a living ethnographic community is converted into the fossilized archaeological record.

Decay Constant—*See* Half-Life.

De Facto Refuse—Tools, facilities, and other cultural artifacts abandoned at place of use although still useful.

Deglaciation—The shrinking of continental and mountain glaciers during the later part of the Pleistocene and the early part of the Holocene epoch.

Dendrochronology—Absolute dating by counting tree rings because one ring equals one year. (*Dendro* = tree; *chronology* = study of time)

Dendrogram—A tree diagram that graphs the degree of affinity among the artifacts or sites being studied in a numerical taxonomy.

Dent—A Clovis age mammoth kill site located in northeastern Colorado.

Denticulate—A toothed flake tool.

Descent Group—Extended family members who are related to a founding kinsman.

Descriptive Type—A type superimposed upon the data by the archaeologist for purposes of dating.

Devolution—*See* Reducing Tradition.

Dibble—A flat-bladed digging stick.

Diffusion—A change process that results when one society borrows ideas or traits from another.

Direct Association—Two or more artifact classes that display the same spatial spread within a site.

Direct Percussion—Manufacturing technique used to shape stone tools by stone or soft hammer blows directed at the implement.

Direct Tradition—A tradition segment that results from persistence of attributes, tool uses, devices, and tool kits without marked change through time.

Discovery—A change process involving the finding of an existing element in nature.

Divination—Foretelling of the future by a priest or shaman.

Divine King—The belief that the bronze and iron age kings were descended from gods and thus were lesser gods themselves.

Dolni Vestonice—A Czechoslovakian Upper Paleolithic site dating between 25,000 and 29,000 years ago.

Dry Farming—Cropping by direct rainfall only, without irrigation.

Dryopithecus—A taxonomic genus composed of extinct great apes of the Miocene epoch.

Dugout Canoe—A water-craft shaped from a tree trunk by fire and adze.

Ecofact—A natural object such as pollen, macro-plant part, animal bone, mollusk shell, or soil sample that displays no evidence of human use. A source of environmental evidence to the archaeologist.

Eemian Interglacial—The last named interglacial of the European glacial sequence. Dated between 100,000 and 70,000 years ago.

Effector—An output component that produces goods and services for a sociocultural system.

Effigy Mound—A human or animal figure sculptured of soil.

Egalitarian—Equal status relations among the members of a society in which everyone participates in decision making. In contrast are non-egalitarian relationships found in unequal status social organizations such as chiefdoms and primitive states.

Elaborating Tradition—A tradition segment created by increasing complexity as new attributes, tool uses, devices, and tool kits are added to the cultural inventory.

El Abra Stadial—The final advance of Wisconsin glacial ice, dated between 10,000 and 11,000 years ago in South America. Equivalent to the Valders stadial of the Folsom age in North America.

Elitism—The rise of privileged status in non-egalitarian societies such as chiefdoms and primitive states.

El Jobo Point—Lithic Period 3 double-pointed projectile point type of South America.

End Moraine—Pile of rock and soil that marks the maximum extent of glacial ice advance. Also referred to as a *terminal moraine*.

Epipaleolithic—A cultural stage in the archaeology of northeast Africa in which tools progressively diminish in size. Began during the late Pleistocene epoch and continued into the Holocene.

Ethnographic Analogy—An inference derived from the study of the behavior of living primitive peoples. Comparing living and dead societies in terms of artifact form, structure, and function.

Ethnology—The study of contemporary, living societies.

Evolution—Modification over time of natural and sociocultural systems.

Excavation—A research method to observe artifacts and their provenience location by systematic digging below the ground surface.

Extensive Excavation—A large-scale dig to trace the distribution of artifacts and strata horizontally. In contrast is the test excavation, which is limited in scope and emphasizes vertical rather than horizontal relationships.

Feedback—A message from the regulator component of a sociocultural system that may amplify (positive feedback) or dampen (negative feedback) the work output of the system.

Fell's and Palli Aike Caves—Two caves dug by Junius Bird at the southern tip of South America. Contained fish-tail projectile points and extinct fauna dated near the end of the Pleistocene epoch.

Ferrassie—An archaeological site in France where a small cemetery of Neanderthal burials was excavated.

Fetish—A symbolic artifact possessing magical powers to ward off harm or cure disease.

Fire Drill—A fire making device consisting of a shaft that is rotated in a drilled wooden base. The heat generated by friction ignites tinder to kindle a fire. The shaft is turned between the hands or rotated by a bow string wrapped around it.

First Family—A single find of 13 Pliocene age Australopithecines assigned to the species *afarensis*.

Fish-Tail Projectile Point—A dart point type found in many Lithic Period 3 sites of South America. These distinctive primary stemmed points mark a time horizon dated between 10,000 and 12,000 years ago.

Fish Weir—A fish trap made of many upright poles, as in a fence.

Fist Axe—A hand-held pear-shaped stone tool made by bifacial flaking. Fist axes date to the latter part of the lower Paleolithic stage in the Old World.

Flakes—The slivers of rock removed from a core, either as waste or to be used as the manufacturing step in the production of finished stone tools.

Fleshing Tool—A toothed bone or antler tool used to remove hides from a slain animal.

Flint Corn—A hard-kerneled maize pulverized with a mortar and pestle.

Floodwater Farming—Agriculture practiced on the river flood plain where the crops are irrigated by the high water table and spring overflow of the nearby river.

Floor—An occupational surface as used by Old World archaeologists.

Flour Corn—A soft-kerneled maize ground between two milling stones.

Flywheel—A wheel mounted on a rotating spindle shaft to provide momentum in the spinning of thread or on a drill shaft.

Foci—*See* Phase.

Folsom—A Folsom age bison kill site located in northeastern New Mexico. The type site for the Folsom phase.

Fontechevade Fossil—A middle Pleistocene age *Homo sapiens* found in France.

Function—Patterned behavior of individuals and institutions in society.

Functional Type—A type that had cultural meaning to the original makers and users. "Read" out of the data by the archaeologist.

Geological Calendar—A calendar that subdivides the earth's 4.6 billion year history.

Give-Away Feast—Community ceremony or festival at which surplus food is presented to others to gain prestige.

Glacial Calendar—The subdivision of the Pleistocene epoch based on successive named advances and retreats of glacial ice sheets.

Glacier—Ice sheet accumulation in the high latitudes and in midlatitude mountains.

Gorilla—A taxonomic genus designating the gorilla great apes.

Gouge—A flute-shaped chisel used in wood working.

Guano—Bird droppings utilized by the prehistoric coastal Peruvians as fertilizer for crops.

Habilis—A slender, big-brained early Pleistocene fossil hominid variously assigned to either the *Australopithecus* or *Homo* genera.

Half-Life—The time period during which one-half of the radioactive atoms in a substance will have decayed to the stable end-product.

Hammerstone—A hand-held stone hammer used to flake a core or core-tool.

Harappan Civilization—*See* Indus Civilization. Named for one of the two capital cities of the early bronze age Indus valley society.

Hematite—Red ochre.

Herbivore—Plant eating animal that feeds by grazing or browsing.

Historiography—A relative event sequence stating what happened first, what happened next, and so on to form an interpretive chain.

Hohokam Tradition—A village farming tradition located in southern Arizona from 300 BC to AD 1400.

Holocene (Recent) Calendar—Subdivisions of the last 10,000 years of the geological calendar. Composed of the Anathermal, Altithermal, and Medithermal periods.

Homeostasis—A self-regulating system in which disturbance in operation is always followed by a rapid return to a state of equilibrium.

Hominidae—A biological family, commonly called *hominids*, that includes all living humans and two genera of extinct prehumans (*Ramapithecus* and *Australopithecus*).

Hominoidea—A taxonomic superfamily that includes the apes and humans.

Homo sapiens—All living humans as well as several fossil sub-species.

Hopewell Phase—The middle Woodland archaeological culture of the Ohio valley dating between 100 BC and AD 500.

Horizon—A unit of time defined by the rapid spread of an art style or technical procedure.

Huaca—A regional Peruvian term for a prehistoric pyramid.

Huaca de la Luna—The moon temple, a mammoth religious complex appearing on the Moche site in north coastal Peru.

Huaca del Sol—The sun temple, a mammoth religious structure appearing on the Moche site of north coastal Peru.

Huari—Capital city of an early Postclassic empire. Located in the south highlands of Peru.

Huitzilopochtli—The Aztec god of war. The name means ''humming bird god.''

Hunch Sampling—Recovery of artifacts and sites by haphazard search.

Hydrostatic Head—Water pressure generated in a gravity flow irrigation system by means of raising a master canal above the field level.

Hypothesis—A provisional conclusion to explain the manufacture, use, or meaning of archaeological data.

Ice-Free Corridor—Formed by the parting of two ice sheets, an open, dry-land passage sufficient to allow the earliest American indians to migrate southward from Alaska.

Ideology—A belief system composed of ethics, values, and attitudes.

Inca State—The last preconquest political empire of the Andean High Culture area. Imperial expansion began in AD 1438 and continued until the Spanish conquest in AD 1532.

Indirect Association—Two or more artifact classes that show mutual avoidance in their spatial spread within a site.

Indirect Percussion—Use of either a hand-held punch or a chest punch to remove flake blades from a prismatic core.

Indus (Harappan) Civilization—Ancient civilization distributed along the Indus river of Pakistan.

Industrial Revolution—A reorganization of labor and an entire restructuring of eighteenth-century English society caused by the application of fossil fuel (coal) power.

Industry—All of the artifact types of the same age made of the same material.

Inference—A logical conclusion derived from given data. Used to explain an artifact in terms of its manufacture, use, and symbolic meaning.

Innovation—A creative process by which existing attributes are recombined to form new artifacts.

Institution—Organized economic, political, religious, or family subgroups of a society whose purpose is to meet the basic needs of its members.

Interglacial—A warming episode of the Pleistocene epoch between successive ice advances. Marked by glacial retreat.

Interstadial—A relatively warm sub-episode superimposed upon a glacial interval.

Invention—A process by which an individual genius creates new tools or symbols.

Irrigation Agriculture—Farming conducted in arid lands by means of ditches that lead water from streams to the fields.

Java Man—A popular name for the first finds of *Homo erectus* by Eugene Dubois in the Trinil district of central Java in 1890.

Jerkey—Thin strips of air-dried meat that have been dehydrated to lighten its weight and preserve it for later consumption.

Kaminaljuyu—An ancient Mayan city now located under Guatemala City.

Kill Site—An archaeological site type where repeated killing and butchering of game has formed a bed of animal bone.

Kiva—A subterranean religious chamber used for social and religious purposes by the Anasazi of the Colorado plateau.

La Chapelle-aux-Saints—A Neanderthal burial site in southwestern France.

Lake Texcoco—The lake of the moon that once filled most of the Valley of Mexico located around modern Mexico City.

Lanceolate—Lance-shaped stone projectile points that tipped spears and darts.

Lateral Moraine—A ridge of poorly sorted rock and soil pushed to the margin of a glacial-filled valley by ice advance.

Lava—Volcanic basalt rock.

La Venta—A ceremonial site of the Olmec civilization, Gulf coastal Mexico.

Lazaret—An archaeological cave site located near Nice, France, that contains lower Paleolithic houses of Riss glacial age.

Least Squares—A regression statistic employed to separate the growth history of a tree from the effects of climate.

Lehner Ranch—A Clovis mammoth kill site located on the upper San Pedro river of southeastern Arizona.

Le Moustier—A Neanderthal burial site in southwestern France. The type site for the Mousterian culture.

Levallois Point—A finished point removed from a prepared core and utilized as the stone tip for a short jabbing spear.

Levallois Technique—The craft of removing many finished tools from a prepared core.

Lindenmeier—A Folsom age campsite located in northeastern Colorado.

Lineage—A descent group that extends to three or more generations.

Linear Border—A line of rock that contours mildly sloping hillsides or grids level stretches of arable land to conserve slope runoff water for farming.

Linguistics—The study of spoken human languages.

Literati—Educated members of an early bronze age society who could read and write.

Lithic Stage—The New World Paleolithic, the cultural stage of the earliest migrants to the New World and their immediate descendants who hunted Pleistocene herd animals.

Living Floor—*See* Floor.

Llano Estacado—The Old Spanish name for the southern high plains of western Texas, meaning "staked plains."

Locality—The amount of geographical space occupied by a single community.

Loess—A columnar soil formed from wind-blown dust accumulating on the tundra zone in front of a glacial ice sheet.

Lovelock Cave—A deeply stratified site containing perishable artifacts of the Archaic stage. Located in Nevada.

Lower Paleolithic—The cultural stage covering the first appearance of stone tools 2.5 mya and extending up to 0.1 mya. Characterized by cobble choppers, then fist axes.

Lucy—Popular name given by Donald Johanson to a nearly complete female fossil assigned to the *Australopithecus afarensis* taxon.

Mace—A stone-headed club with knobs attached for use in warfare.

Macro-Band—A society of many small bands that amalgamate during one season of the year for social and ceremonial purposes. The seasonally scattered units are called *micro-bands*.

Macro-Plant Part—Visible plant part consisting of fossil root, stem, branch, twig, leaf, or flower.

Magdalenian—A named French culture of the Upper Paleolithic.

Maker's Mark—Impressed symbol appearing on sun dried bricks used to construct prehistoric Peruvian pyramids and other examples of religious architecture. Indicated tax payment by each individual community that supplied labor in the public works construction.

Manioc—A staple root crop grown in the Amazon and Orinoco drainage basins of South America.

Manuport—Stone used but not manufactured by proto-humans. Thought to have been used as thrown missiles to bring down game during early Pleistocene times.

Materialism—A research strategy, developed by Marvin Harris (1969), that investigates the interaction of technologies and economics (the material base of society) with the natural environment, seeking ever more complex forms of human organization and belief systems.

Matterhorn—Glacial sculptured mountain peaks. A landscape type named for the mountain in the Swiss Alps.

Mauer Jaw—A massive *Homo erectus* jaw of middle Pleistocene age recovered from a quarry near Heidelberg, Germany.

Mayan Indians—A prehistoric civilization with modern descendants who live on the Yucatan peninsula of Mexico and in adjacent regions of Guatemala.

McKean Technocomplex—A subassemblage of projectile points, including the McKean lanceolate, Duncan, and Hannah types, used as a horizon marker for the middle period of the western U.S. Archaic stage.

Meadowcroft Rock Shelter—An archaeological site in the Ohio river valley in Pennsylvania that has revealed an early archaeological stratum dated between 12,000 and 16,000 years old.

Medithermal—A climatic period of near modern conditions dating from 4500 years ago to the present.

Megafauna—Giant Pleistocene animals including mammoths, bison, camels, sloths, tapirs, dire wolves, and horses.

Megalithic Masonry—Walls and monumental sculpture composed of huge stone blocks. Mostly found in the Andean High Culture area of Peru and Bolivia.

Memory Unit—An information archive for the sociocultural system.

Mental Template—A term coined by James Deetz (1967) to convey the idea of a standard to which the artisan strives when manufacturing or using a tool or symbol. Often used as a synonym for *norm*.

Mesoamerica—A civilized culture area made up of many interacting complex cultures distributed throughout ancient Mexico, Belize, Guatemala, Honduras, and El Salvador.

Mesolithic—The intermediate stone age serving as a bridge between the Old Stone Age and the New Stone Age. In economic terms, the stage of intensive food gathering.

Metric Attributes—Measurable qualities of length, width, thickness, weight, and edge angles—in short, all observations that can be expressed by continuous measurements.

Micro-Band—*See* Macro-Band.

Microlithic—Small stone tool parts made by snapping long flaked blades into segments.

Middle Paleolithic—The middle stone age dated between 100,000 and 35,000 years ago.

Milpa—The Mayan term for slash-and-burn agriculture.

Miocene Epoch—An epoch of the Tertiary period of the geological calendar dating between 18 and 23 mya.

Mississippian Phase—The late Woodland archaeological culture of the lower Mississippi river valley dating between AD 500 and 1650.

Mit'a—A tax of labor and goods levied by the state government in prehistoric Peru.

Mixcoatl—The war chief of the Toltec tribes at the time when they first began to invade central Mexico. The name means "cloud snake."

Mixtec—Postclassic native peoples who resisted the expansion of the Aztec empire into the Mexican state of Oaxaca.

Mochica—The type site for the phase of the same name. Located near the modern city of Trujillo on the north coast of Peru.

Mochica (Moche) Phase—A Classic stage culture found on the north coast of Peru.

Moctezuma I—The first Aztec emperor (AD 1440–1468) to push imperial conquest outside of the Valley of Mexico.

Mogollon Tradition—A village farming tradition that occupied mountains of the American Southwest between 150 BC and AD 1000.

Monogamy—A marriage form limited to a single spouse.

Monte Circeo—A human shrine located near Rome, Italy, that contained a Neanderthal burial surrounded by a circle of animal bones.

Moraine—A pile of rock and soil that has been pushed ahead of the advancing ice sheet or smeared along the margins of an ice-filled valley.

Morphology—The study of form.

Mousterian Phase—An archaeological culture found in Europe and adjacent parts of north Africa and southwest Asia where it was made by the Neanderthal fossil type during Middle Paleolithic times.

Moving Mode—The replacement shift of alternative popularity curves measuring change through time.

Mu—Mythic, supposedly now submerged, continent that supported an ancient civilization. Thought to have been located in the Pacific ocean.

Mungai Knife—A bifacially retouched flake knife type identified from the lowest cultural layer of the Meadowcroft Rock Shelter.

Murray Springs—A Clovis age occupational site located in the San Pedro river valley of southeastern Arizona.

mya—Millions of years ago, a BP scale of measurement used with K/Ar dates.

Nahuatl—The language of the ancient Aztecs and other peoples of central Mexico.

Native Copper—Copper nuggets of sufficient purity to be worked into implements or ornaments by cold-hammering without the need for smelting in a furnace.

Natufian Phase—A preceramic Mesolithic culture of the Near East characterized by small villages of circular houses and the intensive harvest of wild cereal grain.

N-Dimensional Space—The multidimensional space of classification in which *N* is the ultimate number of observations that can be made on the members of any given class of artifacts.

Neanderthal—Fossil humans found in western Germany in 1856. Now classified as *Homo sapiens neanderthalensis*.

Neo-Evolutionism—The mid-twentieth-century revival of the study of cultural evolution by such anthropologists as V. Gordon Childe, Julian Steward, and Leslie White.

Neolithic—The stage of settled, village farming.

Neolithic Revolution—A restructuring of the size and organization of human society as a consequence of agricultural food production.

Neothermal—A new temperature age covering the Holocene epoch of the geological calendar.

Nominal Attribute—A named observation with discrete values such as shape (round, oval, square).

Nonbiface Industries—Stone tool industries characterized by the lack of fist axes and the presence of flake implements. Distributed throughout the Far East beyond India, although some are found in the middle Pleistocene of Europe.

Non-Egalitarian—*See* Egalitarian.

Norm—A cultural rule guiding human conduct.

Normal Curve Pattern—*See* Bell-Shaped Curve.

Nuclear America—The two civilized culture areas of the New World in ancient Mexico, adjacent portions of Central America, and the South American countries of Peru and Bolivia.

Null Hypothesis—In statistical research design, the hypothesis of no difference, abbreviated as H_0. Hypothesis testing requires that this hypothesis, which says that there is no numerical relationship between two variables, be disproved before the alternate hypothesis (H_A) can be accepted.

Numerical Taxonomy—A system of classification by numerically comparing each artifact or site forming the research population.

Nutcracker Man—A newspaper term referring to L. S. B. Leakey's *Zinjanthropus* find.

Nutting Stone—A slab or flat stone with many pecked holes that held nuts for cracking.

Oceania—The island world of the Pacific ocean: Micronesia, Melanesia, and Polynesia.

Old City—The most ancient part of the city of Teotihuacan. Founded in late Formative times.

Old Copper Culture—A late Archaic stage culture of the North American Great Lakes region that made hand-beaten copper implements.

Old Crow—A location along the Porcupine river in the Canadian Yukon where very old spirally fractured bones have been found. The fracture pattern suggests that humans may have eaten the marrow, then used the bones for crude tools.

Oldowan Industry—The earliest stone tools characterized by cobble choppers. First found in Bed I at Olduvai Gorge, Tanzania.

Olduvai Gorge—A fossil locality in Tanzania, Africa, containing many lower Paleolithic archaeological sites.

Olmec—The first widely recognized Mesoamerican civilization located in the Mexican states of Vera Cruz and Tabasco. Dated between 1250 and 500 BC.

Olsen-Chubbuck—A bison kill site of Plano age located in southeastern Colorado.

Omnivorous Diet—A mixed diet of edible plants and meat.

1470 Skull—The field accession number for a remarkable complete skull that Richard Leakey assigned to the *Homo habilis* taxon.

Ontogeny—The life history of a culture, showing its growth, peak, and decline.

Open-Air Living Sites—A human occupational camp found in the open countryside away from natural rock shelters or solution caverns.

Operational Taxonomic Unit (OTU)—The artifact or site actually being compared in a numerical taxonomy.

Optimizer Strategy—An attempt to acquire the maximum possible gain from an array of alternative courses of action.

Otoliths—Fish bones used as a balancing mechanism.

Paccaicasa Complex—The oldest well-dated archaeological assemblage recovered from Flea Cave in the Peruvian Andes.

Pachacuti—The ninth king of the Inca, crowned in AD 1438.

Paijan Point—Lithic Period 3 projectile point type of South America. Large, triangular shape with long stem.

Paleolithic—The cultural stage of the ice-age hunters. (*Paleo* means ''old''; *lithic* means ''stone.'')

Paleomagnetic (Geomagnetic) Calendar—A subdivision of the Cenozoic era based on dated reversals in the earth's magnetic field.

Paleomagnetic Epoch—A major subdivision of the Paleomagnetic calendar.

Paleomagnetic Event—A short duration subdivision that punctuates a Paleomagnetic epoch.

Paleontologist—A zoologist trained as a geologist, who studies extinct fossils in order to reconstruct ancient wildlife and investigate the evolution of plants and animals.

Palli Aike Cave—*See* Fell's Cave.

Palynologist—A botanist who studies fossil pollen grains for plant identification.

Pan—A taxonomic genus designating the chimpanzee great apes.

Parallel-Flaked Series—An unfluted lanceolate-shaped spear point used by Plano hunters on the high plains. Member types include Scottsbluff, Eden, Cody, Angostura, and Agate Basin.

Parent-Daughter Isotopic Pairs—The parent isotope is the radioactive or unstable form; the daughter product is the stable end result of radioactive decay.

Paudorf—A named interstadial of the European glacial calendar, dated between 30,000 and 40,000 years ago. Marked by the mild retreat of ice sheets and formation of incipient soils.

Pedologist—A soil scientist.

Period—A unit of pure time, without cultural content, expressed as an interval with age indicated in absolute years. An example of a period would be AD 1325 to 1400.

pH—A measure of hydrogen ion activity in natural soils. Ranges from very acidic (0) to very alkaline (14) conditions.

Phalanx—A military formation of soldiers aligned so that the spears of the men in alternate rows overlap.

Pharaonic Civilization—Ancient Egyptian high culture distributed along the Nile river from the delta to the first or second cataract.

Phase—An archaeological culture restricted in space appearing within a brief interval of time.

Physical Anthropology—The study of the biological varieties of humans, both present and past.

Phytolith—Opaline rock that preserves the remains of plant cells.

Pikimachay Cave—A natural rock shelter, meaning *Flea Cave*, located in the Ayacucho valley of the Peruvian Andes. Contains some of the oldest well-dated archaeological remains in the New World (ca. 19,600 radiocarbon years old).

Pit House—An architectural structure, invented in the Upper Paleolithic of Europe, consisting of a covered wooden superstructure topping a deep pit. The pit walls form the lower portion of the house.

Plainview Point Series—An unfluted lanceolate-shaped spear point used by Plano hunters on the high plains. Member types include Plainview, Midland, Milnesand, and Meserve.

Plano Phase—A Period 3 Lithic stage culture dated between 7000 and 10,000 radiocarbon years ago. Characterized by unfluted lanceolate spear points. Largely confined to the high plains of the western United States and adjacent regions of Canada.

Play Instinct—A term coined by Alfred Kroeber (1948) to describe the need of the artisan to constantly modify a craft by combining and recombining decorative detail in order to create new and pleasing artistic effects.

Pleistocene Epoch—The geological unit, characterized as the ''ice ages,'' when premodern humans evolved.

Pliocene Epoch—The last geological epoch of the Tertiary period. Dated between 5.0 and 1.9 mya.

Plio-Pleistocene Boundary Marker—The time boundary between the end of the Tertiary period and the beginning of the Quaternary about 1.9 mya. Formed from ''Pliocene'' and ''Pleistocene.''

Pollen—Microscopic spores of seed plants that form a fine yellow dust.

Polychrome—Many-colored painting on decorated ceramics.

Polygyny—Marriage to two or more wives, often sisters.

Pongidae—A taxonomic family covering the various great apes.

Pongo—A taxonomic genus designating the orangutan great apes.

Popularity Curve—A lensing or double-convex history of an artifact type from point of origin through frequency increase to climax, decreasing frequency, and finally extinction.

Population—All of the entities, artifacts, or sites potentially available for study.

Postclassic Stage—The era of imperial states and military rule in nuclear America.

Postcranial—The human skeleton including all but the skull; the skeleton from the neck down.

Potassium-Argon (K/Ar) Dating—Dating of volcanic rocks and ash by the decay of potassium-40 into gas (argon-40).

Potsherds—Broken pottery fragments. In general, the suffix *sherd* (or *shard*) refers to any broken fragment, not just those from ceramic vessels.

Potter's Wheel—A kick-wheel on which a pottery vessel is shaped, a process called ''throwing'' by ceramicists.

Preadaptation—Preparation for an adaptive change before that change is actually needed.

Preceramic—Period of time before the invention and use of fired ceramics in the fossil record. Before middle Neolithic times in the ancient Near East.

Prehistory—Cultures dating before the invention of writing.

Pressure Tool—A tool used to shape and thin another implement by pressing off small chips, a procedure called *retouch* in French.

Primary Refuse—Artifacts discarded at their place of use, such as a workshop area.

Primate Order—A biological classification that includes humans, apes, monkeys, and prosimians such as lemurs, lorises, and tarsiers.

Primogeniture—A form of inheritance by the firstborn of a family.

Prismatic Blade—A flake blade which has been struck from a polyhedral core. In cross section, flakes are prism-shaped.

Prismatic Core—A prepared core with conical shape and fluted sides made during the Upper Paleolithic stage. Also called a polyhedral or many-sided core.

Probability Theory—Statistical techniques that ensure representativeness in drawing artifacts and sites from a population of such objects.

Projectile Point—The chipped stone tip of a spear or arrow shaft. Projected by hurling, throwing with a board, or shooting with a bow at game.

Proto-Biface—The most primitive fist axes, displaying the transformation from choppers to hand axes during early Pleistocene times.

Pueblo—*See* Anasazi-Pueblo Tradition.

Quadan Phase—An Upper Paleolithic culture of the Nile valley, Egypt, that buried its dead, who often show evidence of violent death and warfare, in formal cemeteries.

Quadrant Digging—Digging of round architecture by taking alternate pie-shaped slices to reveal the stratigraphy and its horizontal variations throughout the building.

Quaternary Period—The fourth great period of geological time, covering the last 1.9 million years, during which tool-using humans evolved.

Quechua—Language of Andean indians including the Inca.

Quenching—Plunging a hot glowing metal object into cold water to achieve brittleness.

Quipu—Color coded and knotted rope that served as a mnemonic device for reciting Inca genealogies, liturgical material, and narrative verse. Allowed the recording of decimal numbers for the keeping of statistics.

Radiocarbon Dating—Dating of organic specimens by the decay rate of radioactive carbon (C-14).

Radiometric Dating—Absolute dating based on radioactive decay process of an unstable isotope. (*Radio* refers to "radioactive"; *metric* means "measurement.")

Ramapithecus—A taxonomic genus that includes the early hominids of the late Miocene epoch.

Ramp Model—A formalized theory that culture evolves in a steadily increasing manner.

Random Sampling—An unbiased selection of artifacts or sites according to a table of random numbers.

Rebus Writing—Pictures pronounced as sounds. An early form of pictographic writing.

Receptor—An input component to a cultural system that takes in food and fuel. Basically the role of the economic institution.

Reciprocity—The principle that kinsmen have obligations toward one another for assistance in work, defense, and mutual support.

Red Ochre—An iron oxide mineral pigment; also called *hematite*.

Reducing Tradition—A tradition segment characterized by trait loss and overall simplification; essentially devolution.

Regulator—A control unit that decides the operation of the sociocultural system.

Relative Dating—Placement of an event as before, contemporary, or after another event; an ordering of events in a time series.

Research Design—A plan for conducting research to include problem statement and research methods.

Residual Soils—Soils that form in place by the weathering of bedrock.

Retouch—*See* Pressure Tool.

Revolution—A term by which V. Gordon Childe referred to rapid advances in the evolution of society evidenced by changes in size, structure, and function. Childe recognized two revolutions in prehistory: the Neolithic and the Urban.

Ridged Field System—Farming of wet tropical marsh land by sowing crops on elevated furrows drained by troughs.

Rites of Intensification—Annual ritual events in which community members renew old acquaintances and maintain community solidarity.

Rites of Passage—Annual social events in which young candidates are promoted from one social status to a higher one.

Robustus—A rugged species of *Australopithecus* found in South African caves.

Sacred Precinct—A temple area set off from the secular portion of a city.

Salado—A Pueblo society that migrated about AD 1100 from the Colorado plateau into southern Arizona, where it heavily influenced the local Hohokam.

Sample—A representative part from which estimates can be used to predict the size and behavior of the unknown whole.

Sampling Frame—A list of excavatable squares or units by which the research universe is partitioned. The actual sample squares to be used for study purposes are drawn by chance from this list.

San Lorenzo—A ceremonial site of the Olmec civilization, Gulf Coast of Mexico.

Satisficer Strategy—A prudent but less than optimum course of action.

Scavenging—Obtaining food by small game hunting and collecting of edible plant parts. A diversified strategy in which nearly every edible product is combed from the landscape without discrimination for size or attention to food value.

Secondary Refuse—Artifactual and ecofactual waste at a dump.

Sequence Dating—A form of relative dating devised by Sir Flinders Petrie in which graves are fixed in time according to the stylistically distinctive burial offerings they contain.

Serfdom—A form of slavery brought on by bankruptcy. Once the debt had been satisfied, the serf may return to a freeman status in society.

Shaft Straightener—A socketed wrench used to straighten wooden shafts for use as projectiles or tool handles.

Shaman—A Siberian word meaning "medicine man," "witch doctor," or "magician." In primitive societies, shamans have magical power to cure illness, inflict harm on others, control wild game, and foretell the future.

Shang Dynasty—The first appearance of bronze age civilization in northern China.

Shanidar—A Neanderthal burial site with grave offerings of flowers in the Zagros Mountains of Iraq excavated by Ralph Solecki.

Shell Midden—A discarded pile of shells from the harvest of oysters, clams, and mussels. A common site type for coastal Archaic and Mesolithic peoples of both the New and Old Worlds.

Similarity Coefficient—A coefficient that compares similarity (or dissimilarity) between each pair of artifacts or sites being examined in a numerical taxonomy.

Simple Band—A primitive community of 30 to 100 people who follow a hunting and gathering way of life.

Simple Random Sampling—A form of sampling in which every artifact or site making up the population has an equal chance of being drawn for research purposes.

Site—Artifactual evidence of past human land use or settlement. Usually a find spot indicating some sustained period of occupation.

Site Survey—A research method to discover and record systematically each evidence of human land use and settlement within a locality, region, or culture area.

Slash-and-Burn Agriculture—Dry farming in tropical areas where the forest is cleared by girdling trees and burning the cut, dried brush.

Slope Runoff Farming—Placement of fields on a hillside so that walls prevent precipitation runoff.

Slow Game—Slow-moving game such as snakes, turtles, lizards, and frogs that could be run down and collected by hand.

Smelting—The reduction of metallic ores to a pure form of metal by the application of furnace heat.

Snub-Nosed Scraper—A small end scraper with a stubby scraping edge. A common associate to Lithic Period 3 stage sites found on the high plains of North America.

Soapstone—A soft stone, steatite, used prehistorically in the New World for carving figurines, pipes, and bowls.

Social Structure—Organization of social statuses in society.

Society—Organized group behavior.

Sociocultural—Combining the twin concepts of society and culture.

Sociological Level—The human organizational sector of society made up of such institutions as family, politics, and religion.

Sodality—A voluntary association such as an age-grade club, a secret association, a warrior group, or a religious organization.

Solo Fossil—A middle Pleistocene age *Homo sapiens* found in Java.

Speciation—A process of rapid species evolution.

Spindle—A weighted shaft device employed to twist fibers into thread and twine.

Spokeshave—A concave flake scraper thought to be employed for shaping a wooden shaft for arrows, spears, drills, or spindles.

Stadial—A minor oscillation of intense cold superimposed upon a glacial interval.

Stage—A unit concept expressing similar cultural content across many local and regional archaeological sequences. Employed to measure general evolution.

State—A society organized into sharply delimited socioeconomic classes or castes and administered by a government.

Status Symbol—Material symbol indicative of a person's social position within a society.

Steeling—Smelting a metal object in the presence of an abundance of carbon.

Steinheim Fossil—A middle Pleistocene age *Homo sapiens* found in Germany.

Stele—An erect stone plaque inscribed with text and calendar dates commemorating the building of a Mayan pyramid and altar.

Step Model—A formalized theory that culture evolves by spurts followed by periods of quiescence, thus producing a step profile. Model used by V. Gordon Childe to present his theory of economic revolutions.

Stirrup Spout—A spout made in the shape of a stirrup. A stylistically distinctive part of the ceramic history of prehistoric Peru.

Stone-on-Stone Technique—Use of a stone hammer to reduce a core by direct percussion blows.

Stone Ring—A ring of rocks from Bed I at Olduvai Gorge dating more than 1.8 mya. Thought to have served as a base for the oldest constructed architecture in the world. Probably served as a windbreak, hunting blind, or night protective corral for sleeping.

Stratified Random Sample—The research area partitioned into strata, each of which is randomly sampled proportionate to its occurrence in the universe.

Stratigraphy—The study of layered deposits whose interpretation is based on the principles of superposition and association. The study of very minute banding or laminae within a stratum is called *microstratigraphy*.

Strike-a-Light Kit—A fire-making kit, dated to the Mesolithic stage, composed of flint, meteoric iron, and tinder used to start a fire by percussion striking the iron against the flint to generate a spark.

Strike and Dip—The trend (strike) and inclination (dip) of each stratified layer constituting an archaeological site.

Sumerian Civilization—Ancient civilization of southern Iraq distributed along the Tigris and Euphrates rivers.

Surface of Origin—The buried land surface from which a particular feature (a pit, grave, well, or footing trench) was dug.

Survival—The tendency of a society to endure and prosper in the face of adversity as measured by their increasing numbers and ever widening geographical spread over the face of the earth.

Swanscombe Fossil—A middle Pleistocene age *Homo sapiens* found in England in a Thames river terrace.

Symbol—An object that stands for an idea. Functionally classified as either a status symbol or an ideological symbol.

System—A set of objects or attributes interrelated such that change in one requires a corresponding alteration in all others.

Systematic Sample—A selection of artifacts or sites taken from equal interval parcels within the universe of research.

Systemic Context—The modern institutional setting of an artifact according to Michael Schiffer (1976).

Table-Top Sorting—Classification based on physical groupings of artifacts by placing most similar members into actual piles on a table or large work surface.

Taboo—Social custom that prohibits various kinds of behavior. Negative sanction of a ''thou-shalt-not'' nature.

Talus—A natural deposit of coarse rock formed by erosion at the base of a cliff.

Tarascans—Postclassic native people who resisted the expansion of the Aztec empire into the Mexican state of Michoacan.

Taung—South African cave site that produced the first Australopithecine find, the limestone cast of an infant skull, in 1924.

Tazcatlipoca—A war god of the Toltecs. The name means ''smoking mirror.''

Techno-Economic Determinism—A principle, paraphrased from Marvin Harris (1969), that similar technologies applied to similar environments produce similar arrangements of labor that are justified by similar systems of beliefs.

Tektites—Meteoric stones thought to fall from outer space in showers.

Tempering—The further forging of a metal object by pounding it on an anvil.

Tenochtitlan—The Aztec capital city, located beneath modern Mexico City.

Teotihuacan Site—A large city located 25 miles north of modern Mexico City dating from the late Formative through early Classic.

Tepanecs—Allies of the Aztecs who lived on the banks of Lake Texcoco in the fifteenth century AD.

Terra Amata—An archaeological site of middle Pleistocene age dug by Henry de Lumley at Nice, France. The site name means ''beloved land.''

Terrace—A fossil valley floor which has been eroded by the down-cutting of a river to leave a flat remnant of the valley surface and a clifflike eroded face.

Tertiary Period—The third great period of geological time covering the latest 65 million years during which mammals, including primates, evolved.

Teshik-Tash—A Russian archaeological site on the shores of the Caspian sea where a Neanderthal child was buried, surrounded by a circle of goat skulls.

Test Pit—A hole dug into the ground to explore the depth, thickness, and structure of an archaeological site.

Three-Age Scheme—A stage classification of archaeological remains formulated by C. J. Thomsen based on a progression of stone→bronze→iron.

Thumbnail Scraper—A very small, thumb-size flake stone scraper.

Tiahuanaco—A Classic city located on the southern border of Lake Titicaca, Bolivia.

Time—A measure based on the year (one revolution of the earth around the sun), a little over 365 days.

Tlaloc—The Mesoamerican rain god worshipped by the Mayan and Aztec civilizations.

Tlaxcalans—Postclassic native people who resisted the expansion of the Aztec empire into the Mexican state of Tlaxcala.

Toggle Harpoon—A harpoon head that could be detached from the shaft. Used for hunting sea mammals such as whales, seals, and walrus.

Tool—An artifact used to manipulate and extract raw materials, energy, or both from the physical world. May be hand-held or fixed.

Tool Kit—A set of associated artifact types (carpentry kit, plumber kit) with some work purpose. Grouping of tools that forms some meaningful subset of a total artifact assemblage.

Topiltzin Quetzalcoatl—The feathered serpent god of the Toltecs, Aztecs, and earlier peoples. A supernatural culture hero standing for peace.

Torralba—An elephant-kill and butchering site similar to the nearby Torralba site of middle Pleistocene age dug by F. Clark Howell in central Spain.

Totem—An animal, such as a wolf, snake, eagle, or bear, symbolizing the mythical ancestor of a clan.

Tradition—An archaeological unit concept that persists in time but is limited in space. Employed to measure specific evolution of individual cultures.

Tribe—An egalitarian primitive society organized by descent groups with social integration of the community provided by cross-cutting sodalities.

Tula—The capital city of the Toltec empire, located in the modern Mexican state of Hidalgo.

Tumpline—A strap, braced across the forehead or chest, used to support a bag or basket carried on the back.

Tundra—The barren ground north of the boreal forest in the Arctic. An environment characterized by moss, lichens, and stunted brush along cold streams and rivers.

Two Creeks Interstadial—A mild warming episode marked by a temporary retreat of ice sheets between 11,000 and 12,000 years ago.

Type—Defined by objects: a pattern of artifacts or sites based on groupings showing a high degree of similarity. Defined by object attributes: a cluster of characteristics all of the same age that habitually associate to form a pattern or recurrent set.

Type Site—A location where the first evidence of a named phase was identified. The type site name is often extended to the named archaeological culture, as in the Folsom site from which the Folsom phase was named.

Tzompantli—A skull rack on which the heads of Aztec sacrificial victims were exhibited.

Universal Evolution—According to Leslie White, the evolution of global culture obtained by averaging together all cultures and viewing their composite accomplishments.

Universe—In sampling theory, the area specified for field study.

Upper Paleolithic—The latest stage of the old stone age dated between 35,000 and 10,000 years ago. Also referred to as the Late or Advanced Paleolithic.

Uranium-Lead Dating—Dating of rocks by the radioactive decay of uranium into lead. Useful in determining the age of the earth since it began cooling into a solidified crust.

Urban Revolution—A social transformation resulting in a class structured urban society. Generated by intensive agriculture and, in particular, by irrigation of arid lands or ridged field cropping in the tropics.

Valders Stadial—*See* El Abra Stadial.

Variable—A research observation showing change, either of discrete or continuous measurements.

Varve—Thin, annual layer of mud on the bottom of a cirque lake fed by glacial melt waters.

Ventana Cave—A deeply stratified archaeological site located in southwestern Arizona showing 12,000 years of human occupation.

Venus—Small bone or ivory female sculpture believed to magically insure human reproductivity.

Vertesszollos—An archaeological site located in Hungary, dated to the middle Pleistocene, providing evidence of middle latitude use of fire.

Villafranchian—A named assemblage of extinct early Pleistocene and late Pliocene epoch fauna including an elephantlike animal, a rhinoceros, a horse, and a huge beaver. Marks the time boundary between the Pleistocene and Pliocene epochs of the glacial calendar, a time period dating between 0.85 and ± 4.0 mya.

Viracocha—A heroic god of the Inca people.

Volcanic Ash (Tuff)—Fine, powdery rock material blown out of the vent of a volcano.

Waddi Kubbaniya—A locality near Aswan on the Nile river in Egypt, where Fred Wendorf and his colleagues (1979) found evidence for incipient cultivation of barley and einkorn wheat between 17,000 and 18,000 years ago.

Weathering—The physical and chemical breakdown of parent bedrock, the hard rock crust of the earth, to produce soil.

Wet Rice Agriculture—The growing of rice in flooded fields by means of terraced hillsides.

Wet Site—Water-logged archaeological site containing well preserved perishable artifacts and ecofacts because of the exclusion of oxygen.

Wisconsin Glacial Stage—The last named ice advance of the North American glacial sequence, dating between 70,000 and 10,000 years ago. Roughly equivalent to the Würm/Weichsel of Europe.

Woodland Tradition—A sequence of Formative cultures from 1000 BC to AD 1650 in the Mississippi river basin of North America.

Würm, Weichsel—The last glacial advances of Europe, dating between 70,000 and 10,000 years ago.

Würm I—The first stadial of the last glaciation in the Swiss Alpine glacial sequence.

Y-5 Cusp Pattern—Five cusps arranged in a Y-shape that are typical of the lower molar teeth of fossil and modern anthropoid apes, fossil hominids, and many modern humans.

Z- and S- Twist—Left- and right-spun thread in which the twist is made by either rotating on a spindle shaft or by rolling on a human thigh.

Zinjanthropus—The type fossil for *Australopithecus boisei* found in Bed I at Olduvai Gorge, Tanzania.

Index